Bruce & Fran,

To guide you through your "retirement" years as you look for special antiques!

Merry Christmas 1992.

Love,

Paul, Dawn & Paul

OTHER BOOKS BY RITA REIF

LIVING WITH BOOKS

THE ANTIQUE COLLECTOR'S GUIDE TO STYLES AND PRICES

TREASURE ROOMS OF AMERICA'S MANSIONS, MANORS AND HOUSES

HOME: IT TAKES MORE THAN MONEY

RITA REIF'S
The New York Times
WORLD GUIDE TO ANTIQUES SHOPPING

RITA REIF'S
The New York Times
WORLD GUIDE TO ANTIQUES SHOPPING

RITA REIF

Published in the United States by Times Books, a division of Random House, Inc., New York, and simultaneously in Canada by Random House of Canada Limited, Toronto.

Library of Congress Cataloging-in-Publication Data
Reif, Rita.
Rita Reif's the New York Times world guide to antiques shopping.
Includes index.
1. Antiques—Collectors and collecting. I. New York times. II. Title. III. Title: New York Times world guide to antiques shopping.
NK1125.R373 1987 745.1'025
87-40193
ISBN 0-8129-1251-9

DESIGNED BY NAOMI OSNOS

Manufactured in the United States of America

9 8 7 6 5 4 3 2

First Edition

To Leslie and Timothy

ACKNOWLEDGMENTS

I am indebted to each dealer who welcomed me cordially and gave of his or her time most generously. More than one of these merchants helped plan the schedule for my swift visits in their cities. Several waited into the evening, came early to their shops in the morning or opened their galleries on weekends to accommodate the jet-age timetable I followed. No one, thankfully, ever complained when I telephoned to review or expand on information gathered during my speedy visits.

My thanks also go to the specialists in a dozen categories and the public relations staffs of Sotheby's and Christie's in New York, London, Amsterdam, Zurich, Geneva, Hong Kong, Monte Carlo and Tokyo, who were extremely helpful in preparing lists of dealers in the cities I visited. Everyone was patient with me and generous with information and time, especially Hans Nadelhoffer of Christie's in Geneva and Kazuko Shiomi of Sotheby's in Tokyo.

To Sondra Castile, in Asian Art conservation at the Metropolitan Museum of Art, whose knowledge of the customs of Japan and the dealers in Tokyo and Kyoto prepared me for what became an unforgettable visit, my sincere appreciation. To Robert T. Singer, who assisted further in Kyoto, where he was an American research fellow at Kyoto University, I am most grateful. The trip between Antwerp and Brussels was a friendly experience thanks to Michel Rooryck, who added to my understanding of both cities.

Vienna revisited was memorable, made more so by Kiki Kogelnik, who contributed wit and perception to what we viewed together. Paris—always engaging and endlessly complex—became more negotiable in large part because of the generous assistance and attentiveness of Herve

Aaron. To Mary and Fred Jacobson, who aided my efforts throughout with their gracious hospitality and telephone calls in Munich, Florence and Rome, my warmest appreciation.

Daniel Aharoni smoothed away several practical problems with an ease that was admirable.

My gratitude first and last goes to my editors at *The New York Times*—to Arthur Gelb, Michael J. Leahy, William H. Honan, Annette Grant, Nora Kerr and Robert J. Berkvist, who always encouraged my coverage of the antiques world.

To Marylin Bender, a special vote of thanks for everything.

The editors at Times Books/Random House were supportive throughout. I am most grateful especially to my editor, Elisabeth Scharlatt, and her assistant, Amy Gash, for understanding, guidance and patience. Nancy Inglis masterminded the production so amiably and efficiently that, miraculously, deadlines were met. To Marjorie Anderson's keen eye and alert mind I owe the spare yet warm design of this book, and to Naomi Osnos, the strongly graphic interior. The extraordinary efforts of Don Caswell—gruff griffin that he thinks he is—proved the computer process to be efficient and compassionate. Whatever final patina is there owes much to his cheerful polishing.

My deepest appreciation goes to Marion Donnelly, who made order out of chaos gracefully and on a global scale.

CONTENTS

Introduction xiii
Foreign Exchange Rates xvi

UNITED STATES

Austin-Dallas-Houston 3
Chicago 17
New York 33
San Francisco 119

EUROPE

Amsterdam 139
Antwerp-Brussels 151
Florence-Rome 163
Geneva-Zurich 173
London 183
Munich 247
Paris 259
Vienna 295

MIDDLE EAST

Jerusalem 309
Tel Aviv 315

FAR EAST

Hong Kong 321
Kyoto 329
Tokyo 337

Index 345

INTRODUCTION

My introduction to antiques began when, as a collector of modest means in the early 1950s, I frequented the shops of dealers who had sharp eyes and were generous in sharing their time and considerable knowledge of what they handled. This book owes much to those first memorable encounters, especially with George Basso, whose discriminating eye for Italian Renaissance furniture and Gothic wood carvings transformed a small, dark, cluttered shop on Manhattan's Second Avenue in the East Fifties into a mini-palazzo. Mr. Basso, as well as others who have all long since retired, aroused in me an intense interest in collecting and started me on a pursuit of decorative-arts history that has enriched my life as a writer ever since.

Antiques collecting then was shared with my husband, Paul Reif, a composer. Until his death in 1978, we investigated the antiques districts and flea markets of every town we ever visited, enjoying the dealers behind the counter as much as the antiques they stocked. As a design reporter for *The New York Times,* and, since 1972, the antiques columnist, I met many major dealers from here and abroad who told me about colleagues whose shops I had never visited. It was frustrating and became more so as that list of dealers grew. I knew eventually I would have to find a way to meet these people on their home ground.

This book was written to satisfy my own curiosity about the merchants I had never met in galleries and cities I had never been to. To assemble a sort of Who's Who among antiques dealers worldwide, I consulted museum curators, dealers, collectors and auction houses. From the outset I decided it was absolutely necessary to visit every dealer and to limit myself to cities because it would become physically impossible to venture into the countryside also. The selection was based on the areas in the decorative arts that I cover regularly—from antiquities through Art Deco.

Sheer madness, many friends said. To travel to 22 cities and visit more than 200 dealers would require more time and effort than a full-time working reporter would be able to devote to such a project, they warned. I paid no attention and made 10 trips in all, between June 1984 and June 1987, to cover antiques sources in this country and abroad —in Europe, the Middle East and the Far East.

No one can possibly be an expert in more than one or two areas of the decorative arts, and this writer claims no expertise in any of the categories covered. What I hope is conveyed throughout is what I found in each establishment I visited. The interviews with dealers purposely covered how they came to be involved with antiques, what they handle and why, and what their understanding is of these works.

The antiques these dealers stock may change every season or so—at least partly. Prices may decline or, more likely, rise, and if currencies continue to fluctuate, dealers no doubt will ask different sums for what they sell. Foreign currencies have all been translated into dollars—at the rates effective in September 1986, which are shown in the table on page xvi. If anything remains constant, it will be the dealer's view of the quality and character of the antiques and art works he or she handles. Therefore, the specifics about what was found in each gallery or shop are intended not as a buyer's list but as guideposts to what collectors may expect.

Antiques dealers are enterpreneurial men and women in an extremely personal and competitive business. All are highly individualistic and they all seem to shape the business to their own tastes and personalities. This is often seen in family businesses, when one generation differs dramatically from the next in what each chooses to sell. The dealer's eye is the key that unlocks the world of art for clients. The way they speak of the works they stock may reveal a great deal—or nothing—about this secondhand merchandise.

Unfortunately, after my visits to them, a major London dealer retired and two in Houston moved to other cities. Only one dealer refused to be interviewed and included in the book. However, I am haunted by the possibility that I missed some major dealers in my travels. The very thought should make serious antiques collectors venture beyond the galleries covered here.

RITA REIF,
June 1987

FOREIGN EXCHANGE RATES

Wherever dealers quoted prices in foreign currencies, they were translated according to the rates on September 12, 1986, as published in *The New York Times* on September 13, 1986, a date chosen to be consistent throughout.

COUNTRY	CURRENCY	UNITS OF CURRENCY PER DOLLAR
Austria	schilling	14.68
Belgium	franc	42.63
Britain	pound	0.6764
France	franc	6.7415
Hong Kong	dollar	7.8030
Israel	shekel	1.4930
Italy	lira	1420.00
Japan	yen	155.30
Netherlands	guilder	2.3240
Switzerland	franc	1.6675
West Germany	mark	2.0585

UNITED STATES

THE JENKINS COMPANY

Box 2085
Austin, Tex. 78768
Phone: (512) 444-6616
Hours: By appointment, 9 A.M. to 5 P.M. Monday to Friday

John Holmes Jenkins was ten years old in 1950 when he went into business selling books and coins from his home in Beaumont, Tex., to buy more books. In his collection, he concentrated on works dealing with the Civil War and Texas history, but he sold anything he could get his hands on to satisfy his bibliomania.

At eighteen, when he was still in high school, his first major book—a work he had edited—was published by the University of Texas, *Recollections of Early Texas: The Memoirs of John Holland Jenkins.* These reminiscences had been written by his great-great-grandfather, an Alabama-born adventurer who joined Gen. Sam Houston's army to fight the Mexicans when he was a fatherless thirteen-year-old (his father was killed on the frontier and his stepfather died at the Alamo). The work was acclaimed by historians and reviewed in *The New York Times,* where it was described as "a commendable job for an editor of any age."

By 1963, Mr. Jenkins had finished college and a year of Law School at the University of Texas, all on scholarships. His book-buying and selling had continued unabated and he had publishing ambitions as well. So he left the university but stayed in Austin, opening his rare-book business and the Jenkins Publishing Company.

Both grew swiftly. By 1975 Mr. Jenkins had 500,000 rare books; that quadrupled by 1985. By then he had published 420 titles. On Christmas Eve in 1985, there was a devastating fire in his warehouse affecting about half a million books. He said his rare-book stock still numbered two million books and that most had survived the blaze. Most of the damage, which affected 200 collections, he said, was from oily grime or soot, which is being removed page by page and book by book wherever possible.

"We have the largest number of rare books in the world," he said. "Since 1963 we have sold more than 10 million books and manuscripts for a total of more than $40 million. We issue catalogues twice a month, each of which usually contains about 2,000 books."

Mr. Jenkins is president and sole owner of his two book companies, which he runs with a staff of 17. He specializes these days in assembling partial or entire collections of books for individuals and for institutions. "They tell us they want to collect, and we identify areas we think are interesting," he said, adding that the areas might be the international oil and gas industry, Mark Twain, Colonial American printers, American overland narratives, the Republic of Texas, maps of the world, books by and about women. "I build collections I hope will still be being used for research a millennium from now."

"I am more interested in text than in the condition of books," Mr. Jenkins said. "When I build a research collection, I do not care if there is a chip off the spine of an individual book. In Americana books, condition is definitely secondary to the text. I would rather have a complete copy of a first edition in poor condition than a mint copy in a splendid binding of a modern reprint."

He also does not emphasize books that are more memorable for their esthetic appeal than their contents, although his stock includes all varieties, from medieval illuminated manuscripts through 20th-century books illustrated by artists and boasting stunning bindings.

Books range from $30, perhaps for a history of Michigan in the 1890s, to about $150,000 for a first printing of the United States Constitution.

Clients may visit Jenkins by appointment to see the vast array of stalls that fill a 25,000-square-foot warehouse. Clients who linger while negotiating purchases are accommodated in a hotel suite on the premises. "It's easier than returning to downtown Austin, a 20-minute drive from the warehouse," Mr. Jenkins explained.

W. THOMAS TAYLOR BOOKSELLER

1906 Miriam Avenue
Suite 704
Austin, Tex. 78722
Phone: (512) 478-7628
Hours: 9 A.M. to 5 P.M. Monday to Friday

Walter Thomas Taylor specializes in English literature before 1900 and finely crafted books of all periods, from the late Middle Ages to now. Most of his clients never visit his offices but shop by mail from the three catalogues he publishes each year. Half his sales are to institutions, including libraries, and the other half to collectors.

"I don't maintain a large inventory of books anymore," Mr. Taylor said, adding that the rare-book business has changed in recent years. "Bookdealers were awash in great books in the 1930s—but not today."

"We do try to keep inexpensive books," he said. The stock in books and manuscripts ranges from under $25 to $250,000. Among the least expensive works in one catalogue were a first edition, for $75, of *The Mother of Us All* by Gertrude Stein and Virgil Thomson, one of 1,000 printed in 1947, and a first edition of Robert Louis Stevenson's 1882 *Familiar Studies of Men and Books* for $125.

Of English literature before 1800, Mr. Taylor said, poetry is more difficult to sell than fiction. But a first edition from 1633 of John Donne's *Poems,* a fairly common book, would be very saleable and not inexpensive—about $9,000, he said.

Later works, such as Elizabeth Barrett Browning's *Sonnets From the Portuguese,* have a wider following. One of the three autograph manuscripts of this work from 1850 was bought by Mr. Taylor in 1979 for the Armstrong Browning Library at Baylor University in Waco, Tex.

And the library of Emory University in Atlanta acquired from Mr. Taylor most of the Yeats and Lady Gregory papers in two Sotheby's auctions in 1979 and 1981.

"Half of the really interesting things we handle are manuscripts," Mr. Taylor said, adding that the most important offering he has handled is a collection of 33 letters signed by John Locke, 28 of them to the Irish philosopher William Molyneux, 4 to the philosopher's brother, Thomas

Molyneux, and one to Richard Burridge, an Irish writer-translator. The collection, written from 1692 to 1699, includes unpublished material and is characterized by rich comments on a revision of his greatest work, *An Essay Concerning Human Understanding*. Mr. Taylor's price is about $250,000.

More than once he has handled pages from a Gutenberg Bible. He has sold a vellum leaf from this work, considered the first book printed with movable type, for $50,000 and a paper leaf for $8,000, he said.

"I am as much interested in making new books as selling old ones," Mr. Taylor said. "I like to participate in the creation of books to collaborate with living artists." He works with book designers and graphic artists, including Gérard Charrière, a Swiss designer of bindings living in New York; Michael Wilcox, a Canadian artisan, and Peter Nickel, a graphic artist of Austin. In the books Mr. Taylor produces, all the printing is letterpress and the bindings are leather, cloth or wood boards.

Mr. Taylor, a Texan from Houston who attended the University of Texas, reported in an interview at his book- lined office in downtown Austin that he quit school to start his rare-book business full time in 1972, when he was twenty-one years old. He said he attributes his discovery of rare books to the fact that when he was twenty he inherited one-third of the rare-book collection assembled by his great-grandfather, a lumberman who acquired ornithological and scientific works as well as English literature and fine bindings over 30 years.

"I didn't know anything about books," he said of that windfall of several hundred books. Ideally, he said, a bookseller learns his trade by working for a dealer. But there is another way. "You learn by your mistakes," he said, recalling a copy of a first illustrated edition of Columbus's letter to Queen Isabella reporting the discovery of the New World, which he sold for $8,000—about one-tenth its value. The business operates with a staff of three: Mr. Taylor and Elaine Smyth, the company's "general factotum"—she is the office manager, an editor and the cataloguer—and Bradley Hutchinson, pressman and book designer.

Mr. Taylor said there were a half-dozen good collectors in Austin, including Herman Melville's great-great-grandson, Duncan Osborne, a lawyer. The city also has an excellent library at the University of Texas.

Mr. Taylor's sale terms are standard. He sends books on approval, expects them back within 10 days of receipt if they are not suitable and expects payment within 30 days of receipt. New clients are expected to pay with their orders or supply references.

DALLAS

WILLIAM GRIFFITH ANTIQUES

2913 Fairmount Street
Dallas, Tex. 75201
Phone: (214) 871-2230
Hours: 9 A.M. to 5 P.M. Monday to Saturday

The gallery of Patsy Lacy Griffith, which offers a generous assortment of vintage wares in seven showrooms, occupies a turn-of-the-century prairie-style house in the Vineyard district of downtown Dallas. This area at the north end of town is dominated by antiques shops, offices and restaurants. Mrs. Griffith, a Dallas collector and the widow of William Griffith, an oil man, leaves the buying and selling of vintage wares to Henry Coger, the manager. He and John Bihler joined her in 1978 after moving to Dallas from Ashley Falls, Mass. Mr. Bihler died in 1986.

Griffith's diversified stock is strong in informal 18th- and 19th-century English, French, German and American furniture, as well as ironstone wares, Chinese export ceramics and French and American folk art—weathervanes, decoys and American Indian baskets. Among the offbeat objects reflecting the dealer's taste and flair were a painted 1830s New York State linen press (about $8,000), a pair of Canada geese decoys ($5,000), a collection of French turn-of-the-century lead candlesticks of Daumier-like grotesque figures ($750 to $850 a pair) and an 1810 New England painted blanket chest decorated with a swirl of fig leaves ($7,500).

Prices range from less than $100 for a blue-and-white Canton plate or a 19th- century British horse brass to about $40,000 for a 1780s English oak secretary veneered in tortoiseshell.

Mr. Coger has been in the antiques business since 1950, when he met Mr. Bihler in his hometown of Chicago. Mr.

Bihler had been in his own antiques business for four years, and Mr. Coger was a graduate student at Loyola University. The Arkansas-born Mr. Coger soon gave up his studies to join Mr. Bihler in buying and selling vintage wares and organizing antiques shows.

"We were doing English porcelains, opaline glass, Staffordshire, embroidery pictures—we were very diversified," Mr. Coger recalled. "After that we branched out in all directions and we've never stopped."

This attitude was part of their appeal when they came to New York in the early 1950s to participate in the Madison Square Garden Antiques Show, then the nation's finest such presentation. It was at this show that they met Elektra Webb and sold her such major examples of folk art as the five great Canada geese carvings by Charles Osgood of Salem that became the nucleus of her decoy collection at the Shelburne Museum in Shelburne, Vt. Mrs. Webb later acquired far more from them—more than 50 fine quilts and a hatbox collection.

The dealers settled in New York, maintaining a shop in the East 60s, and later moved their business to Ashley Falls, where their shop was frequented by, among other major folk art collectors, Edgar William and Bernice Chrysler Garbisch, who bought scores of American primitive paintings and watercolors from them.

The partners were in the first East Side House Settlement's Winter Antiques Show in 1954, and remained in the fair, now the nation's most prestigious for secondhand wares, until they moved to Dallas.

Mr. Coger has managed the Tri Delta Charity Antiques Show of Dallas each March since it began in 1976.

MILLY McGEHEE

2704 Commerce Street
Dallas, Tex. 75226
Phone: (214) 871-0513
Hours: By chance and by appointment, 10 A.M. to 6 P.M. Tuesday to Saturday

Milly McGehee seems right at home selling American folk art and sophisticated country furniture in her gallery, a converted 1920s garage in Dallas's SoHo, an area just east of downtown known as Deep Ellum. That name has been used for more than a half century and derives from the Texan pronunciation of a main thoroughfare, Elm Street. Low-slung Art Deco structures, built as warehouses, machine shops and jazz night spots after World War I, now house art galleries, restaurants and boutiques.

"I kept the pressed tin ceiling," Miss McGehee said in a tour of her gallery, which she has occupied since 1985. She also kept the square skylight and let it determine the placement of her office—smack in the middle of the gallery. The sponge-decorated storefront is, however, a modern addition.

Miss McGehee's discriminating eye and wide-ranging taste results in a stock strong in New England, Pennsylvania, Southern and Western folk art, sophisticated country furnishings and Texana. And there are formal works carved by major cabinetmakers, too. Among the assortment of 18th-, 19th- and early-20th-century works that visitors might see are painted chests, twig rockers, cast-iron settees, iron windmill weights, a gilded Hubmobile weathervane, fence posts and such wooden toys as a hand-carved Noah's ark.

"Most of my best stuff stays in Texas," she reported, adding that her customers collect formal and informal furniture and folk art from the East as well as Texana, the sparely wrought but robust furnishings produced by German and British settlers before the Civil War. They are scarce hereabouts.

The dealer, who was born in Natchez, Miss., is more scholarly than most dealers. A graduate of Hollins College, near Roanoke, Va., she spent a year at the Museum of Southern Decorative Arts in Winston-Salem, N.C., and completed her Master of Arts at the Henry Francis Du Pont Winterthur Museum in Delaware in 1975. She was restoration consultant at Old City Park, a complex of 25 historic buildings of the mid to late 19th century administered by the Dallas County Heritage Society, a nonprofit organization. After two years as curator of the Hermitage, Andrew Jackson's home in Nashville, Tenn., she became head curator of the American decorative arts collection, 18th through early 20th centuries, at the Virginia Museum of Fine Arts in Richmond.

"Then I decided I had had enough of working full time in museums," she said, adding that in 1980 she moved back to Dallas and opened a gallery in the Turtle Creek area.

Many of the collectors who shop here share Miss McGehee's taste and sense of adventure in the offbeat objects and furniture she stocks. What they usually find is a selection of weighty 19th-century furniture, for example, an early New England jelly cupboard as sturdy as a safe and a plain-board Vermont tailor's table with a scrap bag on one end. An extraordinary chest of drawers that Miss McGehee thinks must have been crafted in New York State is decorated with stylized flowers and a pair of peering eyes on its fake drawer fronts. Obsolescence does not dim the appeal of many of Miss McGehee's offerings, including a painted gray-blue tailgate board from a Conestoga wagon, complete with its original hinges and wood tool box, nor a painted baby tender, a 20-inch cube framed with wooden pegs.

Miss McGehee also carries major examples of 18th- and early-19th-century high-styled furniture, but they disappear quickly into private collections. During one visit there were a few examples, including one of four known Massachusetts marble-topped mahogany-veneered sideboards less than five feet long and probably made by a member of the Seymour family in the 1790s. It comes with an Israel Sack pedigree and a price tag over $100,000. A Philadelphia Chippendale lowboy with ball-and-claw feet, quarter columns and original brass, made for the Ashurst family of Germantown in the 1760s, was about $35,000.

TRI DELTA CHARITY ANTIQUES SHOW

Henry Coger, manager
P.O. Box 8070
Dallas, Tex. 75205
Phone: (214) 363-3907

The Dallas Convention Center is host for this show each March to benefit the Dallas Museum of Art and Samons Cancer Center at Baylor Hospital. Dallas and Richardson, Tex., alumnae of the college sorority whose name it bears sponsor the show, which lasts four days plus preview. About 55 dealers participate and attract about 10,000 fairgoers.

Preview tickets are $95 each. General admission is $6.

HOUSTON

BALENE INC.

2005 B West Gray Street
Houston, Tex. 77019
Phone: (713) 523-2304
Hours: Noon to 5 P.M. Tuesday to Saturday
Closed last week of July to third week of August

Balene McCormick is a collector-turned-dealer in tribal and ancient art with an eye for boldly graphic and robust textiles, jewelry, pottery and wood carvings.

Mrs. McCormick, a Philadelphian who has lived in Texas since 1957, began pursuing pre-Columbian and African art in 1963, after she and her husband, Sanford, an independent oil producer who used to work for Vice President George Bush, settled in Houston. Her interests have expanded to include antiquities and Oriental and American Indian art.

She opened her gallery in 1981 in a shopping center in River Oaks, one of Houston's finest residential neighborhoods, and offered a provocative selection of tribal art and antiquities. On one visit, there were African wood carvings, including beaded masks from Cameroon and an ancestor post from Kenya. American Indian wares include ancient Hohokam and Socorro pots, kachina dolls, Navajo eye-dazzler blankets and Navajo and Zuñi turquoise and silver jewelry.

Mrs. McCormick is not afraid to stock offbeat wares, such as "wild woolly rugs," as she calls mid-to-late-19th-century hooked Shaker rugs. It is thickly woven with a rich pile and a strong geometric pattern of rectangles within rectangles. Among the more uncommon American Indian works are late-19th-century Navajo children's blankets patterned with triangles, stripes and diamonds, zigzags and crosses priced at $18,000 to $20,000. Notable among the ancient art works was an Anatolian stone bird from about 3,000 B.C.

Jewelry, some of it contemporary, includes American Indian, Far Eastern and African necklaces, bracelets, rings, amulets and pendants. Except for the Southwestern jewelry, most of the pieces have been redesigned and reassembled.

Prices start at $49 for a 40-year-old Indonesian wood spoon. At the upper end are important prehistoric American Indian bowls, pots, jars and large earthenware vessels made by the Hohokams ($7,000) and Socorros ($15,000) from A.D. 900 to 1400.

THETA CHARITY ANTIQUES SHOW OF HOUSTON

Albert Thomas Convention Center
West Hall
Capitol and Bagby Streets
Houston, Tex. 77002

For advance information:
Suite 345
4212 San Felipe Street
Houston, Tex. 77027
Phone: (713) 524-8824, 780-0855 or 465-5731

Since 1953 Houston's five-day show in late September has benefited medical, cultural and educational charities chosen by the local chapter of Kappa Alpha Theta, the national college sorority. The 50 dealers attract 10,000 fair-goers. Preview tickets on the evening before the opening cost $75 for 6 to 10 P.M. and $50 for 7 to 10 P.M. General admission is $5.

Volunteers staff and administer the show under the direction of three administrators: Toni Wallingford, Carroll Yanicelli and Mary Wade Coale.

CHICAGO

MARTHA LANMAN CUSICK

P.O. Box 10926
Chicago, Ill. 60610
Phone: (312) 642-1607
Hours: By appointment

The American Indian jewelry, artifacts and art stocked by Martha Lanman Cusick, a private dealer, have attracted a loyal following of clients, she reported in her booth at the Chicago International Antiques Show. In her display, several period selections of silver jewelry inlaid with coral and turquoise were outstanding, as were Hopi dolls, Navajo masks and weavings, Southwestern pottery, Northwest Coast wood carvings and Plains Indian beadwork.

Mrs. Cusick has followed the route taken by many dealers in recent years and gone private, closing her gallery on Ontario Street, where she greeted collectors for eight years. Now there is more time to spend on buying trips and with clients, undisturbed by interruptions when they meet, she said.

Plains beadwork, which has been gaining enthusiasts in recent years, is a specialty of Mrs. Cusick. She carries small bags embellished with red tassels and blue beads, a child's dance kilt decorated with rolled tops of tin cans, as well as shirts, cradles and slippers. An Eastern Woodlands spoon boasts a carved head on the handle. A set of three Acoma kachina dolls was $1,400.

Mrs. Cusick exhibits the work of contemporary Indian potters—the black pottery of Maria Martinez included a jar at $2,850 and a plate at $3,600—as she has done since she first became interested in American Indian art. At a San Francisco show with Charles Loloma, a Hopi jeweler, historic pottery from the Southwest, which she has handled since 1976 when she began to focus more on period work, included pieces at $900 and $1,100. An ancient 19-inch Socorro storage jar, made between A.D. 1100 and 1250, is decorated with the same colorful lightninglike and terrace motifs used in 20th-century Southwestern pots. The price was $15,500.

JOSEPH W. FELL

3221 North Clark Street
Chicago, Ill. 60657
Phone: (312) 549-6076
Hours: By appointment, 10 A.M. to 5 P.M. "more or less"

"I'm a big frog in a small pond," Joseph W. Fell said. "More than half the rugs I sell are shipped out of Illinois." They are bought by businessmen and decorators from the Midwest, the East and West coasts and Europe.

Mr. Fell was in journalism and publishing when he began to collect antique weavings. "I bought 100 rugs in the first year we were collecting and researching Orientals," he recalled. "In 1968 I decided to retire from publishing. I spent two years studying rugs and learned how to restore them. I worked 16 hours a day."

He said that until those two years had passed, he had "no serious intentions" of selling rugs. Then he told his wife, "I'm going into the rug business." He believes, he said, that antique rugs are disappearing. He thought he could run a different sort of rug business, so he borrowed $10,000 and opened with 40 rugs—half from his own collection.

Mr. Fell has a former photography studio in an 1890s building in the area called Newtown. On a bright day, the colors in his carpets can be read more accurately than in most showrooms because of a huge window, 18 feet high and 20 feet long.

Among his inventory are Persian rugs, including late-19th- and early-20th-century Heriz and Tabriz rugs. Much of his stock is in room-size rugs awash with geometric and floral patterns—ideal for urban dwellings and offices. "These are mostly town rugs, not country rugs," he said, adding that they are sturdy weavings, not too flamboyant in their patterns and more suitable for offices than for mansions in suburbia. About 30 percent of what he sells goes to offices. These rugs tend to be semiantique, which he defines as early 20th century up to World War II. Semiantique room-size rugs—Heriz, Usak or Bijar weavings—start at $7,500 to $8,500 and may sell for as much as $50,000, he said. Antique rugs are $12,000 to about $100,000.

Mr. Fell also keeps a large inventory of European rugs—Aubussons and Savonneries—as well as collector rugs, including kilims, village and nomad rugs, Turkoman weavings from Turkestan and Kurdish rugs from southwestern Persia.

"There were a lot of antique kilims sold as exotica at the Columbian Exposition in 1893," he said. What people recall when selling such a rug, he said, is that their mother or grandmother bought it at that world's fair, covered the piano with it and perhaps later used it as a portiere, then stored it in the attic. Kilims from the turn of the century range from about $4,500 to $12,000.

FLY BY NITE

714 North Wells Street
Chicago, Ill. 60610
Phone: (312) 337-0264, 664-8136
Hours: 10 A.M. to 5 P.M. Monday to Saturday

Visitors to this shop in the River North section sometimes ask first about the Bakelite brooches, the Susi Singer ceramic figures or the Rörstrand vases. But many are far more curious to know why Thomas Martin Tomc, the owner, calls his business Fly By Nite.

The title doesn't seem to fit the shop or its proprietor. Mr. Tomc moved in in 1962, and he has been there five or six days a week ever since. The cluttered interior is an achievement of many years. Mr. Tomc's brusque manner suggests solidity, and no one who has met him will be surprised to learn that he has outlasted the antiques importers who dominated the neighborhood when he came here.

The name of the shop certainly does not suggest pioneering. Yet Mr. Tomc was one of the first to have a highly individualized antiques shop in this neighborhood, which is rapidly becoming the SoHo of Chicago. He was also among the earliest to specialize in 20th-century decorative arts, stocking Wiener Werkstätte, Jugendstil, Art Nouveau, Art Deco and European ceramics from 1900 to 1930. Mr. Tomc still handles some of his other early specialties—poster stamps (he started out as a designer and art director in advertising) as well as other paper ephemera.

So why the name of the shop? Mr. Tomc says the name was above the door when he moved in, and he left it that way.

Once in the shop, visitors may find it hard to leave because there are so many curious things to peruse. Prices range from about $60 for a Czechoslovak glass-and-nickel floral pin to about $10,000 for a French ceramic sculpture. A copy of a Cartier clock in Bakelite was about $375. A Rörstrand black-and-green ceramic vase from about 1930 was $875.

MALCOLM FRANKLIN INC.

56 East Walton Street
Chicago, Ill. 60611
Phone: (312) 337-0202
Hours: 9 A.M. to 5 P.M. Monday to Friday, 9 A.M. to 3 P.M. Saturday
Closed Saturdays from the Fourth of July to Labor Day

15 East 57th Street
New York, N.Y. 10022
Phone: (212) 308-3344
Hours: 10:30 A.M. to 5:30 P.M. Monday to Friday, 10:30 A.M. to 3:30 P.M. Saturday.
Closed Saturdays from the Fourth of July to Labor Day

When Malcolm Franklin opened his first antiques shop in his native Chicago in 1947, he stocked everything British—including Georgian furniture, ceramics, silver and pewter. That's the way dealers did it in the postwar years when antiques shops offered stocks that were far more wide-ranging than they are today. His first location, a block from the converted town house to which the shop moved in 1984, is on the Near North Side in the Gold Coast area once dominated by mansions that have largely been replaced by high-rises.

Trained in the 1920s by Arthur Ackermann of Ackermann & Son, a London dealer who also had shops in New York and Chicago, Mr. Franklin left him in 1927 to sell antiques at Carson Pirie Scott, where he rose quickly to head the store's antiques department. He remained until 1947.

Over the next two decades the antiques business changed dramatically, becoming increasingly more competitive and specialized, and Mr. Franklin chose to focus more and more on 18th-century English furniture. Paul Franklin, his son, who now heads the business, recalled how things were different when he joined the gallery after receiving a Bachelor of Arts in history at Georgetown University. "It was so much easier to be an antiques dealer in 1960," he said, adding that he had worked in the store part time while in high school and college. "There were ample goods for everyone, and when auctions came in New York, you didn't have 10 dealers bidding on everything."

He inherited his father's taste for British furniture dating from 1680 to 1830. The gallery stocks predominantly oak and walnut chairs, tables, bureau-bookcases and chests of drawers of the William and Mary, Queen Anne and Georgian styles. "My father was one of the first to bring walnut furniture to America," he said.

Still reigning supreme here is the British view of patina—a glow won with age, wax and undisturbed dust. "We talk original skin and tell our clients, 'It hasn't been refinished—it has its original skin,'" Paul Franklin said. "We definitely talk construction, too. The quality of the dovetails tells you whether a piece is well or poorly built. A little, precise, thin dovetail will indicate a sophisticated and knowledgeable cabinetmaker."

When Mr. Franklin stops in front of a burled walnut ladies' dressing table, he speaks more of its shapely form and good looks than its construction and finish. The same is true of an early Queen Anne stool with double-cabriole legs—the double S-curve ends in a turned foot. He said of the legs, "See that, how it seems to dance across the floor."

The prices range from $450 for a late-18th-century

Windsor side chair to as much as $100,000 for a good Queen Anne bureau-bookcase.

The younger Mr. Franklin became president when his father retired in 1973 (he died in 1982), and he shares the responsibilities of the business with his sister and partner, Mary Ann Sullivan. Several of their children are in the business, too, in New York and Chicago.

GALLERY VIENNA

650 North Orleans Street
Chicago, Ill. 60610
Phone: (312) 951-0300
Hours: 10 A.M. to 5 P.M. Tuesday to Friday, 11 A.M. to 4 P.M. Saturday
Closed last two weeks of August

Norbert and Michael Gleicher are brothers who live far apart but share interests. Both are physicians and both are intensely interested in the art and design of their native Vienna. The gallery they opened in March 1985 offers early-20th-century Viennese art and design and occasionally Biedermeier designs from 1815 to 1840. They operate it as a sideline, and it helps them keep in touch with each other.

Norbert, a professor of obstetrics and gynecology at Mt. Sinai Hospital and Medical Center in Chicago, organizes the exhibitions, auctions and selling at their gallery. Michael, a pediatrician associated with the Mautner Markhof Children's Hospital in Vienna, does the buying.

The brothers were born long after the art and design movements that they document in their gallery had ended. The Secession movement came and went at the turn of the century, and the Austrian Expressionists flourished from about 1900 to 1930. The Wiener Werkstätte, which produced designs that were precursors of the Art Deco style in Paris and the Bauhaus, closed in bankruptcy in 1932.

Norbert, born in 1948, and Michael, born in 1953, were collectors of Austrian Expressionists and bentwood before they became dealers. They are assisted at the gallery by Leslie Devereux Rutz.

Some of Gallery Vienna's stock echoes displays in the "Vienna 1900: Art, Architecture and Design" exhibition in 1986 at the Museum of Modern Art in New York and in the "Dream and Reality" exhibition, which opened in 1985 in Vienna and later moved to Paris.

During one visit, there were examples of early-20th-century Wiener Werkstätte furniture and objects designed by the founders of the workshop—including a Cabaret Fledermaus set and an adjustable chair called a "sitting machine" by Josef Hoffmann, as well as cabinets and tables by Adolf Loos, Otto Prutscher and Robert Oerley. Sitting machines are among the most desirable designs of this period and start at $25,000.

Less expensive designs by others include bentwood suites of chairs and settees, children's barber chairs, piano stools, coat racks and center tables made by Kohn or Thonet. The accessories shown include ceramics by Michael Powolny and Valley Wieselthier and glass by Hoffmann and Koloman Moser. Sketches, drawings and watercolors by Hoffmann, Carl Otto Czeschka and Egon Schiele are also available.

The prices here range from about $100 for an etching by Willibald Rudinoff to about $30,000 for a rare black-and-white suite of furniture—a bench, two armchairs and a table—by Robert Oerley.

HAMILL & BARKER

400 North Michigan Avenue
Chicago, Ill. 60611
Phone: (312) 644-5933
Hours: 9 A.M. to 4:30 P.M. Monday to Friday
Closed in July and August

Margery Barker and Frances Hamill went into business selling rare books in 1928 and issued their first catalogue that fall. Since then, interest in rare books has grown and the prices have soared.

In 1980, after Miss Barker died, Terence Tanner became Miss Hamill's partner. The 15,000 books in the tower quarters on the 26th floor of the 1920s Wrigley Building—most days it is sun-washed and is always welcoming—covers all periods and price levels. A first edition from 1800 of Richard Alsop's *A Poem: Sacred to the Memory of George Washington* was $65, and a first edition from 1859 of the *Rubáiyát of Omar Khayyám,* translated by Edward FitzGerald, was $16,000. The span between these prices seems filled with books it would take most of us a lifetime to read.

Catalogues, issued irregularly, cover the wide range of Hamill's stock. In 1983, for example, the partners issued a catalogue of 55 rare books and manuscripts to mark the 55th anniversary of the business. Among some of the offerings were an 1899 educational treatise by John Dewey, *The School and Society,* at $250; a complete manuscript of a historical romance, *The White Company* by Sir Arthur Conan Doyle, at $65,000; Joacobus Philippus Bergomensis' woodcuts of famous women—Cleopatra, the Virgin Mary, Eve—issued in Ferrara in 1497 at $27,500, and a first edition of Adam Smith's *An Inquiry Into the Nature and Causes of the Wealth of Nations* from 1776 in a superb contemporary binding at $20,000.

Hamill & Barker handles rare books in all fields in the 2,000-square-foot quarters it has occupied since 1984. Mr. Tanner said Hamill & Barker specializes in Illinois-related material and "we are very heavy in works dealing with American social thought" as well as American imprints. He said the two founders acquired the diaries of Virginia Woolf from her widowed husband, Leonard S. Woolf, and sold them to the New York Public Library in the 1960s after his death. In 1959, they handled the sale of the George Poole Collection of about 500 books on the history of printing to the Lilly Library of Indiana University in Bloomington.

Mr. Tanner has been in the book business since 1970. After finishing college, he first worked building sewers, then did freelance writing and was employed for more than a year by Kenneth Nebenzahl, another Chicago rare-book dealer. He then went out on his own and two years later joined Hamill & Barker.

KELMSCOTT GALLERY

410 South Michigan Avenue
Chicago, Ill. 60605
Phone: (312) 461-9188
Hours: By appointment

Scott Elliott specializes in the drawings, furniture, lighting and accessories of Frank Lloyd Wright and his contemporaries. His studio quarters are in a building in which Wright designed some interiors at the turn of the century. The landmark, built in the 1880s as a carriage factory, was remodeled in the 1890s into the Fine Arts Building of art and drama studios. It still attracts many Chicago artists.

Mr. Elliott's gallery was once the Anna Morgan School of Dramatic Arts, where Ibsen and Shaw were possibly performed for the first time in the United States. The gallery is arranged more like a stage set than a shop, with Wright's slat-back chairs, squarish desks, and Cubist-oriented stained- glass windows dominating. Lighting is by George Mayer, an early-20th-century Chicago architect. Here and there are arresting architectural drawings and posters of the period.

Mr. Elliott was born in Chicago in 1941 and went east in the early 1960s to study art with the Art Students League and Pratt Institute in New York and set design at Yale Drama School. In 1963 he opened his first antiques shop on the Lower East Side. Later he worked privately and for art dealers buying and selling German and Austrian Expressionist drawings and 19th- and 20th- century photography and organizing an exhibition of Wiener Werkstätte furnishings and objects.

After collecting British arts and crafts and spending a year in England, he returned to Chicago in 1979 determined to open a gallery specializing in these turn-of-the-century designs. He named it Kelmscott after the ancestral home of William Morris, whose writings sparked the arts and crafts movement. His interest in Frank Lloyd Wright dominated, however, after he found a rare drawing of the architect's plans for rebuilding Taliesin after the 1920s fire.

"It is like winning a major battle to get every piece of Frank Lloyd Wright," Mr. Elliott said. In one such engagement in 1983 he acquired a rare desk and chair from Buffalo's Larkin building, the headquarters of the soap manufacturer. The desk was $30,000 and the chair $15,000, and they skyrocketed in value. Three years later, Mr. Elliott said, the desk was valued at about $60,000 and the chair between $45,000 and $60,000. Another wood slat-back Larkin chair was $16,000 in 1983 and did not increase so dramatically in value, he said, because too many versions of it became available. "Wright furniture is incredibly rare—too rare to make a strong market for it," Mr. Elliott said.

Mr. Elliott's prices have always seemed high but he said they are usually soon exceeded in auctions. And his manner is sometimes abrasive. He said that most of his sales these days are to museums. Wright's oak side chairs range from $15,000 to $45,000. A 1986 exhibition he organized at the Armstrong Gallery in New York, "Frank Lloyd Wright and Viollet-le-Duc: Organic Architecture and Design From 1850 to 1950," included chairs as well as drawings, lamps, vases and architectural fragments from Wright's buildings.

Most of the Wright stained-glass windows Mr. Elliott handles are $50,000 or more. In 1986 he had two of Wright's most cheerful designs—stained glass patterned in squares and circles from the kindergarten of Queene Ferry (Mrs. Avery) Coonley, usually referred to as the Avery Coonley Playhouse—at $135,000 each.

B. C. HOLLAND INC.

222 West Superior Street
Chicago, Ill. 60610
Phone: (312) 664-5000
Hours: 9:30 A.M. to 5:30 P.M. Monday to Friday, 11:30 A.M. to 5 P.M. Saturday
Closed Saturdays from June 30 to Sept. 15

B. C. (Bud) Holland has been an art and antiques dealer for 30 years, buying and selling modern paintings; Asian, Islamic and African art; Oriental rugs and 20th-century European furniture. Three years ago he moved to his present location, where he now concentrates on fewer specialties: 20th- century European furniture and modern art.

Chicago-area aficionados of European furniture styles are increasing, Mr. Holland reported, noting that he carries works made in Vienna, Italy and France from 1890 to 1950. He stocks whatever he can find of Carlo Bugatti, he said. An exotic 8-foot-6-inch-tall hall mirror in ebonized wood, probably made for the Turin exhibition in 1902, was $18,000. Mr. Holland called it a typical Bugatti extravaganza sprouting "lots of bells and whistles," speaking of the sun-raylike finials that are the designer's trademark. A pair of Bugatti copper-inlaid walnut-and-leather chairs, part of a set of 12 he has been selling, was $9,000.

Mr. Holland does not like everything produced in the period, he said. He strenuously avoids American 20th-century and Bauhaus modern designs of the 1920s and 1930s. His taste is for the sophisticated and more decorative works of Jean-Michel Frank, both the innovative French decorator's own furniture and the pieces he commissioned from such artists as Alberto and Diego Giacometti. The gallery stocks many Cubist-style Frank works when available—wall sconces, table and floor lamps, high-backed low-slung fireplace chairs and tables both high and round and low with rounded ends in the Chinese mode.

Other European furniture includes works by French designers (Emile-Jacques Ruhlmann, Leleu, Dominique and Coard), the early 20th-century Viennese architects (Josef Hoffmann, Otto Wagner and Adolf Loos) and a pre-World War II Italian (Gio Ponti).

Mr. Holland said offerings at the gallery started at about $1,600 for a good Viennese bentwood chair ("a rare one is two or three times that price," he said). Tea tables by Hoffmann from this period were about $2,500. Rarities here may be as much as $20,000.

KENNETH NEBENZAHL INC.

333 North Michigan Avenue
Chicago, Ill. 60601
Phone: (312) 641-2711
Hours: By appointment

"I put together my first map collection when I was ten years old," Kenneth Nebenzahl reported at his aerie high above the Chicago River. "Those 48 filling-station maps cost me nothing."

That may have been the last time Mr. Nebenzahl paid nothing for what he was collecting. Actually, the price is not what deters or attracts true collectors and serious dealers. Starting out that young, Mr. Nebenzahl could hardly escape his fate, which seems absolutely glorious to anyone who visits his book-lined establishment at the top of the tower.

Although he was sidetracked for a while in other jobs—selling menswear and in the wine business—he had been acquiring old books, some rare books and reference books in such depth and quantity that his wife, Jocelyn, told him, "You are a rare-book dealer." Then, he added, "Hans P. Kraus, the Austrian-born New York rare-book dealer, took a paternal interest." Mr. Nebenzahl has been buying and selling American books, manuscripts, maps and prints in the tower at this address since 1960 and in the stunning space on the 28th floor since 1965.

The rare-book business mushroomed because of the Russians, he said. "Sputnik put this business into orbit." After that, hundreds of American universities built research libraries as part of the increase in graduate programs granting advanced degrees in the sciences and humanities. "For 15 years that stimulated the market," he said, adding that the private collectors followed after 1970 and were responsible for the next stage of major growth in the rare-book field.

Mr. Nebenzahl's stock covers all Americana—except the most common books and maps—dealing primarily in American history, discovery and exploration and cartography. He handled a copy of the Declaration of Independence, which he bought on July 2, 1975, for $40,000 and sold to the Chicago Historical Society. He has also handled one of six copies of the first draft of the United States Constitution printed by John Dunlop as well as a first illustrated edition in Latin of Columbus's letter, written on board ship on the return from his first voyage, to Gabriel Sánchez, the treasurer of Ferdinand and Isabella. The letter was printed in Basel in 1493 complete with woodcuts. His great passion in books is the first-person accounts of explorers, such as the journals of Lewis and Clark, which he handled several times before it became what rare-book dealers call critically rare.

Once a year Mr. Nebenzahl issues catalogues of rare American books, pamphlets and prints. The listings show works ranging from about $500 to about $150,000. The map catalogue, issued once or twice a year, lists items from about $300 to $3,600, although others in his stock may be as much as $10,000 to $15,000.

RICHARD NORTON

612 Merchandise Mart
Chicago, Ill. 60654
Phone: (312) 644-9359
Hours: 9 A.M. to 5 P.M. Monday to Friday

Shoppers are advised to call ahead for an appointment at this showroom, where purchases are made only through stores, architects and interior designers.

Richard F. Norton studied to be a civil engineer but became an antiques dealer instead. The switch happened in the late 1920s, when, fresh out of college, he landed a job as a salesperson with Mercier Frères, a prestigious French decorating concern then operating in Paris and New York. In 1931 he was sent to Chicago to open a branch and left Mercier to found his own business in 1933. Four years later he moved the business from Superior Street to the Merchandise Mart, where it remains today. He never regretted his choice of this field, and neither does his son, Richard M. Norton, who heads the family business now.

The younger Mr. Norton, who joined his father in 1965 and became managing director in 1979, continues to stock primarily French and Continental 18th- and 19th-century country furnishings, with some British pieces thrown in. His eye is for highly decorative, boldly wrought and comfortable designs chosen to appeal to the furniture dealers and interior designers from throughout the country and abroad who shop here.

About 40 percent of what he sells goes to offices, hotels and restaurants, and 60 percent ends up in homes. Desks, tables, sets of dining chairs, chests and outsize armoires and sideboards are stocked in abundance. A French 18th-century walnut desk called a bureau plat, its flat top re-covered with natural-colored leather, was $1,600; a pair of English Regency hall chairs was $1,200, and an outsize English mahogany breakfront from about 1800, 8 feet tall and almost 10 feet wide, was $40,000.

"If the hardware is replaced, we tell you," the younger Mr. Norton said. He said reproductions were carefully identified.

Prices range from $9 for old French café saucers to about $65,000 for a mid-18th-century Burgundian buffet in walnut, an admirably simple and robust design that would make a strong statement in any room.

TAYLOR B. WILLIAMS

1624 North La Salle Street
Chicago, Ill. 60614
Phone: (312) 266-0908
Hours: By appointment

Taylor B. Williams has two careers—one in antiques, the other in acting. "Antiques are for my head, acting for my heart," he said, adding that he drops his middle initial when he goes on stage.

None of this was planned, he said. After Mr. Williams received his B.A. in 1958 from the University of North Carolina—his major was drama, his minor history—he went to New York to seek a career on Broadway. Two years later, he went to the Midwest to help start a repertory theater in Arrow Rock, Mo., a restored early-19th-century town best known as the home of George Caleb Bingham, the 19th-century genre painter. Mr. Williams worked hard, both at transforming a mid-19th-century Baptist church into the Lyceum Theater, which has been running ever since, and as an actor. There was, however, very little financial return.

"I decided that I wanted to have another way of making a living," he recalled. "I took $40 and went to a country auction." He came away with a truckload of bargains—a Cannonball bed, a Chippendale blanket chest in walnut and a tilt-top candlestand.

With that $40 investment he thought he'd become a picker, selling things to other dealers. But no one needed his help, he said. "I painted a sign, 'Antiques,' nailed it to a tree in the front yard and I was in the business."

Mr. Williams remained in Arrow Rock for 10 more years, learning about antiques when he wasn't acting. "I made a lot of mistakes but I didn't make them twice." He was prepared, for example, when Harold Sack, the president of Israel Sack, the 57th Street dealers, came to call. He left with a signed Windsor and remembered Mr. Williams when he called from Arrow Rock years later, offering Sack six American Queen Anne chairs for $2,400. He sold them and drove them to New York.

Mr. Williams stocks American formal and sophisticated country things. A case in point is an outsize 1760 Pennsylvania walnut armchair with trifid feet covered with carved stockings and still boasting its original needlework seat of stitched turkey work (now called flame stitch). The price was $18,000. Another is a Connecticut highboy in cherry with a bonnet top, one of the best examples extant with the original brass and finish. It was $175,000.

The English furniture he stocks has to be very unusual, he said, or suitable as a substitute for a far rarer American version "that no one can afford." One example is three-part pedestal dining tables, he said. "You seldom see the American examples." The English ones are about $8,500.

English 18th- and 19th-century porcelains—the kind Americans favored in the period, Worcester and such—are usually in abundance. And sometimes there's a British brass-and-steel model of a steam engine or locomotive at $4,000 to $4,500. English enamel boxes are another speciality at $250 and up.

Mr. Williams said he and his associate, David Bernard, are "professional show dealers," doing 12 antiques fairs a year, and are away at least that many weeks. "When we are home, we are open." he said. Home is an 1880s Second Empire house in the Old Town area, near the Loop, with a century-old elm out back.

CHICAGO INTERNATIONAL ANTIQUES SHOW

Navy Pier
Chicago, Ill. 60611

For advance information:
John D. Wilson, president
Chicago International Antiques Show
6500 North McClurg Court
Chicago, Ill. 60611
Phone: (312) 787-6858

This four-day antiques show in October, begun in 1984 and organized by the Lakeside Group, has international representation. The 100 dealers attract about 20,000 fairgoers.

The opening evening benefits the Art Institute of Chicago, the Antiquarian Society and the Old Masters Society.

Tickets for the opening evening are $75 each. General admission is $6 a person.

NEW YORK

DIDIER AARON

32 East 67th Street
New York, N.Y. 10021
Phone: (212) 988-5248
Hours: 10 A.M. to 6 P.M. Monday to Friday

The New York gallery of this Paris-based French antiques concern occupies a turn-of-the-century five-story town house, a mini-chateau with French Art Deco touches added in the 1930s for Marcel Rochas when the late couturier operated a salon here. It was these modern touches, especially the sweeping ribbonlike railings of its gracious staircase, that won Didier Aaron when he scouted New York for a gallery in 1975. His taste for the exotic is more visible in New York than in Paris, in part because one of his two sons, Hervé, who has headed the New York branch since it opened in 1977, shares his delight in offbeat furnishings, and so do their American clients. At the opening, a coconut-embellished commode that some imaginative artisan in Goa made for a Portuguese official set the tone.

The gallery offers antiques of taste, "antiquaire de goût," Hervé Aaron said. Most date from the first half of the 19th century and include Austrian Biedermeier, French, English and occasionally American furniture selections, but French 18th-century furniture is very much in evidence, along with Old Master paintings and late-19th-century paintings. Here, as in Paris, Didier Aaron provides decorating services.

"New York is probably a little bit less expensive than Paris," he added. The middle range in prices for antiques at the New York gallery is $10,000 to $20,000. The middle range in Paris is $30,000 to $50,000.

SEE Paris: *Didier Aaron, page 259*

BERDJ ABADJIAN

201 East 57th Street
New York, N.Y. 10022
Phone: (212) 688-2229
Hours: 10 A.M. 5 P.M. Monday to Friday

Berdj Abadjian entered the rug business at the age of eighteen in 1955 designing hand-loomed Oriental-patterned weavings in Arta Populara, a Rumanian cooperative in Bucharest. Within a few years he had expanded the operation from 10 people to 2,000. He was president of the cooperative from 1957 to 1962.

In 1963 he and his father and mother decided they would act on a desire of many years and leave Rumania. They escaped via Lebanon to New York, and his father, an expert at rug repair, was offered a job in Chicago. The Abadjians went there, and Berdj Abadjian began to repair rugs under his father. "I learned very fast," he said, adding that several months later he returned alone to New York.

"I did not want to work for anyone," he said. He stayed in a hotel, paying $3 a day, and repaired rugs in his room, earning $5 to $8 a night—"just enough to keep me alive," he said. In learning to repair rugs he had come to know what Oriental rugs are all about. "You either learn it in two or three years or you never learn it," he said. "I was able to buy from dealers. A rug that cost me $200 I would repair and sell to another for $2,000."

In 1964 Mr. Abadjian opened his own business in the West 30s, the heart of New York's wholesale Oriental rug district. He remained there until the changing market indicated that he move to the art-gallery area of Madison Avenue in the 70s, and he called his business Rugs as Art. Prices of antique rugs rose dramatically throughout the late 1970s until the Shah was deposed in early 1979, and the market for some Oriental rugs then declined sharply.

In 1985, Mr. Abadjian moved to 57th Street, taking him to another center of the rug business, where interior designers shop with their clients. "Rugs are now fashionable once again," he said. His showroom is staffed by 12 people, 4 of whom do repairs.

He said he now stocks mostly room-size rugs, 6 by 9 feet, 8 by 10 feet and larger, ranging from about $10,000 to

$40,000. Smaller rugs, perhaps 4 by 6 feet, start at $2,000, he said, adding that most scatter rugs have risen less in price than larger ones, increasing only one and a half times over the last 10 to 15 years. The finer examples of these smaller weavings, which are sought by collectors, have risen faster and cost five to six times what they did in the early 1970s, he said. In the same period, he said, room-size rugs have skyrocketed in price, increasing 10 to 15 times.

Mr. Abadjian said that 30 to 35 percent of his rugs were European (English, French and Bessarabian). The rest are Indian, Chinese, Turkish and Persian. Needlepoints are very desirable, he said, adding that the fashion in rugs now is soft colorings and patterns that are not too busy so they do not fight with paintings and other art objects.

Most of his rugs date from 1870 to 1920, and the Persian rugs include Tabriz, Heriz, Sultanabad, Ferahan and Kashan. Turkish rugs woven after 1920, he said, were made for Americans and Europeans and with chemical dyes that fade faster, producing a softer, more acceptable look.

A LA VIEILLE RUSSIE

781 Fifth Avenue (at 59th Street)
New York, N.Y. 10022
Phone: (212) 752-1727
Hours: 10 A.M. to 5:30 P.M. Monday to Saturday; from Memorial Day to Labor Day, 10 A.M. to 5 P.M. Monday to Friday

West of the Kremlin, this gilt-edged outpost on Fifth Avenue may be the largest source in the world for Russian Imperial treasures—bejeweled Easter eggs, icons, silver champagne coolers and the understated enamels of Peter Carl Fabergé, goldsmith to the Romanovs. The shop's three owners—Paul Schaffer, president; Peter Schaffer, vice president, and Ray Schaffer, their mother, who is secretary-treasurer—say the gallery was founded by A. Zolotnitzky in 1851 in Kiev.

By 1921 Jacques Zolotnitzky, a son of the founder, had moved A la Vieille Russie to Paris. There, Alexander S. Schaffer, a Hungarian professional soccer player and entrepreneur, met him and later traveled to Russia, where he bought works of art for the concern. Mr. Schaffer came to New York in 1926, where he continued to handle Russian decorative arts, working in alliance with his Paris colleagues.

"Mother lent him the money to go into business—$800," Peter Schaffer said recently. Alexander and Ray Schaffer, who were married in 1932, were a formidable team. They opened the Schaffer Collection of Russian Imperial Treasures in Rockefeller Center in 1933. The establishment took its European name of A la Vieille Russie in 1941, when the Schaffers moved to 785 Fifth Avenue, a few doors north of where the shop has been since 1961.

Over the years the Schaffers in New York and Zolotnitzky and a nephew in Paris—that shop closed in the late 1950s—helped develop the international market for Russian jewelry, icons, silver, porcelains, furniture and Fabergé's wonders: exquisite eggs, delicate flowers, winsome animals and enameled boxes and cases.

Since Alexander Schaffer's death in 1972, Paul and Peter Schaffer and Mrs. Schaffer have witnessed enormous growth of interest in this material and soaring prices on all Russian decorative art, especially Fabergé's. They have also helped advance the public's interest and appreciation, especially with their 1983 exhibition, "Fabergé," which presented 560 jeweled, enameled and hard-stone treasures in the largest and most complete retrospective of Fabergé's work ever assembled.

The Schaffers have always carried the refined and the more ornate enameled works by Fabergé to satisfy both the Francophile and Pan-Slavic tastes of collectors. Since the 1970s, Paul and Peter Schaffer have added more furniture—French 18th century as well as Russian and Swedish furniture of the early 19th century.

The Fabergé collectors and others who have shopped at A la Vieille Russie have included David Belasco, Alexander Korda, Marjorie Merriweather Post, the Aga Khan, Barbra Streisand, Diana Ross, Lansdell Christie, Baron Hans Heinrich Thyssen-Bornemisza and Malcolm Forbes.

The prices for Fabergé at this shop start at $1,000; animals range from $5,000 to about $100,000 and flowers from $20,000 to $180,000. Imperial Easter eggs, rarities all, command the highest prices, in seven figures (the highest price ever paid for a Fabergé egg was $1,760,000, which Mr. Forbes paid at Sotheby's in June 1985). More modest works are available for far less, from $35 up for modern miniature eggs of semiprecious stones.

ALEXANDER GALLERY

996 Madison Avenue (at 77th Street)
New York, N.Y. 10021
Phone: (212) 472-1636
Hours: 9:30 A.M. to 5:30 P.M. Monday to Friday, 9:30 A.M. to 5 P.M. Saturday
Closed Mondays in winter, Saturdays in summer

In 1977 Alexander Acevedo closed his hobby shop in the Bronx, where he sold vintage model trains, and moved to 996 Madison Avenue, where he became one of the nation's most aggressive dealers in American art. His stock at the Madison Avenue establishment, which has 996 on the door but no sign out front, reflects his personal interests in paintings of the Hudson River School, Western art, folk art and American Indian artifacts.

In 1984 Mr. Acevedo began buying and selling toys again and exhibiting them with extraordinary flair in an upper room of the gallery. There, with the same care other art dealers reserve for Sung vases or Renaissance bronzes, he shows period trains, trucks, dolls, automatons, windups and Mickey Mouse figures on floor-to-ceiling, softly lighted shelves. He says he is fulfilling a childhood dream in operating what may be New York's first commercial gallery designed to appeal to connoisseur collectors of period toys.

Mr. Acevedo's toy rooms boast the best of 19th- and early-20th-century American, French, German and British playthings that are sometimes faded and chipped but are frequently in near-mint condition. Most were made long before he was born in 1944. They range from $500 to $60,000 or more—adult sums for objects that originally cost from less than one dollar to no more than $100.

When he was small, he says, he didn't have toys—"We were too poor." He did not accept this fate lightly. He coveted both the cars, trucks and trains other children owned and what he saw in toyshop windows. Early on he also cultivated an eye for the best.

"Every Christmas from the age of six on I fantasized about owning Lionel trains," he recalled. "I knew every car in every set from the advertisements. Finally, when I was ten or twelve, my father bought me an inexpensive Marx train set. I was crushed."

Obviously a man of business acumen and daring, Mr. Acevedo said that as a teen-ager he was in a hurry to grow up—he left school after the ninth grade. This dealer who caters to a clientele of motion-picture tycoons, bankers, toy producers, advertising copywriters and business executives also presents the impression of being the boy with his nose pressed against the toyshop window. His love of trains surfaced again after he had left the Bronx and began in 1981 to collect them privately. "But I sold all of what I bought to buy more paintings," he said.

Three years later when he decided to try again, he did so as a dealer. "That way I could buy the great toys, things I could not afford if I did it privately." This made it possible for him to buy a German toy train over the telephone from Sotheby's in London for $39,270, then the highest price ever paid at auction for a toy. Made by Marklin in 1909, the tin-plated model of the 19th-century steam-fired Stevenson's Rocket has a locomotive, tender, open passenger coach and luggage car. It's extremely rare, he explained, because "it was not a big seller when it was new, so very few were produced." That train, the star offering in his stock, was repriced at $60,000 and was sold.

His eye for American Indian art is equally impresssive, judging by his wealth of material produced by Plains tribes. There are beadwork, quillwork, rifle scabbards, saddlebags, horse blankets, clothing, necklaces and an assortment of pipes. The most powerful examples of beadwork and quillwork were produced by the Crows. The Sioux preferred wide white fields against which they played simpler, frequently bold patterns. The most important beaded designs are those using the early, larger pony beads, sometimes in combination with the smallest seed beads, all of which are Venetian glass exports.

Although most of the Plains beadwork is boldly geometric or rich in stylized floral motifs, one pair of Iroquois moccasins of black-dyed moose-hair showed that on occasion these craftsmen borrowed design ideas from

Europe, adapting a French 18th-century brocade to embellish footwear.

The esthetic sophistication of the American Indians has long been recognized. What is equally interesting is the primitive aspects of their beliefs and the effects on their art. "They saw a vision and would paint it on their shield," Mr. Acevedo said, pointing to a stunning shield emblazoned with a buffalo as primitive as a cave painting.

Rarities command high prices whether they be a chief's blanket at $38,500, a hide shirt at $45,000 or a beaded and quilled blanket strip at $25,000.

"When I was a kid I used to tell my mother I wanted to be a cowboy and an Indian," he recalled, adding that he never understood why he couldn't be both.

AMERICA HURRAH

766 Madison Avenue (at 66th Street)
New York, N.Y. 10021
Phone: (212) 535-1930
Hours: 11 A.M. to 6 P.M. Tuesday to Saturday
Closed Saturdays in July and August

Kate and Joel Kopp began collecting quilts and other antiques after they were married in 1968, and they have never stopped. Almost immediately their apartment proved too small for their collections. One day in 1969 they rented a basement storage space on East 70th Street, and the next day they rented the shop next to it.

Their fate, they realize now, was determined by those moves. At first, the store was a gallery where they worked part time, juggling full-time jobs, she as a fashion designer and he as a stockbroker, while also exhibiting at antiques shows. Within months, they gave up their jobs and began developing the gallery into one of the most innovative sources for folk-art textiles in the business.

America Hurrah's stock of period quilts, one of the largest anywhere, had scores of the all-time favorites during one visit. There were stacks of Log Cabin designs, Amish, pictorial, patriotic and Baltimore album quilts as well as miniature crib quilts. Although in 1984 the Kopps paid the auction record price of $30,800 for an album quilt depicting a black family and quickly resold it for $42,000, they make a major effort to handle a large variety of moderately priced quilts at $500 to $700.

"We welcome people who do not have a lot to spend," Mr. Kopp said. "We spend time with them. Usually collecting starts with people buying quilts to cover a bed."

Quilts still constitute more than half of these dealers' sales. They also specialize in such other textiles as hooked rugs, samplers, homespun blankets and bed rugs as well as American Indian works, including cornhusk bags, moccasins, vests and children's clothing. The folk art includes weathervanes, paintings, sculpture, decoys and painted country furniture.

America Hurrah was the first shop in the country to specialize in quilts, the Kopps said. The gallery also pioneered with the first exhibitions of crib quilts, hooked rugs, game boards and cornhusk bags. Their book, *American Hooked and Sewn Rugs,* published by Dutton in 1975, remains a standard source and was reissued in 1986. It followed the 1974 show they organized for the Museum of American Folk Art in New York City, "Hooked Rugs in the Folk Art Tradition," a presentation that opened collectors' eyes to hooked rugs as a folk art.

"Most collectors owned hooked rugs, but they hid them away and most had never hung them on walls until that show," Mrs. Kopp recalled. "They really are folk art when they are good and are far less expensve than paintings."

The Kopps held exhibitions once a year throughout the 1970s and as often as possible in the 1980s, when fine examples of folk art became scarcer.

Quilts, which ranged from $10 to $65 when they began in 1968, have skyrocketed to $500 to $42,000. Hooked rugs are from $200 to $3,500, and weathervanes and folk sculptures are from about $1,200 to $28,000.

Cornhusk bags, which started at $250 when they exhibited them in 1984, have risen to $500 to $1,500. Less expensive offerings—baskets, crocks, advertising signs, spongeware and yellowware—were $100 to $200 each.

ANTIQUE PORCELAIN COMPANY

605 Park Avenue (at 64th Street)
New York, N.Y. 10021
Phone: (212) 758-2363
Hours: By appointment

SEE London: *Antique Porcelain Company, page 189*

ART TRADING (U.S.) LTD.

305 East 61st Street
New York, N.Y. 10021
Phone: (212) 752-2057
Hours: By appointment

Raymond E. Lane left school at sixteen for family financial reasons when he was living in King's Lynn, Norfolk, England, and tried a variety of odd jobs before he began to repair old houses. Once involved with architectural restoration, he soon discovered antiques and how to repair them, which led him to the English ceramics he handles now.

In 1975 he met David B. Newbon, the London ceramics dealer, and began doing restorations for him. It was the beginning of a relationship that continues on quite different terms today, Mr. Lane said. "Mr. Newbon was kind enough to teach me about ceramics," he recalled. An apt pupil, he learned swiftly. In 1979, the London dealer decided to close his shop in London and move to Bermuda. "I bought his business, lock, stock and barrel," Mr. Lane said. Mr. Newbon is now a consultant to Mr. Lane.

In 1980 Mr. Lane moved to Manhattan and set up his New York-based company. He keeps his stock of early English pottery, including Delft, slipware and salt glaze as well as some European faience and porcelain in the space he rents in Cirker's Hayes Storage Warehouse Inc. There he and his wife, Gillian, see clients by appointment. The variety of ceramics stocked covers five centuries and 75 to

80 percent of it is English; the rest is Continental and Chinese. Mr. Lane has a sure eye for robust pottery of all periods and styles, and the couple delight in doing research about these early wares that have begun to upstage porcelains in the affections of ceramics collectors.

One of the earliest vessels he ever handled is a lead-glaze deep brown chevron-patterned pitcher, crafted about 1350, that was exacavated in London. "The pottery is soft and crumbly, like biscuits," Mr. Lane said. Other early works included a Tudor watering can and a 17th-century three-footed cooking pot that seemed unchanged in form and material from those made in the medieval period. The least expensive among the early wares was a rudimentary mug from about 1680 that was $850; the Tudor watering can was $5,200.

Toby jugs, from the 18th and early 19th centuries by Ralph Wood, John Walton and other makers, filled several shelves. Pottery miniature houses, known as pastille burners—they were used to burn scented waxes to relieve unpleasant odors in early-19th-century English houses—came in an assortment of styles and shapes. There were agateware ale jugs, teapots and a stalking lion; a rare redware pew group and Whieldon bulls, lambs and a dovecote for birds. The 17th-century slipware chargers—outsize platters in yellowish cream laced with russet and brown—are among the most arresting vessels in his stock. Their crosshatched borders frame bold portraits—one shows Charles II hiding in a tree flanked by a lion and a unicorn, another depicts a cavalier and a lady—or an outsize tulip.

The amount of ceramics available, once abundant, has been sharply cut in recent years as collectors have rediscovered all types of English ceramics, Mr. Lane said. As recently as 1976 there was one ceramics sale a month at each of London's major auction houses. "Now we are lucky if we have a total of two sales a year," he said. And prices keep rising.

At this source prices range from $500 for a simple pottery figure or a salt-glaze plate to $95,000 for a rich green glazed stove tile made in Nuremberg, Germany, in the late 16th century that depicts America as an Indian. The tile, one of four that originally framed an aristocrat's stove, is an early example of this motif as part of a representation of the four continents.

DORIS LESLIE BLAU

15 East 57th Street
New York, N.Y. 10022
Phone: (212) 759-3715
Hours: By appointment, Monday to Friday
Closed Christmas to New Year's

Doris Blau's gallery is large and not fancy. The lighting is spare. The upholstered chairs and sofas—those not piled high with rugs and pillows—are lumpy and sag a bit. Top decorators bring their clients to shop, and her old customers return over and over. The phone rings a lot, and no one seems seriously distracted. The rugs are rolled and unrolled not too swiftly but with purpose. Everyone seems amazingly patient.

"I see people only by apppointment," Ms. Blau said. "Buying a rug is not a casual matter, and there must be time to do it right."

She is a woman in a man's world, and she does her business her way. She disdains offering encyclopedic knowledge of rugs. "I will never know enough. It is that simple," she said. The candor is disarming. She does not rattle off the names of the rugs in her stock—Tabriz, Usak, Konya, Sultanabad, Ferahan, Agra. Whatever magic the names of those rugs conjure would be lost here. It is impossible to imagine Ms. Blau talking about threads per square inch or about children who once lived across the world in another time and labored as dedicated weavers of these rugs. "The villages were very well organized," she said matter-of-factly.

Buying a rug from Ms. Blau is a serious, highly personal and exciting business. Most of the stock, you are told, dates from about 1875 to 1925, but there are also 17th-century palace-quality Isfahans. The inventory is there to see, rolled up 2 deep along two walls and 10 deep at either end. And if you want a silk rug for your dining room, Ms. Blau will advise against it, explaining that under a dining table the friction of chairs and possible stains might harm such a delicate weaving. Her silk weaves are more suitable for bedrooms, living rooms, offices, dens. The selection of small rugs is modest. Room-size dominates.

Ms. Blau became a dealer while married to Vojtech Blau

from 1964 to 1970. She went into business on her own in 1971. What her clients seek is something not learned in books.

"My major concern is the quest for beautiful color. I am much more concerned with the face of a carpet than with its back," she said. More often than not, she continues, the faces of the rugs that she handles have a subdued palette. "If the palette is not subdued, then where the colors are bright or vibrant there must be a lot of contrast between the light and the dark."

Pattern? "I tend to prefer large-scale pattern, not small." She says she likes the way pattern is woven in Indian Agras—the ivory spaces between the cranberry palmettes and the lines, either midnight blue or bittersweet-Lindt brown, framing the motifs, help everyone see everything more clearly.

Rugs at this gallery are $10,000 and up, with most ranging from $25,000 to $65,000 for those 5 by 7 feet or 6 by 8 feet. Rugs can run as high as $250,000, but Ms. Blau said, "We don't have too many at those prices."

VOJTECH BLAU

800B Fifth Avenue (at 61st Street)
New York, N.Y. 10021
Phone: (212) 249-4525
Hours: 8:30 A.M. to 4:30 P.M. Monday to Friday
Closed last two weeks in August

Vojtech Blau arrived in New York from Prague in 1962 with 15 years' experience as an Oriental rug dealer, much of that time spent working in secret because dealing privately was illegal under the Communists. He was forty years old, had a few rugs and little but his ambition and his eye. He worked for a year in Manhattan's garment center for $60 a week and saved money while he learned English. Then he quit his job and began his own rug business with his savings—$300—and a $3.25 round-trip bus ticket to Asbury Park, N.J.

When he arrived there, a taxi driver helped him find a rug dealer who had an emerald green Tabriz he was willing to sell for $100. "I paid $80 for it," Mr. Blau recalled. "The rug was 100 years old and never had been cleaned. I took it home to Kew Gardens, bought Ivory soap and couldn't wait to clean it. I knew rugs and thought it must be worth $500. When I cleaned it, the rug was worth $1,500." He was paid $1,350; it seemed like a million, he said.

In 1964, after scouring Asbury Park and cities throughout New England, he opened his first shop at 692 Madison Avenue, paying $425 a month rent. Between 1964 and 1969, Vojtech and Doris Blau, his first wife, ran the business together there and in a gallery in the old Parke-Bernet building on Madison Avenue at 76th Street, to which they moved in 1967. Mr. Blau today works with his wife, Jolana, at the Fifth Avenue gallery they have occupied since August 1979.

Mr. Blau's impressive quarters one floor down from the street-level entrance stock fine rugs from the 16th to 19th centuries. The colorful stacks of rugs along the walls of this sprawling space are organized so that all the Tabriz and Persian weavings are in one area, the European rugs in another, the Chinese and Turkish rugs elsewhere. Rugs are also stored in 20 closets, the contents of each of which Mr. Blau seems to recall instantly.

The 200 to 250 rugs in inventory range from about $5,000 for an 8-by-10-foot softly colored Persian Sultanabad of the late 19th century to about $160,000 for a rare Tabriz in soft colors woven about 1880. Mr. Blau's restoration staff works in full view at a long table at the rear of the gallery.

The selection of tapestries here dates from the Gothic period through the 19th century and includes works sought by collectors and suitable for decorating walls of homes and offices, he said.

BLUMKA

101 East 81 Street
New York, N.Y. 10021
Phone: (212) 734-3222
Hours: 10 A.M. to 5 P.M. Monday to Friday; in summer, by appointment

Negotiating Blumka's front door is much easier these days than it was during the 30 years that Leopold Blumka, the dean of Renaissance and medieval art dealers, was in charge and the treasure-filled shop was on East 57th Street. Sherman Lee, former director of the Cleveland Museum of Art, once described it as "a jackdaw's nest of a shop."

The dealer was famous for barring the entrance to anyone he thought was a browser and ordering others to leave when their attire did not meet his standards. Sneakers, for example, were not tolerated. Paul Newman and Thomas P. F. Hoving were both told this on different occasions and complied, returning with proper shoes. "When he learned I was serious, he graciously invited me back in," Mr. Hoving recalled later when he was director of the Metropolitan Museum of Art.

After Mr. Blumka's death in 1973, Mr. Hoving explained why he and others accepted the dealer's gruff manner with respect and affection: "He was one of the great collector-dealers whose connoisseurship enriched many lives." Mr. Hoving said that while he was at the Metropolitan, the museum benefited from what he called the dealer's "historic eye" and "unfaltering sense of quality."

Since Mr. Blumka's death, Ruth Blumka, his wife and partner in business, and their daughter, Victoria, have moved the stock uptown to a maisonette off Park Avenue that is entered through what is surely the most inconspicuous front door of any art gallery in town—solid wood painted black and decorated with only the house number and, much smaller, the Blumka name.

Beyond, everything changes in Blumka's six galleries, which are spread through two floors. The rooms evoke a colorful and sumptuous past of castles and cathedrals. Medieval and Renaissance tapestries decorate the walls, stained glass dramatizes windows and everywhere, on the tops of great tables and inside robustly carved Italian cupboards, are exquisitely chiseled French ivories, early Venetian glass, iron hardware, majolica, reliquaries, medieval steel helmets and great tables and cupboards made for the castles of Italy and France.

"We are big on dragons and lions," Mrs. Blumka said, opening a cabinet filled with lion imagery. Nearby stood a pair of Florentine chairs with the original leather covering—fleur-de-lis motifs decorate the backs and dragons center the seats. These chairs were $12,000 the pair. Other objects are available at much less ($100 for a Renaissance key or lock) or far more (a major sculpture in marble or bronze might be as much as $1.5 million).

Victoria Blumka is the fourth generation of this family in the art and antiques business founded by her great-grandfather. Her father took over at the age of nineteen in 1916. His career was interrupted in 1939 when Hitler invaded Austria. He fled and opened a shop in New York in 1942. Most of the rarities later bought by Robert Lehman, Judge Irwin Untermyer, Jack Linsky, Marjorie Merriweather Post and Anne Johnson when she was Mrs. Henry Ford 2d were found by Mr. Blumka in Europe's castles, monasteries and collections after World War II. Many of the rarities he found then are still—or are once again—available along with scores of other more recent acquisitions.

MARTIN BRESLAUER INC.

P.O. Box 607
New York, N.Y. 10028
Phone: (212) 794-2995
Hours: By appointment

In April 1978 Bernard Breslauer bought the first complete Gutenberg Bible to appear at auction since World War II and was propelled into the limelight on television and in headlines on both sides of the Atlantic. The Gutenberg Bible, acclaimed as the first book printed with movable type and one of the most beautiful, became the most expensive printed book ever auctioned when Mr. Breslauer paid $2.2 million for it.

The Berlin-born New York rare-book dealer was acting for the Wurttemberg State Library in Stuttgart, West Germany, at Christie's auction in New York. Six months later, when he acquired 90 percent of the autograph manuscripts in the sale of Richard Wagner material in the same rooms, the event was not reported because of the newspaper strike in New York.

And that is how the dealer usually prefers his purchases to be treated, even though the rare-book trade is well aware of the specialties he offers in his New York gallery. These include medieval illuminated manuscripts, illustrated books from the 15th to 20th centuries and works with artistic book bindings, major works from the late Middle Ages, the Renaissance and the 20th century. He handles Islamic manuscripts too, he said.

The volumes sought by collectors and dealers change, Mr. Breslauer said. "More and more of the great illuminated manuscripts have been absorbed into public collections," he said. "The very great manuscripts made for royalty have always been in public possession, and those that got unstuck and went into the market were usually acquired by other institutions." Among two areas that collectors have been pursuing with increasing determination are livres des peintres—artist-illustrated books and Art Deco book bindings by Paul Bonet, Rose Adler, Pierre Legrain and others, all of which Mr. Breslauer stocks.

The dealer's father founded Martin Breslauer Inc. in 1898 in Berlin, and Bernard joined the firm in 1935, when he was eighteen years old. Two years later the Breslauers left Germany for London. "We went to England and I continued my studies at London University," he said, adding that his father died in 1940. Bernard Breslauer served in the British Army during World War II and rejoined the family's rare-book business in 1945. He moved from London to New York in 1976.

Collectors of rare books often start modestly, and some books that all buyers seek may be relatively inexpensive. Mr. Breslauer put it this way: "You could find a work for $250 or for much more, $350,000 or half a million dollars."

RALPH M. CHAIT GALLERIES

12 East 56th Street
New York, N.Y. 10022
Phone: (212) 758-0937
Hours: 9:30 A.M. to 5:30 P.M. Monday to Saturday
Closed Saturdays in June, July and August

This jewel box of an antiques shop is much larger than it appears and is filled with the choice wares of one of the nation's oldest major sources for period Chinese art. Allan S. Chait and Marion C. Howe, co-proprietors, hold forth in the gallery that bears the name of their late father, its founder, Ralph M. Chait. The elder Mr. Chait was twelve in 1904 when he arrived in the United States from London, and at eighteen he opened his first shop, at 19 East 56th Street, directly across the street from Chait's present home.

Ceramics have always been a major specialty at this gallery, where one may see neolithic through Tang pottery and Sung through Ch'ing porcelains among the colorful wares filling the shelves and tables on two floors. The selection generally covers almost 2,000 years of kiln-baked vessels and figures, wares dating from the Han dynasty through Ch'ien Lung in the Ch'ing dynasty. Shoppers may expect to spend $1,000 and up for an 18th-century Ch'ien Lung famille rose or K'ang Hsi blue-and-white plate and up to $150,000 for a K'ang Hsi peach-bloom imperial vase.

Some collectors of Chinese ceramics have been known to pay a princely price for a palace pedigree. At this shop a pair of imperial yellow plates, 16 inches in diameter, decorated with five-claw dragons, splendid crockery made for use in the 17th century by a Chinese emperor, was for sale several years ago for $130,000 and would probably sell for more today. In Oriental art a prestigious provenance may also mean the name of a major collector. The Chaits have offered 15th-to-18th-century selections of blue-and-white vases, bowls and plates from Herbert Hoover's collection and famille verte and famille noire porcelains acquired a half century ago by John D. Rockefeller Jr. and sold by his heirs to this gallery.

In 1979, Mr. Chait and Mrs. Howe began stocking

China-trade silver after they acquired a silver pepper caster that they were told was Chinese but that appeared to be English. The small vessel, they discovered, bore the KHC mark of Khecheong, one of the most prolific and imaginative of the silversmiths in the mid to late 19th century. In 1985 they presented the "Chait Collection of Chinese Export Silver," an exhibition marking the 75th anniversary of the gallery's founding. The show of 450 tankards, tureens and other shapes, the first such presentation of China-trade silver outside of a museum in this country and the most comprehensive on the subject to date, traced the development of this silver from the 18th century, when the Chinese began duplicating Western-style pieces for foreigners. By the mid-19th century, these Chinese silversmiths had become more daring and sophisticated, introducing Chinese motifs and styling in their work.

Skillful Chinese copies of Western silver abound in this glittering assortment of silver wares, the bulk of which were produced in Canton, Hong Kong and Shanghai. There are also scores of later pieces that look more Chinese in their embellishment. Most of the examples they handle were bought in the United States and Britain, but others were found elsewhere in Europe.

On some works, East and West meet in an imaginative, sometimes amusing stylistic merger. Beer mugs are fitted with dragon-shaped handles, English tea trays are embellished with pagoda-dominated landscapes, and apostle spoons sprout Chinese figures on their sticklike handles. The most memorable selections in the anniversary show were those that are unmistakably Chinese, including a gilded silver mug sheathed in bamboo branches and leaves by Khecheong and a melon-shaped teapot, produced after 1885, that is awash with repoussé scenes and chrysanthemums. The price range for Chinese export silver is from about $100 for a teaspoon to $70,000 for a gilded tea service.

One of the most recognizable characteristics of Chinese export silver is its weight—virtually all pieces are as much as one-third heavier than comparable Western works. Because these wares are so hefty, Chinese craftsmen improvised other changes—a gracefully crafted foot centers a tray to keep it from sagging and rollers are hidden under the claw feet of a vegetable dish to make it easier to move about.

Also notable here are Chinese export porcelains, including a selection of plates and bowls with armorial patterns. Jades dating from the archaic period through the 18th century dominate among the hard-stone objects shown. Available too are ivories, lacquer plates and vases, bamboo carvings, ancient bronzes, stone sculpture and a small group of scholar's materials, including meditation stones.

DeLORENZO

958 Madison Avenue (at 75th Street)
New York, N.Y. 10021
Phone: (212) 249-7575
Hours: 9:30 A.M. to 5:30 P.M. Monday to Saturday
Closed Saturdays from Memorial Day to Labor Day

DeLORENZO 1950

41 Wooster Street
New York, N.Y. 10013
Phone: (212) 226-2113
Hours: Noon to 7 P.M. Monday to Saturday

Anthony DeLorenzo has a sure eye for 20th-century decorative arts, which he exhibits at two galleries. The pre-World War II works are shown uptown at his Madison Avenue shop, and the French 1950s designs are presented downtown, in SoHo on Wooster Street.

Mr. DeLorenzo, a collector-turned-dealer, opened his first gallery in New York in 1980 and five years later presented a superb show of Jean Dunand's 1920s and 1930s work. The 185 vases, screens, wall plaques and pieces of furniture in the show documented the contributions of this Swiss-born lacquer craftsman to the Art Deco movement. Dunand's superiority in lacquerwork eclipsed that of all other artisans in this period. His shimmering lacquered and hammered-metal designs are embellished with arresting images influenced by Cubism and Surrealism as well as by Japanese and Mayan art.

Outstanding among the works shown were the vases and jewelry, speckled spectacularly with flecks of white eggshell, and the geometric-patterned panels and screens on which he translated a variety of art influences. Notable among the furniture shown were a magnificent black lacquer bed awash with flowers and fish and an austerely simple tortoise-shell lacquered gaming table with fold-up stepped legs that was made for the *Normandie,* the French luxury liner.

Most of the works shown were in a superbly illustrated catalogue ($55). Some were on loan and two-thirds were for sale at $3,500 for lacquered plates to $350,000 for a bar and stools painted with jazz-age motifs under Dunand's direction. Not all were sold, and others have been added since.

Mr. DeLorenzo also stocks jewelry, furniture, lighting, accessories, rugs and decorative sculpture by other top designers, including Emile-Jacques Ruhlmann, Pierre Chareau, Albert Cheuret, Eileen Gray, Jean-Michel Frank, Edgar Brandt and Diego Giacometti. Prices start at about $1,000 for a Daum vase or Dunand plate.

Concurrent with the Dunand show, Mr. DeLorenzo presented another exhibition at his SoHo gallery of the 1920s through 1950s furniture of Jean Prouvé and the post-World War II lighting of Serge Mouille. Both shared an industrial sophistication and were influenced by art—the Surrealism of Miró and Arshile Gorky and the abstract works of Calder.

Prouvé left a legacy of leggy tables, slab-supported desks and bent-plywood and metal-rod chairs that are weighty and powerful. Mouille's black-and-white metal lamps—both the towers of light and the quirky floor and table lamps—are delightful expressions of the 1950s style. The double-barreled presentation was also documented in a graphically arresting catalogue ($25). Prices ranged from $1,000 for a pair of Mouille sconces to $35,000 for a light table by Prouvé.

There are also furnishings by other French designers, including Jean Royère and Mathieu Matégot.

Mr. DeLorenzo's route to Madison Avenue was totally unorthodox. Born and raised in Brooklyn, he finished high school there in 1958 and went to work in construction. Later he became a scrap dealer. He bought his first

Tiffany lamp in 1973 and ever since has been investigating the 20th-century objects he admires and is curious about. He opened a small antiques shop in Cedarhurst, L.I., in 1978 and moved to Manhattan two years later.

ROBERT H. ELLSWORTH LTD.

960 Fifth Avenue
New York, N.Y. 10021
Phone: (212) 535-9249
Hours: By appointment

Robert H. Ellsworth, the Oriental art dealer and author, started out to be a painter and supported himself by buying and selling Chinese art. After 15 years, the entrepreneur in him proved dominant. He then combined his merchandising talent with his writing ability and produced two scholarly studies: the first, *Chinese Furniture,* published by Random House in 1972, and most recently, *Later Chinese Painting and Calligraphy: 1800 to 1950,* published in three volumes in 1987 by Random House.

When Mr. Ellsworth was sixteen, he recalled, he was a runner for New York antiques dealers, did errands for China War Relief and sold snuff bottles. There were no snuff bottles to be seen in his dimly lighted wood-paneled living room, where oyster-colored silk curtains frame his view of Central Park. But what he learned then about detailing, the quality of carving, form and color is visible everywhere in the imposing setting where he works by appointment.

The room is a blend of 18th-century Oriental and Occidental art and furnishings—blood-red Ming porcelains and tea-toned tables; a Queen Anne snake-footed candlestand, pairs of slender-legged tables on pad feet, and a great pediment-topped bookcase-cabinet by William Vile.

The interest in objects began early, as it does with most collectors, Mr. Ellsworth said. He swapped baseball cards and collected stamps in his youth. "I never finished high school," he said, although he went to Yale University and completed eight credits in Chinese in two years.

Mr. Ellsworth has been a private dealer for many years. These days his "stock" is in a warehouse because he travels much of the year to buy and to see clients, including a few top collectors and museums.

The wide range of art works this dealer handles is dictated by the fact that the choice works he buys and sells are scarce and he has a large appetite. He has Chinese, Japanese, Southeast Asian and Indian sculpture dating from the 7th century to the 15th century. His taste appears to favor the classical style, but some stone works are Baroque, too. Mr. Ellsworth also deals in Chinese bronzes and occasionally buys Chinese porcelains, "mostly for myself." Chinese furniture? Very little of the palace-quality Ming furniture he admires is available. If and when it does appear, he may handle it. He concentrates mostly on later Chinese paintings of the 19th and 20th centuries.

Most of the things Mr. Ellsworth handles carry price tags in five figures; some works sell high in six figures, he said.

ANDRE EMMERICH

41 East 57th Street
New York, N.Y. 10022
Phone: (212) 752-0124
Hours: 10 A.M. to 5:30 P.M. Tuesday to Saturday; in summer, 10 A.M. to 5 P.M. Monday to Friday

André Emmerich, a dealer in contemporary art and antiquities, is the third generation of his family in the art business and the first member to handle pre-Columbian art and classical antiquities.

"I began to deal in pre-Columbian art in 1954," the year he became a dealer, Mr. Emmerich recalled. He added classical antiquities in 1958 after moving to East 64th Street. He has been on 57th Street since 1964.

"In the beginning, pre-Columbian was half the gallery's business," he said. "In the 1960s, pre-Columbian was still a major part of the business; in the late 70s, it began to ebb." Pre-Columbian has since become a minor activity, while classical antiquities are shown regularly, but contemporary art now dominates, he said. "Antiquities are a personal business."

Mr. Emmerich was born in Frankfurt and moved as a child with his family to Amsterdam, where his father was an international lawyer. His maternal grandfather, Louis Marx, had had a gallery, Marx Frères, on Boulevard Haussmann in Paris, where he sold medieval, Renaissance and Baroque art from the 1880s to the 1920s. An aunt and uncle, Germaine and François Verna, represented modern French artists in their 1930s Paris gallery, Le Niveau. The Emmerichs left Amsterdam in 1940 for the United States.

Although Mr. Emmerich had worked while at Oberlin College in its Allen Memorial Art Museum, a career in art held no interest for him at first. At Oberlin, Greek history—and art—"caught fire" in his mind when he studied under Prof. George Karo, who had excavated Mycenae in Greece before World War II. After writing for *Time, Life International*, *The New York Herald Tribune* and *Réalités*, he realized belatedly that he really wanted to be in the art business. Later, he returned to writing and produced two books on pre-Columbian art, one of which is a prime reference, *Sweat of the Sun and Tears of the Moon*. Published in 1965 by the University of Washington Press, it was later reissued by Hacker Art Books.

In Mr. Emmerich's 1986 exhibition, "Ancient Vases—Magna Graecia," most of the fourth-century Apulian painted pottery vases were large—a few were huge—and all were notable for their pictorial decoration. The 20 pottery vessels of Hellenistic Italy were produced in the fourth century B.C., about 100 years after more familiar masterpieces were painted in Greece. Compared with their highly refined predecessors, the fourth-century B.C. works, crafted in one of the Greek colonies of southern Italy, are quite charming but decidely provincial in their robust forms, exuberant decoration and rich, sometimes witty, details. The prices ranged from $1,500 for a wine pitcher decorated with a figure of Eros to $32,000 for a water vessel depicting Persephone, Hermes and Hecate.

The gallery usually stocks Roman and Hellenistic marbles and Greek and Roman bronzes. Overall, prices for antiquities range from $1,500 for an Apulian wine picther to $250,000 for a three-quarter-life-size marble Venus.

JOHN F. FLEMING INC.

322 East 57th Street
New York, N.Y. 10022
Phone: (212) 755-3242
Hours: 10 A.M. to 5 P.M. Monday to Friday; appointment advisable
Closed in late July and August

The baronial library where John F. Fleming holds forth, high above 57th Street, is the sort of room some book lovers envision retiring to forever. Glass-faced walnut bookcases groaning with books that are meant to be reread line the walls of the tennis-court-size two-story space. Tall windows open the room to the sky, and nearby stand high-backed generously upholstered 18th-century armchairs on animal-paw feet, inviting one to linger. Banquet-size and smaller tables are piled high with catalogues and leather-covered volumes. Elsewhere, under glass, is a rarity—a manuscript leaf, written on both sides, that is a sketch for Beethoven's "Hammerklavier" Sonata.

This palazzo apartment was both bookstore and the New York home of Dr. Abraham Simon Wolf Rosenbach, Mr. Fleming's mentor and probably the nation's greatest bookseller, for five years until his death in 1952. Dr. Rosenbach, who helped American collectors and institutions understand what rare books to acquire and how to acquire them, did so with passion, often describing the book he was selling with such phrases as "the goddamnedest copy you ever saw."

This is not exactly Mr. Fleming's style, but he respected and loved Dr. Rosenbach. Mr. Fleming went to work for him as a clerk at the age of fifteen in 1925, and remained until his death. Dr. Rosenbach gave Mr. Fleming a college education, encouraged him and made him manager in 1940 and vice president in 1948. For $2 million, Mr. Fleming bought part of Dr. Rosenbach's extraordinary private collection of material dating from the 12th century to the 1950s. The material included 6,000 books, 500 manuscripts and 500 drawings.

Mr. Fleming had come to know many major collectors well and continued to work with Dr. Rosenbach's clients as well as those who came later, including Arthur A. Houghton Jr., former president and chairman of Steuben

Glass; Lessing J. Rosenwald, the late executive of Sears, Roebuck & Company; the late Edwin J. Beinecke Sr. of S. & H. Green Stamps; the Donald F. Hydes; Jane Engelhard, widow of the precious-metals industrialist, Charles Englehard; and Malcolm Forbes, the publisher.

Most book collectors prefer anonymity in buying books, but Mr. Fleming is very public in making acquisitions at auction or in other public arenas. In 1982 at Christie's in New York, Mr. Fleming paid $313,500 for the copy of the Declaration of Independence that is now at the Morgan Library. In 1985 he paid $638,000 for a first folio of Shakespeare's plays at a Sotheby's auction of the library of Paul Francis Webster, the late songwriter, to whom he had sold it in 1965 for $55,000.

Among modern classics there was *The Mookse and the Gripes*—a 24-page typed episode, heavily revised by hand, from James Joyce's *Finnegans Wake*—which he bought at Christie's for $132,000, a record at auction for a work by Joyce. And he acquired the original typescript of Henry Miller's *Tropic of Cancer* at Sotheby's for $165,000, the highest price at auction for a modern manuscript sold in the United States.

The variety of works available from the 10th century to the present—Mr. Fleming's greatest interest is the American 18th century—permits a wide range of prices. Mr. Fleming says he has books ranging from $25 to $350,000.

FRENCH & COMPANY

17 East 65th Street
New York, N.Y. 10021
Phone: (212) 535-3330
Hours: By appointment

French & Company was 80 years old in 1987. It has a glorious history that began when Mitchell Samuels and Percy W. French, two enterprising employees of W. & J. Sloane, bought Sypher & Company and gave it the name that remains today. The founders had the financial backing of Charles M. Ffoulke, a Washington wool merchant and tapestry collector. French & Company's roots go back further, to 1840 and Daniel Marley, whose business was later acquired by Sypher.

When Martin J. Zimet acquired French from the City Investing Company in 1969, the company was in decline, although it had been known as the world's largest dealer in art treasures and one of the nation's oldest and finest. Mr. Samuels, who died in 1959 at the age of seventy-nine, was its dominant personality, and his clients had included such family names as Widener, Morgan, Rockefeller, Vanderbilt, Chrysler, Harriman, Getty, Mellon, Duke and Hearst. It was a Samuels family business in which his younger brothers shared responsibility.

Financial problems always plagued the company and finally overwhelmed the owners in the 1950s. City Investing acquired 50 percent of the company then, and in 1966 became sole owner. A nephew of Mr. Samuels, Robert Samuels, Jr., is the only family member to remain at French today.

Under Mr. Zimet, French is a dramatically different company. He was 38 when he acquired it. The son of a Wall Street investor, he became a broker for Goldman, Sachs & Company after graduating from Lafayette College in 1952. While on Wall Street he formed an oil company and left to run it, reaping a fortune in Texas oil, the profits of which still fuel some of French's activities.

Another difference in French today: under Mr. Samuels, French had a castlelike building on 57th Street east of Third Avenue and two sprawling light-washed floors atop the old Parke-Bernet building, which it once owned, at Madison Avenue and 76th Street. In 1973, Mr. Zimet moved French to three floors of windowless quarters, illuminated by a skylight, in two town houses he had connected. He lives on the top three floors. There is no sign above the door and he sees clients by appointment only, maintaining a staff of seven, about one-tenth the number French used to employ.

The stock includes Old Master paintings, English and French 18th-century furniture and French Art Deco furniture. "We probably have about 70 pieces of furniture and 40 paintings," Mr. Zimet said. In French's heyday, that volume would have been contained in one or two of its score of galleries. "It's different times and different conditions today," Mr. Zimet said.

Why did Mr. Zimet buy French & Company? "I bought

it to have something to do," he said, adding that its stock of tapestries seemed an excellent investment. (He sold one French set, "The Story of Esther" from 1770, to the Shah of Iran.) "I had sold the operating end of the oil company and I had little or nothing to do." Business proceeds at his pace and, since 1981, with his son Henry's help.

"The word gets out that we do have the very best pieces," he said, rattling off a list that included two pieces of 18th-century Charles Cressent furniture, a Jean Dunand Art Deco bed at $125,000 and two partners' desks—an Art Deco design by Emile-Jacques Ruhlmann at $350,000 and a Chinese Chippendale design at $850,000. "We make about 60 sales a year." Among the top offerings were a Louis XV black lacquer commode inlaid with mother of pearl by B.V.R.B. (Bernard van Risamburgh)—one of three made for Madame Pompadour (the other two are in Buckingham Palace and Quirinal Palace in Rome). The asking price? $3 million.

BARRY FRIEDMAN LTD.

1117 Madison Avenue (at 84th Street)
New York, N.Y. 10028
Phone: (212) 794-8950
Hours: 10 A.M. to 6 P.M. Monday to Saturday
Closed Saturdays from June 30 to Labor Day and for the first two weeks of August except by appointment

Barry Friedman, one of the most enterprising dealers in late-19th- and 20th-century decorative arts, stocks important works by major European and American architects and designers who emerged between 1880 and 1960. Among the works from the turn of the century that he offers are both the exuberant furniture and lighting designs of Louis Majorelle, Hector Guimard, Emile Gallé and Louis Comfort Tiffany and the more severe architectural furnishings of Frank Lloyd Wright, Charles Rennie Mackintosh, Josef Hoffmann, Koloman Moser and Otto Wagner. Dutch de Stijl, French Art Deco, Italian Modern and European work of the 1950s and 1960s are also generously represented.

Mr. Friedman, an accountant who became a dealer in 1968 "to finance my collecting," started buying and selling works privately and within a year had opened his first shop in a New York antiques center. In 1970, he and his wife, Audrey Friedman, moved their business to Madison Avenue, founding the decorative arts shop, Primavera, which he left when they separated. After dealing privately again from 1973 to 1976, Mr. Friedman opened a gallery where he has expanded his interests to cover art—Symbolism, Pre-Raphaelite, European realist and Art Deco paintings—as well as 19th- and early-20th-century decorative arts. The present gallery, to which he moved in the summer of 1987, operates with a staff of five, including Mr. Friedman and Jonathan Hallam, the director,

A keen eye and seemingly insatiable appetite for the decorative arts have carried Mr. Friedman a long way. After his initial interest in Art Nouveau iridescent glass, he took major steps forward into the 20th century and was among the first to show Art Deco and 20th-century architectural modern on Madison Avenue. Occasionally, Mr. Friedman organizes exhibitions of this and later material. In 1984 he did "Mackintosh to Mollino—50 years of Chair Design," with catalogue, showing 75 examples of American and European works, a list that read like a Who's Who of the period.

He has a large assortment of works dating from 1890 to 1960, and he usually has a few late works from the 1940s and 1950s or the Italian Modern movement for $500 or less. These styles are now emerging as the next area for major collecting. Prices for the rarest and finest works—by Tiffany, Gallé or Koloman Moser—may be from $250,000 to $500,000.

For the last several years Mr. Friedman has been a major force in establishing auction records for the designers and architects of these periods when exceptional works have come up for sale. For example, in 1985 he paid $76,260 at Christie's in London for a Koloman Moser poster that was included in "Vienna 1900: Art, Architecture & Design," a survey of the period held at the Museum of Modern Art in New York. The price was a record at auction for a poster. At Christie's 1986 sale in Amsterdam of a collection of Gerrit Rietveld's furniture, Mr. Friedman bought some remarkable and rare pieces, including an ebonized easy chair, designed in 1924, for the second highest price of the sale, $42,978. He also bought a plywood worktable-cabinet, a plywood chest of drawers, two military chairs and stools and two Zigzag chairs designed by the architect in 1934.

HIRSCHL & ADLER GALLERIES INC.

21 East 70th Street
New York, N.Y. 10021
Phone: (212) 535-8810

HIRSCHL & ADLER MODERN INC.

851 Madison Avenue (at 70th Street)
New York, N.Y 10021
Phone: (212) 744-6700

HIRSCHL & ADLER FOLK INC.

851 Madison Avenue (at 70th Street)
New York, N.Y 10021
Phone: (212) 988-3655
Hours for all three: 9:30 A.M. to 5:30 P.M. Tuesday to Saturday; in summer, 9:30 A.M. to 5 P.M. Monday to Friday; in August, by appointment

In the 1980s, Hirschl & Adler, a major dealer in American art, became an equally impressive force in American decorative arts. Stuart P. Feld, who was associate curator in charge of the Department of American Paintings and Sculpture at the Metropolitan Museum of Art until he resigned in 1967, joined Hirschl & Adler as a partner and became its owner in the late 1970s. Since then he has expanded the gallery's coverage into three areas.

In 1983 he began offering architect-designed 20th-century furniture, lighting, stained glass and objects at Hirschl & Adler Modern, a gallery headed by Donald McKinney. In 1987 he opened Hirschl & Adler Folk, under the direction of Frank J. Miele, where paintings, furniture, needlework and objects were exhibited. The third expansion is seen in the main gallery, where 19th-century neo-classical through Victorian furniture, silver, porcelain and glass have been on view from time to time and have been offered as part of the gallery stock since 1985.

The first exhibition of 20th-century modern material by architects and industrial designers was of furniture, stained-glass windows and decorations by Frank Lloyd Wright. Since then the gallery has also stocked the works of Charles Sumner Greene and Henry Mather Greene, the turn-of-the-century California architects, as well as major furnishings designed through the 1930s by other American architects and industrial designers.

"At Folk, on the other hand, we are going to have a very broad range of folk-art material," Mr. Feld said. "We are going to continue with a stronger focus on paintings and folk furniture than on quilts and chalkware cats." Folk paintings have always been handled at the main gallery, so it was not surprising to find major works by Ammi Phillips, Erastus Salisbury Field, Thomas Chambers and Rufus Hathaway in stock when the new gallery opened. Added to this were folk furniture, weathervanes and sculpture, including the energetically carved lamb that was in the nation's first major museum show of folk art, which was at the Newark Museum in 1930.

Mr. Feld said that under Mr. Miele, the folk-art gallery would handle major chalkware, glass and quilts, like the Baltimore album quilt that Hirschl & Adler bought at Sotheby's in January 1987 for $176,000 and sold the next day. In fact, another quilt that Mr. Miele said was of equal importance was in stock for the opening of the gallery several months later. "We will be major contenders for the best in folk art," Mr. Feld said. He said he expected the gallery to present exhibitions "about six a year that will document a wide range of material within the broad genre of folk art."

The third expansion was an outgrowth of Mr. Feld's personal interest as a collector in neo-classical furniture of the early 19th century—the Empire and Regency styles as interpreted in the United States. But, as with most things that Mr. Feld investigates, he went further.

"We are basically dealing in 19th century," he said, adding that the gallery offered a small and choice collection of American decorative arts ranging from the late Federal pieces of the early 19th century to the furniture and silver of the Revival styles and Esthetic Realism at the end of the century.

"With an inventory of 5,000 works," he said, "it is not possible to show at any one time everything stocked in different fields. We have objects that are from $1,000 and up. It can vary enormously, depending on what is available." Prices for the most important works may be "well into six figures," he added.

MARGOT JOHNSON INC.

18 East 68th Street
New York, N.Y. 10021
Phone: (212) 794-2225
Hours: By appointment

"Victorian has had a bad press," said Margot Johnson, a pioneer dealer in late-19th-century American furniture. "I think of Victorian as happy furniture, and it makes me smile. A lot of it, especially the American pieces, is romantic or it has an exotic eccentricity that is wonderful."

She said it was the eccentricity that sparked her interest in the 1970s. "I started to buy what I could afford," she said. "Fine wicker tables and chairs were $50 and $100. The same pieces would cost thousands today."

Ms. Johnson was well ahead of the pack as a collector and as a dealer, too. By the early 1980s the field was one of the fastest-growing areas of the antiques world. Her interests soon went well beyond wicker to more formal furniture by some of the best cabinetmakers of the period—Herter Brothers, Alexandre Roux, Pottier & Stymus, Leon Marcotte, George Hunzinger and R. J. Horner.

Shortly after she opened her first gallery on West 40th Street in 1983 she began paying record prices at auction for Herter Brothers furniture, then sold some of these pieces to museums and major collectors. Six months after she moved to that establishment, in fact, the Art Institute of Chicago bought an 1880s rosewood cabinet by Herter that she had purchased at auction. "Every museum in the country seems to be collecting in this period," she commented at the time. And about that time she stocked a Herter Brothers three-piece bedroom set in Japanese style with floral inlays—the same sort of bedroom that Andy Warhol bought for half the price a decade earlier in the 1970s.

After three years in that first gallery, a sprawling space with huge windows on the street floor of an office building, she moved north just in time to be closer to the Metropolitan Museum of Art when its show, "In Pursuit of Beauty: Americans and the Esthetic Movement," opened in October 1986. Ms. Johnson's high-ceilinged one-room space in a turn-of-the-century converted mansion is less than one-fourth the size of her former home, but it is handsomely paneled and far more convenient for clients.

"I have had more visits in two months here than I had in the six months before I moved from downtown," she reported. "New Yorkers are so busy you have to make life more convenient for them, and everyone at some time gets to the corner of 68th and Madison."

She likes vehemently Victorian works in the Revival styles, late-19th-century furniture that is whimsical and made of wicker, light woods, cast iron, wire and brass. Some of her major pieces are stored elsewhere. Among the pieces on view at the gallery were several Herter chests, a bed, vanity and table and a Louis Comfort Tiffany throne chair from the 1880s. "I want to deal only in masterpieces of the period." she said. "Here, I think it will be possible."

When Ms. Johnson, who was born and raised in North Dakota, became a dealer, American furniture produced from 1850 to 1900 had many mysteries and misidentifications. That is changing now as scholars and specialists tackle questions about what was made when, where and by whom.

Prices at this gallery are from $450 for an ebonized plant stand to $95,000 for an inlaid labeled Herter Brothers library table of the Esthetic Movement.

JORDAN VOLPE GALLERY

958 Madison Avenue (near 75th Street)
New York, N.Y. 10021
Phone: (212) 570-9500
Hours: 10:30 A.M. to 5:30 P.M. Monday to Saturday
Closed Saturdays from the Fourth of July to Labor Day; closed Mondays the rest of the year

When the arts and crafts movement flourished at the turn of the century, it filled the offices and dens of America with robust mission-style furniture as well as stained-glass lamps and colorfully glazed art pottery. The revival of interest in this period began in the late 1960s and was well under way by 1976, when this source opened its first gallery on West Broadway in SoHo. Jordan Volpe became the first major dealer in such material and remains the dominant source, holding museum-quality exhibitions at least once a year and offering superb examples of the arts-and-crafts style, which grew out of William Morris's anti-machine proselytizing in mid-19th-century England.

Vance Jordan and Todd Volpe, collectors-turned-dealers, have explored virtually every aspect of the style in imaginatively designed exhibitions organized by experts and accompanied by scholarly catalogues. They presented comprehensive reviews of Gustav Stickley's ladder-back, spindle-back and slat-back chairs, his bookcases, desks and tables along with the designs of his four brothers, which were produced by three other companies. The gallery continues to stock these works. On view, too, are the designs of such other masters of the period as Frank Lloyd Wright, Harvey Ellis, Louis Sullivan and Charles Rohlfs.

American art pottery, another specialty, is covered extensively in exhibitions and in a stock of works by Rookwood, Grueby, Fulper and George Ohr. In 1986, Mr. Volpe and Beth Cathers, a third partner in the gallery, began exhibiting pottery and furniture from the 1940s and 1950s, including works by Peter Voulkos, Paul Frankl, Otto Natzler and Gilbert Rohde.

One of the most memorable shows at this gallery was the ceramic art of the Martin Brothers, a British team of four eccentric brothers who concentrated on fashioning grotesque forms in earthenware a century ago. The 1981 exhibition opened, appropriately, on Halloween night. The gallery had been transformed into the Martins' London shop and a Gothic fantasy setting where eerie sounds, dripping water in a darkened pool, gnarled trees, live moss and mood lighting explained more than words could about the tortured minds of these ceramists.

The pottery included bird-shaped tobacco jars, smirking spoon warmers, sneering and leering two-faced pitchers, satyr-mask jugs and an armadillo-shaped toast rack. They all seemed right at home. These wares, priced from $500 for a small saucy-looking bird to $20,000 for a large sullen-faced bird, have since skyrocketed in price to twice those figures.

Mr. Jordan and Mr. Volpe, who are cousins, said they decided out of desperation to switch from collecting to dealing. "Each of us had floor-to-ceiling stacks of chairs and other artistic piles, and they kept growing," Mr. Volpe said. Mr. Jordan, who ran a theatrical talent agency (he still does), and Mr. Volpe, who had worked until then on sets at the Metropolitan Opera, found that their antiques-choked homes had enough ledge-armed settees, boxy chairs, desks and chests to fill not only a gallery but a warehouse as well.

When the gallery began, chairs, tables and cabinets were $100 to $1,300. Today furniture is from $1,000 for a very good chair and $2,500 for an important table—both by Gustav Stickley—to $50,000 for a rare Harvey Ellis desk or music cabinet or $75,000 for a dining table by Frank Lloyd Wright. Pottery from the 1880s to the 1950s ranges from $1,000 to $15,000.

The staff of seven includes several who restore furniture, lighting, pottery and paintings.

In February 1987 Jordan Volpe moved from SoHo to Madison Avenue near 75th Street to a paintings gallery with "an Old World look," Mr. Jordan said. The walls are covered with dark blue silk and red velvet, and the space is smaller and has a lower ceiling than their former quarters.

MURIEL KARASIK

1094 Madison Avenue (at 82d Street)
New York, N.Y. 10028
Phone: (212) 535-7851
Hours: 10 A.M. to 6 P.M. Monday to Saturday
Closed Saturdays from Memorial Day to Labor Day

"I was always a collector," Muriel Karasik said, surrounded by the proof of her acquisitive nature in her shop, which specializes in 1920s through 1950s jewelry, glass, ceramics, plastics, fashion accessories, lighting, Bakelite radios, furniture, folk art, posters and decorative sculpture. When Mrs. Karasik realized in 1977 that she had run out of space at home for her collections, she decided to make a business out of her consuming interest in objects and jewelry. She reasoned that a shop would help her reduce her holdings and give her a reason to buy more.

Mrs. Karasik's offbeat stock is, she said, dramatically different from what she knew in her home as a child. Her parents, Jack and Belle Linsky, whose stationery business included Swingline Inc., manufacturer of staplers, were impulsive about the formal 18th-century French furniture, European porcelains, bronzes, Old Master paintings and Renaissance jewelry they bought over 40 years. In 1982, two years after her husband's death, Mrs. Linsky gave the collection—said to be worth $60 million at the time—to the Metropolitan Museum of Art.

As a collector, Mrs. Karasik shares with her parents a delight in impulse buying and a curiosity about the human figure, which can be seen in her stock of 1920s and 1930s decorative chrome sculptures by Franz Hagenauer, a Viennese artist. These figures are frequently humorous and invariably lighthearted, a quality characteristic of most of the decorative objects in this shop.

Mrs. Karasik helped advance the rediscovery of Bakelite radios in 1984 when she was host of an exhibition of these passports to the past, "The American Radio Show—Bakelite Radios of the 1930s and 1940s." On view and for sale then—and whenever she can find examples now—were these period radios shaped like Mayan temples, New York skyscrapers, torpedoes and Cleopatra's hairdo. The colors are bold and clear—lipstick red, butterscotch yellow, marbleized green, maroon and white.

Mexican jewelry, another speciality here, was the subject of a 1985 show, "Mexican Silver Jewelry: The American School 1930-1960." Included were the designs of William Spratling, an American architect who settled in Taxco de Alarcón, Mexico, in 1929 and developed his own silver jewelry and guided the work of others, resulting in a boom in silver jewelry in Taxco and throughout Mexico.

Mrs. Karasik and Elaine Mathas, her assistant, buy for the shop. The staff also includes Victoria Karasik, one of Mrs. Karasik's five children.

Prices range from $25 for a pair of Bakelite earrings to $25,000 for one of the panels from the *Normandie,* the French Art Deco luxury liner, Mrs. Karasik said. Most of the items in the shop—the Mexican silver jewelry, figural perfume bottles, the 1930s green lacquered and chromed cocktail shakers, the 1950s Swedish and Italian glass vases, decanters and stemware—are $250 to about $1,000.

GERALD KORNBLAU

305 East 61st Street
New York, N.Y. 10021
Phone: (718) 291-5094
Hours: By appointment

Gerald Kornblau's keen eye for American folk art was developed from his youth, when he went to work in 1944 at the age of twelve as a gofer in a photographer's studio. The still-life work and the accessorizing of photographs that he witnessed and eventually helped with introduced him to a wealth of materials and objects. He served two years in the Signal Corps as a photographer and ran a laboratory during the Korean War. He worked as a photographer until 1958, doing still lifes in advertising. His first antiques shop, at Second Avenue and 49th Street, had English, French and American objects and antiques.

"I taught myself the business," Mr. Kornblau said. By 1961 he had moved to a shop on 58th Street near Second Avenue. He and his wife, Audrey, made weekend shopping forays to New England, Pennsylvania and upstate New York to stock it.

"I used to enjoy buying and selling lots of things," he said. "We would go out on the weekends and buy, come back Monday and sell by Saturday." It was in that shop, too, that American folk art began to dominate his awareness. In late 1964 Mr. Kornblau got hepatitis and had to restrict his activities for the next half year. "I started sharpening the eye to buy less and better," he recalled. He said the most important lesson he learned was "If you see something you respond to, grab it."

Folk-art collectors have learned that message, too. If they see something they respond to in Mr. Kornblau's booth at the Winter Antiques Show each January, they grab it fast before someone else can buy the folk-art painting by Erastus Salisbury Field, the Statue of Liberty weathervane, the cigar-store Indian, the neo-classical architectural relic or the outsize bloodhound garden figure crafted by J. W. Fiske about a century ago. Always one of the most arresting in this show, the booth where Mr. Kornblau has held forth since 1968 is invariably sold out or nearly so by the end of the fair's nine-day run.

The bazaar is the one place the general public can see some of Mr. Kornblau's stock without making an appointment to visit the warehouse where he now sees clients. The dealer gave up his shop after he decided he wanted to spend more time finding art works instead of minding the shop and waiting for clients.

Mr. Kornblau said that as a dealer he tries to buy when his gut tells him he must. And when is that? "When it has good lines," he said, adding that the other elements involved in his visceral reaction are harder to define. The dealer's clients have included virtually all the top American folk-art collectors, including Alice Kaplan, wife of Jacob M. Kaplan, a financier and philanthropist. She acquired several of her most important objects—an Angel Gabriel tavern sign and a great curlew vane—from him.

Mr. Kornblau's price range is typical of the folk-art market. Watercolors start at about $1,000 and architectural relics and other offerings are under $25,000. Some of the finest examples of folk-art paintings are higher.

H. P. KRAUS

16 East 46th Street
New York, N.Y. 10017
Phone: (212) 687-4808
Hours: 9:30 A.M. to 5 P.M. Monday to Friday

When Hans P. Kraus arrived in the United States in 1939 from Hitler's Austria he had only a few books that he had been able to salvage from the rare-book business he started in Vienna in 1932. He landed and began his discovery of America on his 32d birthday, which seemed a good omen to him for it was Columbus Day.

Mr. Kraus said that among his few books was a Columbus letter and that New York newspapers reported the fact. Mr. Kraus then and increasingly after World War II became a figure to be reckoned with in the rare-book and manuscript field, a man who relished publicity on the purchases and sales he made, often for record prices. Never a modest man, he was tireless in building his business with his knowledge of sources, bargaining skills, auction expertise, adventurous style and ruthlessness, wrote one critic from *The New York Times* when his autobiography was published by G. P. Putnam's Sons in 1978.

The bookseller began his New York business in a two-room flat that he soon expanded many times over. Today H. P. Kraus occupies five floors of a converted town house to which Mr. Kraus moved his business in 1945 and two floors in a neighboring building that was taken over in 1964.

Among the other family members still active in the business is Hanni Kraus, his wife, and Mary Ann Mitchell, his eldest daughter.

Dr. Roland Folter, who heads Kraus's antiquarian business, is one of the two Kraus specialists who made the discovery of a missing page and a duplicate page in a Gutenberg Bible that Christie's in New York auctioned in 1978 for $2.2 million, then the record for a printed book.

Mr. Kraus had sold another copy of the Gutenberg a month earlier to the Gutenberg Museum in Mainz, West Germany, for $1.8 million. He had bought it in 1970 from Arthur A. Houghton Jr., then president of Steuben glass and a former president of the Metropolitan Museum of

Art, for the same price. When Mr. Kraus was asked why he let it go at the same price, he replied, "Don't rub it in." His wife had made it clear that he should dispose of it, Mr. Kraus reported. "She said, 'Hans, you are a bookseller, not a bookkeeper.' And that was that."

The money was immediately reinvested in more rare books: the remaining volumes and documents from the collection of Sir Thomas Phillipps, who assembled one of the great libraries in 19th-century England. The purchase of 40,000 books weighed in at three tons in 280 cartons.

"Our specialties are medieval manuscripts, both text works and illuminated, as well as early printed books, especially incunabula, books printed before 1500," Dr. Folter said. Kraus also stocks books on bibliography, natural science, Americana and geography as well as illustrated books, he said. Incunabula is one of Dr. Folter's special interests and among such works he recently sold a rarity, a block book, in which each page was cut into a wood block to be printed. "A very expensive process," he said. The book was suitably priced at $850,000.

Books at this source are from $5 for bibliography to $1.7 million. Most of the rare books and manuscripts are $2,000 to $200,000.

J. J. LALLY & COMPANY ORIENTAL ART

42 East 57th Street
New York, N.Y. 10022
Phone: (212) 371-3380
Hours: 10 A.M. to 5 P.M. Tuesday to Saturday
Closed in August

When James J. Lally opened his gallery in December 1986, it was called the most impressive addition to New York's Asian art scene in decades. He had assembled in this sensitively lighted, understated setting a splendid selection of works of ceramic, bronze, jade, lacquer, wood, silver and gold dating from the neolithic period to the 18th century. The day he opened, more than half the stock in the inaugural exhibition was sold to dealers and collectors, some of whom had lined up for 24 hours before the opening to buy the choicest offerings.

Mr. Lally, former president of Sotheby's in New York, came to Asian art after completing his undergraduate studies at Harvard University and his graduate studies in diplomatic history and international business affairs at Columbia University. In 1970, at the age of twenty-five, he joined Sotheby's in London, where he learned quickly about Chinese art. He moved to New York in 1973 to head Sotheby's Chinese art department. He retained that position—and became a director of Sotheby's Hong Kong—through 1982, when he was named president of Sotheby's in the United States. Mr. Lally left Sotheby's in January 1986 and opened his Asian-art gallery 11 months later.

Ceramics dominate at this source, and the choice works of early pottery, jade and bronze from neolithic through Sung reveal this dealer's preference for bold forms and highly expressive art. In size, these works range from miniature to monumental and include an arresting pair of 40-inch-tall ceramic Tang dignitaries from the eighth century and a postage-stamp-size third-century-B.C. Han seal, a block of carved gold topped by a tortoise with neatly chiseled characters in the base.

Outstanding was a large red pottery Han horse, a powerful figure almost two feet tall from about 200 B.C. boasting admirable musculature, flaring nostrils and fully formed legs. The mottled red surface on this recently excavated sculpture showed traces of earth. "He's quite rare," Mr. Lally said. "So many of the Han-period horses are without legs." Limbless ceramic horses, he said, were originally fitted with wood legs that have since disintegrated.

Among the more provocative of the archaic jade disks was a serenely simple, icy white doughnut almost six inches in diameter. There was an exquisitely detailed silver box of the 14th century with flowers in high relief on the lid. From the 16th century came an aristocratic pair of yoke-back Ming chairs, and from the 18th century a large imperial yellow dish, a ravishing example of the enameler's skill from the Ch'ien Lung period.

"We are going back to a golden era," Mr. Lally said, observing that the Chinese works being offered today are comparable to those available at the turn of the century. Then, as now, excavations uncovered a wealth of tomb material. Although the stock has more tomb works than Ming and later material, Mr. Lally said that may change. "I believe there are great works of Chinese art in every period," Mr. Lally said, adding that he intended to stock only the best and would not handle such smaller collectibles as snuff bottles.

Prices here range from $3,000 for a bronze Han seal to $180,000 for the pair of Tang dignitaries.

FRED LEIGHTON

773 Madison Avenue (at 66th Street)
New York, N.Y. 10021
Phone: (212) 288-1872
Hours: 10 A.M. to 6 P.M. Monday to Saturday
Closed Saturdays in July and August

"I like to search for things other people do not have," Murray Mondschein said on his return from one of his longer, more distant shopping forays—a two-month trip to India and Sri Lanka. He reported that in the oldest jewelry store in Sri Lanka he found a rare double strand of natural pearls that the owner had hidden away since the 1930s.

"That's opulence," he said. "That necklace paid for the whole trip." Finding such extraordinary works is what makes dealers such as Mr. Mondschein succeed. Not surprisingly, the pearls stopped traffic when he placed them in the window of his shop.

Mr. Mondschein did not inherit the lavish taste the necklace represents—and virtually everything else he expresses in his selection of period jewelry. His father was in real estate in the Bronx, where he was born and raised. As a child, he recalled, he admired tropical fish and flowers. "It's simple," he said. "I have always loved beautiful things."

What he stocks in secondhand jewelry is the proof. It includes the Art Nouveau necklaces and brooches by René Lalique, Georges Fouquet and Paul and Henri Vever and the Art Deco designs by Cartier, Van Cleef & Arpels and Tiffany. There are restrained expressions of Art Deco, but the dealer prefers the more luxurious jewelry of the

1920s and 1930s, works made for Indian potentates by Cartier and Van Cleef.

The taste is acquired, he said, adding that he discovered it with the help of Sheik Nasser al-Sabah, a member of the royal family of Kuwait. "I came to understand that great ropes of emeralds and pearls and lots of stones piled on top of each other look wonderful," he said. "I always like that lusciousness of color."

Mr. Mondschein also buys earlier and later jewelry. His offerings range from about $5,000 for a clip, earrings or bracelet, to about $1 million for large diamonds. On one visit, Lalique jewelry included a pair of pins in the shape of wheat at $6,000 the pair, a large plique à jour pin of six leaves at $30,000 and a spectacular dog-collar choker of opals, enamel and diamonds at $125,000. Stunning too was a snake-shaped bracelet of opals, gold, enamel and diamonds and a ring to match, designed by Mucha and made by Fouquet for Sarah Bernhardt.

The Fred Leighton gallery of the 1980s is a far cry from the Mexican crafts and silver jewelry shop in Greenwich Village that Murray Mondschein bought with a partner in 1960. Mr. Mondschein changed things slowly, eventually adding American Indian jewelry, Mexican wedding dresses and Victorian jewelry. In 1973 he left the crafts behind in Greenwich Village and opened a shop on Madison Avenue a block from where he is today.

BERNARD & S. DEAN LEVY INC.

24 East 84th Street
New York, N.Y. 10028
Phone: (212) 628-7088
Hours: 10 A.M. to 5:30 P.M. Monday to Friday; from June to October, same hours Tuesday to Saturday

In the 1970s, Bernard and S. Dean Levy, a father-son team of American antiques dealers, left Benjamin Ginsburg, with whom Bernard had run one of New York's oldest and most respected antiques firms, Ginsburg & Levy. This family business, founded in 1901 by Isaac M. Levy and John Ginsburg, was on Madison Avenue near 68th Street for 50 years.

They opened in handsome quarters on the second floor of the Carlyle Hotel in 1973. They moved again in 1987 to their present address, where the team presents American furniture, paintings, accessories and clocks from the 17th century to about 1820.

New York furniture is a specialty here, as could be seen in Levy's 1984 exhibition, "The New York Chair, 1690 to 1830."

The firm also bought 150 New England furnishings from three rooms that were on view for 25 years at The New-York Historical Society. The works had been assembled by Katharine Prentis Murphy and her brother Edmund Astley Prentis, pioneer collectors of early examples of Americana. There were more than a few gems in the group. One was a rare, small 1690s Massachusetts dower chest. Another was a William and Mary highboy on trumpet legs owned by descendants of Paul Revere, who is said to have used it and a matching lowboy. The lowboy is said to have gone to the family of Henry Wadsworth Longfellow.

Levy's stock usually includes rarities: a Goddard block-and-shell kneehole desk, a Philadelphia highboy, Connecticut and Massachusetts sofas and chests and a variety of chairs and tables from several Colonies. The gallery issues a catalogue once a year in which its variety of offerings are handsomely documented. There are early New York chests and tables showing the lingering Dutch taste for sturdy furnishings of generous proportions and there are later, 19th-century Duncan Phyfe neo-classical works. There are formal Philadelphia chairs and secretaries with sweeping lines borrowed from London cabinetmakers. There are Newport's shell-carved chests and Boston's highboys on tall, gracefully shaped legs.

Prices at this gallery range from $500 for decorative brass and ceramics objects to nearly $1 million for a Boston bombé chest or Newport highboy.

"We were junk dealers when our fathers started the business on the Lower East Side," Bernard Levy said. Within one generation, Ginsburg & Levy were dealing with the nation's industrial barons, including Henry Francis duPont and Henry Ford. The treasures the Levys have handled then and later have become part of the permanent collections of the major museums, including the Metropolitan Museum of Art in New York, the Philadelphia Museum of Art and Boston's Museum of Fine Arts.

MACKLOWE GALLERY

667 Madison Avenue (at 61st Street)
New York, N.Y. 10021
Phone: (212) 288-1124
Hours: 10:45 A.M. to 6 A.M. Monday to Friday; from Sept. 15 to June 15, 10:45 A.M. to 5 P.M. Saturday
Closed the weeks of the Fourth of July and Labor Day

A modest mail-order business was the acorn from which Lloyd and Barbara Macklowe's oak tree grew. Their business today offers one of the largest selections anywhere of Louis Comfort Tiffany lamps, Art Nouveau furniture, glass and sculpure, pre-1930 European modern furniture and bronzes and ancient through Art Deco jewelry.

Mr. Macklowe recalled how it all began in 1965. "We started advertising things—art glass and pottery—in *Hobbies,* a magazine, and selling from home," he said. The prices? He laughed. "Everything was $15 and $20." He was then a vice president in a printing company, and she was an elementary school teacher. They soon expanded, doing antiques shows at Madison Square Garden, Dayton, Ohio, and Indianapolis and Fort Wayne, Ind.

The Macklowes became full-time antiques dealers in 1969, opening a shop at 1088 Madison Avenue with examples of most of what they carry in greater depth and finer quality today. The gallery moved south to 982 Madison Avenue in 1976 and into its present quarters in 1987.

Barbara Macklowe was ahead of most dealers in her awareness of a burgeoning interest in the large variety of early-19th-century and 20th-century period jewelry. Her interest in jewelry began in childhood. "My mother collected antique jewelry," she recalled. The interest matured when she did antiques shows in the 1960s and added inexpensive jewelry, nothing over $25. Today the designs she shows—René Lalique, Georges Fouquet, Cartier, Van Cleef & Arpels, Tiffany and Boucheron as well as unsigned pieces—start at about $500 for cuff links, a signet ring or a stick pin and may go as high as six figures. Most of her sales are from $1,000 to $10,000.

"I've gone very heavily into Tiffany lamps," Mr. Macklowe said, adding that he stocks as many as 50 examples—wisterias, peonies, laburnums, dragonflies and an 18-light lily. There are hanging Tiffany lamps, too, in poppy, grape and nasturtium patterns from $5,000 to $100,000. Another specialty is Art Nouveau furniture—by Louis Majorelle, Emile Gallé, Victor Horta and Georges de Feure. Mr. Macklowe does not mince words about its importance. "I have the largest stock of Art Nouveau in the world," he said, adding that among the unusual offerings was the Majorelle bedroom shown at L'Exposition Universelle in Paris in 1900, for which he was asking $250,000.

The 20th-century modern includes Cubist-inspired, neo-classical and Baroque designs by architects and designers working at the turn of the century (Josef Hoffmann, Otto Wagner, Joseph M. Olbrich and Ettore Bugatti) as well as those who appeared after World War I (Emile-Jacques Ruhlmann, Jean-Michel Frank, Robert Mallet-Stevens, Edgar Brandt, Jules Leleu, Pierre Chareau and Sue et Mare). "We specialize in Wiener Werkstätte and Art Deco furniture and decorative objects," Mr. Macklowe said. "We have nothing past 1940."

D. M. & P. MANHEIM ANTIQUES CORPORATION

305 East 61st Street
New York, N.Y. 10021
Phone: (212) 758-2926
Hours: By appointment

Millie Manheim has been a formidable presence in the New York antiques world since she came to Manhattan in 1948 to run the English porcelain and pottery business she shared with her brothers, David and Peter. Born Emily Manheim ("I loathe the name Emily," she says. "Everyone knows me as Millie."), she was exposed to ceramics from early childhood by her father, Sidney, an antiques dealer in Newquay, Cornwall, England.

"We lived over the shop," she recalled, adding that she did not become actively interested in what her father handled until she was grown and they lived in Bristol. There she came to know the collection at the Bristol Museum, which contained many things similar to those her father stocked—English Delft, glass, pottery and porcelain, most of which was made in and near Bristol.

"My father took us to the museums, the Victoria and Albert and the British Museum, to study ceramics," she said. They had to observe everything, the shapes and patterns of every piece, and would then talk with him about what they had seen, she said. It was a tough way to learn, she said, but it gave her and her brothers ("David was a connoisseur") the foundation that made them go out on their own as partners in 1928 and open their shop at 46 East 57th Street.

By then the Manheims were well known to virtually every British and American collector of 17th-, 18th- and 19th-century ceramics. Some porcelains and pottery they handled are in the collections of the Metropolitan Museum of Art, Boston's Museum of Fine Arts, the Henry Francis Du Pont Winterthur Museum in Delaware, Colonial Williamsburg in Virginia and the Smithsonian Institution in Washington.

Miss Manheim has been in business for herself since 1967. In 1982 she moved to the space she now occupies in Cirker's Hayes Storage Warehouse. The stock, filling shelves and cabinets in two rooms, includes examples of most of the ceramics she has always handled—early English Delft, 18th-century Bow, Chelsea, Worcester, Bristol, Longton Hall and early 19th-century Spode, Worcester and Derby. Prices range from about $1,400 for a small Chelsea dish to about $30,000 for a pair of 1765 Longton Hall candelabra representing the seasons.

Miss Manheim's clients are well aware of how generous she is in sharing her deep understanding and scholarly knowledge of what they collect. Hope Baldwin McCormick went further than most, inviting Miss Manheim to write a book about ceramics. The dealer agreed to do a catalogue of the Staffordshire figure groups of Obadiah Sherratt and his contemporaries that Mrs. McCormick, wife of Brooks McCormick of the farm equipment family, has collected. The privately printed work, published in 1980, is a collector's item of great value in which Miss Manheim offers some of her analyses and conclusions on ceramics.

EDWARD H. MERRIN

724 Fifth Avenue (at 57th Street)
New York, N.Y. 10019
Phone: (212) 757-2884
Hours: 10 A.M. to 6 P.M. Tuesday to Friday, 10 A.M. to 5 P.M. Saturday
Closed Saturdays from June 15 to Sept. 15

"My whole business is based on my eye," Edward H. Merrin said. The antiquities dealer's comment would not surprise visitors to his gallery, which has presented some of the more visually satisfying exhibitions of pre-Columbian objects and textiles and ancient art in New York since he moved to his current shop in 1976.

The dealer's statement was part of his explanation of why he switched from his initial, almost total focus on pre-Columbian art (he also handled some American Indian art) to the more complex area of antiquities. That move was made in 1978, about 10 years after he left his father's jewelry business to become an art dealer. He wanted to broaden his gallery's scope because international traffic in pre-Columbian art was clearly going to continue to present legal problems.

The decision to include classical art and artifacts of ancient Egypt, Rome and Greece was made swiftly; carrying the decision out took much longer, about five years. "I looked and looked," he said, and learned "to tell a fake from a not-fake."

The jewelry, objects, textiles and sculpture stocked here today cover many areas. In the pre-Columbian field there are works dating from 1800 B.C. to A.D. 1500, including Peruvian textiles and feather works, Olmec and Veracruz sculpture and Veraguas (Panama) gold, one piece of which was a stunning double-headed pendant made to be worn as a breast ornament. Antiquities run from fourth millennium B.C. to the late Byzantine of the 12th century and cover a larger area: much of southern Europe and the Middle East. There might be Egyptian jewelry dating to the period of Tutankhamun, and there are usually bronze figures and stone sculptures from Egypt, Greece, Rome and the ancient Near East, including Assyrian, Sassanian and Hittite works, that range in size from Lilliputian to monumental. Etruscan bronzes here date from the seventh to third centuries B.C., the Coptic tapestries from the third to seventh centuries. Medieval works, a newly enlarged category at this gallery, is handled by Mr. Merrin's son, Sam Merrin.

Mr. Merrin also handles objects as simple as clay pots, as was seen in his 1986 exhibition, "The Eternal Urn." "All people did the urn; it's the one object that goes through all art history," he said, speaking of this small, esoteric show of vessels for cooking or storing food, oil, ointments or the ashes of the dead. The exhibition focused on the beautiful shapes and surfaces of what are thought of as quite ordinary objects. "Most of the pots ever made are utilitarian; only a few are wonderful," Mr. Merrin said. "Some things never change. In ancient times and today, very few people have succeeded in making exceptional vessels."

The size of the works ranged from less than two inches (an Olmec cinnabar cosmetic jar) to more than three feet (a fourth-century Greek presentation urn) and their dates from 3200 B.C. to the 18th century. The most memorable was the oldest in the show, a 5,000-year-old pre-dynastic Egyptian vase, a satin-smooth granite ovoid of exquisite refinement.

The selections in that show ranged from about $700 for a Greek wine jug to $195,000 for a sixth-century-B.C. Persian (Achaemenid dynasty) silver vessel with bull handles. Other works may be priced lower or much higher. A feathered strip figure made by the Nazca or Huari people about A.D. 600 to 700 might be $500, and a small Peruvian Chancay textile might be about $350. But a second-century Roman figure of Septimius Severus was $1.5 million. This rare, extremely beautiful headless bronze measures 6 feet 2 inches, and is one of only a handful in the world, Mr. Merrin said.

GALERIE METROPOL INC.

927 Madison Avenue (at 74th Street)
New York, N.Y. 10021
Phone: (212) 772-7401
Hours: 1 to 6 P.M. Tuesday to Saturday and by appointment
Closed in July and August

Wolfgang Ritschka, Georg Kargl and Christian Meyer, all Austrian art dealers, went into partnership in Vienna in 1975. This was two years after Mr. Ritschka had become a dealer, under the name of Galerie Ambiente, handling early-20th-century Austrian decorative arts by architects and designers. These bentwood and painted wood or metal furnishings and accessories by Josef Hoffmann and Koloman Moser, co-founders of the Wiener Werkstätte, have since become one of the most popular areas for collectors of 20th-century modern. The Wiener Werkstätte was Austria's expression of the arts and crafts movement, and it reigned from 1903 until 1931, when it went bankrupt.

In 1981 the dealers came to New York to organize an exhibition of Hoffmann's work. With more than 100 examples of the Viennese architect's furniture, tableware, lighting fixtures, linens, drawings and fashion accessories, this was the most comprehensive show of his work ever held in New York. It was at the Austrian Institute, a cultural center of the Austrian government. Two years later, the dealers did a second show there on Moser, whose works were sometimes more innovative than Hoffmann's.

The displays in both exhibtions offered a preview and a generous sampling of the designs these dealers specialized in at their galleries. The Vienna shop continues under the joint command of Mr. Kargl and Mr. Meyer, and the New York shop, which opened in 1981, is Mr. Ritschka's responsibility.

The Vienna style that developed after the founding of the Wiener Werkstätte has in the 1980s upstaged interest in Art Nouveau and Art Deco at museum exhibitions and at auction. Works by Hoffmann and Moser have brought some of the highest prices ever paid for 20th-century decorative arts, in part because many of their works anticipate by 20 years the modern of the Bauhaus, the German design school of the 1920s, and the decorative excesses of the French Art Deco style.

Galerie Metropol also stocks cabinets, chairs, tables, desks, chests and beds that command more moderate prices of, say, $2,800 for a Cabaret Fledermaus type chair by Hoffmann to $20,000 for a stained black showcase by Moser.

New York is a major center for work by turn-of-the-century Austrian architects and designers, Mr. Ritschka said, noting that many collectors of the style live in the city and others visit to shop for these works. The gallery offers modern furniture by all the major innovators. But, he said, he rarely has major furniture selections on view in the shop for more than a week before customers whisk them away. The supply of suites of salon furniture—two chairs, a settee and sometimes a table—is dependable and at prices of from $7,000 for a set by a pupil of Hoffmann to about $30,000 for an important group.

Invariably, too, there are special bentwood or painted furniture selections designed by major architects or less-well-known designers. On view in Metropol's window on the eve of the Museum of Modern Art's exhibition "Vienna 1900: Art, Architecture & Design" was a 1904 Thonet bentwood table by Marcel Kammerer, an associate of Otto Wagner, that was a mate to one on view in the museum's show. The gallery's table was $6,000. At that time Hoffmann was represented by a Cabaret Fledermaus chair for $2,800, a nest of tables, a bentwood showcase and a blue glass bowl for $1,000. From Adolf Loos there was a three-legged stool at $2,000. The prices range from about $1,000 to $40,000, perhaps for a rocker or an adjustable "sitting machine."

Mr. Ritschka said that the rediscovery of the works of Hoffmann and others was not restricted to the United States. "My grandfather used to have Hoffmann furniture at home," he recalled. "But it wasn't very appreciated in the 1950s. It was in the attic by then." But the style appears to have a stronger following in New York than in the city of its birth.

SEE Vienna: ***Galerie Metropol, page 301***

MARIAN MILLER

148 East 28th Street
New York, N.Y. 10016
Phone: (212) 685-7746
Hours: By appointment, 10 A.M. to 6 P.M. Monday to Saturday

Marian Miller discovered kilims in the late 1950s when she taught English in a private school in Athens and began visiting bazaars throughout Greece and Turkey. The rugs she admired and collected are awash with S motifs, scorpions, stars, combs, hooks, vines, animal heads, spirals, diamonds, hexagons and abstract floral patterns. She returned to the United States in 1959 to work at the Institute of International Education but gave up her job there in 1968 to became a full-time rug dealer, working out of her fourth-floor walk-up apartment at 148 East 28th Street.

"No one knew about kilims in the 1950s and 1960s," Miss Miller, who is from Valparaiso, Ind., recalled. She said these flat woven rugs have been made for centuries on looms, just as tapestries are, by village and nomad women in the Middle East, often for their dowries and not to sell. "The Oriental rug dealers rarely showed them unless you asked if they had any," she added. This explains, the dealer said, why so little was known about them until recently.

Her first customers were architects, designers and folk-art experts who told her that the rich colors and bold geometric designs in kilims married well with modern furniture. Among those who walked up three flights to see her wares in those early days were Charles Moore, former chairman of architecture at Yale's School of Art and Architecture; Ward Bennett, an interior designer; Alexander Girard, an architect and folk-art collector, and Carl Fox, a folk-art expert.

These days Marian Miller's clients climb one less flight to her gallery on the third floor, and most of them are far better informed about kilims, in part because of her efforts.

Miss Miller no longer returns twice a year to shop for kilims in the bazaars of Greece, Turkey, Iran, Lebanon and Iraq, as she did in the beginning. Now she goes on buying trips every other year and concentrates on fine antique kilims woven of vegetable-dyed yarns a century or more ago. She also buys Turkish kilims made today of paler-colored vegetable-dyed yarns, but she stocks none of the kilims woven from the turn of the century through World War II. She said the harsh colors from the inexpensive chemical dyes used then usually fade quickly.

The selection from Turkey includes intricate or boldly patterned kilims, some with the white-ground, some with the lattice motif. Among those from the Caucasus are fine, tightly woven rugs striped in red, blue and yellow, and from Iran come somber-colored kilims with hexagonal patterns.

The prices of Turkish, Iranian and Caucasian kilims are as much as 10 times what they were in the late 1960s, and now are from about $2,000 to about $14,000. Some are prayer rugs and runners, and many are unconventional sizes, measuring perhaps 5 to 6 feet wide and 12 to 15 feet long, which restricts their use as floor coverings. Actually, Miss Miller pointed out, many of the very old weavings are too fragile to use on the floor, so owners frequently hang them on walls. Bag panels and animal trappings used to carry bundles are also stocked here at from $350 to $2,700 each.

LILLIAN NASSAU

220 East 57th Street
New York, N.Y. 10022
Phone: (212) 759-6062
Hours: 10 A.M. to 5 P.M. Monday to Saturday
Closed Saturdays from Memorial Day to Labor Day

When Lillian Nassau retired at the age of 82 in 1982, she was the most energetic figure in the volatile Art Nouveau field. Nobody believed that this doyenne of antiques dealers and the guiding spirit for 30 years in the revival of early-20th-century decorative arts would be able to stay away from her 57th Street shop.

Mrs. Nassau knew better and proved once again that she was a woman of her word. She left the forest of Art Nouveau and Art Deco glass and wood-carved treasures behind her, visiting the shop infrequently. Her son, Paul Nassau, has subtly reshaped the business to his personality and taste. He has worked there since 1971.

What Mr. Nassau finds of compelling interest in the late-19th- and 20th-century decorative arts stocked here are American bronzes dating from the 1890s to World War II. Among those that he considered admirable on one visit were four 1920s life-size bronzes of women by Harriet W. Frishmuth, three of them fountain figures and the fourth a memorial work. They were $75,000 to $100,000 each.

The range for other works at this shop is wide, going from about $50 for a piece of a discontinued pattern of 1930s or 1940s Steuben glass to $450,000 for a three-part Tiffany stained-glass screen, a floral-pattern design from about 1900.

The Lillian Nassau shop on 57th Street and the earlier establishment on Third Avenue became familiar haunts for such famous personalities as Marcello Mastroianni, Barbra Streisand, Andy Warhol, Warner Leroy, a restaurateur, all of the Beatles, the members of Led Zeppelin and of Blood, Sweat and Tears. "It represented to that generation a break with tradition and tremendous excitement, and they felt close to the naturalistic forms," she said.

The stunning quality of the wares stocked awes visitors. Rainbow-hued Tiffany lamps beckon from the back of the shop, and in between are the glorious flowing forms of Emile Gallé's glass lamps and vases; weighty, glittering Steuben glass vessels; frosted glass works of René Lalique; angular, silver tableware of Josef Hoffmann; marquetry-embellished furniture of Louis Majorelle, and a sheer fantasy of form that Carlo Bugatti called a desk.

A showstopper there was a 1920s Egyptian Revival English suite of furniture: a sofa and two chairs in mahogany embellished with bronze and inlaid with mother-of-pearl. The designs echoed some of the fabled contents of King Tutankhamun's tomb, the discovery of which inspired thousands of works, including this suite. The price was $45,000.

Mrs. Nassau pioneered as a dealer in 20th-century styles a decade after she went into the antiques business in 1945 in a small shop on Third Avenue and 56th Street. She bought her first leaded-glass-and-bronze Tiffany lamp for $175 in 1956 and over the years saw such prices increase a thousandfold. As recently as the late 1960s Mrs. Nassau was the only major dealer selling Art Nouveau. Today upper Madison Avenue has more than 10 shops specializing in the style.

NEWEL ART GALLERIES INC.

425 East 53d Street
New York, N.Y. 10022
Phone: (212) 758-1970
Hours: 9 A.M. to 5 P.M. Monday to Friday

Bruce M. Newman has dramatically expanded the decorative antiques business that his father, Meyer Newman, founded in 1937 and headed until his death in 1972. Since then, the younger Mr. Newman has transformed Newel into New York's largest and most important source for theatrical, exotic and outsize period objects. It is six times the size it was in the early 1970s.

A pair of larger-than-life temple Fu dogs guard the entrance to Newel's five-story-plus-basement premises, its home since 1977. Baroque angels dwell in the rafters, and on the floors above are thrones of kings, late-19th-century benches framed with life-size bears and Disraeli's bed, a century-old lavishly carved and painted four-poster probably made in India, its red-and-blue washed surface inlaid with mother-of-pearl. Mr. Newman buys walls from ships, altars from abandoned temples and churches, and the desks of potentates and political leaders—anything, in fact, that he and his nephew, Lewis Baer Jr., vice president, decide has some age and major decorative appeal.

Newel specializes in period furniture, lighting fixtures, decorative sculpture and accessories dating from the Renaissance of the 16th century through the Art Deco period of the 1930s. Most of what is stocked would be considered out of the ordinary by those who frequent the galleries, including some of the nation's top interior designers: Mark Hampton, Mrs. Henry Parrish 2d, Robert Metzger and Mica Ertegun of Mac II as well as set designers and other antiques dealers. The list of private clients who shop here is impressive, too, and includes Barbra Streisand, Rex Harrison, Bob Guccione, Estée Lauder, Baron Guy de

Rothschild, Paloma Picasso, Patricia Nixon and Jackie Kennedy Onassis.

Mr. Newman began working at his father's shop after school and on Saturdays in 1947, when he was fifteen years old. The business, then at Second Avenue and 47th Street, rented more to stage and film productions than it does now, he said. Newel's furniture and decorations have been seen on Broadway in *My Fair Lady, Evita, Annie* and *Nicholas Nickleby* and in scores of films, including the two *Godfather* films, *Annie Hall, Legal Eagles* and *Heartburn*.

One of Mr. Newman's most spectacular coups was finding and selling an entire wall from the Grand Salon of the *Normandie,* the superliner described at its launching in 1935 as the world's most magnificent ship. It was being stripped to use as a troop ship when it burned and sank at its New York dock on Feb. 9, 1942. Fortunately, most of its Art Deco fittings and furnishings had already been removed, including this wall, which consists of 32 sculptured and lacquered brass-framed gesso panels. The stunning gold-and-silver wall, the work of two masters of the Art Deco style, Jean Dupas, a sculptor, and Jean Dunand, a master lacquer craftsman, was reportedly sold for about $2 million to a New York collector.

Mr. Newman was among the first to handle Art Nouveau and Art Deco furnishings, Adirondacks twig and Western horn furniture and the turn-of-the-century British and American arts and crafts style. He still does. These days, decorators and collectors are shopping here also for the 19th-century styles, including German and Austrian Biedermeier, French Empire and Charles X, Egyptian Revival and late-19th-century Venetian furniture that appears to have been made to furnish grottos.

Prices range from $700 for decorative boxes, candlesticks and small bronzes to seven figures for major decorations.

JUAN PORTELA ANTIQUES

138 East 71st Street
New York, N.Y. 10021
Phone: (212) 650-0085
Hours: 10 A.M. to 6 P.M. Monday to Saturday
Closed Saturdays in July and August

Juan Portela brought a shipment of 19th-century European furniture to New York in 1982 to stock the shop he opened on Madison Avenue. There he offered an offbeat mix of Directoire, late-19th-century Turkish salon furnishings and everything with a touch of the exotic in between, including Empire, Regency, Napoleon III and the Revival styles, from Gothic through Louis XVI. "There's a lot of fantasy in the 19th century—that's what I like about the period," he said. Most of his best furniture is earlier than 1850, he noted. But the upholstered furniture—chairs and settees with huge sausage bolsters and covered with Turkish carpeting—is as late as the 1880s.

Mr. Portela became an antiques dealer in 1978 when he was thirty-seven and leased a space at the Louvre des Antiquaires in Paris, where he handled 19th-century furniture and decorations until 1982. Most of these styles had been popular for a decade in Paris, but only Directoire through Biedermeier were being collected by New Yorkers.

His art education began much earlier. "My grandmother introduced me to French 18th-century furniture when I was eleven or twelve," he said. Havana-born, the son of a lawyer and educated in the United States at prep school and Georgetown University's School of Foreign Service, he spent several years working in advertising in New York and Madrid. When he moved to Paris in 1972, he began to buy and sell 19th-century paintings and, in 1977, met Christian Herbaut, a Frenchman who had studied art history at the Sorbonne and was a drawing teacher in a high school near Paris. With Mr. Herbaut as his partner, Mr. Portela slowly switched to buying and selling 19th-century furniture.

After four years on Madison Avenue, the partners decided to move the contents of the shop to two floors of their town house, where Mr. Herbaut works increasingly with trompe l'oeil decoration and Mr. Portela is in charge of the antiques.

Prices range from about $1,000 for neo-classical wooden columns used for lamp bases to about $90,000 for a tall 1790s writing desk of mahogany embellished with gilded brass that is from a Russian palace.

PRIMAVERA

808 Madison Avenue (at 68th Street)
New York, N.Y. 10021
Phone: (212) 288-1569
Hours: 11 A.M. to 6 P.M. Monday to Saturday
Closed Saturdays in July and August

MEISEL-PRIMAVERA

133 Prince Street
New York, N.Y. 10012
Phone: (212) 254-0137
Hours: 10:30 A.M. to 6 P.M. Tuesday to Saturday
Closed in August

Audrey Friedman became a dealer in Art Nouveau and Art Deco in 1968 when she and her husband, Barry Friedman, opened their first shop in a midtown Manhattan antiques center. In 1970 they moved to Madison Avenue, where Primavera has been a fixture ever since. The shop has been under the direction of Ms. Friedman and her associate, Haim Manishevitz, since 1973, when she and Mr. Friedman separated and he left to open his own business.

Then as now the emphasis is primarily on European Art Deco furniture, jewelry and objects. More recently, as designs of the post-World War II period have gained a following among collectors, this shop has added fine jewelry and glass of the 1940s and 1950s.

Most of the great names in jewelry—Cartier, Van Cleef & Arpels, Boucheron, Tiffany & Company, Raymond Templier, Georges Fouquet and René Lalique are found at this shop. Occasionally, too, Josef Hoffmann's jewelry and his silver are represented.

The glass stocked here also includes the top producers and designers—Lalique, Jean Luce, Daum and Maurice Marinot. There is glass from the late 1940s and 1950s by Venini and such other Murano designers as Fulvio Bianconi and Flavio Poli.

French Art Deco furniture by Pierre Chareau, Eileen Gray, Jean-Michel Frank, Jean Dunand, Sue et Mare and Eugène Printz, as well as the iron designs of Edgar Brandt and the furniture and accessories of Hoffmann and Koloman Moser are available at the shop or in the private collection of Ms. Friedman and Mr. Manishevitz.

Since November 1985, Primavera has operated a second shop in SoHo in partnership with Susan Meisel, an artist, and her husband, Louis Meisel, an art dealer. Meisel-Primavera specializes in the colorful Art Deco pottery designs of Clarice Cliff, the British designer. Jewelry includes some of the finer examples of Mexican 1940s and 1950s silver jewelry by Antonio Piñeda, and Antonio Castillo. There are 1950s necklaces, bracelets and brooches produced by Georg Jensen and by such Americans as Sam Kramer and Ed Weiner. Furniture designs include 1950s Italian classics by Gio Ponti and Carlo Molino and some "affordables."

Primavera's jewelry ranges from about $600 for a pair of 1940s gold earrings to more than $50,000, and furniture and objects are $1,000 to $100,000 or more. Major works may be seen only by appointment.

At Meisel-Primavera, prices for jewelry range from $50 to $3,000 and for furniture and objects from about $300 to $50,000.

JAMES ROBINSON INC.

15 East 57th Street
New York, N.Y. 10022
Phone: (212) 752-6166
Hours: 10 A.M. to 5 A.M. Monday to Friday, 11 A.M. to 4 A.M. Saturday
Closed Saturdays from June 15 to Sept. 15

The tonnage of period tableware—Elizabethan to Georgian silver as well as Chinese export and European porcelains—that has passed over the counters of James Robinson Inc. is staggering and impossible to calculate. Far more important and equally immeasurable is the grace and glitter added to the nation's dining scene since the founder of this silver and porcelain establishment arrived in New York from his native London in 1912 and set up shop on Madison Avenue in the East 40s. In 1923 Robinson moved to Fifth Avenue and 57th Street, where the shop remained for 30 years.

James Robinson was far more concerned with buying and selling Chinese export crockery than silver. His shop's emphasis shifted decisively to silver after his death in 1936, when his thirty-two-year-old brother-in-law, Edward Munves Sr., became president. Mr. Munves soon focused more on 17th-, 18th- and 19th-century sterling silver vessels, flatware and tableware, allowing ceramics to play a secondary but important role.

By the time Robinson moved to 12 East 57th Street in 1953, the dealer was also offering glass decanters and Victorian jewelry, both of which continue to be well represented in its stock at its present location, the dealer's home since 1979.

No changes occurred in 1983 when the elder Mr. Munves died. His son, Edward Munves Jr., who had worked full time with him in the gallery since 1952, continues the business in the style to which he became accustomed. The Munveses bought their five-story building in 1984, and two other members of the family of Edward Munves Jr., his wife, Norma, and his daughter, Joan, are part of Robinson's staff. Joan Munves has taken a special interest in Art Nouveau and Art Deco jewelry since she joined in 1980.

Most of the things people seek at this shop—the silver

tureens, trays, coffee and tea services, vegetable dishes, flatware and salts—are for use, not merely display. The same is true of the porcelains, which include French and English 18th- and 19th-century services of dinner plates or coffee and tea cups and saucers. Period sets of 36 pieces—12 plates, 12 soup plates and 12 side plates—range from $18,000 to $95,000 for the set.

Throughout the silver booms of the late 1960s and 1970s, the Munveses said, fluctuations in bullion had little or no effect on the value of period silver. Silver works rose 15 to 25 percent in the early 1970s before bullion prices surged again. In the 1980s silver bullion prices receded to the level of the early 1970s, Mr. Munves said.

Prices for period silver begin at $200 to $500 for serving pieces and decanter labels. At $500 to $1,000 there are cream jugs, wine funnels, toast racks and salt dishes. Sauceboats, baskets, bowls, mugs and small trays command $1,000 to $2,000, and coffeepots, trays, candlesticks and tureens may be as much as $50,000.

ROSENBERG & STIEBEL

32 East 57th Street
New York, N.Y. 10022
Phone: (212) 753-4368, 888-5007
Hours: 10 A.M. to 5 P.M. Tuesday to Saturday; from Memorial Day to Labor Day, 10 A.M. to 5 P.M. Monday to Friday

Not in his wildest dreams could Jakob Rosenbaum have envisioned, when he became an art dealer in Frankfurt in about 1860, the glorious accomplishments of his successors, Isaac, his son, and after World War I, Isaac's nephews, who were Jakob's grandchildren, Saemy and Rafael Rosenberg and Hans and Eric Stiebel.

Four generations of dealers in this family have handled some of the world's finest medieval, Renaissance and 18th-century art treasures. Uprooted from their Frankfurt base by the Nazis in the 1930s, the nephews resettled briefly in Amsterdam (Saemy), London (Rafael) and Paris (Hans and Eric) before opening in New York in January 1939 as Rosenberg & Stiebel. Today the firm lives on with three family members at the helm: Eric Stiebel is chairman (he celebrated his seventy-fifth birthday in 1986); Gerald Stiebel, his son, is president, and Penelope Hunter-Stiebel, Gerald's wife, a former assistant curator of 20th-century decorative arts at the Metropolitan Museum of Art, is director.

Tradition has it that antiques and art objects dominated the stock of the Rosenbaums in their Frankfurt shop and that paintings and drawings were added in this century, becoming increasingly important after World War I. The combination of paintings with palace-quality Renaissance and later 18th-century French furniture, porcelains, medieval enamels and works of art became important by the 1930s to the collectors who were clients, including several generations of Rothschilds (from Frankfurt, London, Paris and Vienna), Calouste Gulbenkian, Henry Ford 2d, Stavros Niarchos, Antenor Patiño, Charles and Jayne Wrightsman, René Fribourg, J. Paul Getty and Baron Hans Heinrich Thyssen-Bornemisza.

The Stiebels have been at their 57th Street address in an off-the-street gallery since 1944. They have gilt-edged and graciously furnished quarters where the aristocrats of banking and industry and museum curators are right at home and hidden from public view. Indeed, it was in this gallery that the Metropolitan Museum of Art acquired the triptych altarpiece by Robert Campin from about 1425 (called the Merode altar after its last private owners), one of its most distinguished treasures at the Cloisters.

"We used to buy every day and sell every day," Eric Stiebel said, recalling his first days in the gallery. "Today I call sales isolated transactions. I am happy if we can buy every few weeks and sell every few weeks." The reason? The major art works this concern is accustomed to handling are scarcer than ever before, and when they do become available, the prices often seem astronomical.

Visitors to this gallery expect to find cabinetmaker's prizes by such ébénistes as Bernard van Risamburgh, Roger Vandercruse (called Lacroix) and Jean-Pierre Latz. There is no in-depth stock of porcelains, but the shop stocks choice examples of Meissen and Sèvres vases, figures, clocks and garnitures as well as Oriental porcelains in French gilded bronze mounts. Porcelains range from about $1,200 for a plate or cup and saucer to $250,000 or more for a pair of Chinese Celadon vases with Louis XV mounts.

Occasionally, too, there are decorative bronze sculptures, such as the 70 Renaissance through late-17th-century figures that filled an exhibition at the gallery in 1985. The bestiary of slithering snakes, a stalking dragon, rearing stallions, screaming birds and a pacing panther are reminders of a period when aristocrats had private zoos—or settled for bronze images of exotic animals. These Renaissance animals range from $2,200 for a small snail shell to $75,000 for a horse.

ISRAEL SACK INC.

15 East 57th Street
New York, N.Y. 10022
Phone: (212) 753-6562
Hours: 9:30 A.M. to 5 P.M. Monday to Friday, 10 A.M. to 4 P.M. Saturday

The three sons of Israel Sack do not collect 18th-century American antiques. And it is not because of the dollars involved, according to Harold Sack, the eldest son and president of Israel Sack Inc. Rather it is that all the family members in the company—Harold, the eldest (he was seventy-five in 1986), his brothers Albert and Robert and Albert's son, Donald—decided not to compete with their customers for the 18th- and 19th-century Newport, Philadelphia and New York furniture they stock.

The Sacks handle some of the finest formal and informal 17th-, 18th- and early-19th-century American furniture—tea tables, highboys, lowboys, chairs, desks and clocks—at their generously stocked, two-story off-the-street gallery. Most of what is shown is furniture made for aristocrats and merchants throughout the Colonies in the pre-Revolutionary period and in the early days of the Republic.

Harold Sack once estimated that 60 percent of the antiques in any major American furniture exhibition had passed through his concern's hands. Sack-pedigree pieces dramatize the American collections of virtually every major collector and museum in the country, including the Henry Francis Du Pont Winterthur Museum in Delaware; Henry Ford's museum and Greenfield Village in Dearborn, Mich.; the Mabel Brady Garvan and Francis Garvan collection at Yale University; the Bayou Bend Collection of Ima Hogg in Houston; the M. & M. Karolik Collection at the Boston Museum of Fine Arts; three Federal rooms and the Russell Sage collection in the American Wing at the Metropolitan Museum of Art in New York and many rooms at the White House and the State Department. The name attracted an elite corps of collectors from the turn of the century on that also included C. K. Davis (guns) and Lansdell Christie (iron ore mining).

"There is nothing like an Israel Sack provenance," said William W. Stahl Jr., the American furniture specialist at Sotheby's. "It's a tremendous plus to have Israel Sack as part of the history of a piece of furniture."

Harold Sack, like his father, who died in 1959, is daring, paying dearly for what he describes as the finest examples. Indeed, the Sacks have never shied away from steep prices, Mr. Sack recalled, adding that his father set the style, earning himself the name Crazy Sack. "My father always dangled a big price as bait," he said.

Israel Sack was born in Lithuania, where he was trained as a cabinetmaker, and moved to the United States in 1903. He settled in Boston and built reproductions and repaired antiques for two years before going into business for himself.

"At that time there were only a few pioneer collectors," Albert Sack said. No important museum had begun collecting 17th- and 18th-century American antiques, he said.

"When I was very young," Harold Sack said, "I wanted to be at the store as often as possible." His father frequently took him on buying forays into the country, teaching him how to recognize masterpieces. "I loved the smell of barns and cabinet shops."

In the last 15 years Harold Sack has, in the name of the family concern and with a gambler's gleam in his eye, raised a score of auction records. When he blinks or raises his pencil at auctions, the prices for American antiques rise. This, in turn, increases the prices of comparable American furniture everywhere, including the Sack stock. In 1977 the company paid $135,000 at Sotheby's for an

18th-century Boston bombé chest of drawers, then the highest auction price ever paid for American furniture. In November 1980 it increased the record to $396,000, the price paid at Sotheby's for a Newport block-and-shell chest of drawers. And in January 1983, Sack established other records, paying, in the same house, a spectacular $687,500 for an 18th-century Newport Chippendale desk, then the record for a piece of American furniture. Two other major purchases that month at Christie's were a Philadelphia Chippendale sofa for $264,000 and a chest-on-chest for $242,000. The Newport desk was sold six weeks after it was aquired—to whom and at what price the Sacks won't say. They have been looking for a replacement ever since.

In January 1986, Mr. Sack was the underbidder on a Philadelphia Chippendale tea table that sold for the sort of price reached previously only on palace-quality French furniture—$1,045,000—in an auction at Christie's. The Sacks had handled the table before. Albert bought it in the early 1950s for $7,500, then an extremely high price, and his father sold it in 1953 for $15,000.

None of the Sacks like to dwell on the past, preferring to look to the future and new challenges, such as finding and buying more masterpieces.

Prices at this gallery start at about $4,000 or $5,000 for a chair or table and generally climb to about $500,000 in the masterpiece level.

S. J. SHRUBSOLE

104 East 57 Street
New York, N.Y. 10022
Phone: (212) 753-8920
Hours: 9 A.M. 5:30 P.M. Monday to Friday and, in November and December, Saturdays

Eric Norman Shrubsole came to New York in April 1936 with $5,000 worth of period silver and orders from his father, Sydney James Shrubsole, to open a New York branch of the antique silver business he had founded in London in 1910.

The first thing young Mr. Shrubsole did—he was twenty-four years old—was to visit all of his father's clients, driving from New York to Dallas, traveling by train to Los Angeles and from there by plane to San Francisco. When he returned to New York, he had sold all the silver and spent all the money.

"It was worth it," Mr. Shrubsole recalled. "I connected with all of our clients. And I met Amelia Earhart. She was one of the five passengers on that flight to San Francisco."

With that sense of enterprise, his father's blessing and more inventory, he opened S. J. Shrubsole at 19 West 57th Street in December 1936. There and at two other addresses on that street the dealer became the formidable force in period silver he remains today.

The proof of Mr. Shrubsole's impact on collectors and museums was seen in "Fifty Years on Fifty-Seventh Street," his 1986 exhibition of 72 important examples of English, Irish and American silver. The tankards, trays, ewers, bowls, baskets, sauceboats, a snuffer and tray, candlesticks and an inkstand made for royalty dated from 1490 to 1829 and were on loan from 24 sources—3 museums, 2 corporations and 19 collectors.

Mr. Shrubsole's passion for silver is seen in his delight in a wide range of styles. He responds enthusiastically to both the plainest wares (he has an unerring eye for form) and the most exuberantly crafted works.

Mr. Shrubsole sold one of the four earliest fully hallmarked English Apostle spoons extant. It was made in 1490, is partly gilded and has a bold fig-shaped bowl and a rod handle ending with the figure of St. Philip. Another early work bought and resold was a Henry VIII beaker that the dealer acquired for $198,000 at Christie's 1982 auction of silver from the J. Pierpont Morgan collection. The four-inch beaker, a model of simplicity with undulating lines chased on its sides, is described as the second- or third-oldest English silver beaker known.

Whether it be a no-nonsense Georgian inkstand crafted by Paul de Lamerie in 1726 for Caroline, wife of George II, with cups for ink and pens, a bell and a rectangular tray or a Queen Anne coffeepot made by William Charnelhouse in 1704 that is one of only two known that is fitted with a spigot, uncommon works abound in this shop.

Mr. Shrubsole's enthusiasm and his sharp eye have resulted in sales to the Museum of Fine Arts in Boston (a gilded ewer and basin), the Minneapolis Institute of Arts (a wine cistern by Paul de Lamerie) and to Judge Irwin Untermyer, whose collection is now in the Metropolitan Museum of Art. Most major American collectors have shopped here, many exclusively.

What shoppers find is a variety of English, Irish and American silver vessels and flatware dating from the 16th century through the early 19th century. The prices range from about $100 for George III silver tongs to $250,000 for a pair of superb Elizabethan tankards.

STAIR & COMPANY

942 Madison Avenue (at 74th Street)
New York, N.Y. 10021
Phone: (212) 517-4400/01/02
Hours: 9:30 A.M. to 5:30 P.M. Monday to Saturday, until 2 P.M. in July and August
Closed Saturdays from Memorial Day to Labor Day

In the fall of 1986 the venerable antiques dealer Stair & Company moved from its town-house home of 50 years on East 57th Street to its new address in a 1921 landmark building on Madison Avenue. Understandably, some collectors and dealers wondered what else might change.

The new premises of one of the oldest and most prestigious English antiques dealers in the United States is quietly impressive. Stair's neo-classical interiors, rich in paneling and crenelated moldings, are in harmony with its new home in a prize-wining English Renaissance building that was designed in 1921 by Henry Otis Chapman Sr. for the United States Mortgage & Trust Company. In 1922 the building was cited by the Fifth Avenue Association as the finest new building in New York.

The imposing limestone structure still houses a bank, the Chemical, on most of its main floor. Stair's discreet entrance is beyond an iron gate that opens onto a quietly elegant hall-gallery that is a bit more formal and less cluttered than its previous quarters. There and on two floors above are 11 galleries, each of a different scale and character, containing Stair's stock of William and Mary through

Regency. The furnishings range from the most conservative and formal architectural pieces to those that reveal a taste for flamboyance, wit and the exotic. Here and there visitors will also find examples of severely simple 17th-century furniture.

Stair's galleries are handsomely detailed mock-period settings filled with 17th-century through early-19th-century English furniture, chandeliers, cut-glass and porcelain decorations, rugs, carpets, prints and engravings. Planned by Stair's former president, Gerald Bland, they express the taste and vision of David H. Murdock, the Los Angeles financier, owner of Stair & Company since 1980.

Prices range from about $1,500 for an English 18th-century Chippendale mahogany side chair to about $280,000 for a Queen Anne green lacquered secretary-bookcase from about 1710. There are Chippendale hall chairs, mahogany with solid wood saddle-shaped seats and pierced backs on no-nonsense straight legs for $55,000 a pair. An architect's table may be as low as $12,500 (if it is as late as 1830) or as high as $50,000.

A diminutive Queen Anne secretary-bookcase in walnut might be $35,000, a pair of Queen Anne mirrors about $60,000. The emphasis here is on the more sculptural and robust Chippendale designs—chests of drawers, chairs, cabinets and partners' desks.

Stair & Company was founded in 1912 in London by Arthur Stair and Valentine Andrews as Stair & Andrews. The dealers opened a New York shop in 1914 at 35th Street and Fifth Avenue, where Mr. Andrews was in charge, and moved in 1922 to 57th Street. Stair occupied quarters in another building on that street before leasing its five-story town house at 59 East 57th Street, where it remained for half a century.

Alastair A. Stair, son of the co-founder, was twenty-two when he came to New York in 1935 to work with his father's partner. When Mr. Andrews retired in 1936, the Stairs bought him out and changed the name of the firm to Stair & Company. Business flourished under the father-son team, with Arthur Stair maintaining the London shop until 1939. After that, he supplied the New York arm with much of its stock.

In 1952 Alastair Stair, backed by Dr. Jules C. Stein, an ophthalmologist who founded the entertainment agency Music Corporation of America, bought out the elder Mr.

Stair's part of the business. Stair expanded, becoming one of the largest English furniture dealers on either side of the Atlantic. In 1970, Stair reopened in London at 120 Mount Street. And in 1983, the younger Mr. Stair retired.

Stair now occupies 7,500 square feet of galleries and offices and continues to operate its smaller shop in London. The Oxford Antique Restorers in New York, Stair's repair shop, handles antiques of all periods and styles. Stair sends a member of its staff to determine what is required and what it will cost.

Stair's clients have included virtually all the major interior designers and most of the major collectors of English antiques. Stair's finest English furnishings have been acquired by Imelda Marcos, Benjamin Sonnenberg and members of the Whitney, Vanderbilt, Ford and Chrysler families.

GARRICK C. STEPHENSON

50 East 57th Street, Seventh Floor
New York, N.Y. 10022
Phone: (212) 753-2570
Hours: 10 A.M. to 5 P.M. Monday to Friday and by appointment

"I have always bought anything that attracted my eye," Garrick C. Stephenson said, explaining how he came to his calling, which he had not planned. After attending Yale and the University of Cincinnati and graduating from Parsons School of Design, his route to the world of antiques passed through the world of decorating. He went to work in 1952 for McMillen Inc. and soon found himself spending a lot of time in art galleries and antiques shops.

Michael Comer, an English furniture dealer, noticed this too and suggested that Mr. Stephenson open an antiques shop. "I have no space, I have no stock, I don't have a great deal of money," Mr. Stephenson told him. Mr. Comer invited him to share his space at Madison Avenue and 55th Street, which he accepted. "I started off in 1959 going to all the auctions and visiting all the dealers up and down Second Avenue."

From these modest beginnings Mr. Stephenson's business grew swiftly in the 1960s, and he was soon traveling to Europe instead of Second Avenue to buy. He moved to 42 East 57th Street in 1967, then moved again in 1976 to his present gallery. The stock is more eclectic than it was when he concentrated more on French furniture. Now the French pieces are mixed generously with Italian, Russian, Swedish, English, Irish and "we are not sure" furniture, all with a certain stylish look. Although most are antiques, there were two 20th-century benches, perhaps from a stage set of the 1960s, that look like pared-down versions of Charles Rennie Mackintosh's cashier's cages, which were designed at the turn of the century for Miss Cranston's Tea Rooms in Glasgow. These interesting selections, 43 inches high, are $8,400 the pair.

Among other uncommon selections was a Louis XVI combination library ladder and bench in mahogany, which was 19 inches high closed and 34 inches high when opened with the steps folded out. Attributed to Canabas, it was $35,000. A handsome pair of Louis XVI mahogany consoles in the English taste on cluster column legs had mirror-back pierced aprons that opened to reveal in one case a fitted silver drawer and in the other a writing desk. Mr. Stephenson's price: $145,000 the pair.

There were a pair of turquoise-painted bamboo-and-wood chairs that looked like they could have been made for Brighton Pavilion, a very Irish marble-topped mahogany console from about 1820 with lion legs, a set of six painted metal Regency-style chairs that looked vaguely Italian and a barrel-like desk chair with a pull-out foot rest that might be Swedish or Russian from about 1800. Mr. Stephenson likes fantasy in furniture—gilded chairs with swans' heads and wings, chests with Japanese and Chinese vintage lacquered panels, low lacquered tables and benches and stools. The prices, overall, range from about $5,000 to about $200,000.

SUGIMOTO

398 West Broadway
New York, N.Y. 10012
Phone: (212) 431-6176
Hours: 11 A.M. to 6 P.M. Tuesday to Saturday
Closed in August

Hiroshi Sugimoto opened his Japanese art gallery in 1979, when he was thirty-one, under the name of Mingei, which means folk art, because folk art was virtually unknown in the United States but "it was my major interest at that time," he recalled.

Five years later Mr. Sugimoto changed the name when he began to add Japanese calligraphy, paintings, medieval Buddhist material and contemporary ceramics. "It is all related," he said. The folk art and furniture, comparable to some of the best found in Japan and still scarce here, continue to constitute 30 to 40 percent of his inventory, he said.

Mr. Sugimoto, a photographer who came to the United States in 1970 to study art, won several fellowships, including a Guggenheim. He maintains the gallery to support his art, he said. His eye for excellence would be hard to match, as can be seen in the three-room gallery, which fortunately is not so sparely furnished as is traditional in Japan. The folk art includes 19th-century farmhouse, office and shop furniture as well as clay pots, lacquered serving vessels, sculptured stone figures, twisted wood candlestands, bamboo baskets, silk-screened robes and wood mortars.

Chests dominate in the selection of Japanese folk furniture. The boxy profiles and the extraordinary hardware are reminiscent of French and German Gothic designs. But the linear detailing of horizontal or vertical bars and the austere elegance of the shaping of iron drawer pulls, hasps, hinges and locks show the Japanese mastery of metalwork.

All the chests are boxes from two to seven feet high, and each is meticulously fitted with drawers, doors, shelves and frequently with secret compartments. The woods are finished in tones ranging from rosewood to mahogany. The actual woods used, unknown in the West, are kiaki (elmlike), kiri (pinelike), kuri (chestnutlike) and sugi (cedar). Most were made for specific needs, such as storing food, clothing, papers or medicines. They range from about $2,000 for a medicine chest about 30 inches square to $20,000 for a two-part, seven-foot kitchen chest.

Some of the chests have wheels and iron pulls at the base to make them easier to move in case of fire, a major problem in northern Japan when these designs were new. There is nothing rustic or mundane in the cabinetwork; in fact, the refinement is astounding. The only nails are those used to affix the hardware to the facades. Cabinet doors lift off with ease, drawer pulls are miniature sculptures and the drawers themselves move as easily as if they had gliders.

In addition to the furniture, there are the robustly carved mortars, barrel-like designs measuring about two feet in diameter, which might double as planters or, with the addition of glass tops, tables.

More impressive still are the Shigaraki clay storage vessels, dating to the 13th and 14th centuries, their surfaces thick with colorful natural ash glazes, and the Tokoname smooth-surfaced 12th- to 15th-century storage jars. Both are named for the towns where they were made. These range from about $3,000 to $30,000. More modest ceramics are priced from $500 up.

TAMBARAN

957 Madison Avenue (at 75th Street)
New York, N.Y. 10021
Phone: (212) 570-0655
Hours: 11 A.M. to 6 P.M. Monday to Saturday
Closed in August

"I was always collecting feathers when we were children and went camping in the outback," Maureen Zarember recalled. A childhood interest in Australian aborigines was sparked by a teacher's stories when she was six years old, she said, and helped awaken her awareness of feathered ritual objects and exotic jewelry. Mrs. Zarember's adult involvement in such material makes for dramatic walls and showcases in her tiny shop. Becoming a dealer did not happen swiftly, but it seems to have been her destiny.

Tambaran's stock of esoteric body ornaments comes from Africa, Asia, North and South America, the Middle East, the Pacific and Australia. Most of the score of cultures represented here were unknown to the dealer when she left Melbourne for Manhattan in 1959 to study textile and fashion design at the Fashion Institute of Technology. A deep curiosity about native peoples made her chart a route through Arizona and New Mexico on her way to New York. "I wanted to see the American Indian," she said. The experience proved both unsettling in that the Indians lived not in tents but in shacks, which she said shocked her, as well as rewarding: "They were wearing their wonderful jewelry."

Twenty years later after a successful career in fashion and textile design and collecting tribal art and exotic jewelry, she opened her gallery on Madison Avenue. Before and since, she traveled the world with her husband, Harold Zarember, a builder, and their two children, visiting Australia annually. Mrs. Zarember has worldwide sources for the beads, body ornaments, ritual headdresses and garments made decades or centuries ago. These works are valued more for design than precious materials, for most are made of feathers, wood disks, semiprecious stones and glass beads that range in size from seeds to golf balls. Some works are gold, silver and precious gems.

Among the African works at this gallery were some uncommon and boldly graphic Ndebele beaded jewelry, including seed-size beads fashioned into thick rolls worn by women as neck muffs, into hand-shaped aprons and into long narrow strips that brides of this South African tribe attach to their hair and wear as trains.

Outstanding among the offbeat selections in Indian jewelry were 19th- and early-20th-century Nagaland material from a northeastern province. The necklaces worn a century or more ago by Naga warriors and their women included great hanks of linguini-thin strands of glass beads, Venetian exports used in trade with these people. Another necklace combined rock crystals larger than jelly beans with lapis lazuli-colored glass beads and bronze bells. Bronze torques, metal-cuff bracelets and a pair of large ivory armlets were also stocked. More formal Indian jewelry included gem-encrusted necklaces, belts of woven silver rope, bracelets and ear ornaments. Notable, too, were jeweled 19th-century southern Indian earrings in the shape of bird cages and a 17th-century imperial Mogul white jade ring inset with emeralds.

Among the ravishing examples of tribal jewelry from the Pacific Islands were silver spiral earrings and a brass serpentine bracelet. Other items included combs, beaded head ornaments, crocodile-tooth necklaces and bone bracelets.

Prices for jewelry and ritual objects range from about $200 for bracelets and necklaces to about $20,000 for Mogul jewelry. Increasingly, too, Tambaran offers ethnographic art and sculpture.

GENE TYSON ANTIQUES INC.

19 East 69th Street
New York, N.Y. 10021
Phone: (212) 744-5785
Hours: 10 A.M. to 5 P.M. Monday to Friday

"I don't like skinny, nervous furniture," Gene Tyson said, giving one reason for having acquired an imposing Irish 1740s painted pine table with boldly carved furry paw feet and a thick green marble top. "It's also eccentric. You see the toenails."

Mr. Tyson's eye for exceptional furniture has been honed over 30 years, ever since friends began admiring what he had acquired for his New York apartment and bought a few pieces. He replaced them and repeated the exercise until it became a habit, and David Webb, the jewelry designer and a friend, urged him to buy and sell full time.

If his beginnings as a dealer sound casual, the selections in his shop express quite a different attitude. Mr. Tyson stocks a great variety of furniture, all of it sculpturally stunning and much of it a tour de force of craftsmanship. On one visit the mix included Irish, English, Russian, Indian, Austrian, French, Turkish and Japanese pieces dating from about 1710 to 1840. "I have the best Venetian mirrors in town," he quipped when a visitor admired a squarish 1710 etched-glass design in which images are seen darkly. "It's untouched."

Mr. Tyson does not brighten time's tarnish on Venetian mirrors, but he does clean blemished wood surfaces. A shapely pair of English Regency chairs with reeded frames in a curule shape needed no restoration, he said. Neither did an English console with a two-inch-thick marble top, a Greek-key apron and legs as weighty as a lion's.

"The more you look, the more you learn. It doesn't happen overnight," Mr. Tyson said after discussing four gilded medallion-back Russian chairs that were ordered in 1790 for Pavlovsk Palace outside Leningrad. "Russian furniture is so exciting." He has carried Russian furniture since he went into business in this shop in 1958, he said, and has made it a major focus since the late 1970s. He took down six Russian books on period decorative arts, most of them published since the 1970s, to show comparable chairs and other designs. Even more compelling was a Russian neo-Gothic table from the 1830s, its Gothic arched front dramatized with contrasting woods and gilded bronzes.

Speaking of a 1780s Japanese chest with an asymmetric design, marquetry of fans and geometric images that any French ébéniste would envy, he said, "We have had only one other of these cabinets in 30 years."

Mr. Tyson's clients have included Brooke Astor, Paul and Rachel Mellon, the John Hay Whitneys, the William S. Paleys, Bill Blass, Ann Getty and Annette Reed. Today clients can buy a pair of French Empire stools for $7,800 or spend as much as $250,000 for a Chippendale cabinet.

URBAN ARCHAEOLOGY

137 Spring Street
285 Lafayette Street
New York, N.Y. 10012
Phone: (212) 431-6969
Hours: 10 A.M. to 6 P.M. Monday to Friday, noon to 6 P.M. Saturday and Sunday

The neon guitar pulses red, green and blue in the window of Urban Archaeology, New York's most sophisticated architectural junkyard. The eight-foot-plus sign, a relic from the Popps Music Store of Dayton, Ohio, may convey 1950s rock-and-roll "but the mechanism says it's 1930s," said Gil Shapiro, co-owner of the SoHo establishment founded in 1977.

He should know. Before the neon was plugged in, he said, he had craftsmen dismantle and restore the sign to its original throbbing intensity. That's the way he and his partner, Leonard Schechter, treat almost everything they stock. They scrub, repair and polish the iron grillwork, marble columns, stained-glass windows, plumbing fixtures and the interiors of ice-cream parlors, barbershops and Paris department stores, most of which date from the Civil War to World War II. Salvage is their stock in trade. They acquire their bounty directly in travels throughout the city and the country and from pickers who scour demolition sites and junk yards in the United States and abroad, searching for outsize artifacts.

"We're not the first to sell architectural elements," Mr. Shapiro said, adding that the recycling of buildings was almost as old as architecture itself. "But no one ever wanted to get involved with restorations, alterations and installations. We do." Most of the more elaborate sculptures and fittings on Urban Archaeology's two floors and in its two warehouses end up in health clubs, gambling casinos, resort hotels and restaurants.

But homes, too, are transformed by these artifacts. James Havard, an artist, sleeps in the barbershop he bought for his TriBeCa loft. Pierre Cardin bought a pre-World War II slot machine that shows a horse race. John McEnroe chose a nickelodeon and a five-foot oak bar, Robert De Niro some gleaming turn-of-the-century brass shower fittings and Henry Winkler two doorknobs monogrammed W from the Woolworth Building. Several celebrities, including Barbara Walters, David Brenner, Diana Ross and the team of Nickolas Ashford and Valerie Simpson, were carried away and bought late-1920s peach-colored mirrors, lavishly etched with underwater scenes, that came from the lobby of the Brooklyn Fox Theater.

What's left? Tons. Hard by the front door are a banquet-size library table, a cluster of Art Deco bronze railings from Au Bon Marché department store in Paris and some vehemently Victorian bathroom fixtures balanced on lion's paws. "Two of the best sinks I ever saw I found here, and then there's that old bathtub," said Paul Simon one Saturday afternoon when he stopped in to check the refinishing of the hardware for his milk-white porcelain tub. He likes its gently crazed surface, he said; it's all part of its period charm.

The ceiling throughout this sprawling emporium is hung with scores of chandeliers and stained-glass fixtures. The walls are covered with leering gargoyles, part of a neo-Gothic copper crown from the 29th floor of the Woolworth Building, oak walls from 19th-century bars and barbershops and beige marble panels punctuated by green lacquered mirrors from an Art Deco beauty parlor in Harlem. Two billiard tables are stacked in one corner, oak filing cabinets in another, and the floor groans with stonework: keystones, stair posts, columns and fireplaces. Time is telescoped here as an Elizabethan Revival four-poster bed stands beside pre-World War I cash registers and a 1950s bubble-model Wurlitzer jukebox.

"We're open seven days a week and closed the last day of February, Christmas and," Mr. Shapiro said, pausing, "New Year's Day—perhaps."

Prices range from 10 cents to $1 million, a ridiculous range but one that makes most visitors feel welcome. There are Lilliputian plastic Indians from the 1950s, the kind you might find in a box of Cracker Jacks, at 10 cents each. And what's left of the interiors of the Paris department store they will part with for $1 million. Most things are somewhere in between. Pedestal sinks range from $300 to $3,000, stone keystones start at about $250. Oak filing cabinets range from $450 to $850.

FREDERICK P. VICTORIA & SON INC.

154 East 55th Street
New York, N.Y. 10022
Phone: (212) 755-2549
Hours: 9 A.M. to 5 P.M. Monday to Friday

Anthony G. Victoria heads the antiques firm that his father, Frederick P. Victoria, founded in 1933 and developed into one of New York's most prestigious concerns for French and Continental antiques and reproductions. Over the years, it became a source frequented by the nation's top decorators and collectors.

Albert Hadley of Parish-Hadley Associates Inc., interior designers, once described the founder as "a taste maker and an expert in this field." Billy Baldwin, another habitué, had Mr. Victoria make étagère bookshelves for Cole Porter's apartment at the Waldorf-Astoria based on a Regency rosewood and brass whatnot unit. The bookshelves became one of the most copied designs in interiors of the post-World War II period.

At his death at the age of seventy-six in 1980, the dealer's business occupied five floors, and the antiques he had handled there had become part of the collections of the Duke and Duchess of Windsor, Brooke Astor and the William S. Paleys.

"My father had a very decorative eye," Tony Victoria said. "We have a strong reputation for French furniture but not what you would call all of the F.F.F.—fine French furniture. We almost never stock little tables with marquetry tops." However, if a little table is painted and has charm, the gallery may have it.

"We always try to have among the most unusual chairs around," he said. Decorators and collectors also shop here for consoles and commodes, cabinets, chandeliers, wall lights and objects—bronzes and English and Continental ceramics. Prices range from about $1,000 for an 18th-century-style small side table made a century later to about $200,000 for an outsize Régence oak bookcase 9 feet high and 8 feet wide that was part of the boiserie, or paneling, of a room completed about 1715.

"Most classic French antiques dealers avoid stocking single chairs," Mr. Victoria said. "I love singles. An unusual chair becomes an element of sculpture." And for good reason, he said, adding that chairs are the most personal, the most provocative and the most difficult of all furniture designs to produce.

Mr. Victoria's first exhibition at the gallery, a 1984 show that marked the firm's fifty-first birthday, reflected this special delight. Included in "The Master Chair-Maker's Art, France 1710-1800" were chairs made for invalids, musicians, barbers, hairdressers and nursing mothers. There were chairs for dining and reclining, for work and for seating two snugly.

Although Mr. Victoria cannot restage that show from stock at will, he is able to find some arresting examples most of the time.

Like his London-born father, who was of Italian parentage and started out as a magazine art director instead of an antiques dealer, Tony Victoria never intended to go into this business. However, after he received his M.B.A. from the Wharton School in 1969, he spent a year working for his father, left to work elsewhere, and returned after three years.

"He was older and I was older and I knew this is what I wanted to do." When the company was changed to a corporation in 1978, "& Son" was added to its title.

MICHAEL WARD

9 East 93rd Street
New York, N.Y. 10028
Phone: (212) 831-4044
Hours: By appointment
Closed the last two weeks of August

Michael Ward takes a scholarly approach in the cataloguing and all preparations for his twice-a-year exhibitions. These miniature museum shows in his town house gallery—two high-ceilinged turn-of-the-century parlors—often focus on medieval art, the subject of his graduate studies for a Ph.D., which he completed in 1978 at New York University's Institute of Fine Arts.

These shows also frequently cover antiquities, another

major interest. He held two fellowships at the Metropolitan Museum of Art, the first at the Cloisters and the second in the museum's Department of Medieval Art. Mr. Ward's taste for excellence owes something also to the six months he spent in 1979 working for the late Mathias Komor, a New York dealer who shared Mr. Ward's interests in ancient and medieval art.

After working for Mr. Komor, Mr. Ward became a private dealer, operating from his apartment-home in Brooklyn Heights. "I couldn't get any of the collectors to cross the Brooklyn Bridge," he recalled. "I was carrying the things around with me. So I decided I better find a place in Manhattan to be more accessible."

Since 1983 when Mr. Ward moved his gallery to Manhattan, he has organized exhibitions that reflect his work in museums while demonstrating a lively interest in exploring familiar and esoteric collecting areas. The materials he combines include ancient art from Egypt, Greece and Rome, Bronze Age and Celtic works and medieval art to about 1500. "Occasionally, we have Renaissance things," he said. "You have to spread your nets pretty wide because there is a scarcity of fine things."

Mr. Ward's shows reflect this breadth and his curiosity about the usual and uncommon material of these periods. For example, he organized the predictably popular "Ancient Glass and Its Legacy" six months after he presented offbeat materials in "Jewels of the Barbarians: A Dark Ages Treasury."

An exhibition in 1984 of 18 glorious illuminations from the 13th-century Bible of Conradin resulted in these boldly painted images being reunited with the magnificently decorated Bible from which they had been cut and separated in the 18th century. The Bible, a work combining Byzantine and Western European traditions, was made for the young Conradin, the son of Conrad IV, a Holy Roman Emperor, before his military defeat and execution at the age of sixteen in 1268. When Henry Walters bought the Bible in 1902, the missing illuminations were thought to be lost. After the exhibition, Mr. Ward, in association with Maggs Bros. of London, handled the reuniting of the book when J. Paul Getty 2d made a gift of the illuminations to the Walters Art Gallery of Baltimore.

The works at this gallery range from about $500 for an Egyptian New Kingdom wooden carving of a hand to about $600,000 for Greek, Roman and Egyptian sculpture.

THOS. K. WOODARD ANTIQUES CORPORATION

835 Madison Avenue (at 70th Street)
New York, N. Y. 10021
Phone: (212) 988-2906
Hours: 11 A.M. to 6 P.M. Monday to Saturday
Closed Saturdays in July and August

Thomas K. Woodard and Blanche Greenstein, collectors turned dealers, are co-owners of this lively gallery that stocks American antiques—painted and Shaker furniture, baskets, folk art and hooked rugs as well as quilts.

Why was Miss Greenstein's name not used in the title? "It was Blanche's choice," Mr. Woodard said. "One reason was she liked the look of my name. I guess she also thought that Woodard and Greenstein might have sounded like we were reporters for *The Washington Post.*" That thought seemed important when they became shop owners in 1974, the year President Nixon resigned.

The team's disparate backgrounds seem to result in a harmonious mix of wares. Mr. Woodard is Iowa-born and came to New York after college to go into the theater, where he eventually met Ms. Greenstein, a native New Yorker who became a stylist for photographers after college before switching to antiques.

"Quilts are really our first love," Mr. Woodard said. "There is nothing like that thrill of discovery and sharing it with others. However, it is getting harder and harder to find really great quilts." Even the garden-variety quilts are always more expensive than they once were. They start at this shop at $500. "We used to have stacks for under $100," he added.

After seven years at their first shop on Lexington Avenue at 74th Street, they moved in 1981 to Madison Avenue. Many collectors came to know their taste from the Winter Antiques Show, where they have exhibited since 1977.

Period country kitchenwares and accessories are also stocked here when the prices are realistic. Mr. Woodard and Ms. Greenstein have an eye for pottery, including spongeware pitchers and bowls at $300 each and 19th-century French jaspé starting at $250 each.

Mr. Woodard and Ms. Greenstein are frequently responsible for furthering trends in collecting with exhibitions that include moderately priced and more expensive folk art as well as some spectacular works. In 1981 they organized an exhibition of 19th- and 20th-century crib quilts to mark the appearance of their book *Crib Quilts and Other Small Wonders,* published by Dutton. They wrote *Twentieth-Century Quilts 1900-1950,* a 1987 book for Dutton, and were guest curators for the 1979 exhibition of Hawaiian quilts at the Museum of American Folk Art in New York.

In June 1986 they invited three upstate New York antiques dealers—Suzanne Courcier, Robert Wilkins and Richard Rasso—to do the only exhibition of Shaker furnishings of the 19th century held in New York during the period when "Shaker Design" was on view at the Whitney Museum of American Art in New York.

Prices here range from about $300 for a mid-19th-century New England stool covered with hooked upholstery to more than $20,000 for an important piece of furniture. Most furniture—painted and unpainted chairs, blanket chests, beds and cupboards—is in between. They sold a graduated stack of Shaker oval boxes, boasting their original paint, for $42,000 in 1984, and a mid-19th-century Baltimore album quilt for $26,000.

FALL ANTIQUES SHOW AT THE PIER

Passenger Terminal Piers
12th Avenue between 52d and 55th Streets
New York, N.Y. 10019
Phone: (212) 777-5218
Hours: Noon to 10 P.M. Thursday to Saturday, 11 A.M. to 6 P.M. Sunday

For advance information:
Sanford L. Smith & Associates
152 Second Avenue
New York, N.Y. 10003
Phone: (212) 777-5218

The all-Americana Fall Antiques show, which began in 1979, is held in the third week of October on one of the piers on the Hudson River. Folk art and country wares dominate among the best of the 110 dealers, who come from more than 20 states. The wares also include 18th- and 19th-century Revival styles and other periods through the 1950s.

The preview party from 6 to 10 P.M. Wednesday benefits the Museum of American Folk Art. Benefit tickets are $100 each; admission other times is $8.

MODERNISM: A CENTURY OF STYLE AND DESIGN 1860-1960

Seventh Regiment Armory
Park Avenue between 66th and 67th Streets
New York, N.Y. 10021
Phone: (212) 777-5218

For advance information:
Sanford L. Smith & Associates
152 Second Avenue
New York, N.Y. 10003
Phone: (212) 777-5218

Introduced in 1986, New York's newest "antiques" show offers a century of wares from 1860 to 1960. The fair, held the third week in November, offers American and European wares presented by about 75 dealers from 12 states and abroad, 8 from Europe. The periods covered include the late-19th-century Revival styles, architect-designed furniture, arts and crafts, Art Nouveau, Wiener Werkstätte, Art Deco, Bauhaus and the 1940s, 1950s and 1960s.

The preview party on the Wednesday night before the opening benefits the Brooklyn Museum's Department of Decorative Arts. Tickets are $100 each.

For the show itself, the hours have been noon to 10 P.M. Thursday to Saturday and 11 A.M. to 6 P.M. Sunday. Admission is $8.

WINTER ANTIQUES SHOW

Seventh Regiment Armory
Park Avenue between 66th and 67th Streets
New York, N.Y. 10021
Hours: 11 A.M. to 9 P.M. Monday to Saturday, 11 A.M. to 6 P.M. Sunday

For advance information:
East Side House Settlement
337 Alexander Avenue
Bronx, N.Y. 10454
Phone: (212) 665-5250

The Winter Antiques Show, the nation's most prestigious presentation of antiques, is held in late January. The bazaar, which began in 1955 and is managed by Russell Carrell, is open to the public for nine days, including two weekends.

Most of the 74 dealers who participate are Americans, but there are several Europeans, too.

Before the opening there are three preview parties, all on the same day, for collectors and dealers eager to see and buy before the general public is admitted. The Benefactors' Tea is at 4:30 P.M. and costs $500. The Patrons' Party is at 6 and costs $250. The Preview Party is 7:30 to 9:30 and costs $150. The proceeds of these festivities go to the East Side House, which does social work in the South Bronx. Admission at other times is $8.

The Winter Antiques Show attracts more than 32,000 people each year. The booths are stocked with a mix of American painting and sculpture and folk art and American, European and Far Eastern furniture, ceramics, silver and decorations.

CHRISTIE'S

502 Park Avenue (at 59th Street)
New York, N.Y. 10022
Phone: (212) 546-1000
Office hours: 9:30 A.M. to 5:30 P.M. Monday to Friday
Viewing hours: 10 A.M. to 5 P.M. Monday to Saturday, 1 to 5 P.M. Sunday
Sales: September to June

CHRISTIE'S EAST

219 East 67th Street
New York, N.Y. 10021
Phone: (212) 606-0400
Office hours: 9:30 A.M. to 5:30 P.M. Monday to Friday
Viewing hours: 10 A.M. to 5 P.M. Monday to Saturday, 1 to 5 P.M. Sunday
Sales: September to July

WILLIAM DOYLE GALLERIES

175 East 87th Street
New York, N.Y. 10128
Phone: (212) 427-2730
Office hours: 9 A.M. to 6 P.M. Monday to Friday
Viewing hours: 10 A.M. to 5 P.M. Saturday, noon to 5 P.M. Sunday, 9 A.M. to 7:30 P.M. Monday, 9 A.M. to 5 P.M. Tuesday
Sales: Mostly on Wednesday year-round

PHILLIPS

406 East 79th Street
New York, N.Y. 10021
Phone: (212) 570-4830
Office hours: 9 A.M. to 5 P.M. Monday to Friday
Viewing hours: 9 A.M. to 5 P.M. Monday to Saturday, noon to 5 P.M. some Sundays
Sales: September to July

SOTHEBY'S

1334 York Avenue (at 72d Steet)
New York, N.Y. 10021
Phone: (212) 606-7000
Office hours: 9:30 A.M. to 5:30 P.M. Monday to Friday
Viewing hours: 10 A.M. to 5 P.M. Tuesday to Saturday, 1 to 5 P.M. Sunday
Sales: September to June

SAN FRANCISCO

DILLINGHAM & COMPANY

470 Jackson Street
San Francisco, Calif. 94111
Phone: (415) 989-8777
Hours: 9 A.M. to 5 P.M. Monday to Friday

Before Gaylord Dillingham became a full-time dealer in British and Continental furniture, he taught social studies and was a college counselor at a high school in Chicago. Born and raised in Honolulu, Mr. Dillingham went to Harvard and, before going on to graduate studies in psychology at Stanford University, he took two years off to teach. The pause changed the course of his life. While in Chicago he met an antiques dealer and became a collector of English furniture with a great curiosity about the history of William and Mary through Georgian furniture styles.

That summer of 1973, he went to San Francisco and worked for an antiques dealer before entering Stanford. He studied psychology for four months. "I hated it—it was not for me," he said. "Jobs were few and far between, so I went into business for myself."

Four years later his antiques business was flourishing, but he wanted to crack the books again. "I decided that if I was ever going to be any more than a provincial dealer, I would have to go back to school and study decorative arts. I didn't grow up in the business, so my way of learning the history of English furniture was to study it."

In January 1977 he took a three-month course at the Study Center of the Fine and Decorative Arts, a private school in London sponsored by the Victoria and Albert Museum. A year later he returned to the Study Center for a nine-month course, earning a Bachelor of Arts equivalency diploma in fine arts, decorative arts and architecture. In 1981 and 1985 he studied at the Attingham

Summer School, which is organized and run by Americans to study English period houses and their contents.

The primary focus at his gallery is English furniture, but Mr. Dillingham also carries Dutch, Portuguese and French furniture, all dating from about 1700 to 1840. Occasionally, he buys pieces made after 1840. An 18th-century Dutch architect's model of a 17th-century building—it may be a town hall—is the sort of tour de force of woodworking skills that Mr. Dillinham cannot resist. He offered it for $7,500.

His stock is predominantly good examples of provincial and London furniture. He says he would love to buy more "really important examples of English furniture" but adds that he does not know whether the market in San Francisco is ready for them.

One of his English rarities was an early-18th-century scarlet lacquer cabinet-on-stand, which was available for $39,500. Another unusual design was a mahogany card table, made after 1740, with a concertina action and four robustly carved claw-and-ball feet. "It's never been refinished," he said, citing a major asset of the piece, which was $18,000.

Among other early pieces were a small inlaid stool at $950 and a 1685 laburnum-veneered oak chest of drawers, looking like it was finished in tortoise shell, at $9,500.

The 18th-century finds included a nice big George III dining table from the 1790s with carved and fluted legs at $15,000. Mr. Dillingham said it was in mint condition and had never been refinished. From the 19th century, he offered an 1840s cabinet with lively Gothic tracery on the front panels. Mr. Dillingham said it might have been designed by Pugin, but he did not know whether it was made in his workshop or by another hand. The price was $6,750.

Prices range from about $150 for a snuff box to about $40,000 for the early 18th-century lacquer cabinet-on-stand.

ROBERT DOMERGUE & COMPANY

560 Jackson Street
San Francisco, Calif. 94133
Phone: (415) 781-4034
Hours: 9 A.M. to 5 P.M. Monday to Friday

At first, buying and selling antiques was Robert Domergue's way of supporting himself as a painter. Now he not only thoroughly enjoys French and Continental antiques for what they are but he also tries to handle ever more highly styled pieces in a city where, until now, there has been sharp resistance to formal furniture.

A native Californian, Mr. Domergue graduated from the University of California at Berkeley in 1970, spent two years at the San Francisco Art Institute, then went to France for a year to paint. In 1973 he returned to California and continued to paint, opening his first antiques business in San Francisco in 1975. He has been at his present location since 1979.

"We can't sell B.V.R.B. commodes here yet," Mr. Domergue said, speaking of Bernard van Risamburgh, one of the most important ébénistes producing palace-quality furniture under Louis XV. Mr. Domergue's stock, he said, includes French and other Continental furnishings dating from the 17th century to 1830 and priced from $200 to $75,000. Most pieces, including a French Empire settee from about 1815, are in four figures (the settee was $6,500), he said.

One of the more formal pieces on view was a demilune commode made in Russia or Sweden about 1800 with a two-layer gallery top, its rounded drawer fronts embellished with brass inlay, its legs short and angular. It was $22,000.

An 18th-century Italian fruitwood library table was $9,375. Two look-alike library tables, robustly carved in Russia, he said, were made at different times—one in the late 17th century, the other in the 19th century. The older one was $19,700, the copy $5,700.

French chairs, always in demand by designers and collectors, included two notable selections in easy chairs, a Louis XV bergère by Louis Cresson at $15,000 and a wider example, a Louis XV marquise, painted in two tones of blue and signed by Nogaret, a Lyons maker, at $20,000.

In addition to furniture, Mr. Domergue stocks some unusual decorations. An 18th-century Dutch five-foot-tall dummy board, a realistic painting of a nursemaid and child, was made either to fool anyone looking into an unoccupied house or possibly to be used as a fire screen. It was $21,000.

DRUM & COMPANY

415 Jackson Street
San Francisco, Calif. 94111
Phone: (415) 788-5118
Hours: 9 A.M. to 5 P.M. Monday to Friday

John Drum Jr. has been in the antiques business in San Francisco since 1981—first on Sacramento Street and since 1984 in what used to be the showroom of Jack Lenor Larsen. Like most of his colleagues, Mr. Drum does a great deal of business with interior designers, about 50 percent, he said. And many of his customers are from out of state. When they come on their own, they frequently seek accessories, which are priced here at $100 and up for a porcelain figure or a dish.

A nine-piece French glass toiletry set was $425 and four French tin puppets—a young girl, a man in a top hat, a bread seller and a postman—with articulated arms and legs, all dating from about 1860, were $1,200 for the set. A miniature late-19th-century Renaissance Revival bookcase, probably a New York piece, was $1,800. Another miniature, called a Kilmarnock chest after the place in Scotland, was made of tin, had five drawers and was about 10 inches high. It was $650.

Although Mr. Drum's stock included some contemporary furniture made from period pieces, he said most of his stock is period furniture. The taste here is for decorative furniture of the 18th and 19th centuries, be it rococo or neo-classical. Some noteworthy antiques on view included a Swedish rococo bombé chest in walnut for $22,500 and an 18th-century Italian fruitwood commode for $8,750.

From the 19th century came several German pieces. A Bavarian armoire from about 1800 painted bright blue was $3,450; a North German Biedermeier chest was $3,850; a neo-classical Swedish mirror framed in gilded wood, from about 1820, was $2,250, and a French Charles X chest of drawers for gentlemen's trousers was $3,250.

LOUIS D. FENTON

432 Jackson St.
San Francisco, Calif. 94111
Phone: (415) 398-3046
Hours: 9 A.M. to 5 P.M. Monday to Friday

Louis D. Fenton's eye is restless and his mind is, too. Throughout his 25 years in the antiques business, 5 in partnership with Spiro Arbus, Mr. Fenton has resisted too narrow a framework for his antiques ventures. Now, in his own two-story gallery since 1971, he sells Buddhas and Baroque furniture, 18th-century English partners' desks and 19th-century African textiles, Directoire steel beds and Tibetan palace figures.

"Twenty percent of my sales are in the Bay area and the rest goes out of state and out of the country, to London, Paris and Australia," he said. "Some of my major pieces are going to Iowa and Arkansas, too."

The mix of periods, styles, woods and geographical origins was highly appealing and definitely unusual, even in a town where most antiques dealers have a theatrical flair. There was, for example, a proper 1750s partners' desk that seats four, with leather inserts, for which Mr. Fenton asked $24,000.

An Austrian Biedermeier chest of drawers framed in columns and with painted black embellishments was $15,000. The variety also included a Louis XIV chest of drawers at $45,000, an English Sheraton desk from the late 18th century at $15,000, a George II Welsh dresser from about 1740 at $27,000 and an Austrian 1790s cabinet with ebony inlay at $15,000. A pair of highly decorative and important Tibetan mythological temple figures, painted animals that look like dogs with horses' tails, was $120,000.

Born in a small Utah town, he received his Bachelor of Arts at the University of Utah in 1959, then moved to San Francisco to work at the antiques shop of Harry and Susan Barnett, a top source for American furniture. He stayed four years, starting with such odd jobs as polishing brasses but graduating swiftly to more serious pursuits. He accompanied the Barnetts when they traveled to Europe, and Mr. Barnett taught him how to look at furniture, turning it upside down and dismantling pieces, too. When Mr. Barnett retired, Mr. Fenton went into partnership with Spiro Arbus.

Mr. Fenton's gallery is in an 1890s building, a generous two-story space but much smaller than the premises he had a decade ago when he was importing antiques by the 40-foot container. "After I did that for a while, I realized this can no longer be a volume business."

ED HARDY/SAN FRANCISCO

750 Post Street
San Francisco, Calif. 94109
Phone: (415) 771-6644
Hours: 10 A.M. to 5 P.M. Monday to Friday

Ed Hardy's considerable fantasy never included the possibility that he would one day work in a garage on a San Francisco hilltop near Union Square. Well, it is no ordinary garage—the Chartered Bank of London kept its motor vehicles there before Mr. Hardy leased the 6,000-square-foot space with 17-foot ceilings and converted it into a gracious gallery that looks more like an English country house than an urban parking garage.

The results prove that what starts out as a barren spread with poured-concrete floors can be dramatically altered with oak parquet flooring and a million dollars' worth of furnishings. Of course, some of the architectural details are quite special, too. French 19th-century paneled pine doors add charm, and the five red marble columns that may formerly have graced an 18th-century aristocrat's palazzo in Verona, punctuate the scene with period elegance.

"In San Francisco it is rather difficult to specialize," Mr. Hardy said. What works best for his clientele, he said, is a mix of periods and styles. Mr. Hardy and his assistant, Suzanna Allen, cater mostly to interior designers, who make about 60 percent of the purchases.

Mr. Hardy's gallery and the way he stocks it reflect his experiences and personal taste. After receiving his Bachelor of Arts from Colgate University, he took summer courses at Rhode Island School of Design. He spent three years in the United States Navy during the Vietnam War, then spent two years at the California College of Arts and Crafts in Oakland, ending in 1972. He went to work at Sotheby's in Los Angeles and four years later, after heading its West Coast Oriental art department, went on his own as an antiques dealer.

The Jackson Square area, where he opened in a two-story space on Montgomery Street in 1976, was then the center of the decorative arts and antiques trade. When many of the decorative arts sources moved in 1983, several antiques dealers did, too, including Mr. Hardy, whose larger quarters are now on one level and more accessible to tourists.

Period furniture is Mr. Hardy's strength but he also carries accessories, including small decorative boxes, at $100 and up. Furniture and art works command much more, in four or five figures up to about $75,000, the price asked for a Ming Wan Li black lacquer and mother-of-pearl cupboard, embellished with phoenixes, peonies, bows and rocks, dating from about 1600.

The considerable variety of styles here included several French designs, one of them a Louis XV provincial walnut mantel with a rich patina, at $7,500, and a neo-Egyptian demilune console, a tour de force of 1790s detailing, including scrolls and swags on its apron and hieroglyphics on its tapered supports, at $18,000.

Among the offerings sold as pairs were two early-19th-century klismos-style Italian chairs, painted creamy white and partly gilded, for $20,000 the pair, two 1820 gilded Swedish consoles with carved dolphins as base supports at $36,000 the pair and two Tang funerary figures, court ladies about 12 inches tall and washed in a straw glaze, that were $6,500 the pair. Decorative sculptures also sold in pairs include composition-stone figures from the Regency period, 19-inch-tall eagles from about 1815 at $4,000 and 40-inch-long sphinxes at $20,000. From the belle époque at the turn of the century come pairs of overscale lanterns ribbed in copper and fitted with textured opaque glass for $4,000 the pair.

The most imposing period work on view was a singular Palladian-inspired relic, a George II mahogany breakfront, with a broken pediment at the top, that was more than nine feet long and was $66,000.

"I'm a hopeless purist in some things," Mr. Hardy said, adding, "but not in all." He stocks some altered antiques, such as Ming center tables that have been cut down by others decades ago to a height suitable for use as coffee tables.

JEREMY NORMAN & COMPANY

442 Post Street
San Francisco, Calif. 94102
Phone: (415) 781-6402
Hours: 10 A.M. to 6 P.M. Monday to Friday

Jeremy M. Norman has specialized in rare books and manuscripts on medicine, other sciences, economics and social science most of his years in the rare-book business, which he enetered when he was nineteen in 1965. Mr. Norman's catalogues, written by him and by Davida Rubin, his senior cataloguer, have been issued twice a year since he opened his own business in 1971. They are articulate, handsome and, where appropriate, witty as well.

Mr. Norman has clients throughout the world but most, he points out, are where the greatest number of physicians are—in the United States. Currently popular medical subjects among collectors include, he said, neurology, neurosurgery, ophthalmology, cardiology, dermatology, orthopedics, internal medicine, obstetrics and gynecology, pathology, plastic surgery, general surgery, otolaryngology, urology and psychiatry. Collectors start earlier than they used to, he said. When he began in business, most were in their 60s. Now, he said, many are in their 30s and 40s.

To command a premium price as a rare book, a second-hand book must satisfy one or more of several criteria. First is scarcity. Books printed in editions of 25,000 or more do not become rare, Mr. Norman says, although not all scarce books become valuable. Those that do, he says, have substantive or esthetic importance or are sought because of where or when they were printed or who owned them. On substance, one criterion is being a first—the first edition of a classic in English literature, the first account of a historic exploration or voyage of discovery, the first publication of a great scientific or medical discovery or the first English translation of a foreign literary work. Esthetic importance usually comes from a book's typography, the exotic paper or vellum on which it is printed, its illustrations or its binding. Condition determines price whenever a book is hard to find in fine condition with a perfect dust jacket.

Books and autograph materials at every price level are stocked, and the rarity of something does not always mean it is the highest priced. A facsimile reprint of Marie Curie's thesis detailing the discovery of radium was offered at $50; a first edition of Johannes Kepler's *Dioptrice,* from 1611, tracing the passage of light through lenses and systems of lenses, was $6,000; an autograph leaf from Darwin's *Origin of Species,*" from before 1859, was $5,750, and a first edition of Gaspare Tagliacozzi's 16th-century classic on plastic surgery, *De curtorum chirurgia per insitionem,* was $19,500. This market is generally in books under $50,000, Mr. Norman said, although some works command much more. He cited William Harvey's *De motu cordis,* published in Frankfurt in 1628, which might cost $150,000 to $200,000.

Are rare books a good investment? "I am a rare-book dealer and not an investment counselor," Mr. Norman said. "I sell rare books for their current market value and cannot predict the future." He points out that the investment-minded must be aware that rare books pay no dividends and are relatively unliquid. Nevertheless, he adds, "fine copies of rare books have had considerable success as inflation hedges." Furthermore, he pointed out, even during periods of relatively low inflation, as in the mid-

1980s, prices continued to rise because demand far exceeded supply.

BERNARD M. ROSENTHAL

251 Post Street
San Francisco, Calif. 94108
Phone: (415) 982-2219
Hours: By appointment, 9 A.M. to 5 P.M. Monday to Friday

Bernard M. Rosenthal's family has been buying and selling books for four generations, ever since his great-grandfather, Joseph Rosenthal, a licensed tailor in Fellheim, near Munich, grew prosperous on a sideline—selling antiques, probably including books. The family's bookselling business began formally with Joseph's son Ludwig, who was nineteen when he opened his own shop in 1859 and issued an impressive first catalogue of 3,000 books. It gave some hint of the impact this family would soon have on this business. By 1867 Ludwig was established in Munich, and his two brothers, Jakob (he later changed it to Jacques) and Nathan, had joined him there. They remained together until 1895, when each went his own way and all flourished in Munich, then the center of the German book world.

Medieval and Renaissance books and manuscripts, a specialty of Bernard Rosenthal, were the major interest of his grandfather, Jacques. On Jacques's first trip to Paris in 1878, he met Léopold Delisle, chief librarian of the National Library, who invited him to seminars on medieval manuscripts. Bernard's interest comes also from his maternal grandfather, Leo Olschki, a native of East Prussia, who went to Italy in the 1880s and became one of the great book dealers of Florence.

Rosenthal and Olschki were major competitors at auctions and for clients—J. Pierpont Morgan and Henry Walters bought from both. But their friendship resulted in a marriage: Leo Olschki's youngest daughter, Margherita, wed Jacques Rosenthal's son Erwin, and they remained in the business, living over the Munich shop. Each of the young couple's three sons made a mark in the book business. Albi, a musical manuscript specialist, settled in London, Bernard in San Francicso and Felix, an architect, was in charge of the family book business in Zurich until it closed in 1984.

Bernard left Munich at thirteen in 1933 for Florence, where he stayed until he was eighteen. After finishing high school in Paris in 1939, he moved with his family to California and he went to college at the University of California at Berkeley. Later he spent three years in the United States Army and after World War II went to Berlin as a French interpreter for the United States delegation to the Allied Control Council.

Mr. Rosenthal went into the book business in 1949, apprenticing at his family's shop in Zurich. Two years later he went to work for two years at Parke-Bernet Galleries in New York as a cataloguer. Since 1953, he and his wife, Ruth, have been in their own rare-book business, in New York until 1970, in San Francisco since then.

Mr. Rosenthal issues catalogues once a year, but most of his rarest books and manuscripts are not included because they are often bought before the catalogue appears. In addition, some he does not want to sell. "I'm known for Middle Ages and Renaissance books and rare books about the period," he said.

He stocks books of paleography for enthusiasts of ancient writing and everything to do with the Latin or Greek Codices. He also specializes in bibliography and the history of the early book, including early efforts to systematize catalogues of books and authors.

Among some of the choice rarities he had on one visit was "Mirabilia Urbis Romae," a 15th-century vellum scroll used by pilgrims to Rome as a guide to its churches and as a prayer book. It was $9,000. A generously illustrated edition of Sebastian Brandt's "Ship of Fools," printed in Basel in 1507 with manuscript additions on practically every page by Wolfgang Mayer, an early 16th-century Cistercian scholar-monk, was $15,000. Incunabula are available at $1,500 and up, but a Psalter printed in 1520 on vellum in the German city of Halberstadt is special. It was for Roman Catholic use, and after the city turned Protestant, someone changed all the passages by hand. This 19-pound volume was $12,000.

Mr. Rosenthal's prices start at $8 for a new scholarly reference book and go to $60,000, what might be asked for a collection of 200 manuscript leaves and documents from the 9th to the 15th centuries.

"I like early books printed before 1600 that show evidence of use, especially writing in the margins," he said. "You know they've been read."

NORMAN SHEPHERD

458 Jackson Street
San Francisco, Calif. 94111
Phone: (415) 362-4145
Hours: 9 A.M. to 5 P.M. Monday to Friday

Montauk Highway
Watermill, L.I. 11976
Phone: (516) 726-4840
Hours: 10 A.M. to 5 P.M. daily

"The one thing I love is the overscale look," said Norman Shepherd, an Iowa-born antiques dealer who opened his first shop in New York on East 57th Street a year after leaving the United States Army in 1947. A decade later Mr. Shepherd switched to decorating but went back to antiques in 1963 when he opened Et Cetera, a name he has since dropped for his shop in Watermill, L.I. There and at his Jackson Square gallery in San Francisco, which he added in 1980, Mr. Shepherd caters to decorators and collectors with an eye for the currently fashionable in period decorative arts.

His clientele in San Francisco responds readily to his generous assortment of outsize furniture, including 18th-century English pine cabinets, "the French-influenced ones," and Continental extravaganzas in bookcases, breakfronts, wardrobes, partners' desks and dining tables. They are rarely disappointed.

Take, for example, the stripped pine bookcase from a 1760s Glasgow house designed by Robert Adam. The bookcase may well have been by the master British architect-designer also. The neo-classic detailing and fretwork on this 15-foot-long storage piece were not disturbed when the bookcase was stripped of its painted finish in the 1930s. Mr. Shepherd's price was $62,500. A later pair of Venetian pine bookcases with black lacquer details, dating from about 1800, are 110 inches high and 52 inches wide. They were $40,000 the pair.

Sets of chairs are always in demand and this source handles them as often as possible. A set of eight 18th-century English oak side chairs with woven rush seats were $8,000 the set.

The shop usually has offbeat decorations, and on one visit there were two painted wood doors from a British 1810 ducal coach that were quickly acquired by two sources, a winery in Napa Valley and a riding club in Michigan. A set of six French 18th-century Révillon wallpaper panels, mounted on canvas and depicting mythological scenes of gods and goddesses, were $37,500. And an 18th-century, 12-panel Coromandel screen more than nine feet tall was $125,000. Brass candlesticks here are also unusual because they are crafted of weighty bell metal—they ring to the touch. They are among the least expensive offerings at $375 the pair.

Mr. Shepherd said he has been buying and selling Biedermeier since he went into business 40 years ago. The neo-classical style, distinguished by light woods accented by ebony or black paint, reigned from about 1810 to 1840, primarily in Germany and Austria-Hungary but also elsewhere, even in Northern Europe. Until recently, Mr. Shepherd was ahead of his time. His gallery stocks a hefty selection that might include a German Biedermeier secretary with a fall front framed by black columns from about 1835 at $11,500, a set of four German chairs with fanned backs at $9,500 the set and a Swedish octagonal table on a pedestal base with three leaves at $9,000. A German cylinder top beechwood desk with a pull-out writing shelf was $6,000.

Why San Francisco? "We sell so much out of state—we ship to the East and to Texas—that we might say why not San Francisco," Mr. Shepherd said. He sometimes considers pulling up stakes in the East and concentraing all his efforts in San Francisco.

HOUSE OF SUNG

3661 Sacramento Street
San Francisco, Calif. 94118
Phone: (415) 922-4422
Hours: 10 A.M. to 5 P.M. daily

Charles Luke Fong was sent to San Francisco in 1929 at the age of sixteen after living with relatives for four years in New Haven. He was old enough by then and knew enough English to work at his uncle's shop in San Francisco's Chinatown. It was the Sing Chong Company on Grant Avenue and California Street, which had been founded in 1905. His parents in Taishan Xian, a small town in Guangdong Province, had sent him to be educated in the United States.

Mr. Fong was paid a dollar a day and worked seven days a week at his uncle's shop, he recalled during a visit to his present antiques shop, a second-floor hideaway overlooking a courtyard in the Pacific Heights section. The shop is one of San Francisco's lesser-known repositories of period wares and one where knowledgeable Oriental-art buyers go, especially for Sung ceramics of the 10th to 13th centuries.

When he arrived in the United States as a boy, Mr. Fong said, he was an aspiring artist, and in San Francisco he spent most of his salary on painting lessons, $3 twice a week. That left him $1 a week to live on. "My uncle brought me over to be a watchdog," Mr. Fong said. He did better than that, learning the business of Chinese art and antiques and advancing swiftly to the position of salesman. In 1943 he was drafted and remained in the United States Army three years, leaving as a sergeant. Two years after his return, he left his uncle's business and founded his own, the House of Sung. He has been at his present address since 1976.

Mr. Fong's stock of ceramics usually includes a selection of small Tang clay tomb figures, about eight inches high, and small vessels, at $400 to $500 each. A wine jar, its original green-glazed surface now silvery gold, dates to the early years of the Han dynasty, which began in 206 B.C., and is about $5,000. Small Han tomb figures of farm animal—a dog, horse, rooster or hen—are $400 to $500 each. A South China Sung tea bowl splashed with black and brown glaze was $1,250.

He also handles 18th-century white nephrite and green jadeite jewelry and scholar's utensils. Small touchpieces of a lotus leaf or a fish are from $200 to $750; a white jade belt buckle was $1,500 and a white jade cylindrical scholar's cup for brushes is $2,000 to $3,000. Mr. Fong also carries tiger's lapis lazuli objects such as 18th-century brush washer vessels from $1,200 to $10,000.

THERIEN & COMPANY

411 Vermont Street
534 Sutter Street
San Francisco, Calif. 94107
Phone: (415) 956-8850
Hours: 9:30 A.M. to 5:30 P.M. Monday to Saturday on Sutter Street, Monday to Friday on Vermont Street

Robert R. Garcia, James G. Huseby and Bruce G. Tremayne, who head Therien & Company, a source mainly for Northern European furniture and decorations, have been in business together since 1978. Mr. Garcia and Mr. Huseby met while working at Gump's in the mid-1960s when that decorative arts and antiques store was still in its heyday. In 1978 their paths crossed again when Mr. Huseby went to work with Mr. Garcia and Mr. Tremayne in an antiques shop on Montgomery Street in Jackson Square that was then called J. F. Howlands & Associates. The name was changed in 1979 to Therien, for Howard Therien, a director of the company who left in 1980.

Therien's two galleries attract different shoppers. The Sutter Street space is smaller and more accessible to tourists, and its offerings reflect this. Silver wares and accessories can be found there, along with some important pieces of period furniture and porcelains. Such furniture and porcelains are the main stock in trade at the Vermont Street gallery, where interior designers are responsible for about 95 percent of the business.

Therien opened the Vermont Street showroom in 1984 and redesigned it to look like an 18th-century European house, complete with a covered driveway. The Swedish, Russian, Danish and other European designs there date from the late 17th century through the first quarter of the 19th century. A set of four 1815 fruitwood chairs, embellished with the Russian double-headed eagle traced in penwork on the back splats, were $22,000.

The pedigree on a gilded Russian tripod-based table—its three supports are winged women—states that it was once in the collection of the Royal Palace of Drottningholm near Stockholm, Mr. Garcia said. The price for the neo-classic design, which dates from 1790, was $22,000. A pair of Swedish early-19th-century chairs of more humble origin, painted cream and pale yellow, were $6,500 for the two.

Among the earlier designs was an early-18th-century Swedish bureau plat, a table desk, in black lacquer with gilt trim, measuring 69 inches long and priced at $28,000. A Swedish rococo 1760s commode with a gray marble top, crafted in rosewood by Lorens Norden, a major cabinetmaker of the period, was $28,000. An English mahogany kneehole desk fitted with secret drawers and fire-gilded mounts, a transitional mid-18th-century design, was $36,000.

Therien also handles less imposing furniture, with French and English country-made tables at $2,000 and up. One of the most expensive offerings the house has handled was a coromandel 12-panel screen of the K'ang Hsi period, a late-17th-century work, that was $110,000. There are also more modest porcelains, 19th-century plates, for example, from $150.

SAN FRANCISCO FALL ANTIQUES SHOW

2 Pier Three
Fort Mason Center
Marina Boulevard at Buchanan Street

For advance information:
Enterprise for High School Students Inc.
3275 Sacramento Street
San Francisco, Calif. 94115
Phone: (415) 921-1411

Since 1981 this four-day antiques show in late October has benefited Enterprise for High School Students, a non-profit job-referral service for students. The 64 dealers attract about 10,000 fairgoers in a show managed by Russell Carrell.

Preview tickets for the eve of the opening are $100 each or, for patrons' tickets that allow unlimited access to the show, $500 for two. General admission is $10.

BUTTERFIELD & BUTTERFIELD

220 San Bruno Avenue (at 15th Street)
San Francisco, Calif. 94103
Phone: (415) 861-7500
Office hours: 8:30 A.M. to 5 P.M. Monday to Friday
Viewing hours: 10 A.M. to 5 P.M. Friday and Saturday, noon to 5 P.M. Sunday, 10 A.M. to 7 P.M. Monday

Major auctions are held in early March, June, September and November. Smaller auctions are every six weeks on Tuesday, Wednesday and Thursday.

Warehouse auctions are on the second and fourth Tuesdays of each month at 164 Utah Street.

EUROPE

AMSTERDAM

KUNSTHANDEL AALDERINK

15 Spiegelgracht
1017 TP Amsterdam
Netherlands
Phone: (31-20) 23-02-11
Hours: 10 A.M. to 5 P.M. Monday to Friday, 10:30 A.M. to 5 P.M. Saturday

"I think it is a good feature that you can start here as a small collector and stay here as a bigger one," Wim Bouwnan, a lawyer who became a dealer, said. He went to work in 1970 for Jacob Aalderink, then eighty-three and one of Amsterdam's more prominent dealers. Mr. Aalderink had been in the business since 1929, catering to museums and, among other customers, King Gustav VI of Sweden. Mr. Bouwnan remained after the retirement of Mr. Aalderink, now deceased, and he continues to stock most of the categories favored by his predecessor: Indonesian, Japanese and Chinese art. One category he dropped was African art.

"I have been a collector since I was about eight years old," Mr. Bouwnan said, adding that his parents had a huge art and antiques collection. His first acquisitions as a boy were, he said, "Dutch tiles and pewter things."

The two-story shop, dating to about 1913, is filled with virtually all the kinds of Asian art collected today: furniture, sculpture, paintings, jewelry, ceramics, textiles, other works and "whatever I think is attractive and suitable," he said. But he doesn't carry Oriental export ceramics, he said. There are Chinese archaic bronzes, Tang horses and Sung ceramics, Indonesian textiles, Japanese tea ceremony wares, 19th-century bronzes, lacquer works and netsukes. Netsukes, toggles used to fasten a purse to a kimono sash, are extremely popular among Dutch collectors, Mr. Bouwnan said, adding that he organized an exhibition of about 500 examples, all documented in a catalogue, in December 1985.

The offerings at this shop range from about $85 for a small Siamese ceramic cup or jar to about $65,000 for a Tang horse.

ARONSON ANTIQUAIRE

Nieuwe Spiegelstraat 39
1017 DC Amsterdam
Netherlands
Phone: (31-20) 23-31-03
Hours: 10 A.M. to 5 P.M. Monday to Friday

David Ronny Aronson, chairman of the Dutch Antiques Dealers Association, specializes in Dutch Delft, Chinese porcelains, European furniture and silver. Mr. Aronson's grandfather Leon Aronson founded the family's antiques business in 1881 in Arnhem, near the German border, and moved it to Amsterdam in 1926. The family business today is run by Abraham Aronson, the son of the founder; his wife, Noen; their son David, and his wife, Irene.

Abraham Aronson recalled spending the war years in hiding with his wife's family in a suburb of Amsterdam. "We were with nine people in an attic," he said.

Before the war the shop was in a house nearby, and Mr. Aronson said, "I remember very well that my father sold to Marshall Field in Chicago." He entered the business in 1939 at the age of seventeen, and David joined him in 1956 when he was ten.

Ceramics at this shop cover a wide range. There is the Dutch Delft, both the blue-and-white and the polychrome, from the 17th and 18th centuries, German 18th-century ceramics and Chinese porcelain from Ming through Ch'ien Lung, dating from about 1600 through 1800.

Among the most important works stocked on one visit were a pair of Ch'ien Lung dishes with saucers that were $20,000 the pair, a Dutch Baroque 17th-century oak-and-palisander cupboard from the Zeeland area in the north that was $20,000 and a Dutch 17th-century oak dining table that was $30,000. The least expensive works were $400 to $500 for a small blue-and-white vessel or dish.

BLITZ ANTIEK EN KUNSTHANDEL

Nieuwe Spiegelstraat 37a
1017 DC Amsterdam
Netherlands
Phone: (31-20) 23-26-63
Hours: 10 A.M. to 6 P.M. Monday to Friday, 10 A.M. to 5 P.M. Saturday

"When I was twelve years old, my father, a surgeon, started collecting Chinese porcelain," Dries Blitz recalled in his shop in the heart of Amsterdam's antiques district. "I bought my first pot when I was thirteen. At fourteen, I decided that I wanted to be a dealer."

In 1968, when he was twenty and had completed his studies at Rotterdam University, Mr. Blitz went to London to work for Bluett & Sons Ltd., a prominent Chinese ceramics dealer, at the Grosvenor House Antiques Fair. He stayed on and worked at Bluett for 10 years before returning to Amsterdam with his English wife, Diana, in 1978 to open his own shop.

Mr. Blitz specializes in Chinese ceramics but does not stop there. "I also like objects that are a little unusual," he said. These might be 16th-century bronzes, 17th- and 18th-century lacquer boxes, 18th-century cloisonné objects and 19th-century Cantonese silk embroideries of birds, trees and flowers. He also carries some 18th-century Japanese porcelains and Oriental soapstones, ivories and bamboo wares.

Some Oriental ceramics do not appeal to him and he does not handle them. He says he can't sell something he does not find appealing.

"I don't have Dutch taste because I deal with earlier work, including Sung ceramics," he said, adding that he handles very few of the later Ch'ing vessels.

Prices for 12th-century Sung porcelains here range from $500 to $10,000. Ming porcelains may command higher prices. For example, an early 16th-century imperial blue-

and-white dragon dish might be about $14,000.

An example of the sort of rarity Mr. Blitz stocks was an early 18th-century garniture made to decorate a mantel. It was three 36-inch-high Japanese porcelain vessels to which lacquer panels were added in the Netherlands. This set was sold to a palace in the Netherlands, he said.

FRIDES LAMÉRIS

Nieuwe Spiegelstraat 55
1017 DD Amsterdam
Netherlands
Phone: (31-20) 26-40-66
Hours: 10 A.M. to 6 P.M. Monday to Friday, 10 A.M. to 5 P.M. Saturday

Frides Laméris, a glass collector turned dealer, began buying 17th- and 18th-century European glass when he was twenty years old. His passion for engraved, cut and exquisitely blown European bowls, vases and glasses is undiminished since he gave up his job in a bank in 1963 when he was forty-two to become a dealer. His interests have since broadened to glass made earlier than the 17th century, including Roman, and to ceramics, both European and Chinese. There are, for example 16th-century Murano goblets, 17th-century Dutch bottles and 18th-century French, German, Dutch and Italian drinking glasses on view in this glittering crystal-lined emporium, a two-story shop in Amsterdam's antiques area.

The shop carries mostly Continental designs from the first to 19th centuries. Among the rarities here during one visit were a Venetian tazza from about 1540 that was $9,000, a Dutch miniature tankard with a silver lid from about 1600 at $15,000 and a wheel-engraved glass depicting nautical motifs from about 1760 at $10,000.

Prices range from $100 for an 18th-century opaque twist glass to $30,000 for an early enameled or diamond-engraved glass.

FRANS LEIDELMEIJER

Nieuwe Spiegelstraat 58
1017 DH Amsterdam
Netherlands
Phone: (31-20) 25-46-27
Hours: 11 A.M. to 6 P.M. Monday to Saturday

Frans Leidelmeijer and Daan van der Cingel, collectors turned dealers, specialize in Dutch and other decorative arts dating from 1890 to World War II. Mr. Leidelmeijer, a dealer since 1970, and Mr. van der Cingel, a former manager of a computer center for a construction company, opened their present gallery in 1980, stocking Rozenburg's arts and crafts porcelains, bronzes by Theo Vos's, Leerdam's Art Deco glass, Jan Toorup's posters and mirrors and Gerrit Rietveld's and Mart Stam's early modern furniture.

The Dutch arts and crafts style, called Nieuwe Kunst (1890 to 1910), is well represented here with Rozenburg's eggshell-like white porcelains embellished with botanical motifs designed by Sam Schellink. Important examples of a cup and saucer would be about $1,000, a vase as much as $10,000. Among more florid Art Nouveau works are Toorup's drawings, posters and mirrors.

Theo Vos's documented the ballet in his decorative bronze sculptures of the 1920s, as can be seen in a 1925 figure of a dancer, her hair fanned Cleopatra style, her skirt swirled. The price: $20,000.

Gerrit Rietveld's de Stijl furniture, although never mass-produced and uncommon in the market, does appear from time to time at this gallery. Mr. Leidelmeijer said he had recently sold two prototypes of the designer's 1918 Red-Blue de Stijl chair, that three-dimensional Mondrian. Rietveld's ebonized plywood easy chair, a quieter study of similar abstract elements from 1924, is also scarce and from time to time Leidelmeijer has handled one. In both cases few were made. Later, in the 1950s and 1960s, other versions were made with Rietveld's permission by Gerard A. van de Groenekan, the architect's original cabinet-maker. These chairs are uncommon in the marketplace, too.

The original Red-Blue chair now costs over $50,000;

the easy chair, about $40,000. Rietveld's Zigzag chair from 1934, another uncommon work, is about $25,000, and his military chair is about $10,000. Rietveld's chromed-metal-tubing chair from 1927, its back bent like a paper clip, its plywood seat and back painted bright yellow or red, sells for about $10,000.

Mart Stam's bent-chromed-metal-tubing chair appeared in 1926. One version, with a linen back and seat stretched between its chromed sides, is a minimal updating of the Italian Renaissance folding chairs. The price, when a chair is available, is about $10,000.

Modern furniture of the 1920s and 1930s by Hendrik Wouda both echoes the past and anticipates the future. His 1927 slat-back chairs look like variations on the arts and crafts style of Gustav Stickley and Frank Lloyd Wright, but his upholstered leather-covered seating of 1930 could be precursors of the Italian Modern chairs and sofas of the 1960s.

Leerdam's mold-blown and free-blown studio art glass vessels of the 1920s are gaining in international popularity among collectors who also admire the works of René Lalique. Examples here might include the simple speckled vases of Chris Lebeau (an amethyst-colored vase in a triangular design would be about $3,000) or the frosted glass bowls and vases of Andries D. Copier ($2,000 to $6,000).

JOSEPH M. MORPURGO

Rokin 108
1012 LA Amsterdam
Netherlands
Phone: (31-20) 23-58-83
Hours: 9 A.M. to 5:30 P.M. Monday to Friday
Closed from mid-July to mid-August

There is no sign above the door, but antiques enthusiasts who know Amsterdam well need no map to guide them to Rebecca Morpurgo, a woman of indeterminant age and abundant energy. Her shop, one of Amsterdam's best-known, stocks Dutch and other European furniture, Dutch Delft, European and Oriental porcelains, Dutch silver, Oriental rugs and virtually anything antique that collectors seek.

Mrs. Morpurgo dates her entry into this business to her marriage to Lion Morpurgo in 1929. He was already working for his father, Louis M. Morpurgo, in the antique and modern silver business founded in 1869 by his father, Joseph M. Morpurgo. The business is now in its fourth generation with Rebecca and Lion's only child, Anny Wafelman-Morpurgo, sharing the management of the bustling two-story emporium since shortly before her father died in 1957.

Among the most distinctive offerings are the many selections of Dutch 17th-century oak and walnut furniture, including tapestry-covered chairs and massive library and refectory tables, some with melon-carved legs. Many of the furnishings of a Dutch room at the Toledo Museum of Art were acquired at this shop, which has been at the same location since 1929. One of the more unusual works was a 17th-century barber's chair that was not for sale.

Prices range from about $700 for a carved amethyst-colored-glass Chinese 19th-century snuff bottle to about $16,000 for a fine German glass vessel.

KUNSTHANDEL J. POLAK

Spiegelgracht 3
1017 JP Amsterdam
Netherlands
Phone: (31-20) 27-90-09
Hours: 10 A.M. to 6 P.M. Tuesday to Saturday and by appointment

Jaap Polak has a large appetite for exotic works, and he has grown to know them well in his 20 years as an antiques dealer. His colorful two-story shop is filled with unusual examples of Egyptian scarabs, tribal art, Oriental sculpture and paintings, Benin bronzes and Hindu Javanese sculpture from the 7th to 15th centuries. He considers himself an expert on Dutch Delft and also handles medieval through 18th-century glass vessels.

Mr. Polak is the first person in his family to become an art dealer. He did so quite young, in 1965, when he was eighteen and worked at Art Gallery A. Vecht while he studied art history, Sanskrit and Southeast Asian archeology at Amsterdam Univerity.

His shop was filled with many treasures, including a Dutch 17th-century japanned lacquer cabinet, each panel painted with a Dutch floral still life. There were Indian miniature paintings from the Mogul, Pahari and other schools, and medieval ivory diptychs, a Netherlands oak sculpture of SS. Joachim and Anne, a 14th-century French Madonna and a Nottingham alabaster depicting the coronation of the Virgin.

Other notable works included a very large Stockholm silver beaker from about 1775, a Nuremberg Renaissance tazza with hunting scenes from 1575, a 1480 bronze lion-shaped Rhineland aquamanile, an early-15th-century Yung Lo bronze head of a royal lady, a dressing table signed by Topino from about 1774 and a rare Enghien tapestry from about 1550 depicting Old and New Testament images.

The variety is stunning and so is the price range. Shoppers will find a 15th-century horse bell in gilded bronze at about $130, and an important medieval sculpture might be as much as $150,000. But most items in the shop go for $3,000 to $11,000.

KUNSTHANDEL INEZ STODEL

Nieuwe Spiegelstraat 65
1017 DD Amsterdam
Netherlands
Phone: (31-20) 23-29-42
Hours: By appointment

Inez Stodel, the daughter of Meyer Stodel, a Rotterdam antiques dealer, is the first dealer in her family to be based in Amsterdam and to specialize in period jewelry. Her stock dates from antiquities through the 1930s.

In 1964 she opened a shop for her father in Amsterdam that offered everything old: furniture, porcelains, silver, Oriental art, Eskimo art, clocks, furniture and drawings. In

1971 her father gave her the Amsterdam shop and she began specializing in jewelry.

Mrs. Stodel's tiny shop is filled with wonderful ornaments that reflect her eye for arresting design. She had an unsigned pair of ancient Roman earrings made of carved rock crystal and gold, a 1925 Cartier diamond brooch in the shape of a 1909 airplane, an enameled bow and a pair of Napoleonic iron earrings with gold-colored fittings and lacelike shells and drops.

Specialties at this shop include Peking glass-bead necklaces strung on knotted silk. Some of the necklaces have the green glass beads that look like jade. They range from about $30 to $750. Enameled butterflies, popular on and off since the turn of the century as pendants and brooches, are from $80 to $100. And there is usually an assortment of English arts and crafts jewelry designs: pendants, necklaces, bracelets and brooches.

"I am limited in Amsterdam to what is fashionable and beautiful," Mrs. Stodel said. "I love all periods. It just depends on the design."

The limitation, if there is one, does not keep the red-haired dealer from showing works that would stop traffic in any major antiques shop. For example, she briefly showed an early-20th-century René Lalique horn comb embellished with white gold and diamonds, the mate to one in the Calouste Gulbenkian Collection in Lisbon. The comb, as with most rarities, was sold within days—to the Rijksmuseum.

The 19th-century works might include a pair of 1810 Empire coral bracelets with clasps in the shape of the sun, an 1880s carved-rock-crystal face by Carlo Giuliano or a long strand of faceted French jet beads from 1850. "I have the most beautiful amber necklace I have ever seen," Mrs. Stodel said, producing a strand of amber flat disks found on Sicily in the 18th century.

The price range is as wide as the time span covered here, going from $3 for some fantastic "early plastic" object from the 1920s to about $70,000 for a rare Lalique work or a Byzantine gold and cloisonné enamel pendant.

SALOMON STODEL ANTIQUITÉS

Rokin 70
1012 KW Amsterdam
Netherlands
Phone: (31-20) 23-16-92
Hours: 10 A.M. to 5 P.M. Monday to Friday

Jacob Stodel heads the family business that bears his father's name and was founded in 1860 in Amsterdam by Bernardictus Stodel, his great-grandfather. When Salomon Stodel went to work in the shop in 1906 when he was sixteen, the Stodels still stocked virtually anything old.

Today, while dealers become ever more specialized, Mr. Stodel continues to offer a great variety of porcelains, furniture, clocks, antiquities, wood carvings and silver. He has a second shop stocked with materials used in decorating in Amsterdam called Stodel Décor, Spiegelgracht 23-25, and one in London, at 116 Kensington Church Street.

Jacob Stodel has an excellent eye for French and Dutch 17th- and 18th-century furniture, Italian Renaissance bronzes and European silver of the Renaissance through the 18th century, all of which he offers in his main Amsterdam shop. (In London he stocks French and Continental furniture with fewer collector's items, he said.)

Far and away the most important offerings are European and Chinese ceramics, which he offers at his Amsterdam and London shops. There are Delft and other faïence wares from the 17th and 18th centuries and German and French porcelains from the 18th century. Shoppers visit here in search of 16th-century polychrome albarello pharmacy jars, some depicting legends. A large vitrine was filled during one visit with 18th-century Delft polychrome lions in black, blue and white at $52,000, some Ming imperial yellow vessels, 17th-century Delft plates and porcelains from several 18th-century German factories, including Meissen.

Prices range from about $1,750 for a small 17th-century Delft dish to $13,000 for an Urbino early-16th-century majolica plate.

CHRISTIE'S AMSTERDAM B.V.

Cornelia Schuytstraat 57
1071 JG Amsterdam
Netherlands
Phone: (31-20) 64-20-11
Office hours: 9 A.M. to 5 P.M. Monday to Friday
Viewing hours: 10 A.M. to 4 P.M.
Sales: September to June.

SOTHEBY'S AMSTERDAM

102 Rokin
1012 KZ Amsterdam
Phone: (31 20) 27-56-56
Hours: 10 A.M. to 4:30 P.M. Monday to Friday, 10 A.M. to 4 P.M. some Saturdays and Sundays

ANTWERP-BRUSSELS

BERNARD BLONDEEL

Schuttershofstraat 5
B-2000 Antwerp
Belgium
Phone: (32-3) 233-25-54
Hours: Noon to 6 P.M. Tuesday to Saturday
Closed sometimes from July 20 to Aug. 20

The architectural spareness of Bernard Blondeel's high-ceilinged modern gallery enhances each of the Gothic and Renaissance treasures arranged in it. Gothic wood carvings and Hispano-Moresque pottery are set out on a banquet-size English 17th-century refectory table against walls hung with richly detailed Tournai and Flemish verdure tapestries. Here and in the rooms beyond are meticulously carved boxwood figures, French 14th-century ivory reliefs and 13th-century Limoges champlevé enamels.

Mr. Blondeel is a dealer with an exceptional eye for the sort of 12th- to 17th-century artwork that once dominated the taste of European and American collectors. These days such works are scarce—many of the finest were acquired by museums—and fewer dealers understand and handle them.

But when Mr. Blondeel became a dealer at twenty-two in 1973, he handled later material. He had been studying medicine for three years when he joined his mother, Marie Louise Blondeel, in the antiques and decorating business she founded in the late 1950s. Two years after he came in, his mother retired, and he began to reshape the general character of the stock to his taste: the Gothic and Renaissance. His present gallery was designed for him by an architect when he moved into this space in 1983.

The harmonious mix of tapestries, furniture and pottery included several memorable 17th-century pieces of furniture: an Augsburg cabinet, a Flemish tortoise-shell-embellished ebony cabinet and a robustly carved table. Most of the art works here are earlier, including three realistic oak carvings of soldiers from the Lower Rhine, each full of movement with heads cocked, arms on sword hilts or raised to strike another.

Prices start at about $500 for a 16th-century Hispano-Moresque plate, decorative ivory object or chair. Tapestries range from about $10,000 for a 17th-century Flemish verdure weaving to about $200,000 for a Gothic mille-fleurs tapestry.

GALLERY BOB CLAES

Hotel Rosier
Rosier 21-23
2000 Antwerp
Belgium
Phone: (32-3) 225-01-40
Hours: 11 A.M. to 6 P.M. Monday to Saturday and by appointment

Bob Claes's presentation of antiques—especially of the French Empire and Charles X periods—starts just inside the front door of the Rosier. This luxury hotel, furnished in the grand manner by Mr. Claes, is a converted two-story mansion that dates from the 17th century and has additions from a century later. It was the home of Antwerp's mayors when it was new.

The elegant residence has served many uses over the years. In this century it was a school and later a rest house for the White Sisters of Africa, a Roman Catholic order from whom it was bought in 1972 for conversion into a hotel.

The transformation of the interiors from functional quarters into elaborate period settings with the latest in modern amenities, including an indoor swimming pool, reveals Mr. Claes's taste in antiques and his skills in decorating. The 18th- and 19th-century furniture, carpets, wall sconces and chandeliers and the Old Master paintings that decorate the lobby, salons, dining room and guest rooms transport visitors back to earlier times when this house was a center of Antwerp's social and political life.

The shop on the main floor is a boutique-size space where Mr. Claes and his partner, Alfons Scheers, have ever-changing arrangements of French Empire, Charles X and Russian neo-classical furniture and decorations. There were several Charles X pieces, including a console table that was $5,000 and a work table at $4,000. There was also a set of six Restoration armchairs dating to about 1815, a gilded bronze Russian clock from about 1810 and a pair of late-18th-century vases that Mr. Claes said were made for one of Napoleon's chateaus.

Prices range from $500 for porcelain dishes to $200,000 for the Russian clock.

AXEL VERVOORDT

Kasteel van's Gravenwezel
St. Jacobsteenweg, 2232's Gravenwezel
Antwerp
Belgium
Phone: (32-3) 658-14-70
Hours: Preferably by appointment 9 A.M. to 12:30 P.M. and 1:30 to 6 P.M. Tuesday to Friday, 11 A.M. to 6 P.M. Saturday; open house the first two weekends in December
Closed in July

Axel Vervoordt is an antiques dealer with exceptional flair, an enormous appetite for art dating from antiquity through the 20th century and a keen merchant's instinct that spurs him on in worldwide buying treks. Whatever he sells, he has lived with for a while. When it doesn't sell, he added, "it was meant to stay with us."

The settings he has chosen for exhibiting his extraordinary stock are as exciting as the materials they frame. Until 1986, the antiques shop filled a complex of 22 buildings on a winding street in the medieval part of Antwerp. Its interiors were white-walled and magical, from the 13th-century vaulted cellars where he stored the blue-and-white Ming porcelains salvaged from a 17th-century shipwreck in the South China Sea through the warren of rooms on the floors above, chock-full of gilded silver vessels, Roman statuary, 12th-century-B.C. archaic jades, Gothic chests, English Chippendale bookcases, Japanese screens, Khmer vases and tortoise-shell-veneered Flemish chests. The best of 30 centuries and a score of cultures was housed in harmony under the dealer's roof.

In 1986, Mr. Vervoordt moved everything seven miles from downtown Antwerp to his castle, Kasteel van's Gravenwezel, which boasts a medieval moat. There he, his wife, May, and their two children live over, around and in the "shop," which consists of about 100 rooms that were started in the 12th century and evolved architecturally until the 17th century. Until 1984, when he bought it, the castle and its 350-acre estate had been the family home of Baron Gilles de Pelichy for two centuries. Now it houses his shop, home and workshops, where a staff of 20 is kept busy five days a week.

The remoteness of this castle delights the dealer, for he loves the land and the challenge of redoing another ancient building. And he knows that wherever he goes, collectors will follow him to see what he has found, be it a 10th-century-B.C. 20th-dynasty Egyptian bronze of Sekhmet, a 15th-century East Anglia English oak monastery table or 16 gilded silver vessels made in 1632 by the Huguenot silversmith David Willaume. All were for sale but, Mr. Vervoordt said, his outsize Shigaraki ash-glaze storage vessels awash with Rothko-like colors were not. He wants to have these 15th-century Japanese earthenware pots with him a while longer, he said.

Collectors who have shopped at Mr. Vervoordt's establishments include members of the Rothschild and Lauder families as well as Yves Saint Laurent and the Agha Kahn. It is difficult to go away empty-handed with so much from which to choose, including 12th-century Khmer vases, a Flemish Gothic oak chest, a Japanese 16th-century dragon-embellished screen, a painted Venetian secretary-bookcase, glass canes, Delft tiles, vessels devised from tree roots, Yüan-period Chinese calligraphy and a 19th-century prehistoric-looking stuffed anteater.

Prices range from about $60 for Ming wine cups from the shipwrecked vessel to high in six figures for major examples of Egyptian sculpture or rare fine silver objects.

J. ZEBERG N.V.

Melkmarkt 37-39
2000 Antwerp
Belgium
Phone: (32-3) 233-82-30
Hours: 9:30 A.M. to noon and 1:30 to 6 P.M. Monday to Saturday; from June to August, 9:30 A.M. to noon Saturday

In 1941, Jenny Van Wichelen Zeberg, vice president of Belgium's Chamber of Antiques Dealers, took over the antiques business founded by the Anthonissen family in 1887. She built it into a sprawling enterprise that fills three buildings in the center of town. Her husband, Erik Zeberg, a Dane who has lived in Belgium since 1942, left his work in the shipping business in 1974 and helps her and their two daughters in the antiques business.

Notable among the elaborate French and Italian Renaissance furniture was a Henry II prie-dieu (pew) at $4,000, several small 16th-century Louis XIII desks at $3,000 to $7,000 and a boldly carved 16th-century northern German cabinet at $10,000. Those in search of elaborate alabasters usually find a large selection at this shop; Flemish 16th-century alabaster reliefs filled a large showcase. There were 17th-century Dutch marquetry-embellished chairs and tables, Chinese 18th-century blue-and-white porcelains, tapestries, brass candlesticks and Renaissance to 18th-century European silver.

GISÈLE CROËS

Boulevard de Waterloo 54
1000 Brussels
Belgium
Phone: (32-2) 511-82-16
Hours: 10 A.M. to 12:30 P.M. and 2:30 to 6:30 P.M. Monday to Friday, 2:30 to 6:30 P.M. Saturday

"I started as a junk dealer with $1,000," Gisèle Croës recalled one Saturday morning, surrounded in her green-

and-beige gallery by the dramatic proof of how far she had traveled in 20 years. The Chinese artworks gathered so harmoniously there—Tang pottery figures, 18th-century Chinese jades, archaic bronzes, Sung porcelains and imperial Ming chairs—are the sort of ingredients many dealers mix with jarring results.

Before Mrs. Croës sold junk, she said, she was a journalist. In 1964 she went to China and worked there for Beijing Radio. In 1966, she returned home to Brussels and decided for personal reasons to join a friend selling period wares of indeterminate age and character—junk—in a Brussels flea market.

Although that alliance ended in a few months, Mrs. Croës had found her world, the world where art and history merge in a merchant's hands. The years in China were well spent, although she never dreamed when she lived there that she would one day be buying and selling the works she had admired, mostly from afar.

Mrs. Croës went on her own in 1973, opening her first shop on the Place du Grand Sablon, the Brussels antiques center. She moved several times to more fashionable quarters in converted 19th-century mansions and has been in her present gallery since 1987.

Most of the works were memorable for their form or rich colors, including a Wei third-century horse, a pair of 17th-century imperial armchairs of huang huali wood, Ming monochrome blood-red porcelain bowls, a pale green Mogul jade in the shape of a chrysanthemum and an early-19th-century Japanese red-and-gold-lacquered kimono cabinet. The kimono cupboard, formerly in the collection of Barbara Hutton, was one of the more expensive pieces of furniture on view at about $60,000. Furniture here starts at about $6,000, the price asked for Chinese export Regency period garden seats of papier-mâché and lacquer. Chinese Tang pottery figures might be $100,000 or more.

CHRISTIAN DE BRUYN

Rue van Moer 7
1000 Brussels
Belgium
Phone: (32-2) 512-44-68
Hours: 2:30 to 6 P.M. Tuesday to Saturday

Christian de Bruyn and his wife, Germaine, have been antiques dealers since 1956. Mr. de Bruyn, who has headed the Belgium Antiques Dealers Association since 1967, studied art before he became a dealer, specializing in 16th- to 18th-century European furniture, artwork and decorations.

The antiques here are in the grand style. On one visit the walls were hung with numerous 16th- and 17th-century tapestries. Many Brussels historical weavings were on view, and one was from a series of eight by Matthias Roelants after cartoons by Rubens. It cost $37,300.

Mr. de Bruyn also stocks 17th-century French ivory figures, 18th-century tortoise-shell boxes, 17th- and 18th-century boxwood carvings, 16th-century wood carvings and Renaissance and later decorative objects. The furniture selections included late-16th- to 18th-century tapestry-covered chairs and elaborately carved and inlaid desks, cabinets and chests.

Prices range from $215 for an ivory box to about $170,000 for a Flemish tapestry.

GALERIE DeWINDT

Rue Lebeau 77-79
1000 Brussels
Belgium
Phone: (32-2) 513-36-12
Hours: 11 A.M. to 12:30 P.M. and 3 to 6:30 P.M. Tuesday to Saturday

In Brussels visitors may think the clock stopped at the turn of the century with the Art Nouveau period. However, Jacques DeWindt and France Borms prove in their shop on the Grand Sablon that European furniture, lighting and jewelry of the 1920s to 1950s were as innovative as anything that happened earlier. In some cases, the furniture and accessories they stock were born in Brusssels.

Mrs. Borms studied drawing and became a dealer in Art Nouveau in 1965 when she was twenty-three, opening the first shop specializing in Art Nouveau and Art Deco in Belgium. Mr. DeWindt joined her in business that year, when he was twenty. Recently, Winston Spriet, an architect, has been a consultant.

The shop offers an offbeat selection of 20th-century decorative arts, from 1920 to 1960. The mix is of serious signed works by some of the major French designers and unsigned furniture, jewelry and accessories. Most are either undeniably handsome or evocative of a period or style.

During one visit, for example, there was a set of four René Herbst nickel-plated chairs at $4,700, a chromed-metal Art Deco lamp at $1,000, a 1920s aluminum screen by Robert Mallet-Stevens, a French ivory bracelet from the 1930s at about $150 and a 1950s necklace of clear plastic beads at $30.

At the shop and in their private collections, these dealers also have an early modern wood bookcase and chrome-tubing framed table by Eileen Gray, and a Jean Dunand tour de force of lacquer and eggshell, a bowl 30 inches across. One of the later designs was a 1950s chaise by Poul Kjaerholm, the Swedish designer.

A Bauhaus chair by Marcel Breuer was $1,200, Austrian Secessionist furniture was $300 and up, silver jewelry by Georg Jensen was $100 and up and fine 1930s watches ranged from $100 to $3,000.

GALUCHAT

182 Avenue Louise
1050 Brussels
Belgium
Phone: (32-2) 647-45-40
Hours: 10 A.M. to 6:30 P.M. Monday to Saturday, 11 A.M. to 1 P.M. Sunday

West of Vienna and north of Paris, the largest representation in Europe of quality works by Josef Hoffmann and his Viennese turn-of-the-century colleagues and, to a lesser extent, the French Art Deco designers is at Nele Haas-Stoclet's gallery, Galuchat.

Mrs. Haas-Stoclet, the granddaughter of Adolf Stoclet, who commissioned Hoffmann to design the 1905 Palais Stoclet, his acknowledged architectural masterpiece and a Brussels landmark, grew up in that house. The dining room walls are dramatized by Gustav Klimt's glorious wall mosaics, and the furnishings throughout, even the teaspoons, cups and saucers and ashtrays, were all designed by Hoffmann. She has been a dealer in this field since 1977.

"I used to live in the house of my grandfather," Mrs. Haas-Stoclet said. After her grandfather died in 1948, when she was four, her father, Jacques Stoclet, looked after the house. Since his death in 1961, her mother, Anne Stoclet, has assumed that responsibility. "I try to follow the same spirit as was expressed in the Palais Stoclet," she said.

Her intimate knowledge of the best of early-20th-century Viennese design could be seen in the works in her gallery. There were such Hoffmann works as his Cabaret Fledermaus chairs and tables, a maple dressing table, parlor suites of settees and chairs, a sitting machine, wall cabinets, silver tableware, silver cigarette boxes, glassware and a spectacular brass-framed dance card from 1909.

The prices for the Hoffmann designs vary considerably depending on whether they were made in quantity, as in the case of some parlor furniture, or are scarce examples. A Cabaret Fledermaus chair was $1,200.

Among the works by other designers were a perfume box and coat rack by Koloman Moser, a painted white parlor suite of spindle-framed chairs and a circular table by Robert Oerley, Thonet chairs and settees and a Dagobert Peche silver cup.

Prices range from $590 for an unsigned case covered with sharkskin (galuchat in French) and $1,760 for a clear blue glass by Hoffmann to $45,000 for a Ruhlmann cupboard.

VILLARS

14 Place du Grand Sablon
Grote Zavel 14
1000 Brussels
Belgium
Phone: 932-2) 512-14-17
Hours: 10 A.M. to noon and 3 to 7 P.M. Monday to Saturday

In the 16th century when houses on the Grand Sablon had names, the three-story shop of Villars on this historic square was known as the Green Angel, as can be seen by the large ceramic plaque that says Groene Engel. Today Villars, under the direction of Gilbert Sarraute-Mourchette, stocks some of the finest examples of French 18th- and 19th-century furniture, from Louis XIV to Napoleon III.

Villars, one of the first antiques dealers to move to the Sablon, has been at this address since 1960. The house provides an uncommonly intimate and charming background for the furniture he stocks, most of which, he said, has excellent pedigrees.

With or without important provenance, selections here are strong on eye appeal. There was a Louis XIV Boulle commode inlaid with gilded copper at $25,000, a Charles X dressing table at $4,000, a Louis XVI roll-top desk by Jean-Henri Riesener at $50,000 and an early-19th-century English invalid's chair at $5,000.

Prices ranged from $100 for 17th-century Indian quill-covered boxes, $300 for a Chinese 18th-century dish and $5,000 for a late-18th-century mahogany writing box to $50,000 for the Louis XVI roll-top desk.

Mr. Sarraute-Mourchette suggests that those who speak

only English phone ahead so that his colleague, Pierre de Formanoir, can be on hand.

ZEN GALLERY

10 Rue Ernest Allard
1000 Brussels
Belgium
Phone: (32-2) 511-95-10
Hours: 2 to 6 P.M. Tuesday to Saturday

André Cnudde and Luc Van Mulders began buying and selling Oriental art and decorations privately in 1975. They moved to this shop in 1982, stocking Japanese screens and scrolls as well as Chinese furniture, porcelains, Tang terra cottas and tomb figures.

Most of the more than 40 Japanese screens on view during one visit were full size and from the 18th and 19th centuries. They ranged from about $4,500 to $58,000. Two notable early-19th-century designs were a two-panel black-and-white screen depicting a tiger for $7,000 and a six-panel gold scenic that was $11,500. A small selection of earlier screens included a 17th-century six-panel screen of blue and white flowers in a marsh against a gold sky at $32,700 and a 17th-century six-panel mountainscape at $17,500. Japanese scrolls range from about $900 to about $4,200.

Chinese ceramics include 14th- to 15th-century Celadons and blue and yellow monochromes as well as Tang terra cottas at about $28,000 for a horse and $4,500 to $7,000 for tomb figures.

FLORENCE-ROME

GALLERIA LUIGI BELLINI

Lungarno Soderini 5
50124 Florence
Italy
Phone: (39-55) 21-40-31
Hours: 11 A.M. to 1 P.M. and 3 to 7 P.M. Monday to Saturday
Closed in August

Mario A. Bellini was born into a family of antiquarians who have been buying and selling art and antiques in Florence since the 18th century. The antiques establishment that Mr. Bellini heads dates formally to 1786 and has occupied the three-story Solderini mansion overlooking the Arno since Mr. Bellini's father, Luigi Bellini, moved there in 1908.

The mini-palace is furnished in a grander style than any Florentine aristocrat of the Renaissance or 18th century would probably have achieved. The walls are covered with icons and Madonnas, landscapes, still-life paintings and tapestries. The rooms are furnished with Italian Renaissance chairs, tables, credenzas and cassones that were made for aristocrats and cardinals.

The red-velvet-covered walls of one intimate gallery are a perfect background for the Renaissance reliefs and carvings exhibited there. On table tops and in cabinets are Faenza, Urbino, Deruta and Gubbio majolica vessels, Italian Renaissance bronzes and Della Robbia enameled terra cotta figures. Bronze candlesticks, small sculptures and massive marble statuary dramatize a dozen galleries in a setting that sugests many secret treasure rooms.

Mr. Bellini, a hearty man with an engaging manner, is the grandson of Giuseppe Italiano Bellini, who made the Bellini name famous in the booming antiques trade in the late 19th century. Luigi Bellini built on this legacy when he took over. From about 1910 until after World War II he dominated the antiques trade in Italy.

His two sons, Mario and Giuseppe, continued in this tradition, and in 1959 were co-founders of Florence's International Antiques Fair, which is held every two years in September at the Palazzo Strozzi. Mario's wife, Dodina, a Bolognese woman and the daughter of a gunpowder manufacturer, is usually at the gallery with her husband.

The Bellini clientele has included Gustav VI of Sweden, Leopold III, King of the Belgians, J. Paul Getty, William Randolph Hearst and Imelda Marcos. Purchases made here are now in the collections of the National Gallery in Washington, Boston's Museum of Fine Arts and the Metropolitan Museum of Art in New York.

Among the outstanding Italian Renaissance furniture selections on view was a banquet-size 16th-century Florentine table over 100 inches long with a coat of arms and scroll-carved legs ending in lion's paw feet. It was about $190,000. Cassones, chests with lift-up lids, included some 15th-century examples with paintings by Apolonio di Giovanni and Rosello di Jacopo Franchi. Others were embellished with intarsia, painted coats of arms or carved figures. There are Dante chairs, the 16th-century folding chair on which Hollywood's 1930s director's chairs are based, and wood-slatted Renaissance folding Savonarola chairs, too.

Art treasures at this gallery and elsewhere require export permits. Minor works pose few problems. Mr. Bellini says that most of the major works are acquired outside of Italy and that he has documentation—a temporary import license—to prove where they were purchased, thereby easing export.

Prices range from about $1,000 for a small table or perhaps a piece of majolica to $1,000,000 or more for an Old Master painting or major sculpture.

GUIDO BARTOLOZZI & FIGLIO

Massimo Bartolozzi
18 Rosso Via Maggio
50125 Florence
Italy
Phone: (39-55) 21-56-02
Hours: 9 A.M. to 1 P.M. and 4 to 7:30 P.M. Monday to Saturday
Closed in August, Monday morning in winter, Saturday afternoon in summer

The Bartolozzi family celebrated its centenary as antiques dealers in 1987—100 years in business and, amazingly, 100 years at the same address. Guido Bartolozzi, the founder, was succeeded by his two sons, Renato and Carlo. In 1963, Renato's son Guido, then forty-two years old, took charge of the business. In that year, too, the Bartolozzi business added a fourth generation when Massimo came to work for his father.

The Bartolozzis' shop and their gallery nearby in Guido Bartolozzi's home, a 16th-century palace at 11 Nero Via Maggio, reflect the taste of the owners and the current market for antiques. There were some highly decorative works and some more important antiques, too. There were, for example, four painted doors dated 1745 and signed by Pannini that were $50,000; a pair of Roman 17th-century busts that were $10,000; a late-17th-century table top signed by Andrea Cherubinus that was $30,000; a Tuscan red lacquered bookcase from about 1780 for $100,000, and a Sicilian brass bed of the Biedermeier period for $6,000.

Prices here range from about $1,000 for decorations to high in six figures for an important sculpture.

FALLANI BEST

Borgognissanti 15R
50123 Florence
Italy
Phone: (39-55) 21-49-86
Hours: 9:30 A.M. to 1 P.M. and 3:30 to 7:30 P.M. Monday to Saturday
Closed Monday morning in winter, Saturday afternoon in summer

Paola Fallani said she named her shop Fallani Best not as a boast but to add an element of "some fantasy" to her name. She adopted the name when she went into business in 1968, and it has stuck. The decorative arts she stocks from the mid-19th to mid-20th centuries have given her shop the reputation of being the best in the field.

Mrs. Fallani changes the stock in her gallery as works become available, bringing different designers and materials into focus. She has carried the major designers' works in 19th- and 20th-century decorative sculpture, glass vessels by Emile Gallé and Andreas Schneider of Daum; lacquer decorations by Jean Dunand and Art Deco furniture by Emile-Jacques Ruhlmann and C. R. Colinet. From time to time there will be exotic turn-of-the-century furniture by Carlo Bugatti and Art Nouveau fantasy objects: outsize Medusa-shaped terra cotta vases and a moon-shaped mirror framed in a bronze female figure with a base of a crescent moon.

Mrs. Fallani has decided to add a specialty: jewelry by 20th-century artists. Among those whose works she intends to show, she said, are Arnaldo Pomodoro, Afro, Capogrossi and Roberto Fallani, her husband.

Prices at this shop range from about $1,000 for a vase or a box to tens of thousands for an important piece of furniture or jewelry.

GIANFRANCO LUZZETTI

Borgo S. Jacopo 28/A
50125 Florence
Italy
Phone: (39-55) 21-12-32
Hours: 9 A.M. to 1 P.M. and 3:30 to 7:30 P.M. Monday to Saturday
Closed Monday morning in winter, Saturday afternoon in summer

Gianfranco Luzzetti founded his antiques business in 1960 in Milan when he was twenty-eight. The gallery where he stocks majolica, bronzes, furniture, decorations, marble works and Old Master paintings has antiques in the Florentine taste. Renaissance furniture from Tuscany includes boldly scaled and robustly carved walnut designs that are architectural in form. There were great tables, credenzas and cassones, the chests with lift-up lids.

Majolica dishes and platters, earthenware vessels elaborately embellished with armorial designs, scenes or mythological images are among the highly decorative Italian Renaissance works found here.

Like many Italian dealers, Mr. Luzzetti does not discuss prices except when actually selling.

FABRIZIO APOLLONI

Via Babuino 133
00187 Rome
Italy
Phone: (39-6) 679-2429
Hours: 10 A.M. to 1 A.M. and 3:30 to 7:30 P.M. Monday to Saturday
Closed Monday morning in winter, Saturday afternoon in summer

"I am the third generation in the business and 20 years here," said Fabrizio Apolloni. He became an antiques dealer in 1948, following in his father's and his great-grandfather's footsteps. The Apolloni concern was founded in 1861 by his great-grandfather Jerome Apolloni and the business was resumed by his grandchild, Wladimiro Apolloni.

As with all these family antiques businesses, the stock changes slightly or even dramatically with each generation and with swings in collecting fashions. Nineteenth-century paintings were the specialty of the founder. "My father specialized in 18th-century paintings and furniture," Mr. Apolloni said.

The art offerings are older still under Fabrizio Apolloni. "I specialize in Italian works of art and European Old Master 17th- and 18th-century paintings and drawings." He said he thinks Italian dealers follow their own taste in what they offer more than dealers do in London or Paris. "In Italy there is another sort of culture," he said. "It is not only for the market reasons that we decide what to show but it is because we are curious in many fields."

The things Mr. Apolloni is most curious about these days, he said, are Roman works of art of the 17th, 18th and early 19th centuries. He is, of course, not alone. Other dealers and certainly collectors, dealers and decorators from New York, London and Paris admire the sort of sculpture he carries: the Venetian blackamoors, Florentine late-16th-century busts and outsize marble vases made of Egyptian onyx. "My firm handles mainly Roman sculpture, not archeological but from the 18th and 19th centuries," he said. These are the figures and urns that are becoming all the rage in decorating on both sides of the Atlantic.

Mr. Apolloni did not discuss prices.

PIERO BETTI

Via Babuino 153/154
00187 Rome
Italy
Phone: (39-6) 678-6251
Hours: 9:30 A.M. to 1 P.M. and 3:30 to 7:30 P.M. Monday to Saturday
Closed Monday morning in winter, Saturday afternoon in summer

In May 1986 Piero Betti moved from Florence to Rome, opening in the heart of Rome's antiques shopping neighborhood on the street where many of the top names in the field have shops.

Mr. Betti's stock has always been well laced with decorative antiques and accessories that add spice to interiors. These works include Japanese screens, outsize Imari vases, marble vessels, furniture with Chinese and Japanese lacquered panels and most European styles. The dealer, who became an interior designer in the 1970s, has the eye for such decorative works and selects them with enviable confidence.

Mr. Betti, who has worked with Valentino, lived in the United States during the 1970s and knows American taste. After he returned to Florence in 1981, he redecorated Gucci Palace, near the Ponte Vecchio, for Roberto Gucci, son of Aldo Gucci, a project that was widely publicized.

Among the more arresting objects was a Dali work from 1950: a bronze beast with the head of an elephant and the legs of a giraffe balancing a plastic obelisk on his shoulder. A pair of long-beaked imperial Japanese birds, Gustave Miklos bronzes, were arresting, ageless long-legged creatures dating from about 1928. Two enormous black Belgian marble fountains, strongly classical designs of the Art Deco period, were 75 inches tall and cost $50,000.

Mr. Betti's selection of furniture is wide-ranging and included a Louis XV commode by Jacques Dubois with Chinese lacquer front panels for $50,000, a 1730 gilded rococo console and a malachite-topped round table from about 1800 with a mahogany frame and a marble column for the base. The table was made for Pavlovsk Palace and cost $40,000.

ALBERTO DI CASTRO & FIGLIO

Piazza di Spagna 5
00187 Rome
Italy
Phone: (39-6) 679-2269
Hours: 10 A.M. to 1 P.M. and 3:30 to 7:30 P.M. Monday to Saturday
Closed Monday morning in winter, Saturday afternoon in summer

This prestigious antiques firm is more than a century old. Founded in 1878 by Leone di Castro, it bears the name of his son, Alberto di Castro Sr. Since the death of Alberto Sr.

in 1975, his son Franco, then forty-five years old, has headed the family business. Now Franco has been joined by his son, Alberto, the fourth generation of the di Castro family.

The di Castros' elegant gallery is an excellent source for knowledgeable collectors seeking 17th-, 18th- and early-19th-century furniture, mirrors, paintings, decorative objects, lighting and clocks. It represents the aristocratic Italian taste. Most of the selections come from Italy: Rome, Venice, Naples, Florence. There are, however, some French pieces from time to time.

Although the works on view cover a range of finishes (marquetry inlays or painted and gilded finishes) and more than a century of stylistic developments, from the 17th-century Baroque through 18th-century rococo and neoclassical, there is a unity of taste. Everything seems a bit understated, more serene than exuberant.

Mid-to-late-18th-century designs dominated among the more appealing selections. There was, for example, a late-18th-century commode enlivened with painted decoration, a transitional chair from about 1770, a ladies' desk and a rococo commode.

The di Castros also offer a selection of 18th- and 19th-century Roman marbles: urns, vases, bowls and footed compotes. Prices were not discussed.

ANTONACCI EFRATI

Via del Babuino 146 R
00187 Rome
Italy
Phone: (39-6) 678-1595, 678-9087
Hours: 9 A.M. to 1 P.M. and 4 to 8 P.M. Monday to Saturday; afternoon hours in winter, 3:30 to 7:30

"We started in 1916," Giuseppe Antonacci said recently of the business his grandfather Emanuele Efrati, a textile dealer, founded during World War I. Americans collected tapestries and fine fabrics then, the dealer said, and his grandfather did a lot of business with them.

"I was born into the business," Mr. Antonacci commented, adding that his mother, Mrs. Luigio Efrati-Antonacci, ran the business from the founder's death until 1965, when he took over. He said he made his first trips to Paris in 1948 and 1949 and has retraced his steps many times since. Now there is a fourth generation of the family in the business: two of Mr. Antonacci's three children, Paolo and Francesca. They work with him while Filippo, another son, studies architecture.

The Italian taste in furniture and decorations as seen at this gallery is more opulent and dramatic than the Parisian taste. "It must have a rich look and be a quality piece," Mr. Antonacci said, citing a Lepinne regulator clock, pairs of angels decorating the wall, pairs of chairs and decorative sculpture. The mix of styles included French, German, Austrian and Italian neo-classical, Baroque and rococo chairs, tables and commodes. "We always keep one eye on the foreign market," he said, adding that they visit exhibitions abroad and are aware of the changing fashions in decorating and collecting.

Outstanding among the uncommon selections at the gallery, where the walls are hung with gilded mirrors and tapestries, were neo-classical marble decorations inspired by Piranesi (urns, vases, footed bowls and mantels) as well as crystal chandeliers. A German Würzburg commode from 1750-60 in violet-hued ebony was poised on transitional legs. A crystal chandelier crafted in Genoa about 1780 was framed in gilded metal.

The wide range of offerings commands a wide range of prices, from about $1,000 for a pair of candlesticks or a bronze clock up to about $500,000 for a beautiful piece of French furniture or marble sculpture.

GALLERIA ANTIQUARIA "F. TUENA"

Via Margutta 53 B
00187 Roma
Italy
Phone: (39-6) 679-5116
Hours: 11 A.M. to 1 P.M. and 4 to 7:30 P.M. Monday to Saturday
Closed Monday morning in winter, Saturday afternoon in summer

Massimo Tuena was born into the business that his father, Federico Tuena, founded in 1936 and moved to this address in 1946. Federico headed the shop until his death in 1950. Now along with Massimo Tuena there is a third generation, Filippo, his son, who came to work at the gallery in 1980.

"Statues are our specialty," Massimo Tuena said on his premises, a splendid house full of sunlight with huge marble and stone columns, figures, architectural sculpture and furniture. It was erected in 1858 as a house of artists' studios. It is an ideal setting for the extraordinary garden statues and impressive furniture seen here. There were, for example, a gilded Florentine table that was $9,000 and a sofa from the Palazzo Torlonia in Rome that was $15,000.

A pair of 16th-century vases in Egyptian granite were $40,000 and, Mr. Tuena said, would pose no problem shipping out of the country because they "were purchased abroad." This means that no special export permit is required, he said.

GENEVA-ZURICH

GALERIE GRANDES EPOQUES

Grand Rue 8
1204 Geneva
Switzerland
Tele: (41-22) 28-72-07
Hours: 2:30 to 6:30 P.M. Monday, 10 A.M. to 12:30 P.M. and 2:30 to 6:30 P.M. Tuesday to Friday, 10 A.M. to 5 P.M. Saturday

Bernard Oberson, whose father was Swiss and whose mother was French, was raised in Gruyère, Switzerland. He became a dealer in French 18th- and early-19th-century furniture in 1959, opening first on the Côte d'Azur near Nice and adding a second shop in Geneva in 1965. He maintained both until 1980, when he closed the shop in the south of France.

Mr. Oberson's classical taste is seen in all the offerings of furniture by Georges Jacob and other ébénistes. A handsome early Empire mahogany desk on chest, attributed to Jacob, had a drop-down writing surface and an interior fitted with many small drawers. The price was $140,000.

Notable too were six painted white chairs with squarish backs, transitional legs and seats covered in blue velvet that were attributed to Georges Jacob. The set dates to about 1780 and was $22,500. A pair of demilune consoles with gilded decoration, attributed to Jacob, was $7,000. A choice pair of small Louis XV corner cupboards by Pierre Macret with squarish legs embellished with bronzes doré was $22,500. The shop also stocked several other desks and tables, all restrained examples of the late 18th and early 19th centuries.

Prices range from about $3,000 for a pair of Louis XVI chairs to about $170,000 for a Louis XV commode with gilded bronze mounts.

MAX KNOLL ANTIQUITÉS

25 Grand Rue
1204 Geneva
Switzerland
Phone: (41-22) 21-05-22
Hours: 9 A.M. to noon and 2 to 6:30 P.M. Monday to Friday, 10 A.M. to noon and 2 to 4 P.M. Saturday

"Every year there are fewer collectors," Max N. Knöll said in his shop, where 13th- to 17th-century bronzes, enamels, silver and glassware are the specialties. "It would be much easier to sell Biedermeier," he said.

Founded in Basel, in 1923 by Mr. Knölls's grandfather Max Knöll, the antiques business was then mainly faïence and porcelain. His son, Max Knöll, began a separate business in Bern in 1950 with picture frames, to which he added early glass and silver. He later moved to Basel but did not join his father in business. After the founder died in 1977, his son and grandson took over the antiques business, eventually closing the Basel shop and moving in 1981 to Geneva. Max N. Knöll worked at Christie's in London for two years, starting as a porter in 1979. In 1980 he became assistant to the head of its silver department in Geneva, and returned to work with his father in 1981.

Today Max Knöll is a father-son alliance. The father, whose major specialty is silver and early works of art, does much of the buying and research, while his son remains in the shop. The early glass and objects of art included German, Austrian, Dutch, French and Italian selections dating from the 14th to 18th centuries. There are German late-15th- and 17th-century vessels embellished with colorful coats of arms and sometimes with horses and beer barrels. Often the coats of arms are known. A group of 1590 vessels was made for a member of the aristocratic Saxony family of Von der Schulenburg Einsiedel and bears their coat of arms; the vessels were about $27,000 each. There are examples of pale green Römer glass vessels on footed bases of the 17th century, pale green formed-glass narrow-necked bottles of the 18th century and Swiss 18th-century enameled Flüli glasses, usually thought of as Stiegl in the United States.

Notable too was a 15th-century stained-glass panel for

$1,500, small glass vessels from $720 and a 16th-century Italian enameled glass at $4,500.

PETER ZERVUDACHI

La Galerie du Lac à Vevey
5-7 Rue du Lac
1800 Vevey
Switzerland
Phone: (41-21) 51-09-58
Hours: 9 A.M. to noon and 2 to 6 P.M. Monday to Saturday and by appointment

Peter Zervudachi, a Greek dealer whose family had large land and cotton holdings in Egypt, has spent much of his life since childhood in Switzerland. In 1955, he and his wife, Muriel, settled in Vevey in an 18th-century house formerly known as the Galerie Seiler.

The Zervudachis began using the residence as a combination home and gallery in 1961. Ever since they have greeted an international clientele with their extraordinary stock of antiquities as well as 18th-, 19th- and early-20th-century furniture, silver, boxes and objets d'art. Early on, Mr. Zervudachi was a prominent figure at antiques fairs and at auctions selling and buying some of the world's finest treasures.

In 1977 at Christie's in Geneva he acted as the agent for the Cleveland Museum of Art and Baron Hans Heinrich Thyssen-Bornemisza in the purchase of a pair of Louis XV silver tureens by Juste-Aurèle Meissonnier for $1,104,000, a record at auction for silver for many years.

At this handsome establishment, the rooms were arranged with a grand mix of furnishings and objects in a wide range of styles and periods that blended in enviable harmony. The English furniture included a large mid-18th-century chair that opened into a bed that was $20,400, a traveling desk fitted with many small drawers dating from about 1790 and some Regency chairs. Unusual examples of French furniture began with an outsize Louis XVI lawyer's cupboard, an 1870s pillar-based table and mirror in painted wood in the Egyptian style made in Paris for the

Palace of Gezira in Cairo that was $7,000, a Napoleon III ebonized cabinet embellished with gilded bronzes and pietra dura, Venetian 18th-century furniture, Russian 17th- to 19th-century furniture and Bessarabian and kilim rugs are standard in the stock here.

Among the notable decorations were a Louis XV Boulle clock at $108,000, 19th-century French tôle lamps, a Tiffany silver coffee service in the Japanese taste from 1890, a Cartier table clock of crystal, agate and lapis at $19,600, and a Fabergé egg made by the work master Julius Rappaport about 1908 that was $80,000.

EDGAR ABRAHAM MANNHEIMER

Falkenstrasse 12
8008 Zurich
Switzerland
Phone: (41-1) 252-5888
Hours: 9 A.M. to 5:30 P.M. Monday to Friday

Edgar Abraham Mannheimer, who was born in Czechoslovakia and is a Holocaust survivor, spent the war years in Auschwitz working as a shoemaker. "Shoes saved my life," he recalled in his sprawling shop filled with ticking timepieces. When the war ended in 1945, he was nineteen and returned to Czechoslovakia, where he became a car dealer. He left in 1948 when the Communists took over, to settle in Munich. He opened a liquor shop and started dealing in antiques, too. In 1956 he married a Swiss woman and in 1957 moved to Zurich. He has been at his present location since 1982.

Mr. Mannheimer is one of the world's top dealers in period watches and has been a dominant force in this field since the mid-1960s. His stock includes 16th- to 20th-century watches, automatons and clocks—table, wall, floor and tall-case models. He also conducts auctions twice a year, selling watches, vintage cars, furniture, jewelry and porcelains. Among some interesting examples on view were a vase-shaped late-16th-century Augsburg or Prague clock, a gilded 1620 tower-shaped clock, a 1680 box-shaped brass clock on ball feet and several early-19th-century astronomical clocks.

Other curiosities abound here. There were, for example, numerous early-20th-century cash registers and a number of musical instruments, including an 18th-century harp.

Mr. Mannheimer sold an important 17th-century automaton-clock to the Smithsonian Institution. The amusing timepiece, probably German, is made of wood and leather in the shape of a dog with eyes that blink and a mouth that moves.

Mr. Mannheimer attends all the major auctions and pays steep prices at public sales for some of the choicest examples. He paid $159,500 for a British tourbillion watch by Smith & Son, and in December 1986 paid $170,500 for a 19th-century Swiss tourbillion watch by Paul Ditisheim.

Prices here range from about $50 to about $300,000.

FRITZ PAYER

Pelikanstrasse 6
8001 Zurich
Switzerland
Phone: (41-1) 221-1382
Hours: 2 to 6 P.M. Monday, 9 A.M. to noon and 2 to 6:30 P.M. Tuesday to Friday, 9 A.M. to 1 P.M. Saturday

Fritz Payer began handling period silver in auction houses in 1962, working first for a Stuttgart house for three years, then for the Galerie Koller in Zurich, where he remained seven years. In 1972 he opened his first antiques shop in a 15th-century house, specializing mostly in 16th- and 17th-century European silver and gilded silver vessels. He has been in his present shop in the heart of the city's shopping district since 1978.

The glittering early silver tazzas, cups, beakers and bowls that he stocks were produced in Augsburg, Nuremberg, Breslau, Hamburg, Vienna, Prague, Basel, Lucerne and Zurich—all the centers where silversmiths worked in the Renaissance and the 17th century. What is remarkable is how different the color of the silver is from one center to the next and the variety of styles demonstrated by these competing craftsmen.

Several years ago he sold a rare tazza crafted by Christoph Lencker in about 1590 for $100,000.

Mr. Payer had handsome examples of vessels, some with details of exotic animals. Among the more memorable selections were a silver-mounted coconut cup with a warrior figure on top made in Zurich in 1610 to 1620; a pair of gilded nautilus cups from Lucerne dating to 1620 to 1630, and a 1570 beaker in the shape of a dromedary.

Prices here start at about $1,500 for a small beaker. The most important pieces—such as a tazza by Lencker or the camel-shaped beaker—are as much as $100,000.

GALERIE RÖMER

Rämistrasse 23
8001 Zurich
Switzerland
Phone: (41-1) 41 60 87
Hours: 9 A.M. to noon and 2 to 6:30 P.M. Monday to Friday

Roland Römer and Heidi Römer-du Carrois have been dealers together since 1980. Before that, they worked at the Galerie Koller, an auction house where he was a specialist in European sculpture, furniture and bronzes and she headed the paintings department.

The Römer gallery reflects the partners' adventurous taste in French 18th-century tapestries and European 18th- and early-19th-century furniture and sculpture. There was an 18th-century commode that looked more French than Swiss, and for good reason. The 1760s chest was produced by Mathäus Funk of Bern, who was influenced by the French ébéniste Charles Cressent, the owners explained. French furniture included a rare Empire bureau plat, a table-desk, signed by Georges Jacob that was made for the Château de St. Cloud.

Outstanding among the artworks was a tapestry, one of a set of five woven in Nancy between 1703 and 1710 to celebrate military victories in Lorraine. They were taken to Vienna, where three hang in the Museum of Fine Art.

Notable too was an uncommon 18th-century Austrian rococo mirror finished with many coats of lacquer and fitted with gilded bronze and enameled candleholders and flowers.

Bronzes included offerings from a 16th-century Italian study of Mars by Giambologna to a 20th-century Rodin of Balzac. Among the 19th-century animal sculptures were several by Antoine-Louis Barye. Also shown was *Danseuse,* a bronze by Edgar Degas with an unusual brown patina.

Prices for bronzes ranged from about $6,000 to $300,000. French bureaux plats are available from $30,000 to $180,700, the price asked for the Jacob table-desk.

HEIDI VOLLMOELLER

Kurhausstrasse 17
8032 Zurich
Switzerland
Phone: (41-1) 251-3103
Hours: By appointment

Bahnhofstrasse 16
8001 Zurich
Switzerland
Phone: (41-1) 211-1929
Hours: 10 A.M. to 1 P.M. and 2 to 6 P.M. Monday to Friday

Precious vessels, bronzes, terra cottas, textiles and jewelry from throughout the ancient and medieval world are the specialty of Heidi Vollmoeller, an art dealer who was born in Stuttgart and was educated in Zurich and Paris. She began her career in 1958 as an antiquities dealer, setting up shop in one room in Zurich and focusing on Coptic textiles and glass from the Middle East.

Her stock today appears, with a few notable exceptions, to be limited only by what she admires, what is considered ancient and medieval art and what is available. The wide-ranging selection covers many cultures: Egyptian, Greek, Roman, Etruscan, Byzantine, Persian, Coptic and pre-Columbian. The assortment of objects is equally impressive and includes ceramic tiles, bronze mirrors, terra cotta figures, painted vases, stone fragments, marble sculpture, tapestries, iridescent glass and virtually any kind of gold and silver jewelry made by early peoples.

The main gallery on Bahnhofstrasse stocks much of Ms. Vollmoeller's early jewelry. There were Greek ornaments worn in the hair or the ears dating from about 400 B.C., a gold Greek necklace of large and small palm leaves from about 200 B.C., Byzantine earrings from the sixth century, Lilliputian glazed buttonlike Persian ornaments in the shape of crosses and circles from 800 B.C. and pre-Columbian necklaces combining dark green jade and gold.

The larger works are kept at Ms. Vollmoeller's house on Kurhausstrasse (where she receives her mail) and included an ancient Greek vase decorated with two horses' heads, a Syrian bronze lamp rich in green patina on an iron candelabrum made in Pompeii in the early Roman period, ancient Greek black- and red-figured vases and Coptic textiles, one of which was awash with swastikas and bordered with scrolls.

The prices for jewelry range from about $1,800 to about $10,000. The larger works command even higher prices.

CHRISTIE'S INTERNATIONAL

8 Place de la Taconnerie
1204 Geneva
Switzerland
Phone: (41-22) 28-25-44
Hours: 9 A.M. to 12:30 P.M. and 2 to 5:30 P.M. Monday to Friday
Sales: Mid-May and mid-November at:
Hôtel Richmond
8-10 Rue Adhemar Fabri
1201 Geneva
Switzerland
Phone: (41-22) 31-14-00
Viewing hours: 10 A.M. to 6 P.M.

SOTHEBY'S GENEVA

Hôtel Beau Rivage
13 Quai du Mont Blanc
1201 Geneva
Switzerland
Phone: (41-22) 32-85-85
Hours: By appointment
Sales: May and November

LONDON

DIDIER AARON

21 Ryder Street
London SW1 Y6PX
Phone: (44-1) 839-4716
Hours: 10 A.M. to 6 P.M. Monday to Friday

SEE Paris: *Didier Aaron, page 259*

NORMAN ADAMS

8-10 Hans Road
Knightsbridge
London SW3 1RX
Phone: (44-1) 589-5266
Hours: 9 A.M. to 5:30 P.M. Monday to Friday

The period English furniture stocked at this shop, which is across the street from the west entrance to Harrods, includes mostly restrained examples of early-18th-century Queen Anne through early-19th-century Regency styles. Stewart Whittington, the managing director, favors the best of oak, walnut and mahogany tables, desks, chests and chairs, resisting almost everything lavishly embellished with lashings of ormolu or elaborate lacquer fronts. Increasingly, Mr. Whittington said, Americans seek such understated 18th- and 19th-century furniture, and purchases by Americans account for more than half his sales.

Mr. Whittington pointed out that the shop has carried designs with impressive pedigrees, and at all times, he added, there is a generous assortment of works with excellent patina. Among the furniture boasting a great past and the right period glow that Norman Adams has handled were a high-backed elm box chair owned in the early 18th century by Dr. Samuel Johnson and a Sheraton writing table that was made for William Pitt the Younger about 1790 and is now in the Governor's Office at the Bank of England.

Connoisseurs among collectors of English furniture are more concerned about the patina than the pedigree, Mr. Whittington said. The patina is the bronzelike luster that is part of the aging process of oak, walnut and mahogany, a finish produced by rubbing, dusting and waxing coupled with the oxidation of the wood and the effect of the sun's rays. When a patinaed surface survives, the mellow glow may distinguish it as among the very best in English furniture. Stripping, on the other hand, cannot be corrected, for a patina cannot be simulated by skill, only by time. "We hang our whole reputation on the color and surface of what we sell," Mr. Whittington said.

At one Grosvenor House Antiques Fair, this dealer sold a Sheraton satinwood worktable known as a Carlton House desk because the first example of this design was made for the Prince Regent to furnish Carlton House. It went for over $150,000 to a European collector who lives in London.

Mr. Whittington usually has more than a few fine worktables and secretaries from which to choose. There may be, for example an aristocratic Queen Anne bureau-bookcase dating to about 1710, a simple Chippendale kneehole from about 1774, a 1785 Hepplewhite cylinder-front bureau or an ornate brass-inlaid Regency writing table from about 1815. And it does not stop there. Virtually every furniture form of the 18th century is well represented: chairs, tables, chests, bookcases and mirrors.

Shoppers may expect to find chairs from $4,500 and tables from $3,000. But most antiques command higher prices, from $7,500 to $150,000. A bird-embellished rococo gilt mirror carved in the Chinese taste is about $60,000. A Chippendale serpentine chest of drawers with a bombé front is about $85,000.

Mr. Whittington's interest in antiques began in 1964 when he was an aspiring collector and worked as an account executive in a London advertising agency. He met Norman Adams while the two were inspecting the same piece of furniture at Sotheby's in London.

"I couldn't afford to buy it but was definitely interested," Mr. Whittington recalled. They became friends and Mr. Adams soon made an offer. "He caught me at a moment when I was about to change jobs," Mr. Whittington continued, adding that he decided to "give it a whirl for a year or two" and went to work at the establishment he has headed since Mr. Adams's death in 1979.

Norman Adams's 56-year-career as an antiques dealer was not without its share of anachronisms. He was the son of Walter Adams, a Bristol schoolmaster who had become an antiques dealer, first in gold jewelry, then furniture, to supplement his income.

The younger Mr. Adams met some of the American dealers who came to Bristol to buy English antiques and decided to save them the trouble by setting up a wholesale English antiques business in the United States. In 1923 he opened his first shop, on Charles Street in Boston, one of the first antiques dealers to cater exclusively to the trade. The idea brought him immediate success and also attracted major private collectors, including John D. Rockefeller Jr. and Henry Ford, whom he turned away because they were not dealers.

Collectors were not ignored long in the United States. Two years later, Mr. Adams opened a New York shop for everyone at 155 East 54th Street and maintained his Boston and New York businesses until World War II, when he closed them. Eventually, Mr. Adams reversed his original formula at the London establishment he started in 1928. He decided in 1955 that times had changed and now he would deal with collectors only. It's a policy that Mr. Whittington still follows.

ALEXANDER & BERENDT

1 Davies Street
London W1Y 1LL
England
Phone: (44-1) 499-4775
Hours: 9:30 A.M. to 6 P.M. Monday to Friday, Saturday by appointment

Frank Berendt entered the antiques business after finishing his studies in history at Oxford and before making up his mind whether or not to become a barrister and go into politics. He went to work in 1947 in the antiques business that his father, Siegfried Berendt, founded early this century. "It was an old-fashioned antiques business; buying and selling wholesale Continental furniture and porcelains," the younger Mr. Berendt recalled.

It is no longer, but changes came gradually. "I discovered the things I was bad at and the things I was good at," he said. By the early 1960s he was specializing in French and Continental furniture as well as monumental sculpture and architectural decorations.

"I love big things and unsaleable things," he said. "I'm not interested in buying things because they are in fashion." The gallery where he has welcomed visitors since 1968 expresses his flair for outsize and exotic works that appear to have aristocratic pedigrees and frequently do.

Regal prizes on one visit included a Louis XV bureau plat with gracefully curved legs and generous touches of gilded bronze decorations and a magnificent pair of four-foot French gray-white marble vases made in 1716 by Nicolas Coustou, sculptor to the court of Louis XIV.

Another imposing work was an early humanist 17th-century work, a life-size bust of a man by Thomas Boudin. Mr. Berendt's stock also included an elaborately carved 1750s Louis XV bed, attributed to Jean Baptiste Tilliard II. It has since been sold to the J. Paul Getty Museum in Malibu, Calif. There was also an elegantly simple Louis XVI armoire by Riesener. The prices here range from about $10,000 to $2 million or more.

Don't bother looking for Mr. Alexander. He has always been a fiction.

ARMIN B. ALLEN

3 Bury Street, St. James
London SW1 Y6AB
Phone: (44-1) 930-4732
Hours: 10 A.M. to 5:30 P.M. Monday to Friday

Armin Allen, a New York dealer in pottery, porcelain, works of art and ornamental and botanical drawings, moved to London in September 1986. "My children are half English and we wanted to be closer to my wife's family," he said. "When this shop became available, I realized it is in an ideal location and did not hesitate to grab it."

Mr. Allen said that many of his American and European clients visit London frequently. "The people who collect pottery and porcelain are very European," he said. "The Americans who buy very much like to shop in London—they like the whole ambiance here, the atmosphere is just right." And the costs of doing business in London, particularly rent, are far lower than in New York, he commented.

The Allen shop is where Robert Williams of Winifrid Williams, the English and Continental porcelain business his mother founded, had been for 16 years until he retired. Mr. Allen carries some of the same things his predecessor did but has his own special taste in European ceramics.

"I don't deal in dinnerware and tea services," he said. "I deal in the rare individual pieces in French ceramics, particularly Sèvres and faïence." Robust and Baroque forms in faïence and German and Italian ceramics makers are also represented with some unusual serving dishes, accessories and figures. Mr. Allen has always had an eye for the unusual and handles some majolica, buying for specific clients, not for stock.

Prices range from $1,200 for a Rouen plate to $200,000 for a pair of white Vincennes hunting groups after Oudry that Madame de Pompadour is believed to have owned.

Mr. Allen took his first job in antiques in 1965 at the shop of Frank Partridge, then a New York dealer in 18th-century English furniture and decorations. From 1969 to 1971, he worked at Sotheby's in London in its porcelain department. Back in New York, he headed Sotheby's European pottery and porcelain department from 1971 to

1978 and the works of art and ceramics departments from 1978 to 1980.

Mr. Allen continues to hold drawing exhibitions twice a year (botanical in April, ornamental in November) at his former gallery, at 33 East 68th Street, and exhibits at the Winter Antiques Show in New York each January.

ALBERT AMOR LTD.

37 Bury Street
St. James's
London SW1 Y6AU
Phone: (44-1) 930-2444
Hours: 9:30 A.M. to 4:30 P.M. Monday to Friday

When antiques businesses change hands, they tend to change character, too, as new owners reshape the stock to their personalities and tastes. Albert Amor dates back to the 1880s, when its founders offered 18th-century furniture, paintings and porcelains.

After Mr. Amor died in the early 1920s, his successor, Leslie Perkins, established the specialty areas for which the business was known for the next half century: English and Continental ceramics. Amor was antiquary to Queen Mary, who continued her patronage until her death in 1953. By then, Mr. Perkins had died, in 1951, and his son John had taken over.

Anne Margaret George, the managing director since 1973, came to work at the shop in 1956. Mrs. George's father, Archibald F. Allbrook, was an important porcelain collector who became a dealer in 1945 after leaving the oil business (he had chartered oil tankers for Esso in London).

Mrs. George worked first for her father in his shop in South Kensington and pursued research on porcelains. "I kept running from my father's shop into the Victoria and Albert," she recalled in her meticulously arranged two-story premises. She also helped organize exhibitions.

After she bought out the Perkins family at the death of John Perkins, Mrs. George narrowed the focus of the shop even further to concentrate on 18th-century English porcelains.

"We have far more collectors on our books today than we did 10 years ago," she said. Many are Americans and Canadians, but some are Australians. Not all buyers are serious collectors; many acquire porcelains as decorations, she said.

The stock these days focuses on only Worcester, Chelsea, Bow, Derby, Longton Hall and Bristol dating from the first period of Dr. Wall Worcester and his associates (1751 to 1784). The selection is generous, including tableware, vases, mantel decorations and figures. Mrs. George is assisted at the shop by Robyn Robb.

Prices go from under $1,500 for a Worcester Sèvres-style cup and saucer to about $30,000 for a magnificent garniture of five Worcester vases. Beginning collectors can start by buying a blue-and-white pickle tray, cream jug or butter dish by the Worcester, Bow or Lowestoft factories at $300 to $450.

"I often say to people, as long as the quality is there, don't worry if there is a chip. Quality is the keynote."

ANTIQUE PORCELAIN COMPANY

149 New Bond Street
London W1Y OHY
Phone: (44-1) 629-1254
Hours: 9:30 A.M. to 6 P.M. Monday to Thursday, to 5 P.M. Friday
Closed in August and between Christmas and New Year's

Ten years after Hanns Weinberg's death in 1976, the company he founded specializing in European porcelains and faïence still has the largest selection in the world of table wares and figures produced by 18th-century English and European factories. Rotraut Beiny, his daughter, remains president of the antiques concern. Mr. Weinberg opened his London shop in 1945 and expanded in 1957 with a five-story-plus-basement establishment on 57th Street in New York. He stocked his new place from top to bottom with porcelains and furniture made for European royalty and aristocrats.

In London and in New York, Meissen selections date from 1710 to about 1757, but the table wares and figures from Frankenthal, Nymphenburg, Höchst, Vienna, Berlin, Fürstenberg, Ludwigsburg and Kelsterbach (which started later) all continue through the 1760s to possibly 1800.

The New York branch is under the direction of Michele Beiny, Mr. Weinberg's granddaughter, and has been moved to an apartment where the porcelains are arranged in vitrines and on the tops of French 18th-century tables and commodes in much the manner they were in Mr. Weinberg's gallery.

Mr. Weinberg, who became the world's most influential dealer in porcelains by the 1960s, was born in Germany and was a successful lawyer and a collector before the Nazis came to power. In 1938, he fled with his wife, Lisa, his daughter, Rotraut, and his son, Martin, to London. There, in 1945 he opened his first antiques establishment on New Bond Street.

It was in that shop that he began attracting the prestigious following that soon included the Queen Mother, Princess Margaret, the Duke of Windsor, King Gustav VI of Sweden, Umberto of Italy and scores of industrialists and bankers, including Henry Ford 2d, Jayne and Charles Wrightsman, Paul Mellon and several members of the Rockefeller and the Rothschild families.

Miss Beiny said she prefers Meissen table wares to figures and is more partial to the Baroque period than the later rococo. There are exceptions to everything and she showed delight in a number of figures, especially Bustelli's gracefully modeled commedia dell'arte subjects.

"We still have the life-size pelican swallowing a fish," Miss Beiny said, speaking of one of the rarities, a life-size bird modeled by Kändler in 1732. "I don't think we'll ever sell it."

Meanwhile, there are so many other works available. The most notable selections from Höchst, Ludwigsburg and Kelsterbach ("my mother's favorite factory") are figures, some rococo Italian comedy subjects.

"Now the taste is increasingly for the eccentric, a piece that was experimental, even if it has flaws, especially if it has charm." This applies to early French and English soft paste factories.

The French factories, Vincennes/Sèvres, Clichy, St. Cloud and Chantilly, and early English such as Chelsea,

Bow, Longton Hall, Derby and first period Worcester are also well represented at the two branches. Prices range from about $550 for a Chelsea seal to high in six figures for an important garniture of vases or large sculptured pieces. A garniture of three Sèvres vases with memorable chinoiserie decoration on a pale blue ground was $385,000.

ARMITAGE

4 Davies Street
Berkeley Square
London W1Y 1LJ
England
Phone: (44-1) 408-0675, 629-0958
Hours: 10 A.M. to 5:30 P.M. Monday to Friday

Rahim Saadat and Martin Beck have been a major force in antique silver since they went into business together in 1979. The Iranian-born Mr. Saadat came to London to study economics in 1970. He became an antiques dealer selling furniture and paintings in the 1970s. He found his specialty in silver, buying at a time in the mid- to late 1970s when interest in all period silver was soaring and a great deal of material was becoming available as prices rocketed upward.

Although there is not an abundance of silver visible in their two-story shop, Mr. Saadat and Mr. Beck handle a great variety of English and Continental silver of all periods, dating from the 14th century through about 1885.

"We are like brokers," Mr. Saadat explained, adding that this approach makes it possible for them to handle extremely rare works without tying up all their money in inventory. They are extremely active in auctions and buy many of the highest-priced silver offerings in partnership with other major London silver dealers. "We had one 14th-century spoon, made about 1380," Mr. Saadat recalled, that was sold to an investment trust he did not identify for about $40,000.

One of the most active buyers of silver in recent years, Mohamed Mehdi al-Tajir, Ambassador to London from the United Arab Emirates, has bought from Mr. Saadat.

What is available through Armitage is mostly 18th- and early-19th-century material. Mr. Saadat said that they do buy Victorian things, dating to as late as 1885, provided they feel the works have quality and will increase in value.

The cutoff date of 1885 is important because in recent years Americans have dominated the buying of British silver, and they must pay duty on works that are not antiques, which the United States Customs Service defines as 100 or more years old. Furthermore, Mr. Saadat said, museums in the United States are moving into 19th-century and later silver, which has sparked interest among collectors in post-Georgian silver.

Although men used to dominate among silver collectors, "we have as many women collecting silver now as men," Mr. Saadat said.

"Silver has been going up and down in value in recent years," Mr. Saadat said, commenting on the volatility of the market. "I like to be sure that the people who buy from me don't go wrong."

Prices at Armitage start at $1,500 to $2,000 for a good pair or a set of four small open salts. They climb to $1 million for a dinner service.

BERNHEIMER FINE ARTS LTD.

32 St. George Street
Mayfair
London W1R 9FA
England
Phone: (44-1) 499-0293
Hours: 10 A.M. to 5:30 P.M. Monday to Friday

SEE Munich: ***Bernheimer, page 247***

DAVID BLACK

96 Portland Road
Holland Park
London W11 4LN
England
Phone: (44-1) 727-2566
Hours: 11 A.M. to 6 A.M. Monday to Saturday
Closed sometimes in August

David Black started small when he became an Oriental rug dealer, selling in a flea market. He began on Portobello Road in 1966. "The stock was valued at $800," he recalled. "It was pretty awful." Few would admit this, and fewer still would survive to learn as much about a subject as Mr. Black has about Oriental rugs. He has completed seven books, the most recent of which he edited, *The Macmillan Atlas of Rugs & Carpets,* published in 1985 by Macmillan in the United States and by Country Life in London.

Mr. Black came to rugs after working in advertising, retailing, on a magazine, in a kibbutz in Israel and as an interior designer. After five weeks of selling rugs in his first shop, he was cleaned out in a robbery. "I've always been grateful to those burglars," he said. The stock improved slowly. "I learned from other people, mostly customers. I was lucky enough to have a few well-informed clients. I went for what others were not buying." This included geometric patterned rugs, tribal rugs, kilims and Caucasians, he said.

"When I first bought kilims, other dealers laughed. To them it was dead stuff." Clients felt otherwise.

Mr. Black moved to his present site in 1972 and rebuilt the two-story building. The lighting, natural and otherwise, brings out the best in these 19th- and 20th-century weavings, most of which are vividly colored and boldly patterned but some of which are extremely subtle in the motifs and hues.

Antique rugs at this shop are mostly 19th-century. "I've stayed away from the 18th century," he said. "There are so many interesting things made in the 19th century." Although aniline dyes were used after 1860, most of the antique rugs stocked here were colored with vegetable dyes, he said.

He has Persians, Caucasians, Turkomans, kilims, durries and embroideries. Many were acquired locally but some were found abroad. "Last year I traveled to Turkey four or five times," he said, describing his journeys as "voyages of discovery."

Very few quality rugs here are under $1,500, he said. Most range from $4,500 to about $45,000. The selection is wide, including a Bessarabian tapestry of figural motifs bordered in flowers, Persian rugs awash with mille-fleurs patterning, and a Qashqai geometric woven in bold motifs in strong reds and blues.

H. BLAIRMAN

119 Mount Street
London W1Y 5HB
England
Phone: (44-1) 493-0444
Hours: 9 A.M. to 6 P.M. Monday to Friday and by appointment

"People do tend to call us at any hour—from America, from Australia," George Levy said of the business he heads. It specializes in Regency and 19th-century Revival styles and Esthetic Movement furniture and decorations. His wife's grandfather founded the concern more than a century ago, and he says, "It is still a family business." Customers are aware, he explained, that he, his wife, Wendy, and their son, Martin Levy, are often in the shop before 9 A.M. and after 6 P.M.

Harris Blairman, a Polish immigrant, would have approved. He sold mainly Continental porcelains, 19th-century paintings and late-19th-century French reproduction furniture when he arrived in Britain in 1884 and settled in the fashionable resort of Llandudno, Wales.

Mr. Blairman moved to London in 1910 to Regent Street and continued at the shop until his death in 1926. The founder's sons, Walter and Philip, ran the business together, selling mainly English 18th-century furniture there, in a branch in Harrogate and after 1930 on King Street, where they remained until Walter's death in 1934. Philip Blairman moved the shop to Bond Street, where he pioneered in popularizing Regency furniture. During World War II he operated a shop in New York on 57th Street, returning after the war to London, where he headed the business until his death in 1971.

George Levy, who came to work at Blairman in 1950, stayed on despite an early lapse when he broke a Chinese mirror painting. ("He was tolerant of my ineptitude," Mr. Levy said jovially.) The dealer has continued to maintain a small but select stock of Regency pieces. Since 1975 when Martin Levy, then twenty-one years old, joined the concern, Blairman has pioneered again, adding choice examples of late-19th-century furniture and decorations by architects and designers who worked in the Esthetic Movement and Revival styles.

"If we are to maintain the quality to which we are accustomed, we cannot have a large stock," Mr. Levy said. The Regency pieces on view included a six-foot-wide rosewood breakfront cupboard with a marble top that was $25,000, a rosewood worktable with lyre-shaped sides and brass trim at $30,000 and a rosewood writing table at $75,000. Smaller works, such as a Regency inkstand, start at about $2,250.

The later-19th-century offerings include, when available, furniture by Edward William Godwin and Charles Rennie Mackintosh. The prices on decorations start at under $500 for metal vases and lamps and climb to $100,000 or more.

BLUETT & SONS LTD.

48 Davies Street
London W1Y 1LD
England
Phone: (44-1) 629-4018, 629-3397
Hours: 9:30 A.M. to 5:30 P.M. Monday to Friday

Roger B. Bluett is the third generation of art dealers in a distinguished family of British merchants who have handled Oriental art for more than a century. At first, Bluett's focus was on Japanese art. Family tradition has it that Alfred Ernest Bluett, who founded Bluett in 1884, dressed the original production in 1885 of *The Mikado* by Gilbert and Sullivan. The founder did carry Ch'ing ceramics originally, preferring famille rose and famille verte to Ming porcelains.

"The railroads hadn't opened up the tombs yet," Roger Bluett said. "That came about 1900. Between 1905 and World War I, much Tang material came to light and Alfred's sons, Edgar and Leonard, who were to run the firm for some 50 years, were pioneers in introducing these early wares of the Tang and Sung periods."

Roger Bluett joined the business in late 1946 after four years in the Royal Navy. It was headed by Leonard and Edgar Bluett, his father and uncle, and he was in partnership with them at their deaths in the 1960s.

"We have an old-fashioned image," said Mr. Bluett, adding: "In my view, the most important thing in any antiques concern is a strict code of ethics." He said clients relied on Bluett's "international reputation for integrity" and its reputation for having scholar-dealers. "We don't pretend to be academics, but we do try to keep up with all the information that continues to come out of China."

The firm has been at the same address since 1923 and is headed by Mr. Bluett, chairman, and two other directors, Brian Morgan and Anthony Carter, who are the three owners. "We specialize in ceramics and carry all periods," Mr. Bluett said, "but our personal interests are in the earlier periods." Tang figures, Sung porcelains, Ming blue and white are all represented. The stock also includes jades from neolithic through Ch'ing as well as ancient bronzes and artifacts in lacquer, ivory and other materials.

"There was a lot of stuff on the market—I bought quantities," he said of the boom in Chinese art sales in the late 1960s. "The biggest influence of all was the emergence of the Japanese dealers. In Japan the prices were already much higher than in the West." He said Sotheby's auctions in the 1970s in Hong Kong also increased prices tremendously.

Spiraling prices means that there is virtually nothing available these days at Bluett under $150. Small Sung ceramics are $150 to $1,500. An 18th-century blue-and-white Ch'ing vase might be $500. A fine set of five imperial Ming yellow plates was $40,000. The bulk of what Bluett sells is from $1,500 to $30,000, but many major items are considerably higher.

ESKENAZI

Foxglove House
166 Piccadilly
London W1V 9DE
England
Phone: (44-1) 493-5464
Hours: 9:30 A.M. to 5:30 P.M. Monday to Friday

Giuseppe Eskenazi was twenty-one when he arrived in London from Milan in 1960 to help his father, I. Eskenazi, open a gallery known the world over today as a source for some of the finest Chinese art available anywhere. "My father never used his given name in business," the son recalled, adding that they moved to London "to be closer to the heart of the art market."

At his father's death in 1967, Giuseppe Eskenazi assumed command of the business. His family has other roots in the Oriental art market: the Eskenazi gallery in Milan was founded in 1925 by Giuseppe's great-uncle Vittorio.

Mr. Eskenazi, a candid, energetic enterpreneur with an eye for antiquities, has been partly responsible for the dramatic change in international taste in the last 20 years from an almost exclusive concentration on Ming and Ch'ing ceramics to a stronger focus on ancient works: Shang bronzes, Tang tomb figures, archaic jades and ancient precious art objects. Mr. Eskenazi said his success was fortuitous. "It wasn't of my own making," he explained. "The time was ripe. The collectors were ready for ancient material, at least after a while. You can never force such things, you have to also be lucky."

Mr. Eskenazi was more than lucky. He pursued what he liked best: the antiquities that had been collected by Americans and Europeans 70 years ago but were not widely shown on the market after World War II. "I filled in a gap, and American museums became my best customers," he said. Other clients included such major collectors in the United States as Avery Brundage, Dr. Arthur M. Sackler, Hans Popper, Fredrick Mayer, Earl Morse and John D. Rockefeller 3d. Throughout this period, he has gradually helped push back the historical parameters in Oriental art by offering objects to museums and collectors that most people once considered too esoteric and unappealing.

Mr. Eskenazi is highly visible professionally—he organizes museum-quality art exhibitions in his gallery and travels to most major auctions of Chinese art, bidding openly on the finest offerings.

Typically, he says, the finest works sell the fastest. Within two days after his 25th anniversary exhibition of masterworks opened in 1985, 16 of the 28 works had been sold. They ranged in price from $15,000 for a fourth-century-B.C. bird-shaped silver belt hook to $750,000 for an archaic bronze wine vessel cast with boldly worked dragons and masks from the 11th century B.C. Two were bought by the Cleveland Museum of Art: a palm-sized Tang gilt-bronze recumbent bull from the eighth century and a jade ring in the form of a dragon dating to the Warring States Period, fourth century B.C. The rest were sold to collectors from the United States, Japan, Hong Kong, Switzerland, Italy and France.

Mr. Eskenazi continues to offer some of the finest Ming wares as well. Among some recent prizes were four choice Ming porcelains acquired from Herbert Hoover 3d of Pasadena, Calif., two bowls, a vase and a box with cover, all of which had been collected by his grandfather, President Hoover. A blue-and-white early-15th-century palace bowl, awash with figures of women and children playing in a palace garden, is one of the most extraordinary of such bowls to reach the market in recent years, he said. The vase, a narrow-necked design from the late 16th century decorated with scenes of scholars in a garden, is almost identical to one in the National Palace Museum in Taiwan. The bowl and vase were each priced in six figures.

Mr. Eskenazi's stock is not all rarities, but it has very few ordinary objects. Prices for Chinese works begin at about $5,000 and may include Han bronzes, a small gilt figure or a mirror, as well as Tang pottery figures, a Sung porcelain tea bowl or a blue-and-white Ming dish.

The gallery offers a healthy selection of quality Japanese lacquer boxes, screens, sculpture and netsukes, which are palm-sized toggles used to attach pouches, purses and boxes to pocketless kimonos. These miniatures are fashioned of ivory, wood, metal, soapstone, bone, coral, horn and glass to depict virtually every known plant and animal as well as folk heros, mythological deities and Noh theater masks. These Lilliputian carvings range from about $700 to $120,000.

MICHAEL FRANSES

The Textile Gallery
4 Castellain Road
London W9 1EZ
England
Phone: (44-1) 286-1747
Hours: By appointment

"I probably buy 30 classical carpets a year, and I sell 30 classical carpets in a year," Michael Franses said, surrounded by about half that number, all extraordinary weavings, at the Chicago International Antiques Show. Mr. Franses said that he had about 12 important clients in the United States who buy major items each year and that he expected at least six of them to come to the fair to see his selection of textiles, which may include pre-Columbian, Coptic, French Gothic, Persian, Chinese and early Scandinavian weavings.

The Textile Gallery, which was founded in 1972, is run by Michael Franses and his wife, Jacqueline, who are partners. Although the Franseses do not have a formal exhibition space in London, they present their best items at fairs, and they show every year at the International Antiques Fair in Maastricht, the Netherlands, in March or April. This permits Mr. Franses to limit the selling to specific periods, he said, and "leaves me free the rest of the time to travel in the long search for important textiles."

In London they see clients by appointment at their home. Of the 250 choice items they usually have, roughly a third are going through various stages of conservation and about 100 are classical carpets from all the major weaving centers from Spain to China.

The Franseses have organized and participated in more than a dozen exhibitions, most in London but also in Dublin, Paris, Milan and Munich, many of them concentrating on kilims and village rugs. Classical carpets from the gallery are now in the collections of the Victoria and Albert

Museum in London, the Metropolitan Museum of Art in New York, the L. A. Mayer Museum in Jerusalem, the Carpet Museum in Teheran, Iran, the Thyssen-Bornemisza Collection in Lugano, Switzerland, and the National Museum in Kuwait.

What they have exhibited in galleries and shows covers an impressive range. There might be, for example, a fifth-century Coptic fragment showing the haunting face of a woman; a mid-15th-century German tapestry depicting a unicorn and a woman; a pre-Columbian feather cape; 16th- and 17th-century village rugs from Anatolia; a silk 17th-century Mogul hunting carpet, its surface a study of palmettes, deer and leaping tigers, from Lahore, India; an extraordinary 18th-century medallion weaving from Central Asia framed in outsized flower faces, and a wool-on-linen betrothal tapestry dated 1818 that covered the cushion used in the carriage taking the bride to her wedding.

Mr. Franses's taste is for the finest and for weavings, whether made for a village wall or a palace floor, so fresh in their imagery they could have been conceived yesterday. "I believe the earliest carpets were the finest," he said. Prices start at $4,000 to $5,000 for fragments. The average price for rugs is $30,000 to $70,000. But the most important classical carpets can be as much as $350,000.

The Franses family has been in textiles for at least three generations. "My grandparents immigrated to England from Istanbul," he said. He began selling rugs, he said, when he was still at school, and worked for his family in 1965. Since 1969 he has been on his own and in 1975 was the co-founder of the International Conference on Oriental Carpets. He discovered the earliest known Islamic carpet, which he said was woven no earlier than the seventh century and no later than the ninth century. It was acquired in 1986 by the Fine Arts Museums of San Francisco.

In 1977 Mr. Franses founded the handsome and scholarly quarterly *Hali,* an international magazine of antique carpets and textiles, and was its publisher and co-editor until 1985. He gave up these functions "to devote more time to study and searching out outstanding examples of textile art."

CHRISTOPHER GIBBS LTD.

118 New Bond Street
London W1Y 9AB
England
Phone: (44-1) 629-2008
Hours: 9:30 A.M. to 5:30 P.M. Monday to Friday
Closed August and the first week of September

"I've always liked large lumps of stone," Christopher Gibbs said at his sprawling century-old gallery where the bounty of architectural rock relics fills hallways and corners. "I love things that need cranes to be moved." The mammoth sculptures include mostly ancient Roman, Greek and medieval works.

Mr. Gibbs also has a taste for large eccentric furniture, as could be seen everywhere in that high-ceilinged space awash with sun from a skylight. Against a far wall were an imposing pair of 12-foot-long 18th-century painted pine couches supported on oak elephant heads, in the style of William Kent.

Standing about were many outsize desks, cabinets and cupboards, including a stunning 1763 neo-classical medal cabinet designed by William Chambers, an imposing 1740s architect's desk made for four people and a sculptural English country chair dating from about 1820 that was crafted of bare elm with a curved back and rakishly angled legs.

Furnishings that boast a theatrical flair come in many shapes, sizes and finishes. There were, for example, a Chippendale gilded rococo mirror at $60,000 and a pair of Regency rosewood sofas that showed their Greek roots with uncommon grace. Outstanding too was a wonderful 1754 pair of purposely black Gothic chairs from Horace Walpole's great house, Strawberry Hill, their high backs pierced with tracery ($100,000 the pair).

"I try to have precious and rare things," Mr. Gibbs said. "I don't put limits on what I handle—in cheapness, in dearness or in age."

Mr. Gibbs's family was in banking, but he preferred to follow his own delights. He had always been a collector and became a dealer in 1958 at the age of twenty. He began by taking a place in Islington, in north London, then Chelsea, and moved to his present gallery in 1976.

The offbeat works here are wide-ranging and include a bounty of pictures. There were, for example, architectural drawings for Windsor Castle from 1810 by the incredibly pretentious Wyatteville, an early picture of Stonehenge and another of Brighton Pavilion. Among the paintings was a bird picture depicting "crazy ducks and things" by Stranover, from about 1720, at $35,000 and a 1700 work by Peter Casteels depicting two blackamoor busts at $100,000. Among the sporting pictures was Stephen Pearce's *Coursing at Ashdown Park,* a 19th-century work depicting dozens of grand folks all dressed up on lots of horses chasing a hare. It was $220,000.

Unconventional objects in Mr. Gibbs's stock can be virtually anything. There was a great long piece of twisty wood, one end carved with a ram's head, that was the tiller on the Duke of Leinster's yacht around 1800.

The period works at this gallery range from about $150 for an engraving to $750,000 for a small Holbein portrait.

MICHAEL GOEDHUIS LTD.

Colnaghi Oriental
14 Old Bond Street
London WIX 4JL
England
Phone: (44-1) 409-3324
Hours: 9 A.M. to 6 P.M. Monday to Friday, appointment advised

Michael Goedhuis, a London dealer who specializes in Japanese, Chinese, Indian and Islamic art under both his name and Colnaghi Oriental, has been extremely busy on both sides of the Atlantic in recent seasons. Spurred by major museum exhibitions in New York, London and Geneva in all of the areas in which he specializes, there has been quickened international interest among collectors in Oriental art at his London gallery. His offerings are sparely arranged on two floors against neutral backgrounds.

Mr. Goedhuis has also exhibited at two antiques fairs in the United States, the International Antiques Show in Chicago and the Winter Antiques Show in New York. When

Mr. Goedhuis is in New York, he sees clients and shows some of his stock at Colnaghi (U.S.A.) Ltd., 26 East 80th Street. Colnaghi, dealers in Old Masters and Oriental art, was broken up and sold in two parts in 1980 by the owner, Jacob Rothschild of London, to Richard Herner, an Old Masters dealer, and to Mr. Goedhuis, who then opened Colnaghi Oriental as a separate gallery.

One reason for Mr. Goedhuis's stepped-up activities in the art market, he said, was his role as the agent for the mysterious owner of a Persian art collection bought in early 1986 for $7 million by the Smithsonian Institution. The collection, described by Robert McC. Adams, the secretary of the Smithsonian, as "perhaps the most significant purchase in the history of the Smithsonian," was begun in the 1890s by Henri Vever, a Paris jeweler who died at eighty-nine in 1943. It was acquired by the museum from his heir. The seller, according to Lawrence Brinn, his New York lawyer, is the last remaining member of Vever's family but does not bear that name and insists on anonymity. The Smithsonian's Asian art authorities added that he is an American, possibly a New Yorker, who divides his time between the United States and Paris.

This extraordinary assemblage—39 full volumes, 291 Persian miniature paintings, 98 illuminations and calligraphies, 29 bookbindings and 4 textiles—is regarded as possibly the finest Islamic art collection in private hands to be formed this century.

As the owner's agent, Mr. Goedhuis prepared the inventory, catalogue and appraisal of the art works and showed them to the Smithsonian representatives at his London gallery. The Vever collection will go on view in 1988 in the Smithsonian's new Museum of Asian Art, which is to bear the name of its primary benefactor, Dr. Arthur M. Sackler, the New York collector.

Mr. Goedhuis (he pronounces it GOOD-house) came to art after a brief career as an investment banker. Dutch-born and educated in Britain at Eton and in France at the Sorbonne, the dealer left the world of finance in the early 1970s and went back to school to study art at the Courtauld Institute of Art in London. He joined Jacob Rothschild in 1975 to work in his London-based art investment company, Poliarco, which owned Colnaghi.

The exotic art works he offers are primarily Japanese and Chinese but he also stocks Indian, Anglo-Indian and occasionally Islamic objects. A rare 15th-century jade cup from Central Asia was $50,000; a 16th-century Turkish miniature from the Kevorkian collection depicting a marriage scene was $25,000 and several examples of Islamic calligraphy were $1,000 to $7,500. Among the Anglo-Indian antiques he shows is an octagonal rosewood gaming table with a marble top that he says was made for an aide to Queen Victoria. It was $20,000.

Another period table made for British use in India is a tour de force of craftsmanship. Its base is formed of carved peacock heads, its round top is inlaid with 34 kinds of exotic wood. The price was about $50,000. A pair of 17th-century ebony chairs made in the Dutch East Indies with red silk seats and backs were $15,000 each. Less costly offerings might include an 18th-century incense burner in the shape of a mythical animal at about $1,000.

GERALD GODFREY/FAR EASTERN ART

104 Mount Street
London W1Y 5AH
Phone: (44-1) 409-2777
Hours: 9:30 A.M. to 5:30 P.M. Monday to Friday

SEE Hong Kong: *Charlotte Horstmann and Gerald Godfrey, Ltd., page 324*

GRAHAM & OXLEY

101 Kensington Church Street
London W8 7LN
England
Phone: (44-1) 229-1850
Hours: 10 A.M. to 5:30 P.M. Monday to Friday, 10 A.M. to 1 P.M. Saturday

"When I went to the Victoria and Albert Museum at the age of fifteen or sixteen, I lingered over the porcelain," Michael Graham recalled, adding that the memory has had great meaning ever since he and Joseph Oxley went into business together in 1965. Since then this team has become one of the more prominent London dealers in ceramics. In 1978, they founded this shop, where they stock their specialty, 18th- and early-19th-century English porcelains and ironstone services.

"I think in this business you can decide that you are going to do well and you can make it happen," Mr. Graham said. The way these men have made it happen is to follow their own instincts. They share an eye for quality and have "remarkable uniformity of taste," Mr. Graham said. Both feel that there has been a great swing back to simpler things, including English creamware with botanical decorations. Their stock reflects this conviction.

Prices range from about $100 for an Imari tea stand from about 1810 that might be used as an ashtray or $300 for a Worcester blue-and-white cup and saucer from about 1770 to about $22,000 for a Bristol white porcelain figure of Lü Tung-pin dating to about 1750, one of only nine extant.

Many dealers and decorators cross the Atlantic to buy dinner services here, and a great deal of what they find is ironstone, a heavy, hard and opaque earthenware that is prized for its strength. Such services are plentiful, Mr. Graham said, because they were produced in abundance from 1813 to 1845.

"Seventy to 80 percent of our clients are Americans," he said. "American collectors use porcelain as it was meant to be used, as decorative accessories." At this shop, a 95-piece ironstone dinner service by the Mason factory in the grasshopper pattern, circa 1820, would be about $17,000.

OTTO HAAS

49 Belsize Park Gardens
London NW3 4JL
England
Phone: (44-1) 722-1488
Hours: By appointment, 9:30 A.M. to 5:30 P.M. Monday to Friday

A. ROSENTHAL LTD.

9 Broad Street
Oxford OX1 3AP
England
Phone: (44-865) 243-093
Hours: 9:30 A.M. to 6 P.M. Monday to Friday

Albi Rosenthal's specialty in the world of rare books and manuscripts is music—manuscripts, printed scores, books, biographies of composers and musical personalities and autographs from Scarlatti through Stravinsky.

Music, an interest Mr. Rosenthal shares with his wife, Maud, and his younger daughter, Julia, who helps run the family business, also dominates his private life and has since he began studying violin at the age of seven. The dealer said that knowing music as a performer adds immeasurably to his appreciation of musical manuscripts. "Bach shaped his letters in a way that shows much of the construction of the actual music," he said.

This double involvement with music served him well in the discovery in 1951 of a Mendelssohn Violin Concerto in D minor. He was visiting a descendant of the composer who showed him a musical manuscript, and he recognized it as a previously unknown work written by Mendelssohn when he was thirteen. Mr. Rosenthal discussed the work with Yehudi Menuhin, who spent part of the interview standing on his head, and Menuhin bought it. "He played it all over the world," Mr. Rosenthal said.

"Chamber music is one of my relaxations," the dealer said, adding that he usually takes his violin on business trips across the Atlantic or the English Channel so he can play in the evenings with friends. Since 1947 he has performed with, among others, the Oxford University Orchestra, of which he was president in 1987.

Mr. Rosenthal was born into the world of rare books and manuscripts in Munich, where the family business was based from 1867, eight years after its founding, until 1934, when his father left. (The rich legacy that he and his brother, Bernard Rosenthal, share from this family of booksellers is covered more fully in the entry on Bernard Rosenthal of San Francisco.)

The two brothers left Munich in 1933—Bernard going to Florence and Albi to London, where he studied at the Warburg Institute, now part of London University.

Albi Rosenthal began his own rare-books and musical-manuscript concern in London in 1936. He moved to Oxford in 1941, and in 1955 he acquired Otto Haas of London, the outstanding firm in this field.

Mr. Rosenthal's autograph prices range from about $100 for a letter by Massenet upward. Prices for manuscripts range to $548,000, the price he paid for an extraordinary manuscript, Stravinsky's *Rite of Spring,* at an auction at Sotheby's in London in 1982, representing the Paul Sacher Foundation of Basel, Switzerland. Less than a year later Mr. Rosenthal was the agent for the foundation in its purchase of one of the largest known bodies of musical material, the Stravinsky archive, which he acquired for $5.25 million from the estate of the composer.

HEIRLOOM & HOWARD

1 Hay Hill
Berkeley Square
London W1K 7LF
England
Phone: (44-1) 493-5868
Hours: 9:30 A.M. to 6 P.M. Monday to Friday, noon to 6 P.M. Saturday

David Sanctuary Howard of Heirloom & Howard has become the world's most quoted expert on armorial ceramics and export wares. His own lineage includes a few notables: his great-grandmother was a cousin of Anthony Trollope, the English novelist. And, he reports, a survey made at the turn of the century of all the living descendants of Edward III proved "my mother was one of them, one of 50,000."

Mr. Howard's shop specializes in export crockery and stocks ceramics made for Chinese use only when they bear images of Western places or people or are Western in their shaping (a tea strainer, for example, or a mustard pot). Armorial saucers are available at $50 to $200. Mugs, salts and teapots are $450 to $2,000. Tureens run from $3,000 to $6,000.

Blue-and-white 17th-century wares are still undervalued, in Mr. Howard's opinion. He offers barber's bowls at $600 and up, ewers and basins from $600 to $2,000. Rarities have included two drug jars bearing the arms of Peter the Great that were $1,000 and $2,000.

He also handles portrait engravings, seals, rings, dies, coach panels, shields and harness fittings—anything with a coat of arms on it that he can identify. At last count his stock numbered 30,000 items, mostly ceramics and engravings, and he had 8,000 people in his computer that he was hoping he would be able to match with these crests. Mr. Howard seems tireless in his travels and has lectured extensively in the United States. He discovered that everywhere he went, he met Americans with British roots, some with aristocratic progenitors. "My passion is getting lots of people happy with the little things, finding the heirlooms for as many families as possible at a reasonable price."

Mr. Howard will stock a damaged coffeepot with a proper crest and part with it for $50. He said nothing in the shop was more expensive than $8,000.

The urbane and genial Mr. Howard became interested in heraldry in his student days at Stowe. In 1956 he embarked on a major research project: documenting all the armorial porcelain produced in China that he could find in Britain. He crisscrossed the country many times, visiting castles and manors of aristocrats and collectors and photographing their tableware. The results of that extraordinary research was a book hailed as the major opus in the field, *Chinese Armorial Porcelain,* issued in 1974 by Faber & Faber. When he finished this book in 1973, he left his full-time position as the commercial director of an educational publishing concern to become a full-time dealer in armorial wares, especially porcelains. He started with an investment of about $35,000 "and never put a penny more into it," he said. Today he operates the shop and continues his research with a staff of six.

His second major book, *China for the West,* was written with John Ayres, head keeper of ceramics at the Victoria and Albert Museum in London. It was published in 1976 by Sotheby Parke Bernet Publications in London. This book documented the Mildred and Rafi Y. Mottahedeh collection of Chinese export wares.

Lest anyone mistake Mr. Howard for those mail-order sources who, for a fee, poke around in your family tree and find a coat of arms that supposedly fits, he warns clients: "Not everyone with a family name has the right to use a coat or arms." He is as strict with himself as with others, refusing to wear the red-and-white insignia with six crosses that has been the Howard coat of arms since the 14th century, when the family took root in Norfolk.

"I'm from the subsidiary branch and have no right," he said.

JONATHAN HORNE

66 B & C Kensington Church Street
London W8 4BY
England
Phone: (44-1) 221-5658
Hours: 9:30 A.M. to 5:30 P.M. Monday to Friday

"I became interested in antiques through archeology," Jonathan Horne said, explaining what had sparked his involvement in period wares that eventually led him to handle English pottery dating from the medieval period to about 1830. After working as an archeologist on a Roman site and on a postmedieval site in southern England in the 1950s and 1960s, Mr. Horne began to buy and sell antiques.

He began in 1968 with what he calls corny things—copper kettles and oil lamps—in the flea markets of Portobello Road and Bermondsey. He did this while working full time as a manager in a department store, where he learned stock control.

"The joy of being a dealer in London is that you can specialize," he said. "You collect your own customers." These customers, more than 75 percent of whom are Americans, come in search of robust English brown stoneware, which dates from about 1660 to the 19th century. It was made in London, Nottingham, Bristol and Staffordshire. He also stocks English Delft, which was often made in the same workshops as the stoneware.

Stoneware prices range from about $150 for a small cup to $7,500 for a carved Nottingham jug from the early 18th century and bearing an inscription. Delft ranges from about $30 for an 18th-century tile to about $30,000 for an inscribed money box. He also carries creamware, Whieldonware, slipware, medieval material and Staffordshire figures. Mr. Horne has produced several catalogues of his shows on English Delftware tiles, early English pottery and English brown stoneware of the 17th and 18th centuries. "People are bored with porcelain," Mr. Horne said, adding that the fine detailing is less interesting for today's collectors. "I've never known anyone in pottery to go on to porcelain."

BRAND INGLIS LTD.

9 Halkin Arcade
Motcomb Street
London SW1 X8JT
England
Phone: (44-1) 235-6604
Hours: 9 A.M. to 6 P.M. Monday to Friday

Brand Inglis is a lively dealer who operates his shop with the same energetic enthusiasm he demonstrated when he was president of the British Antique Dealers' Association and chairman of the Grosvenor House Antiques Fair from 1983 to 1985. He began in this field working in the silver department at Spink & Son Ltd. and later at How of Edinburgh Ltd. and was a director of Thomas Lumley before he opened his own antique silver business in 1975. Mr.

Inglis is the author of *Guide to English Silver,* and he has lectured on this subject.

The traditional silver works stocked by most British silver dealers—the 17th-, 18th- and early-19th-century candlesticks, soup tureens, salvers and vegetable dishes—are well represented in Mr. Inglis's stock. Occasionally he offers vessels signed by such 18th-century master silversmiths as Paul Lannuier and his contemporaries, and he also handles early-19th-century works by Paul Storr.

Mr. Inglis is well known for the offbeat pieces he stocks: an ecclesiastical patent dating to about 1635 was $4,000. He said his prices go from about $150 to as much as $200,000.

Among the more unusual pieces he has handled in recent years were a South German silver and partly gilded rosewater dish and ewer from 1575 that he sold to the Toledo Museum of Art in Ohio; a silver-gilt massive candelabrum by Paul Storr that was bought by Colonial Williamsburg, and an Augsburg tortoise-shell casket with gold inlay and gold-mounted bottles inside from about 1745 that he sold to the Minneapolis Institute of Arts.

JEREMY LTD.

255 King's Road
London SW3 5EL
England
Phone: (44-1) 352-0644, 352-0127
Hours: 8:30 A.M. to 6 P.M. Monday to Friday, 8:30 A.M. to 5 P.M. Saturday

Geoffrey Hill founded Jeremy in 1946 after returning from military service. At first, while he learned about furniture and his own taste, "he was dealing in junk," his son Michael said. After 40 years, those days seem like a century ago. The quality and the taste of 18th- and early-19th-century English and French furniture seem as secure and distinctive as the patina on most of the furniture stocked here.

Mr. Hill, now chairman, shares the responsibilities of this business with his two sons, Michael and John, who are in their forties. "I think we are purists," Michael Hill said. "We look for furniture that has never been disturbed. If something has been repolished, the piece has to be absolutely marvelous for us to handle it."

At Jeremy, where French and English furniture has always been stocked, Americans buy about 60 percent of what is sold. The Hills have seen American taste change noticeably in recent years from French to English. "Perhaps Americans have decided that English furniture isn't quite as grand as French furniture and that's why it has become popular," Michael Hill said. He said another factor may well be the increased scholarship in recent years on English furniture.

The variety of furniture spread through galleries on the three floors of this shop is considerable. The taste is for somewhat elegant examples of English furniture: satinwood and tulipwood veneers, ormolu fittings and embellishments, inlaid pictorial decoration and much mechanical ingenuity. The French pieces are, in sharp contrast, somewhat understated examples of 18th- and early-19th-century designs.

Among some of the more appealing selections were an Empire marble-top console with ormolu decorations on the columnar base, a Regency lantern with an ormolu shade, a George III satinwood and rosewood secretary embellished with ormolu decorations and a purple wood dressing table by Pierre Langlois fitted with a pull-out reading slide and mirrors. Notable too was a pair of Adam 1780 commodes inlaid and banded with satinwood, tulipwood and rosewood that was $280,000 the pair.

Prices here range from about $1,500 for a decorative object or piece of porcelain to about $375,000 for a highly important piece of English, French or Russian furniture.

JOHN JESSE AND IRINA LASKI LTD.

160 Kensington Church Street
London W84 BN
England
Phone: (44-1) 229-0312
Hours: 10 A.M. to 6 P.M. Monday to Saturday, 11 A.M. to 4 P.M. Saturday in summer

"I became a legend in my own time," John Jesse said, recalling how he began collecting and dealing in Art Nouveau and Art Deco long before most others in London became aware of these styles. He started in 1963 when objects of sinuous shape from the turn-of-the-century Art Nouveau period and the jazz-age Art Deco period between the world wars were just beginning to be rediscovered in Paris, London and New York. "These were the only things I could afford to buy," he explained.

Mr. Jesse had finished art school and was working in an art gallery. On Saturdays he sold jewelry, glass, ceramics and collectibles on Portobello Road. He learned swiftly and became a full-time dealer in 1965, opening a shop at 164 Kensington Church Street, next door to his present shop. A year later he organized an Art Deco exhibition that attracted, among others, Andy Warhol and Henry Geldzahler, curator of 20th-century art at the Metropolitan Museum of Art in New York. "Henry Geldzahler bought everything in my window," Mr. Jesse said.

Both styles became bywords among collectors, and Mr. Jesse's shop was the source they visited when in London. He remained there until 1979, closed for two years, and returned in 1981 in partnership with Irina Laski, whom he met when they were both dealers on Portobello Road. "It makes the most fantastic combination," he said.

The shop is crowded with a century of wonderfully witty and offbeat jewelry, table accessories and decorations in ceramic, glass, metal and sometimes wood and plastic from 1880 to 1980. Mr. Jesse's eye for glamorous, zany and great objects is drawn to the chic and the trivial, both usually the best of their kind.

"We try to have a little bit of everything," Mr. Jesse said, pointing to Demêtre Chiparus and Frederick Preiss ivory-embellished bronze sculptures, Georges Fouquet combs and jewelry, René Lalique glass and jewelry and Josef Hoffmann silver boxes, which he said can be as much as $22,000. Then he produced some 1940s costume jewelry —earrings, a bracelet, a necklace—that carried price tags of $100 to $200.

In addition to 1880s scent bottles, a clothes brush in the shape of a duck and the sort of things that were made to fill rumpus and family rooms just before and after World War II, this shop is well stocked with color-pulsing or icelike vases by Tiffany, Gallé, Daum and Loetz; glittering silver and pewter works by Archibald Knox for Sir Arthur Lasenby Liberty and other metal arts and crafts objects by Charles Ashbee. Among the prizes they have handled recently, he said, were one of the wrought-iron panels designed by Edgar Brandt for the elevators at Selfridges, a bat-embellished cameo glass lamp by Gallé and an Alfonso Mucha poster of Sarah Bernhardt.

LEWIS M. KAPLAN ASSOCIATES

50 Fulham Road
London SW3 6HH
Phone: (44-1) 589-3108, 584-6328.
Hours: 11 A.M. to 6 P.M. Monday to Saturday

Lewis M. Kaplan, a New York lawyer who was senior counsel to the Dreyfus Fund in the 1960s, moved to London in the 1970s and became a private dealer in contemporary art and in 20th-century decorative arts. His partner, Gordon D. Watson, heads their shop, which stocks furniture, objects and jewelry dating from 1900 to 1960. They opened their shop 1978, the year Mr. Watson left Sotheby's, where he was a specialist in ancient art as well as Tibetan and Middle Eastern ceramics and glass.

When the shop was new, Mr. Watson said, he tried combining antiquities with 20th-century objects. "It didn't work," he recalled. "The other was very academic and this material is more accessible."

Collectors of French and Danish 20th-century silver are among the first to agree. Mr. Watson specializes in Puiforcat and Georg Jensen silver, offering both the early curvaceous Art Deco designs that reflect tradition and the Cubist-modern, geometric-styled vessels and flatware produced in the late 1920s and 1930s.

Puiforcat tea sets range from about $4,500 to $15,000, depending on the pattern, size, number of pieces and whether the handles are of wood, semiprecious stone or ivory. Jensen silver flatware in the Acorn, Bernadotte and Continental patterns is about $10,000 to $15,000 for a 200-piece service. He also handles 1940s modern silver tea services by Calderoni of Rome that anticipate later Italian Modern styling.

The shop offers a wide range of wares, including turn-of-the-century objects from the English arts and crafts movement, 1920s jewelry by Georges Fouquet, perfume bottles made for Lanvin, 1940s jewelry by Cartier and Van Cleef and 1950s Italian ceramics by Guido Gamboni and Mellotti.

"Ruhlmann? We used to have many pieces of Ruhlmann's furniture," Mr. Watson said. "But they are scarcer now. We have the odd piece of furniture from time to time." René Lalique's glass, once a specialty here, has been the subject of so many ups and downs in prices that Mr. Watson stocks far less of it now than he once did.

Prices range from about $500 for a scent bottle or a Daum glass vessel to over $50,000 for a signed piece of Cartier or Van Cleef jewelry from the 1940s.

JOHN KEIL LTD.

154 Brompton Road
London SW3 1HX
England
Phone: (44-1) 589-6454
Hours: 9 A.M. to 5:30 P.M. Monday to Friday

John Keil stocks some of the very best examples of English furniture, dating from the late 17th century through the early 19th century. He began in the antiques business working for a short while with his father, H. W. Keil, now dead, at his shop in Worcestershire. He left in 1960 to open his own establishment in London. He shares the running of this shop, and another at 10 Quiet Street, Bath, with his co-director, Michael Hughes.

They report that about 70 percent of what they sell goes to Americans. "A lot of this business is with decorators who buy for their clients," Mr. Keil said. Some clients buy major pieces from the brochure that Keil sends out twice a year.

Many Americans shop for English furniture in London because they see a far greater selection in the shops and at the antiques fairs than they do in New York, Chicago or San Francisco, Mr. Keil said. "There have always been collectors of English furniture in America, but for many years it did not have a strong appeal to the general public," he said. "Now it does."

"Regrettably, it would seem, antiques are now regarded as a commodity, with their scarcity ensuring that prices for the best pieces are always on the increase," he said.

Mr. Keil said he sometimes buys in the United States, but carefully. "We like to see a fine quality of timber with good color," he said. "A repolished piece loses its patina."

Prices range from about $1,500 for an early-19th-century tea caddy to about $500,000 for a red lacquer bookcase by Giles Grendey. Choice offerings may include suites of furniture, as was the case with the 1778 suite of 10 armchairs, 1 side chair, a pair of stools and a large settee that was sold for $235,000.

E. & C. T. KOOPMAN & SON LTD.

53-65 Chancery Lane
London WC2 A1QS
England
Phone: (44-1) 242-7624, 242-8365
Hours: 9 A.M. to 5 P.M. Monday to Friday, 9 A.M. to noon Saturday

"The ups and downs in the price of silver bullion have as much to do with the value of antique silver as today's price of lumber does with the value of Chippendale furniture," said Jacques Koopman, the Dutch-born dealer.

Mr. Koopman knew what he was talking about when he made this comment in 1982, a month after he paid

$429,000, a record price, at Christie's in New York for a pair of silver-gilt tureens by Jean-Baptiste-Claude Odiot. The purchase of these French silver vessels occurred when silver as a metal was selling for less than $10 an ounce, down from $50 an ounce, the peak price for silver established in January 1980.

Mr. Koopman's aggressive manner in auctions, where he frequently pays record prices for French and English silver, is matched by his flair for choosing the finest silver to appear on the market. He and his brother, Edward Koopman, are a formidable team in the auction rooms and at their London shop.

Jacques Koopman was fourteen years old when he arrived in London from Amsterdam after World War II. His parents died in a concentration camp in the war, and he spent four years in hiding. He joined his older brother, who had left Amsterdam in 1940 for England, and settled in Manchester, where he became a jewelry dealer.

The brothers are the second generation of antiques dealers in their family but the first to specialize. They started in business together as jewelry dealers—Jacques even learned diamond cutting—before switching to silver in 1951 in their shop in Manchester. Business mushroomed and they opened a second shop in London in 1957. Today, the Manchester office and the London shop are among the world's most influential in English and Continental silver. Other family members who work there are Edward's wife, Catherine Turner Koopman, their son, Michael, and Jacques's daughter, Elisabeth.

The Koopmans' sprawling London establishment is on the main floor of the Silver Vaults, the building where they opened an annex two floors below the street in 1957. They moved upstairs in 1981. Their many galleries display glittering 18th- and early-19th-century silver vessels, flatware and decorations in floor-to-ceiling showcases. Their stock is rich in rococo and neo-classical examples expressing the full repertory of the silversmith's virtuosity and bearing the signatures of most of the great London silversmiths of the period, including Paul de Lamerie, Matthew Boulton, Hester Bateman, Paul Storr and scores of others.

The Koopmans' enterprise and persistence was proven in their dealings with the Middle East. To attract buyers, they exhibited their silver in Dubai on the Persian Gulf in the early 1970s. "We didn't sell one silver teaspoon,"

Jacques Koopman recalled. They returned in 1975, slowly found customers for their abundant silver and eventually helped Mohamed Mehdi al-Tajir, Ambassador to London from the United Arab Emirates, form one of the largest private silver holdings assembled in decades.

Prices range from $100 for a small object, such as a spoon, to more than $500,000 for an important pair of vegetable dishes or tureens. A set of three Queen Anne sugar shakers was $5,700. A Queen Anne chocolate pot was $54,000. A pair of Hester Bateman sugar basins from 1788 was $1,740.

L'ODÉON

173 Fulham Road
London SW3 6JW
Phone: (44-1) 581-3640
Hours: 11 A.M. to 6 P.M. Monday to Saturday

Noël Tovey, an Australian, arrived in London in 1959 and joined Sadler's Wells as a dancer. After a knee injury in the 1960s, he switched to acting, directing and choreography.

He also started collecting Clarice Cliff ceramics. "I loved the colors," he said of these British 1920s and 1930s boldly painted pitchers, platters, plates, cups and saucers decorated with motifs and palettes influenced by Matisse and Léger. They cost pennies, he recalled. He was 20 years ahead of the rest of the world.

In 1970 he translated some of what he made performing in London in the original production of *Oh! Calcutta!* into collectibles and doubled his money. There was a shop available with a rent of $16 a week at 56 Fulham Street. "I decided to go into it in an academic way," he said. "I read everything I could get my hands on." In 1980 he moved to his current shop.

Mr. Tovey stocks a variety of 20th-century decorative arts: glass, china and metal work dating from 1900 to 1950. The Wiener Werkstätte is represented with glass and china designs by Koloman Moser (a blue-dotted ceramic mug was about $450) and Josef Hoffmann (a ruby red glass vase was about $1,100). From France come glass designs by René Lalique and Daum. There are works by Peter Behrens, Karl Köpping and Frederick Preiss, and there are glass designs produced by Loetz and Venini and metal Art Deco designs by Edgar Brandt.

The Clarice Cliff pottery fills floor-to-ceiling shelves on one wall and included a cookie jar at about $375, a vase at about $2,200. Rare patterns such as Persian are from $800 to $7,000 and Age of Jazz is from $2,000 to $20,000 for a complete set of five figures.

MAGGS BROS. LTD.

50 Berkeley Square
London W1X 6EL
England
Phone: (44-1) 493-7160
Hours: 9 A.M. to 5 P.M. Monday to Friday

Maggs is one of Britain's and the world's oldest rare-book dealers still owned and managed by the original family. Founded by Uriah Maggs in 1853, Maggs today is run by his fourth-generation descendants—John Maggs, the senior family member, and Bryan Maggs, his cousin—and three nonfamily directors. There is a fifth generation at work at Maggs, John's son, Edward, and his daughter, Elizabeth. John Maggs hopes the house will one day add a sixth generation when Benjamin John Carroll Maggs, born to Edward Maggs in March 1987, is old enough.

The town house that Maggs has occupied since just before World War II was the home of Prime Minister George Canning in the early 19th century. "We still have the stable where he kept his horses," Mr. Maggs said, adding that the three floors in the mews are also piled high with books. The house is famous for another reason. "It's supposed to be the most authentic haunted house in London—but we've never seen the proof," he said. Haunted or not, the building is handsome and large: four floors lined with books.

The three nonfamily directors (the bookseller became a limited company in 1935) are Paul Harcourt, Maggs's classicist and expert on Greek and Latin; Robert Harding, the house expert on 17th- and 18th-century English literature, and Hugh Bett, expert on travel books of all periods.

Maggs's specialties include all the areas on which its experts focus: Elizabethan and 18th-century English books; 19th- and early-20th-century English literature and bibliography and military books of all periods. Autographs, both letters and documents, and miniature European illuminated manuscripts are also handled in depth. English bookbindings of the 18th and 19th centuries, a period of major interest for today's collectors, is a field in which Bryan Maggs's judgment is valued by many. At Sotheby's record-breaking 1987 auction in Monte Carlo, Mr. Maggs made several major purchases from the Marcel Jeanson collection of 600 manuscripts and books, one of the world's finest libraries on hunting, shooting and fishing, including Gaston Phébus's *Livre de Chasse* dating to 1400, which is described as the most influential medieval book on hunting.

"We also give attention to the $20 books," Mr. Maggs said. "We can and do sell books to beginners among collectors." Maggs does not stock books on medicine, science and architecture in depth.

The period after World War I saw many great private libraries dispersed at auction, and Maggs handled its share, selling many books to King Manuel II, Portugal's deposed ruler, when he was forming his great library in London. Maggs is Booksellers by Appointment to Her Majesty Queen Elizabeth II.

John Maggs said his uncle bought a Gutenberg Old Testament at auction in 1947 for $88,628, then the auction record for a printed book. He sold it, bought it back and resold it to Carrie Estelle Doheny. Mrs. Doheny, the widow of a California oil industrialist, viewed the Gutenberg as the most important work in the Doheny rare-book collection.

MALLETT & SON ANTIQUES LTD.

40 New Bond Street
London W1Y OBS
England
Phone: (44-1) 499-7411
Hours: 9:15 A.M. to 5:15 P.M. Monday to Friday

MALLETT AT BOURBON HOUSE LTD.

2 Davies Street
Berkeley Square
London W1Y 1LJ
Phone: (44-1) 629-2444
Hours: 9:30 A.M. to 5:30 P.M. Monday to Friday

"We are told that we are the finest dealers in English furniture in the world," said Peter Maitland, managing director of Mallett's on New Bond Street, leading the way through its exquisitely elegant premises where many members of the royal family, many more of the landed gentry and still more of the American aristocrats of banking and industry shop for British antiques. The furnishings have the air of being ordained, not arranged.

On New Bond Street, the emphasis is on highly refined and perfectly decorated rooms, most of which are lavish, echoing everyone's image of the estates of Britain's landed gentry. There are sporting pictures and flower paintings and portraits on the walls, chandeliers lighting the dining tables and pottery, silver and gilded bronzes decorating the settings. Mallett leaves to its clients the opportunity of adding fuddy-duddy eccentricities that add individualism to their collections, and it expects time to contribute patina.

The 11 galleries in the 7,000 square feet on two floors accommodate about 500 pieces of furniture and almost as many other period objects. Each gallery is furnished in a different style: a Queen Anne early-18th-century parlor, an Adam period dining room, a mid-18th-century Chippendale library and an 18th-century bedroom.

Outstanding among the finer selections were a George III octagonal rent table from about 1760 that was $72,000, an exceptionally fine 1760s Chippendale carved and giltwood mirror that was $112,500 and a 1690s William and Mary walnut kneehole desk at $42,000. The range of prices at this gallery is from $7,500 to about $750,000.

On Davies Street, where David G. F. Nickerson is managing director, the furnishings are Continental and are spread through a rabbit warren of rooms that present a scene in sharp contrast to the New Bond Street quarters. This comfortable sprawling house, the home of the Duke of Westminster until 1958, when Mallett's acquired the lease on the building, is filled with complete rooms that are busy, eclectic and crowded with objects organized in a way only the Wild Hare could fathom. Visitors may not understand, but they appreciate that these settings, six galleries on two floors, are perfectly executed right down to the flower-filled vases and baskets.

The two stores, which together sell about $9 million worth a year, share a strong emphasis on decoration, which they repeat for their clients in realistic, frequently dramatic schemes filled with period furniture and all the amenities to add glitter and excitement.

Mallett and Son Antiques Ltd. came into being in Bath in 1865. In that year, John Mallett, a jeweler and silversmith, set up shop on Milsom Street. His son, Walter Mallett, joined his father in the late 1870s or early 1880s, "quickly assuming complete control," a company history relates. He expanded the business to include old silver and furniture and moved it in the 1890s to the Octagon, a 1767 church that had fallen into disuse.

Mallett opened a London branch at 40 New Bond Street in 1908. After Walter Mallett's death in 1930, Francis Snoek, who married Mallett's daughter and changed his name to Mallett, became chairman of the antiques concern.

From 1955 to 1986, Francis Egerton headed the concern, which by then had 30 shareholders and 5 partners, reshaping it as a modern business. Under Mr. Egerton's direction, Mallett expanded briefly in the early 1970s to Geneva and New York.

"The timing was wrong," David Nickerson recalled. "The slump came and we pulled back."

In April 1986, Mr. Egerton resigned, and the partners

under him—Mr. Maitland, Mr. Nickerson, Lanto Synge, John Yorke and Peter Dixon—acquired 51 percent of Mallett. The remaining 49 percent was purchased by Sears Holdings.

About half of what Mallett sells goes to Americans. Of the 10 pieces sold at one Grosvenor House Fair, 4 went to Americans. The highlight of that booth, indeed of the fair, was a Boulle-type bureau-bookcase, an Antwerp piece that carried a price tag of $750,000.

Mr. Nickerson has an eye for the extraordinary and the offbeat. A red lacquer early-18th-century Berlin secretary-bookcase, a tour de force of chinoiserie detailing, with a fall front, three drawers in the base and a plain cornice, was $240,000. An exuberant and rare walnut bookcase with a carved caryatid cornice executed in Turin about 1800 was $150,000. A French walnut dining table from about 1800 has tapered legs fitted with brass rollers, and the table extends from a half-ellipse measuring 4 feet 8 inches to a 20-foot-long banquet size to seat 24. The price is $50,000.

Smaller objects and accessories in glass, metal and procelain range from $500 to $10,000.

PARTRIDGE (FINE ARTS) LTD.

144 New Bond Street
London W1Y OLY
England
Phone: (44-1) 629-0834
Hours: 9 A.M. to 5:30 P.M. Monday to Friday

An Edwardian mood of elegance laced with exuberance pervades the premises over which John Partridge reigns in the heart of London's art and antiques district. Beyond its neo-classical stone facade and arched portal, collectors and curators from throughout the world shop for English and French 18th- and early-19th-century furniture, porcelains, silver, tapestries, paintings and works of art in galleries rich in the architectural amenities of England's great manor houses.

"Today, there's no one else who deals in all the things I

deal in," Mr. Partridge said, acknowledging the major change in antiques dealing since World War II. More and more dealers have narrowly specialized, and few now offer all categories of period furnishings for fine homes.

Partridge's entrance hall, a soaring space of Ionic columns, molded plaster ceiling, parquet floors, pilaster-framed niches, leaded-glass windows and a marble mantel, is one of 14 galleries on three floors. There and in the other silk-lined and linenfold-paneled rooms, Partridge's stock of antique furniture, much of it lacquered or gilded and boasting aristocratic pedigrees, graces settings enlivened with crystal chandeliers, gilded rococo mirrors, marble statuary and needlepoint rugs.

Partridge was opposite Christie's on King Street for several decades until it was bombed in World War II. It then moved to its present home on New Bond Street, directly across the street from Sotheby's, Christie's rival in the auction business.

"We were hit the same night Christie's was and lost two-thirds of our stock," Mr. Partridge recalled. "My grandfather had wanted this building all his life, and it was available." The gallery had been built before World War I for P. & D. Colnaghi & Company, but the art dealers were forced to abandon it when the company had financial reversals in the 1930s. "We acquired this building for £1,000 a year during the war when the bombs were still dropping and it was used as the air raid warden's canteen," he said.

Mr. Partridge, a barrel-chested and balding man with thick eyebrows, an intense gaze and unflagging energy, heads the privately owned antiques concern founded at the turn of the century by his grandfather, Frank Partridge, a man remembered as a tough, daring businessman who bought with taste and boldness. The younger Mr. Partridge assumed command in 1958 at the age of twenty-eight at the sudden death of Claude Partridge, his father, who had taken over only four years earlier when the founder died.

"I think the whole art field has changed since my grandfather's time," Mr. Partridge said. "There was a small nucleus of collectors then. We might have had 100 collectors on our books. Now when we send the catalogue out, we mail it to 5,000."

There have been other changes. His grandfather maintained a New York branch, which he opened in 1920 at 6 West 56th Street. John Partridge closed it in 1968, deciding that he preferred to travel to clients—and they to him—now that jet travel has quickened the process. It's a policy that appears to work for him, he said, noting that over the last 15 years American buying has increased substantially and now constitutes 70 to 80 percent of his business.

The range of prices for the more than 900 items in stock goes from about $1,500 for a small silver box to $1 million or more for a very important piece of French furniture. A Louis XVI black lacquer secretary-commode, made for Talleyrand, was $950,000, and a pair of Chippendale chairs, with stuffed back and seats and open sides, was $90,000 the pair.

"To be a successful art dealer you must be a bit crazy and you must feel very passionate about the objects," he said. "I buy any work of art that I really like and I don't buy anything I don't like."

Mr. Partridge has two heirs, and the older, Frank, is the fourth generation in the business.

PELHAM GALLERIES

163-165 Fulham Road
London SW3 6SN
England
Phone: (44-1) 589-2686
Hours: 9 A.M. to 5:30 P.M. Monday to Friday, by appointment Saturday
Closed the first three weeks in August

"I've been looking at antiques since I was in my pram," Alan Rubin said, recalling his beginnings in the family antiques business in which he is now the only remaining active member. Pelham was founded in 1928 by his father and uncle, Ernest and Henry Rubin, on Charlotte Street, then a wholesale center crowded with antiques dealers. The Rubin brothers moved to Fulham Road in 1933, and over the next half century the street became one of the most important antiques centers in England.

"They had the habit of buying in a very broad spectrum, " Mr. Rubin recalled. "There was a variety of pieces and a quantity of fine antiques that is unimaginable today."

After Alan Rubin finished his studies at Cambridge, where he read philosophy and took a fine-arts course, he began working at Pelham. "I had made my first purchase at sixteen and came to work here at twenty-one in 1970."

Mr. Rubin's taste for the offbeat and exotic is seen in Pelham's stock of coromandel screens, clocks and musical instruments. He also carries English and European furniture dating from the 17th century through the 1830s. Among the later works are many Regency and William IV designs. Uncommon pieces include musical instruments, including one of only two surviving examples of an English chamber organ made in London about 1790 with a cabinet by John England & Sons. The window was filled with five unusual clocks, framed in porcelain, gilded metal, tortoise shell, ivory and wood by British and French 18th- and 19th-century clockmakers.

At this gallery, antiques ranged from about $500 for a Regency Boulle inkstand to about $270,000 for a late-17th-century coromandel screen showing children at play. An uncommon Regency library table was $32,000 and a Roman table, its top inlaid with ancient marble specimens in Naples about 1800, was $90,500.

S. J. PHILLIPS LTD.

139 New Bond Street
London W1A 3DL
England
Phone: (44-1) 629-6261
Hours: 10 A.M. to 5 P.M. Monday to Friday

S. J. Phillips, one of the world's top sources for period jewelry and silver, has been on New Bond Street since 1869, when it moved to No. 113. The current address, opposite Sotheby's, has been home since 1966. This business has specialized in silver and antique jewelry since its founding and has been run by descendants of Solomon Joel Phillips since his death in 1909.

For the next two decades, his son, Edmund, called Teddy, was at the helm, and after his death in 1934, the concern was headed by the two sons of S. J. Phillips's daughter, Nita Phillips Norton—Martin and Richard. Richard died in 1985.

The Nortons operate Phillips very much as a family business. Martin Norton, who was 75 in 1986, is chairman, and all the other Nortons—his sons, Nicolas and Jonathan, and his nephew, Francis, the son of Richard—are directors.

Phillips's taste in silver is for the refined English and Continental examples. "We tend to leave the big, heavy, ugly stuff for others," Francis Norton said. One of the earliest works ever handled by Phillips was a 13th-century Savernake horn dating from the period when the Savernake Forest in Wiltshire was a royal hunting land. It was sold to the British Museum.

The range in prices for silver is wide, going from $37 for a "spoon of character" to seven figures for a splendid mid-18th-century tureen by Thomas Germain or Paul de Lamerie.

Phillips is even better known for its stock in ancient through early-19th-century period jewelry and precious objects. Rarities in Greek, Roman and Egyptian antiquities and Renaissance jewelry are sold to the world's top collectors and museums. Exquisite tiaras, necklaces, bracelets, pendants and rings bear royal and aristocratic pedigrees as glittering as their enameled and stone-washed surfaces and as impressive as their prices.

Phillips bought about two-thirds of the Russian crown jewels when they were auctioned in 1927 at Christie's—and resold them quickly. Another prize handled by this dealer is an 1811 ruby-and-diamond necklace presented by Napoleon to his second wife, Empress Marie Louise, and remounted a few years later for the Duchess of Angoulême.

Jewelry prices range from $100 for a paste button of the 1820s to $750,000 for a late Georgian ruby bracelet from about 1820.

Phillips also stocks old Sheffield plate, gold boxes, snuff boxes and miniature enamel paintings in small frames or for jewelry.

BERNARD QUARITCH LTD.

5-8 Lower John Street
Golden Square
London 1R 4AU
England
Phone: (44-1) 734 2983
Hours: 9:30 A.M. to 1 P.M. and 2 to 5:30 P.M. Monday to Friday

Bernard Quaritch Ltd., a name to be reckoned with among British booksellers, began in 1847, seven years after the Prussian-born founder emigrated to London from his native Worbis in Saxony. After he landed, he dropped the *s* from Quaritsch. With his apprenticeship behind him in Germany, he became a general bookseller, handling everything at his London shop. Over the next half century his boundless energy and dedication earned for him the title in the trade of the Napoleon of Booksellers. His clientele included Gladstone, Disraeli and Napoleon's nephew, Prince Louis-Lucien Bonaparte. The poet Edward FitzGerald became a friend, which led to Quaritch's becoming the first publisher of the *Rubáiyát of Omar Khayyám,* which FitzGerald translated from the Persian.

Quaritch's son, Bernard Alfred, succeeded him in 1899 when he was twenty-eight and headed the store for 20 years. After his death, it hummed along profitably, run by a succession of managing directors. In 1976 Quaritch was acquired by its present owners, Lord Parmoor and Simon Sainsbury.

Today there are about 30 part-time and full-time employees, most of them book people, each with a specialty. Among them is Arthur Freeman, a Bostonian and former professor of English literature at Boston University, who has been a consultant since 1975, when he moved to London to live and write.

The plums in Freeman's field that Quaritch handled earlier in this century, including Shakespeare's *First Folio,* do not surface often these days, he said. In 1981, Quaritch paid $210,000 for the Prescott *First Folio,* one of the few copies to appear in recent years.

"Half of our business is with Americans," Mr. Freeman said. Quaritch handled the sale in 1986 of the Carl and Lily Pforzheimer library of early English books and manuscripts to H. Ross Perot and earlier sold the Pforzheimer Gutenberg Bible for $2.4 million to the University of Texas.

With Hans P. Kraus, Quaritch was the agent for the buyer of the 12th-century *Henry the Lion Gospels* in the Sotheby's London auction in 1983 for $11.9 million, an auction record for a manuscript and the most expensive art work ever auctioned until van Gogh's *Sunflowers* went under the hammer and brought $39.9 million at Christie's in London in 1987.

Others at Quaritch are specialists in Continental books, travel, science, natural history, art and architecture, anthropology, economics and philosophy.

These specialists work in a Quaritch's fourth home, a 100-foot-long converted wool warehouse. The books here start at $50 and range up to six figures.

WILLIAM REDFORD

9 Mount Street (at Berkeley Square)
London WIY 5AP
England
Phone: (44-1) 629-1165
Hours: 10 A.M. to 5 P.M. Monday to Friday

William Redford, the son of a financier, came into the antiques business in 1945 when very few people had any money to spend. He joined Gerald Kerin, one of London's most respected dealers in antiques in all fields. At that time, Mr. Redford said, antiques meant anything made before 1800. "In those days, that's where we stopped." Today Mr. Redford, who specializes in Continental furniture and decorations, stops a little later, about 1820.

In 1961 he and Mr. Kerin moved from Davies Street, around the corner, to the present location. For all its charms, Mount Street is not easily fathomed by strangers to the neighborhood because the numbers "are difficult," Mr. Redford said. They go up one side and down the other, so that directly across the street from his premises at No. 9 is No. 125.

Mr. Redford has been on his own since 1971. The large

windows do attract a few people, he said, but most of his clients make appointments, telephoning from across the English Channel and other parts of the world. What they find is an inviting mix of Louis XIV through Empire lacquered, gilded, painted and mahogany furniture mixed with porcelains, gilded bronzes, mirrors, sconces and candelabra.

What clients count on here is the fine condition of the dealer's offerings—for example, a Louis XVI mahogany console desserte, embellished with a 17th-century pietra dura plaque, that was made by the royal cabinetmaker Guillaume Beneman. The bronzes, thick with gold, have never been cleaned, Mr. Redford said. Notable too was a large Louis XVI gilt-bronze-mounted kingwood console from the collection of the Duke of Abercorn that had been bought by one of his ancestors at the French Revolution sales. There was a signed pair of Louis XV carved and gilded bergères by Falconet in a design Hepplewhite copied for his easy chairs. Notable too were a rare 1764 marquetry commode by Kemp and handsome clocks of the Louis XVI and Empire periods.

"I sell with an unconditional guarantee," he said. "We don't sell the goods; the goods sell themselves." Prices range from $7,500 for a pair of candlesticks to $200,000 for the signed Louis XVI console.

ALASTAIR SAMPSON ANTIQUES

156 Brompton Road
London SW3 1HW
England
Phone: (44-1) 589-5272
Hours: 9:30 A.M. to 5:30 P.M. Monday to Friday

"The really compulsive collector becomes a dealer," said Alastair Sampson, explaining his decision to become an English ceramics merchant. "When I was a practicing barrister, I became more and more obsessed with antiques and went into partnership."

Mr. Sampson's initial involvement with period English pottery began after he had completed his studies of history and law at Cambridge in the 1950s. He remained a barrister in London for 15 years. In 1967 he sold his collection of Leeds pottery in four sessions at Christie's so he could get married. "My wife wanted to hang her things in the cupboard," he said. "We also needed the money."

His move to the other side of the counter came in 1969 when Mr. Sampson began a partnership with David Seligmann as Sampson & Seligmann. In 1971 he changed partners and the name of the business to Jellinek & Sampson. Since 1982 the business has been known as Alastair Sampson Antiques with Mr. Sampson offering pottery; Tobias Jellinek, "the uncrowned king of oak furniture," stocking 17th- and early-18th-century pieces; Antoine de Vermoutier selling needlework, and Christopher Banks other period decorations.

Today the pottery Mr. Sampson stocks is sought by many more collectors than when he started in business. And since 1980 more and more of these people have paid extraordinary prices for what they collect. These robust wares—English Delft, Staffordshire slipware, salt-glaze figures, Whieldon animals—date from the late Middle Ages, from about 1400, through the end of what English pottery collectors call the classic period, about 1830.

"We carry an enormous stock," he said. The earliest wares, he said, are hefty jugs and pitchers, some of them mounted in silver. The 17th- and 18th-century Delft blue-and-white bottles, bowls and mugs, the polychrome chargers, slip-decorated Staffordshire jars, bowls and honey pots are handsomely decorated with boldly drawn patterns, strong colors and relief decoration.

Mr. Sampson made several important purchases at Sotheby's 1986 auction of the collection formed over 40 years by Tom Burns of Rous Lench Court in Worcestershire. The dealer outbid all competitors for a salt-glaze pew group that was expected to bring at most $55,000 but sold for $179,520, then an auction record for English ceramics.

"No one with a small purse should be daunted about coming into the shop," Mr. Sampson said, adding that his pottery starts at $40 and "the ceiling is $180,000." Many collectors come to meet Mr. Sampson, whose column on collecting in *Punch* has enhanced his popularity.

SPINK & SON LTD.

5, 6 & 7 King Street
St. James's
London SW1 Y6QS
England
Phone: (44-1) 930-7888
Hours: 9:30 A.M. to 5:30 P.M. Monday to Friday

Spink & Son, one of the world's oldest antiques concerns and London's best-known source for a wide variety of period wares, continues to have a major influence in the art market in antique English silver, Oriental art, Islamic jewelry, coins and medals.

Spink was founded in 1666 by John Spink, a goldsmith, and the family business in silver and jewelry prospered. Over two and a half centuries, Spink moved from time to time as London changed and the firm expanded, settling in 1927 at its present address.

It was a family-controlled business until 1978, when it was acquired by Andrew Weir & Company, a shipping, insurance and investment company. Descendants of Spink's founder have always been on its staff and today include two great-grandsons "several times over," Anthony Spink, who heads the English paintings department, and his cousin Michael, who heads the Islamic art department.

Spink's wide-ranging stock also includes jewelry, Chinese and Japanese ceramics and European and Oriental textiles.

"We stock everything the Chinese ever made from 2,500 years ago to about 1916," said Roger Keverne, who heads Spink's Oriental art department and is a member of its board of directors. He showed an imperial quality Ch'ien Lung Celadon vase, flared at the mouth and embellished with a dragon, an eighth-century Tang vase in cream and amber more than two feet tall, and a 14th-century Ming blue-and-white trumpet-shaped vase. Each was $50,000 or more. There are 17th-century lacquer cabinets (a fine pair was $150,000) and pairs of fine Tang horses, which were even higher in price. Spink recently sold a duck, made in about the fourth century, for $67,500 and a Tang horse for $37,500. "There is a big market between

$750 and $15,000, and we try to have wares at those prices, too," Mr. Keverne said.

China export wares are less expensive and many are choice. A pair of porcelain plates made for the British market in famille rose enamels with scenes of European buildings and Canton's ports was about $12,000 the pair.

The stock also included a rare Tibetan 12th-century iron dancer's mask, the eyebrows, beard, mustache and lips inlaid with gold. "We have never before seen a mask of this quality, antiquity or in this medium," said Anthony Gardner, director of the Southeast Asian art department. The price was $18,000.

Notable too was a pair of Japanese 19th-century Meiji bronzes, exuberant studies of the god of wind playing a flute and the god of thunder beating a drum, at $127,500 the pair. Much of its Oriental art is less costly, from about $150, Mr. Keverne said.

Spink's antique silver includes vessels and flatware that may range from an ivory-handled silver crumb scoop from 1931 by Omar Ramsden at $675 to a Queen Anne wine cistern and fountain of 1707 at $825,000. Chinoiserie silver is a specialty here and included a James II silver monteith made by George Garthorne of London in 1685. The weighty bowl, which measured about a foot in diameter, was handsomely decorated in the Chinese taste on all eight panels and carried a price tag of about $75,000. A set of 12 18th-century gold spoons, the only hallmarked set to appear, was $37,500.

Coins are sold by Spink at its shop, at its London auctions, which are held twice a month, and at several of its branches, including Zurich, where ancient and European coins are handled. Among the most important coins handled by Spink in London was a Henry III gold penny, the oldest surviving British coin, of which only seven examples from his reign (1216-1272) are known. It brought the equivalent of about $98,000 at auction.

STAIR & COMPANY

120 Mount Street
London W1Y 5HB
Phone: (44-1) 499-1784/5
Hours: 9 A.M. to 5 P.M. Monday to Friday
Director: Robert Luck

SEE New York: *Stair & Company, page 98*

JACOB STODEL

116 Kensington Church
London W8 4BH
England
Phone: (44-1) 221-2652
Hours: 9:30 A.M. to 5:30 P.M. Monday to Friday, Saturdays by appointment

SEE Amsterdam: *Salomon Stodel Antiquités, page 148*

ROBIN SYMES

94 Jermyn Street
London SW1 Y6JE
England
Phone: (44-1) 930-5300
Hours: 10 A.M. to 5:30 P.M. Monday to Friday

3 Ormond Yard
London SW1 Y6JT
Phone: (44-1) 930-9856
Hours: By appointment

Robin Symes is the sort of person about whom some people say, "Everyone knows him but no one knows anything about him." Mr. Symes wears such a reputation lightly. Since he probably knows more about the people he buys from and sells to than they do about him, everything seems quite in order. In the antiquities field, in fact, discretion is not only desirable, it is demanded.

Mr. Symes was born in 1939 in Dorchester, the son of a furniture maker. His soft lilting accent bears the traces of that Hardy countryside in southern England. "I was a painter and went to art school," he recalled. "In the last year, I married and had to earn some money." Working as a waiter, he discovered some copies of 15th-century wooden East Anglia angels that were to be burned, and he bought one, beginning his career as an art dealer. He was soon selling medieval material to both Paris and Brussels.

By the mid-1960s, ancient art dominated his dealing both because of the shortage of medieval works and his natural curiosity about this material. Antiquities had attracted his attention much earlier, when he was eleven or twelve, the dealer recalled. "I had a little museum with tesserae from a Roman pavement and a Roman horseshoe," he said. "It was terribly modest, all built into an empty fireplace of my bedroom."

Antiquities are stocked at both of Mr. Symes's galleries, with the major works reserved for Ormond Yard. Intaglios and amulets are the least expensive items, from about $90 to $120, and many selections are under $3,000. The stock at Jermyn Street, where Chantal Spar is in charge, includes ancient jewelry, gold rings and necklaces, decorative marble sculptures, small vessels and terra cottas.

Mr. Symes specializes in Egyptian, Greek, Roman and Middle Eastern art. These works surround him at his Ormond Street place, a house with steep and narrow stairways and great charm that was built as an art-supply company and dates to about 1820. The storage cupboards that remain from the previous owners are as sturdy as medieval chests. The private relics here also include a set of Charles Rennie Mackintosh chairs around a conference table. Of particular note from his stock was a Roman bronze folding stand from the first century surmounted by three beautiful statuettes of horses. With a marble top resting on the horses, it functions as a table.

"I deal with very few people; that's why so few people know me," Mr. Symes said. "I think the trick of being a good dealer is getting on with what you are doing, very quietly, very discreetly."

TZIGANY FINE ARTS

28, 29 Dover Street
London W1X 3PA
England
Phone: (44-1) 491-1007
Hours: 9:30 A.M. to 6 P.M. Monday to Friday

In 1982 Russian furniture and all of its Swedish, Austrian and German imitations began a stunning ascendance in popularity in interior decorating on both sides of the Atlantic. In 1985, Antoine Chenevière opened Tzigany, the only shop west of Moscow now specializing in furniture and objects crafted for the Romanovs and their friends between 1780 and 1840.

Mr. Chenevière was not new to Russian furniture. The dealer, who is half-Swiss and half-Bulgarian, had been selling the taste of the Czars in imperial and more modest quality tables, chairs, desks and cabinets since 1975, when he was twenty-five years old. That was when he opened his first business in Geneva. In 1974 he worked for Didier Aaron, a Paris dealer who stocks major examples of the

French furniture that the Russians adapted and in some cases improved.

Mr. Chenevière began his move to London from what he calls the "city of clocks, chocolates and bankers" in October 1985, and for a year operated both shops before deciding to close the one in Geneva.

"I am one of the very few dealers in Russian furniture," Mr. Chenevière said, adding that he meant "anywhere." In Geneva this proved to be curious, he said; in London, exciting.

Once installed in his gallery in Mayfair, the dealer became more ambitious. In 1987 he said he was writing a book on Russian furniture. At that point, he noted, his stock included more than 20 late-18th-century Russian pieces, the Louis XVI and Directoire style that the Russians did with more heft and more gilded embellishments.

There were chairs with sunburst backs, swan's necks and lion's heads, a table mounted engagingly with porcelains and gilded bronzes. Everywhere was evidence of a bounty of small objects Russophiles cannot live without: malachite vases, lapis lazuli boxes and some special clocks. The examples of the Empire style, as it was interpreted in the early 19th century in St. Petersburg, were equally impressive: the cylinder-front desks, tables and chairs were sometimes outsize and invariably architectural.

What distinguishes the Russian works stocked here from the Continental interpretations of French furniture made in Germany, Austria and Sweden is the weighty elegance and imperial taste that adds aristocratic grandeur and some fantasy.

These days, Mr. Chenevière said, he is visited by collectors, designers and their clients from throughout London, the Continent and the United States. Furniture prices range from $20,000 to $200,000 and higher. A pair of secretaries was $600,000.

The gallery's name, gypsy in Hungarian, "has always had the scent of dreams, the smell of adventure for me," Mr. Chenevière said.

WARTSKI

14 Grafton Street
London W1X 3LA
England
Phone: (44-1) 493-1141, 493-1142, 493-1143
Hours: 9:30 A.M. to 5 P.M. Monday to Friday

A. Kenneth Snowman, chairman of Wartski and the third generation in the family business, grew up surrounded by Peter Carl Fabergé's engaging jeweled baubles and extraordinary enameled objects as well as the exquisite gold boxes and jewelry that are stocked at this gallery. Founded in 1865 by Mr. Snowman's grandfather Morris Wartski, who emigrated from Byelorussia to Bangor, Wales, the gallery prospered selling jewelry and silver. Morris Wartski died at ninety-four in 1945 in Llandudno, Wales, where the gallery was.

In 1909, Morris Wartski's daughter Harriet married Emanuel Snowman, and a year later Snowman opened a branch of Wartski in London on Bond Street. Queen Mary shopped there, and, at Wartski's other galleries, so have Queen Elizabeth the Queen Mother and the Prince and Princess of Wales.

Russian jewels, works of art and Fabergé became a major specialty under Emanuel Snowman, who visited Russia in 1925 and was the first person the Soviet Government allowed to export Russian art works. In the 1930s Fabergé animals, carved of semiprecious stones and fitted with diamond and ruby eyes, were sold at Wartski's for one to five pounds each, then the equivalent of $25 to $60 each. Today's price? Add about three zeros.

When Emanuel Snowman died at eighty-four in 1970, A. Kenneth Snowman took over the gallery. He had completed his studies at London's University College School and trained as a painter. He has exhibited at the Royal Academy.

Mr. Snowman organized the 1977 Fabergé exhibition at the Victoria and Albert Museum in London and was guest curator of the 1983 Fabergé exhibition at the Cooper-Hewitt Museum in New York. The popularity of these exhibitions helped propel values of Fabergé's imperial Easter eggs to seven figures in widely publicized auctions.

Two of Mr. Snowman's four books, written since the 1950s, are on the Russian jeweler.

Mr. Snowman's prominence as an authority on Fabergé led to his involvement in a legal action after his 1977 authentication of a Fabergé work that was auctioned by Christie's in Geneva. The auction house described the work before the sale as an imperial Easter egg and Mr. Snowman concurred. He continues to say that the egg is authentic, but he has now dropped the word "imperial" in his description. Shortly before the egg was to be auctioned again at Christie's in New York in 1985, he publicly stated that the egg was a work made by Fabergé that had been "elaborately sophisticated," by which he meant that people other than Fabergé had added to it.

Mr. Snowman's two books on antique gold boxes cover the sort of precious works that Wartski stocks. A past chairman of the British Antique Dealers' Association, he is a founder of the Burlington House Fair, which is held every other year, and has been its chairman since 1984.

Wartski's clients at this shop have included most major collectors of Fabergé and fine gold boxes. Malcolm Forbes, the publisher, who has amassed one of the world's largest and most important private collections of Fabergé, bought two eggs for $2.16 million here in 1979. They were the exquisite 1897 Coronation Egg and the delicate pink enameled 1898 Lilies of the Valley Egg. Other clients have included Jayne Wrightsman, the William S. Paleys, members of the Whitney and Astor families. Jacqueline Kennedy Onassis, Frank Sinatra and Marjorie Merriweather Post.

One-third of Wartski's stock is Fabergé, one-third is antique gold boxes (made in France, England, Germany, Austria, Scandinavia and Russia) and the remainder is period jewelry and silver, Mr. Snowman said. The Castellanis and Giulianos, the 19th-century jewelers who excelled at interpreting ancient Egyptian, Greek and Roman jewelry, are represented. Geoffrey Munn of this gallery is usually on hand to explain the material, about which he has written extensively.

RAINER ZIETZ

39 Tite Street
London SW3 4JP
England
Phone: (44-1) 352-0848
Hours: By appointment

"Art history is not something of the past; it is for today," said Rainer Zietz, a dealer-collector born in 1944 in Bad Lauterberg, the son of a physician. He studied at the University of Heidelberg, majoring in European and Far Eastern art history and archeology. After completing his studies in the late 1960s, he became interested in 20th-century modern design and was among the first to handle the early-20th-century furniture and silver designs of Josef Hoffmann, the Austrian architect, and his Viennese colleagues in the Wiener Werkstätte.

In 1969 Mr. Zietz left Heidelberg for Hanover to become a dealer, stocking mostly much older things. He handled Venetian 15th- and 16th-century glass, medieval art and Italian and French Renaissance works of art, selecting them in private collections and at auctions.

In 1978 he was among the most active bidders at the Baron Robert von Hirsch sale at Sotheby's in London, purchasing medieval art for several West German museums, including the Museum of Applied Arts in Berlin, the Herzog Anton Ulrich Museum in Brunswick and the Museum für Kunst Gewerbe in Hamburg. He bought the most expensive object in the sale, a Mosan medallion, for $2.2 million.

By then, although still living in Hanover, he kept an apartment in London. He moved to London in 1980. He said dealers have a responsibility to do more than sell a work of art—they should help people acquire collections.

Mr. Zietz's richly appointed gallery-home includes examples of virtually all the periods and types of works of art that he has sold over the last 20 years. An eclectic mix of English, French and Neo-Gothic furniture is combined with Renaissance bronzes, tapestries, gleaming silver vessels and outsize vintage ceramics.

"Ninety-five percent of what I sell goes to museums,"

he said, taking a long puff on his inevitable cigar. He buys against the trends, he said, and assembles sizable numbers of the works he seeks, then sells the collection to one source, telescoping into many months or a few years what it usually takes collectors decades to accomplish. This is what he did with the 15th- and 16th-century majolica collection of 28 pieces that he sold to the J. Paul Getty Museum in Malibu in 1984. These colorful pottery vessels, platters, pharmacy jars and bowls, which are embellished with boldly drawn portraits, scenes, stylized fruits and flowers and classical motifs, had been out of fashion since before World War I and have now made a comeback.

Uncommon works he has handled before they became even moderately noticed include French 18th-century Palissy pottery, migration-period jewelry from the 6th to 10th centuries and Viking and Celtic works of art. He also stocks African sculpture and Carlo Molino's 1950s furniture and 1950s and 1960s Scandinavian, Italian and Czechoslovak glass.

Mr. Zietz says he deals in objects for beginning collectors with a small budget as well as what he calls "unique masterpieces that fill the gaps in the collections of the world's leading museums." Prices range from what is considered moderate in various categories, he said, without being specific except in the area of Florentine majolica, where they go from $10,000 for a 15th-century glass bottle to seven figures for antiquities and medieval art works.

LONDON SILVER VAULTS

Chancery House
53-63 Chancery Lane
London WC2 A1QS
England
Phone: (44-1) 242-3844
Hours: 9:30 A.M. to 5 P.M. Monday to Friday, 9 A.M. to 12:30 P.M. Saturday

The London Silver Vaults is a complex housing the shops of 35 silver and jewelry dealers both on the main floor and in vaultlike spaces two floors below street level. Each dealer offers a different mix of antique, secondhand and modern sterling and silver-plated wares. The building has become one of the more popular tourist attractions in London, a space its tenants sometimes refer to as Aladdin's Cave.

The underground warren of shops was opened a few doors away from its present site in 1885 as the Chancery Lane Safe Deposit. Its strongrooms and safes were rented to professionals, merchants and others who were traveling abroad and wanted safe storage areas for documents, jewelry and other valuables. Jewelry dealers nearby soon dominated as tenants, using the spaces for stowing valuables at the end of each business day. Later, an increasing number of silver dealers moved in, and by World War II some had opened shops there. The building was partly destroyed by bombing during the blitz, and a new building was completed in 1953.

Most of the dealer-tenants offer silver and Sheffield plate objects and jewelry at moderate prices. The range goes from $6 up for a wine coaster or $10 and up for a napkin ring but is usually high, in three or four figures for anything of more than souvenir quality. Although earlier wares are sold here, the focus of most dealers is Victorian and 20th-century silver.

BURLINGTON HOUSE FAIR

Royal Academy of Arts
Burlington House
Piccadilly
London W1V ODS
England
Phone: (44-1) 734-9052
Hours: 11 A.M. to 8 P.M. opening day, 11 A.M. to 7 P.M. other days

For advance information:
Burlington House Fair
6 Bloomsbury Square
London WC1 A2LP
England
Phone: (44-1) 430-0481

This 12-day fair in early September begins on a Wednesday and runs through two weekends. It and the Grosvenor claim roots in the 1934 Antique Dealers' Fair, which was held at the Grosvenor House Hotel in mid-June every year through 1978 except during World War II. In 1979 a hotel strike kept the fair from opening, and the Burlington House Fair was begun the next year at the Royal Academy of Arts. It is now held in odd-numbered years, alternating with the Biennale Internationale des Antiquaires in Paris. Representatives of *Burlington Magazine,* the art publication, sit on the board of the fair and have a voice in what is shown and by whom. The name Antique Dealers' Fair is registered and usable only by Burlington Fair.

The fair is under the patronage of Queen Elizabeth the Queen Mother and offers the wide-ranging stocks of more than 60 dealers from Britain, the Continent and the United States. On view in their booths are a handsome, eclectic mix of offerings: European Old Masters, Oriental and Middle Eastern art and British and Continental furniture, ceramics, silver and decorations, all in the very British setting of the glorious 1760s interiors of the Royal Academy.

Admission is about $10 opening night and about $8 thereafter.

GROSVENOR HOUSE ANTIQUES FAIR

Grosvenor House
Park Lane
London W1 3AA
England
Phone: (44-1) 499-6363 only during the fair
Hours: 5 to 8 P.M. opening day, 11 A.M. to 8 P.M. Monday to Friday, 11 A.M. to 6 P.M. Saturday and Sunday

For advance information from the sponsor:
British Antique Dealers' Association
20 Rutland Gate
London SW7 1BD
England
Phone: (44-1) 589-4128

Organized by:
Evan Steadman & Partners Ltd.
The Hub
Emson Close, Saffron Walden
Essex CB1 01HL
England
Phone: (44-7) 992-6699

This 11-day fair opens on a Wednesday in early or mid-June each year and runs through two Saturdays. It and the Burlington House Fair both claim roots in the 1934 Antique Dealers' Fair, which was held at the Grosvenor House Hotel each year through 1978 except during World War II. Renamed the Grosvenor House Antiques Fair in the early 1970s, the show was canceled in 1979 because of a hotel strike. The Grosvenor House Antiques Fair returned in 1983 and has had an attendance of as many as 15,000.

The 86 dealers exhibiting offer some extraordinary selections and are said to do an excellent business at this fair, more than at the Burlington. The smaller and larger booths on the two levels of the ballroom are stocked with mostly English furniture, but some European and Oriental furniture is seen. Other dealers show British, Continental and Oriental ceramics, silver, metal wares and decorations.

A preview party is held from 7 to 9:30 P.M. on Tuesday before the opening. Tickets are $75 and available from the organizers. Admission thereafter is about $12.

CHRISTIE'S

8 King Street
St. James's
London SW1 Y6QT
England
Phone: (44-1) 839-9060
Office hours: 9 A.M. to 5 P.M. Monday to Friday
Viewing hours: 9 A.M. to 4:30 P.M. Monday to Friday
Sales: September to July

CHRISTIE'S SOUTH KENSINGTON

85 Brompton Road
London SW7 3LD
England
Phone: (44-1) 581-7611
Viewing hours: 9 A.M. to 7 P.M. Monday, 9 A.M. to 5 P.M. Tuesday to Friday
Sales: Year-round

PHILLIPS

7 Blenheim Street
New Bond Street
London W1Y OAS
England
Phone: (44-1) 629-6602
Hours: 9 A.M. to 5 P.M. Monday to Friday, 9 A.M. to noon Saturday, special sales noon to 5 P.M. Sunday
Sales: Year-round.

SOTHEBY'S

34-35 New Bond Street
London W1A 2AA
England
Phone: (44-1) 493-8080
Hours: 9 A.M. to 4:30 P.M. Monday to Friday, noon to 5 P.M. some Sundays
Sales: September to July

MUNICH

BERNHEIMER

Lenbachplatz 3
8000 Munich 2
West Germany
Phone: (49-89) 59-66-43
Hours: 10 A.M. to 5:30 P.M. Monday to Friday

More than a few turn-of-the-century antiques dealers were giants and a different breed from those we see today. Some became so powerful and their stocks were so varied that their establishments resembled palatial department stores filled with an abundance of antiques and art treasures of many centuries and a score of cultures.

That kind of extraordinary business is what Lehmann Bernheimer developed in a dignified high-ceilinged house he built in 1889 a few blocks from the store he opened in 1864. Still housing the business today, it has marble floors, a sweeping staircase and ballroom-size galleries.

The original store's site, now in the center of downtown Munich but then on the city's outskirts, was chosen, or so the story goes, because it was where the dealer had gone with his father to peddle wares in a street market when he was a boy.

The business was lost to the Nazis after Kristallnacht, when the founder's son, Otto Bernheimer, and the entire family were taken to Dachau. Astonishingly, they were allowed to leave the country after the payment of a great deal of money.

After the war, Otto Bernheimer returned, and in 1950 the family began slowly rebuilding the business. His grandson Konrad Bernheimer now heads the business, one of the largest antiques concerns in Germany. He said the five-story gallery's stock, impressive in size by most modern standards, is far smaller than it was at the turn of the century, when J.P. Morgan and William Randolph Hearst shopped here. He said he wouldn't have it otherwise. "Today we think quality is more important," he added. His two sisters, Iris and Maria, who own the business with him, agree.

Bernheimer's inventory of quality Oriental rugs, tapestries and textiles attracts buyers from throughout Europe and the United States. Collectors also shop here for Chinese porcelains, French and German Renaissance and European 18th-century furniture, Gothic and Renaissance sculpture and period decorations, including bronzes and majolica.

"We were the first ones to make an exhibition in the mid-1970s of kilims," Mr. Bernheimer said, entering the ballroom-size rug gallery where these tribal rugs were stacked and where an even larger number of room-size weavings were hung, including Herize, Tabrize, Bokhara, Turkoman, Kazak and Anatolian rugs. With the flick of a switch, the rugs a client wants to see are moved into the spotlight.

Bernheimer does a large business in decorative rugs from Persia, Turkey and China, and the areas in between. Mr. Bernheimer said prices go from $1,000 to about $125,000. Among the collector-type tribal weavings, prices start at about $250 for small pieces of camel trappings and bags. A fine Caucasian rug 6 feet by 9 would be about $25,000.

The Chinese porcelains here are the pictorial variety of the K'ang Hsi and Ch'ing periods, and they ranged from about $100 to about $100,000. The French furniture is formal, rich in inlays and embellished with gilded bronzes of the Louis XV and Louis XVI periods, at $2,500 to about $250,000.

In 1986 Bernheimer expanded, opening a shop in London in Mayfair, at 32 St. George Street.

BRIGANTINE

Turkenstrasse 40
8000 Munich 40
West Germany
Phone: (49-89) 28-48-16
Hours: 11 A.M. to 6:30 P.M. Monday to Friday
Closed for two weeks after Christmas

Monika Fahrenson's stock of French Art Nouveau, German and Austrian Jugendstil, Wiener Werkstätte and other turn-of-the-century decorative arts is one of the largest of the period in Munich. Most of the major designers are represented in her offerings of lighting, tableware, vases, jewelry, decorative sculpture and prints that were produced in France, Belgium, Germany, Austria and Denmark. She also handles later Art Deco wall lighting, Danish silver by Georg Jensen and decorative sculpture.

Mrs. Fahrenson's shop, which she has occupied since 1978, has a large selection of jewelry and buckles, cigarette cases, hat pins, pendants embellished with dragonflies, scarabs and flowers. The turn-of-the-century whiplash styling was visible in silver candelabra, lighting fixtures and decorative bronze figures and some Majorelle chairs. The organic shaping of a silver inkwell, a bronze figure of Loïe Fuller by Raoul Larche that functions as a lamp and the Emile Gallé vases and lamps were among the strongest examples of the Art Nouveau style on view. The Austrian architectural look of the Wiener Werkstätte appears in Josef Hoffmann's cobalt-tinted glass vases and silver vessels and in Michael Powolny's cherubic ceramic figures.

Prices range from about $25 for German and English turn-of-the-century decorative tiles to about $40,000 for a Gallé or Daum lamp.

EBERHART HERRMANN

Theatinerstrasse 42
8000 Munich 2
West Germany
Phone: (49-89) 29-34-02
Hours: 10 A.M. to 6 P.M. Monday to Friday, 10 A.M. to 1 P.M. Saturday
Closed for two or three weeks in August

Eberhart Herrmann was twenty-four years old and a lawyer in 1967 when he joined his mother in her Oriental rug shop, a business she started in 1953. They continued together until her death in 1979, developing what has become one of the world's most important sources for exceptional weavings, a place where many rug connoisseurs stop when they come to Munich. Mr. Herrmann moved to his two-story gallery in 1955, and in 1975 the area became a pedestrian zone.

"When I joined the business, I decided to buy only what I really like," Mr. Herrmann recalled, saying that his mother soon left most of the buying to him. "In that way I have no trouble selling anything in my stock."

In the late 1960s it was not possible to handle only collectors' carpets, but by the mid-1970s it was.

What Mr. Herrmann likes and stocks today is a wide-ranging selection of collectors' rugs—Persians, Chinese, Turkomans, Caucasians, Anatolians and tribal weavings—which an ever-increasing number of European, American and Middle Eastern buyers seek. Most date from the 18th and 19th centuries, but he has some classical rugs—"when they are very good"—that were woven earlier, in the 16th and 17th centuries. He also handles European tapestries and Oriental wall hangings.

Since 1978, Mr. Herrmann has organized exhibitions each October that are widely praised by experts and are documented in catalogues that quickly become collectors' items. In 1984 he exhibited about 100 rugs acquired over 12 months that included an astounding variety of weavings, many of exceptional quality and design. Among them were many notable for their glorious colors, their geometric or figurative patterns and their bold or subtle combinations of images. Most were impressive for their bold impact, fine condition and originality.

In that assemblage were Turkish, Caucasian, Persian Qashqai, Turkish, Turkoman and Chinese weavings as well as Tibetan pieces, Uzbekistan embroideries and Baluchs. Each category had different types of works, with the Persians including Afshars, Luris, Kurdish tribal weavings, a T-shaped salt bag, a Bijar and a Senneh kilim. There were outsize weavings and saddle bags, palace-quality floor coverings and tribal wall hangings.

What distinguishes the stock here from that of most other galleries, Mr. Herrmann said, is that he does not carry any weavings merely to appeal to those looking for rugs to decorate their homes or offices. "Just old is not enough; just decorative isn't either," he said. "We are selling art pieces. We are art dealers in the field of carpets and textiles."

Mr. Herrmann views rugs the way collectors and painters did before World War I, when Munich and Vienna were major centers for Oriental rugs. He said Matisse and other artists came to the 1910 Islamic art exhibition in the Glaspalast and came away talking about the extraordinary colors.

The prices range from $250 for a bag face to about $150,000 for early classical pieces that are extremely rare or in extraordinary condition. Some pieces may even cost more, he said without giving figures. He cited a late-16th-century Ottoman prayer rug he sold to the National Museum in Kuwait. But most of the rugs sold here are between $3,000 and $30,000.

FERDINAND NEESS

Franz Josephstrasse 19
8000 Munich 40
West Germany
Phone: (49-89) 33-30-89
Hours: 10 A.M. to 1 P.M. and 3 to 6:30 P.M. Tuesday, 3 to 6:30 P.M. Thursday and Friday, 10 A.M. to 1 P.M. Saturday and by appointment

Ferdinand Neess, a collector turned dealer, has one of the finest private assemblages of Art Nouveau furniture, lighting, decorative sculpture, porcelains and metalwork in the world. He began acquiring his collection in 1962, long before most Europeans even knew the name of the turn-of-the-century style. He has shopped the finest sources in Paris, Brussels, New York and Vienna and knows this material intimately.

For the most part he stocks accessories: ceramics, glass, bronzes, jewelry, tableware, silver vessels and boxes. His shop is a stunning and glittering white-walled showcase for precious objects.

Mr. Neess, a descendant of German industrialists, was in banking when he began collecting Art Nouveau. "I started collecting with French and German Art Nouveau," he said. "I learned by myself by attending museum exhibitions and meeting dealers. My personal taste is more inclined to French and German Art Nouveau and Symbolists than anything else."

When he began there were virtually no books on these subjects to guide collectors, he said, so whatever he learned was acquired through collecting.

GALERIE OSTLER G.M.B.H. "ALTE UND NEUE KUNST"

Ludwigstrasse 11
8000 Munich 22
West Germany
Phone: (49-89) 28-56-69
Hours: 2 to 6 P.M. Monday, 9 A.M. to 12:30 P.M. and 2 to 6 P.M. Tuesday to Friday, 10 A.M. to 2 P.M. Saturday

Munich's long love affair with Oriental rugs can be seen in part in some of its galleries, where many fine examples may be found. Herbert Ostler collaborated with Agidius Geisselmann, a painter, in writing *The Art of the Oriental Carpet and the Art of Modern Times,* which was published privately in 1980. It is a handsomely illustrated book based on an exhibition of rugs displayed with photographs of paintings, and it shows a relationship between 20th-century art and Oriental rugs.

Mr. Ostler, who has been in this business since 1954, has a selection of rugs from the 19th century and earlier at his large, dramatically lighted gallery. "I do not deal in decorative rugs; I have collectors' pieces only," he said. "I have many American customers who buy from me."

He has handled Persian 17th-century vase carpets, many 19th-century Shirvans, as well as Anatolian, Caucasian and Turkoman weavings.

An outstanding rug on one visit was a Turkoman with red embroidered flowers on white linen that was about $4,500. Prices range from about $500 for a Caucasian saddle bag or fragment to about $60,000 for a 17th-century Caucasian dragon rug or a 16th-century Mamluk rug.

GERHARD ROEBBIG

3 Prannerstrasse 5
8000 Munich 2
West Germany
Phone: (49-89) 22-75-09
Hours: 10 A.M. to noon and 4 to 6 P.M. Monday to Friday, 10 A.M. to 1 P.M. Saturday

Kardinal Faulhaberstrasse 15
8000 Munich 2
Phone: (49-89) 29-97-58
Hours: 10 A.M. to noon and 2 to 6 P.M. Monday to Friday, 10 A.M. to 1 P.M. Saturday

Gerhard Roebbig specializes in 18th-century German porcelains in his shop on Kardinal Faulhaberstrasse and handles 18th-century French and German furniture in the shop on Prannerstrasse, which he opened in 1972 when he was twenty-four years old. Mr. Roebbig studied to be a restorer of paintings and studied art history at Stuttgart University, he said, then became involved by chance with porcelains.

After a member of his family died, he was asked to examine some porcelains. "I was very impressed with the material, the quality and the different types." He has been buying and selling porcelains ever since. The most important works he carries are Meissens of the early period, 1710 to 1745, and he sometimes carries examples as late as 1760.

A rare pair of stoneware flasks that look like iron and were made by Böttger were about $55,000 the pair, he said. Another unusual work was a Meissen figure modeled by Georg Fritsche depicting an old Chinese man with a bird and dating from about 1732. Mr. Roebbig had four commedia dell'arte figures, the most valuable of which was a Harlequin nine and a half inches tall for $70,000.

"Collectors come here to buy," Mr. Roebbig said. He said serious buyers do not wait for him to call; they check his stock all the time because they know other collectors do, too. "There are quite a few young people who have become interested," he said. "Today dealers are no longer the only ones with knowledge. The collectors are very well informed."

Mr. Roebbig says research in dating porcelains has produced ways to identify which kind of porcelain was used. "When we know the minerals used, we can put a fairly exact date on a piece," he said.

Prices range from about $750 for small mid-18th-century Meissen figures to high in six figures. The biggest problem Mr. Roebbig has these days, he said, is finding choice examples. "This year only 20 percent of what was offered a year ago came on the market," he said.

SCHLAPKA KG

Gabelsbergerstrasse 9
8000 Munich
West Germany
Phone: (49-89) 28-86-17
Hours: 10 A.M. to 6 A.M. Monday to Friday, 10 A.M. to noon Saturday

Since 1979, Axel Schlapka has specialized in Biedermeier furniture, the neo-classical architectural furniture style that swept Central Europe between 1815 and 1840. It was then that he opened his own antiques shop after working with his father, an Oriental-carpet dealer, for three years. His timing proved excellent because Biedermeier was just then beginning to increase dramatically in popularity throughout Europe and the United States.

Mr. Schlapka is now one of the most knowledgeable dealers specializing in the style and is able to identify the makers of most pieces by their carving, woods and finishes. Until recently, he said, most of his customers bought Biedermeier furniture to live with, not to collect. "This is a new field for collectors," he said, noting that he stocks pieces only up to 1840.

What Biedermeier buffs admire are the light woods, the neo-classical taste and the architectural detailing—pediments, gables and columns—in the commodious clothes cupboards, secretaries, cabinets, parlor tables, settees and chairs.

"The style was more glamorous in Austria than in Germany," he said at his two-story shop. It was only in southern Germany that cabinetmakers ebonized columns, the edges and feet or used ebonized inlays and veneers, he said.

German furniture producers in the south favored cherry and walnut; in the north, they used mahogany or, when a lighter wood was desired, ash. Berlin craftsmen worked with birch, mahogany and cherry, he said, while in Austria, walnut was almost always preferred.

"A fine piece of Biedermeier will always be veneered," he said. "The most important pieces are not easy to find because few were made. Biedermeier furniture was bourgeois furniture. The people then were not very rich."

Mr. Schlapka sells mostly to Germans, and the majority of what he offers is acquired privately, he said. The armoires are $3,000 to $15,000, chests of drawers are $2,000 to $3,250 and secretaries are $4,000 to $15,000. Sets of four or six chairs are $750 to $1,500, settees are $3,500 to $10,000 and center tables range from $3,000 to $7,000.

KUNSTHANDLUNG H. W. SELING

Oscar von Miller Ring 31
8000 Munich 2
West Germany
Phone: (49-89) 28-48-65 133698
Hours: 9 A.M. to 1 A.M. and 2 to 6 P.M. Monday to Friday

Helmut Seling, an Austrian-born dealer and expert in European silver, especially Augsburg, has been at this gallery since 1964. He is on hand most days selling or studying his own 17th-, 18th- and 19th-century silver and gold works and discussing these wares with students and collectors. His pursuit of these glittering vessels and utensils began in 1952 when he bought his first piece of silver, a teaspoon.

"I'm an art historian," Dr. Seling said at his gallery, where he produced from his library his most important work, *Augsburger Goldschmiede,* a three-volume study of the period published by C. H. Beck of Munich in 1980. It covers the masterpieces of what is considered to be the golden age of this art form.

Dr. Seling completed his art studies at Albert Ludwig University in Freiburg, then went to work in London at an art gallery that sold Dutch Old Master paintings. He returned in 1960 to write the Augsburg work and, a few years later, to open his shop.

"In those days it was much easier to find objects than it is now," he said. The collecting boom that sent prices for silver soaring reduced the supply swiftly, he added. Dr. Seling's inventory is small but choice compared with those of some London dealers. And he spends a great deal of time researching individual pieces or collections for others, including the early-16th- and 17th-century European gold and silver collected by J. P. Morgan at the Wadsworth Atheneum in Hartford, Conn. Dr. Seling's catalogue of the collection, which was not exhibited publicly until 1987, was completed for the exhibition.

The gallery's stock of English and Continental silver included an Augsburg 16th-century cup with cover by Jeremiah Nathan at $47,500, a late-19th-century German box used for cigarettes at $1,900 and a tiny teapot made in Cassel in 1780 by Isaac Beauclaire at $8,250. Among the most sought-after vessels are the coffee- and teapots, some with coats of arms. A set of a small coffeepot and a large one and a sugar bowl was $15,000. Prices range from $500 to about $75,000.

GALLERY WOLFGANG KETTERER

Briennerstrasse 25
8000 Munich 2
West Germany
Phone: (49-89) 59-11-81
Office hours: 8:30 A.M. to 1 P.M. and 2 to 5:30 P.M. Monday to Friday
Viewing hours: For main sales in June and November, 10 A.M. to 5 P.M. every day one week before the sales

This auctioneer has 10 sales a year, usually in April, May, June and November. All sales are on weekdays, and the main ones, in June and November, are on Monday, Tuesday and Wednesday.

The specialties are 20th-century art (especially German and Austrian Expressionists), decorative arts (Art Nouveau and Art Deco), books, tribal art from Africa and Pacific and pre-Columbian art.

PARIS

DIDIER AARON

118 Rue du Faubourg St.-Honoré
75008 Paris
France
Phone: (33-1) 47-42-47-34
Hours: 9:30 A.M. to 12:30 P.M. and 2:30 to 7 P.M. Monday to Friday
Closed in August

The Paris gallery of Didier Aaron, a major international dealer in French 18th- and early-19th-century furniture, occupies a five-story converted limestone mansion that dates to about 1840. The gallery, which was Pierre Cardin's showcase for his fashion collections in the 1950s and his furnishings in the 1970s, was taken over by Mr. Aaron in 1987. The interiors of this Restoration-style building have been transformed in the understated style of Jean-Michel Frank, the French decorator of the 1920s and 1930s who used all-wood backgrounds, preferably oak, in 18th-century-style interiors.

"We were the first in the 1960s to mix modern decoration with antiques, to use Charles Eames chairs with Louis XV commodes," Mr. Aaron said. The eclectic taste the dealer advanced more than 20 years ago, at the beginning of the antiques boom, helped a generation of collectors select dramatic examples of furniture, sculpture and decorations without regard to age or origin.

Mr. Aaron has counted among his clients Baron Edmond de Rothschild, Givenchy, Charles and Jayne Wrightsman, Barbara Piasecka Johnson, the J. Paul Getty Museum, the Metropolitan Museum of Art in New York and the Victoria and Albert Museum in London.

The stock is predominantly 18th-century French with a generous selection of rococo and neo-classical chairs, gilt-embellished writing-table-desks, Louis XV commodes faced with Chinese lacquer panels and Charles X center tables. In addition, there are life-size Italian Renaissance busts, elegant 18th-century English mirrors, weighty 17th-century Flemish cabinets and German Baroque ivory figures. "We buy all the time all over Europe," Mr. Aaron said, "and I think it is the biggest strength of the firm." Prices range from $1,000 for a Japanese lacquer box to $1.5 million for a Louis XV lacquer-faced commode by Desforges. The middle range of prices here is $30,000 to $50,000.

French 18th-century styles were just beginning to upstage all others in 1946 when Mr. Aaron, at the age of thirty-two, became a dealer. He was following in the footsteps not of his father, who was a banker, but of his mother, Jeanne Aaron, who dealt in Chinese art and was the daughter of a silver dealer. Didier Aaron had studied art and law and spent World War II in the French underground. He started out selling knickknacks from a back room in his parents' Paris apartment, and from these modest beginnings the ebullient, eagle-eyed dealer became a major figure in the Paris trade, offering pedigreed, palace-quality antiques to aristocrats and tycoons of all nationalities.

By the early 1960s, French antiques shared the spotlight in international decorating with 20th-century modern. Both categories were well represented in Aaron's former mansion quarters at 32 Avenue Raymond-Poincaré, his gallery from 1969 to 1987. The design and sales staff there numbered about 30, as it does now.

Both of the dealer's sons, Olivier and Hervé, have joined him in the business, with Olivier in charge of paintings (Old Masters, 18th and early 19th century) in Paris, and Hervé heading the New York branch since it opened in 1977. In 1985 Didier Aaron added another city to his conquests: London, opening in a three-story space in St. James's.

Didier Aaron's taste is visible in all these galleries. But there are differences, especially between Paris and New York. The former is filled with mostly French 18th-century designs, furniture in the grand style, grand antiquaire. In addition, there are a small number of earlier and later designs, from the 17th century and the early 19th century. New York offers antiques of taste, antiquaire de goût, with a strong emphasis on the first half of the 19th century.

"We both do decorating, we both do Old Master paintings," Hervé Aaron said, adding that the New York gallery also offers late-19th-century paintings; Paris does not.

SEE New York: *Didier Aaron, page 33*

SEE London: *Didier Aaron, page 183*

AVELINE

20 Rue du Cirque
75008 Paris
France
Phone: (33-1) 42-66-60-29
Hours: 9:30 A.M. to 7:30 P.M. Monday to Saturday
Closed in August

The extravagant taste of Jean-Marie Rossi, a towering figure of a man with a flamboyant manner, are evident everywhere in the crowded rooms on two floors of Aveline. Outsize mid-18th-century famille rose vases dramatized the entranceway, an area rich in furnishings embellished with gilding and mother-of-pearl. A 17th-century pair of gilded iron pedestals were used to display busts of two Roman emperors.

Notable in a gallery on the floor above were a 19th-century mahogany desk by Bellanger, its legs robustly carved as griffins with lion's-paw feet, and a superb Louis XVI console embellished with Japanese lacquer panels arranged asymmetrically on its front. The cabinet, framed in bands of gilded bronze topped with marble and fitted on the sides with shelves fenced with lacy ormolu, is a signed work by Claude Charles Saunier. Mr. Rossi was asking $400,000 for it. The stock also included a barometer by Roentgen and a pair of Empire pedestals enhanced with gilded metal mounts by Pierre-Philippe Thomire.

Mr. Rossi switched from law studies to antiques when he was twenty-six years old after he had furnished his parents' home with period artifacts. In 1956 he and Maurice Aveline founded Aveline. Mr. Rossi assumed full command after Mr. Aveline retired in 1976.

The price range goes from about $10,000 for a piece of

Louis XIV porcelain to more than $1.5 million for a Martin Carlin commode embellished with plaque de Sèvres.

The dealer says it seems to be nearly impossible to find exceptional furniture and decorations. His shop is visited by virtually all the museums and the major collectors of French 18th-century cabinetmakers' prizes. Mr. Rossi has sold to many museums, including the Grand Trianon at Versailles, the Louvre, the Nyphemburg Museum and the J. Paul Getty Museum in Malibu, Calif. Among the collectors he has served are Baron Hans Heinrich Thyssen-Bornemisza, the Swiss industrialist; Giovanni Agnelli of Fiat; and Antenor Patiño, the Bolivian tin industrialist.

JACQUES BARRÈRE

36 Rue Mazarine
75006 Paris
France
Phone: (33-1) 43-26-57-61
Hours: 2 to 7:30 P.M. Tuesday to Saturday
Closed in August

Jacques Barrère has been an Oriental art dealer since 1966, when he joined his family's business. He and his wife, Marie, have been on their own at this address since 1978.

When Mr. Barrère began buying and selling Oriental art, he focused on Ming bronzes and cloisonné vases. He visited Japan in 1970 and sold many pieces to the Arita Pottery Museum in Kyushu. He has since traveled five times to Japan to study Japanese art and to see clients interested in Japanese porcelains and Chinese antiquities. Today his gallery offers a much larger range of Oriental art wares—Han and Tang pottery and figures, ancient Shang and Chou bronzes, Kakiemon porcelains from Japan, cormandel screens, Ming lacquer wares and 18th-century Chinese furniture.

"The market for Chinese and Japanese art was built in France before World War II," Mr. Barrère said. After French artists discovered Oriental art in the late 19th century, French designers, decorators and art dealers helped popularize this material and furthered the collecting of works from the 16th to the 19th centuries.

The variety of wares stocked by Mr. Barrère reveals both his eclectic taste and the difficulties a dealer has today in finding sufficient marketable period works in fewer categories. He had 17th-century Chinese lacquers and 18th-century Chinese altar tables, a 17th-century 12-panel coromandel screen, Tang horses, ancient Chinese wine vessels and Japanese porcelains. In 1987 he began to concentrate more on Chinese archeological works, neolithic through Wei period pieces.

Dominating the shop was a two-ton Buddha, an early Ming bronze from Beijing that is 10 feet tall. The temple relic was brought to Paris by a French general in 1907. Mr. Barrère said he had refused many offers to buy it, adding that the price that might persuade him to part with it would be about $1 million. The bulk of Chinese and Japanese works are far more moderate, starting with small Japanese porcelains for about $3,000, ancient Chinese bronze vessels for $80,000 and Tang horses at up to $300,000.

BEURDELEY

200 Boulevard St.-Germain
75007 Paris
France
Phone: (33-1) 45-48-97-86
Hours: 10 A.M. to noon and 2:30 to 7 P.M. Tuesday to Saturday
Closed July 20 to Sept. 6

Massive 19th-century Japanese mortars function as chairs and a table in the upstairs gallery at this establishment, where Jean-Michel Beurdeley and his father, Michel Beurdeley, began receiving clients in 1963. The elder Mr. Beurdeley, who came into the business in 1936, is now an expert at Paris auction rooms and does appraisals.

The mortars from Okada and everything else at this Oriental art gallery—Tang funerary vases, Chinese bamboo brush holders, an outsize 14th-century Siamese pottery bowl and an 11th-century Burmese temple Buddha—convey a sense of earthiness that lingers long after a visit to the two-story premises.

Most of the sculpture was from the 8th to 13th centuries, was carved from wood and stone and came from Southeast Asia. It included Khmer, Indonesian, Javanese and Chinese works. The Thai carvings were 13th century or later and Champa sculpture (from what is now Vietnam) dated to before the 10th century. One Japanese 17th-century Shinto painting of a Zen deity painted by Hakuin is a work Mr. Beurdeley described as popular art.

The younger Mr. Beurdeley has an eye for the extraordinary in all the areas he stocks, no matter the age, scale or country of origin, as could be seen in richly glazed brown, green and white Tang eighth-century funerary vases and urns, a blond-wood 19th-century Chinese desk, a huge Siamese pottery bowl or a six-inch Ming hourglass-shaped blue-and-white vase.

Prices range from about $1,000 for an 18th-century bamboo brush holder depicting a landscape with a man on a horse, to about $1.3 million for a third-century big bronze drum from Southeast Asia.

"Today you must go out and find the pieces and find the customers," Mr. Beurdeley said, adding that he travels a great deal and this represents a change from the way the art and antiques business once operated. "To find the objects is the exciting part; to sell, not at all."

GALERIE MARIA DE BEYRIE

23 Rue de Seine
75006 Paris
France
Phone: (33-1) 43-25-76-15
Hours: 2 to 7 P.M. Monday, 10 A.M. to 1 P.M. and 2 to 7 P.M. Tuesday to Saturday
Closed in August

Maria de Beyrie began selling Art Nouveau furniture by Louis Majorelle and Hector Guimard and Art Deco and 20th-century furniture by architects in 1970 from her space at Les Halles. From the outset she sold to such museums as the Quai d'Orsay Museum and the Virginia Museum of Fine Arts in Richmond. In 1980 she moved to her present location, where she stocks 1920s and 1930s European modern furniture, most of it by architects and some by designers.

She has chairs and tables by Gerrit Rietveld, Jean-Michel Frank, Robert Mallet-Stevens, Herbert Bayer, Paul Iribe, Pierre Chareau, Pierre Legrain and Emile-Jacques Ruhlmann. Outstanding among these designs were a mechanical chair by H. V. Metz & Company, a steel-and-wood chair with a canvas seat by Anton Lorenz at $3,000, an aluminum chair with a wood seat by Marcel Breuer and a zinc-framed chair with a white cloth sling seat and back by Mallet-Stevens.

René Herbst, a 1920s French designer whose name is still virtually unknown in New York—he was the leader of the Union of Modern Artists—was represented with a metal-frame chair with elastic banding replacing upholstery. Chareau's spare design in an ingenious mahogany console, a precursor of the Parsons table, had pull-out panels at the ends and swing out shelves. Paul Iribe and Pierre Legrain worked together on a stunning and stylish chaise longue covered in button-down satin that echoes, with its spare Macassar ebony frame and square legs, Legrain's interest in African tribal art.

Prices range from about $1,500 for a chair by Adolf Loos to about $220,000 for a fireplace frame by Hector Guimard.

CAMOIN

9 Quai Voltaire
75007 Paris
France
Phone: (33-1) 42-61-82-06
Hours: 10 A.M. to 1 P.M. and 2:30 to 7 P.M. Monday to Saturday
Closed in August

Alain Demachy's establishment is a stunning stage for antiques and period decorations. The entrance is dominated by a double staircase displaying chandeliers, sconces, paintings and sculpture, an architectural device that adds excitement to any interior.

"I studied architecture," Mr. Demachy said during a tour of his gallery, which shows his special talent for interior design and decoration and his eye for theatrical furniture. He decided to pursue commercial interior design and began in 1955 with Didier Aaron. Mr. Demachy made a dramatic switch in 1980, when he was offered Camoin, a very famous antiques gallery that dates to the turn of the century. He had two days to accept the offer of the owners to buy the shop or not, he recalled. "I had told them once, if you decide to sell, call me—never thinking they would," he said. "It was like a revolution in my life. I decided to be more of an antiques dealer than a designer."

He has never regretted the move, he said. "I want to be eclectic. I want to enjoy, be happy. I don't want to be one period. My taste is simple." He favors the classicism of the late 18th century. "Weisweiler, Riesener, Canabas, Leleu is my taste," he said. He demonstrated the special delights of a late-18th-century table by Cramer, pulling out the leaves like the writing surface of a desk.

The house is large, with many galleries filled with curious furnishings: clocks with gilded mounts, a small Louis XV love seat, malachite accessories, Chinese paintings, English bookcases, French chairs with balloon seats, a Venetian cabinet and a big English cabinet from the mid-19th century. "It was a gift for Victoria the Queen by a Lyons cabinetmaker," he said.

Mr. Demachy has many desks—French 18th century, Charles X, English ones, too. There was a Carlo Bugatti design for a wardrobe with copper, painted leaves and flowers on glass panels and amusing hieroglyphics in metal. The asking price was $80,000 he said.

Most of the antiques here range from $1,650 to $25,000, but some treasures may run as high as $170,000 or even much more.

ARIANE DANDOIS

61 Rue des Sts.-Pères
75006 Paris
France
Phone: (33-1) 42-22-14-43
Hours: 10 A.M. to 12:30 P.M. and 2 to 7 P.M. Tuesday to Saturday
Closed in August

Ariane Dandois, a dealer in highly decorative and offbeat Japanese, Chinese and European furniture, was in public relations before she became an antiques dealer in 1974. At her gallery she shows Japanese and Chinese chests combined sometimes with English or French bases, Japanese screens, Italian and Russian furniture, English chandeliers and Indian sculpture.

Miss Dandois's eye for the most arresting lacquerwork is exceptional. She showed a traveling early-17th-century shogun's cabinet, awash with geometric detailing and his crest, standing on an early-17th-century English base. Another black lacquer cabinet decorated with a landscape was resting on an elaborately carved and gilded English base. There were Chinese coromandel lacquer cabinets on English bases and a rare 18th-century Japanese brown lacquer cabinet, its front surface depicting cranes with bamboo, a pine tree and the love sign of a turtle with a long tail.

Nearby was an amusing Japanese 19th-century bronze turtle, one of many highly decorative bronzes of the period stocked by Miss Dandois. A pair of Ming chairs and a Chinese table dramatized the shopwindow, Japanese screens decorated two walls and nearby were two pairs of huge English wooden urns and a 19th-century mahogany Russian writing table with elaborately carved animal-paw feet and gilded detailing.

Lacquer trays crafted in Japan in the 18th and 19th centuries are memorable here, whether decorated with exquisitely worked leaves on the underside and fruits on the top or with many squares of Japanese poems. They range from $6,000 to $9,500.

Japanese screens are another specialty, and the gallery stocks an impressive selection of about 100. "I am selling 60 percent to Americans," she said, adding that prices range from about $15,000 to $200,000. There was a 12-panel coromandel screen as well, an early-17th-century, nine-foot-tall design showing court scenes, musicians and calligraphy, its base dramatized by boldly carved cutouts. It was $250,000.

Prices start at about $1,000 for a small bronze or a basket. Lacquered chests range from $30,000 to $100,000, and the most important works may command up to about $250,000,

GALERIE JEAN-JACQUES DUTKO

5 Rue Bonaparte
75006 Paris
France
Phone: (33-1) 43-26-96-13
Hours: 2:30 to 7 P.M. Monday, 10:30 A.M. to 12:30 P.M. and 2:30 to 7 P.M. Tuesday to Saturday

When Jean-Jacques Dutko switched in 1971 from a career as a writer and executive in advertising and publicity to art and antiques, he focused on furniture and painting of the 18th century for the first three or four years. Then he added Art Nouveau furniture and glass by Daum, Gallé, Gabriel Argy-Rousseau and Décorchemont as well as Symbolist paintings. In 1978 he switched to the Art Deco period, preferring, he said, the simple architectural shapes.

The 1920s furniture he has stocked since then is by the top designers and producers: Jean Dunand, Emile-Jacques Ruhlmann, Pierre Chareau, Charlotte Perriand, Eileen Gray, Robert Mallet-Stevens, Coard, André Groult and Sabino. Eugène Printz, who Mr. Dutko thinks was "one of the most creative and inventive designers of the period," was well represented in the gallery's stock with desks, a vitrine, chests, armchairs and a buffet. The dealer has completed a book on Printz with Guy Bujon, a friend, a work being published by Editions du Regard of Paris. It is called *Printz.*

"I think in the next few years all the important Art Deco

furniture will be at the prices of French 18th-century furniture," Mr. Dutko said.

Mr. Dutko's taste is for the shimmering and voluptuous modern that was developed in Paris about 1925. Outstanding among the designs here were a round, glass-topped table with an S-shaped, chromed-steel base at $20,000, a metal-based minimal lamp by Jean Perzel at $10,000 and a wood bench in an X-shape by Coard at $20,000.

ANNE-SOPHIE DUVAL

5 Quai Malaquais
75006 Paris
Phone: (33-1) 43-54-51-16
Hours: 2:30 to 7 P.M. Monday, 11 A.M. to 1 P.M. and 2:30 to 7 P.M. Tuesday to Saturday

The furniture and lighting of some of the most important designers who worked in Paris and elsewhere in Europe from 1900 to 1940 are represented in the stock of Anne-Sophie Dumas, a dealer who has been buying and selling 20th-century designs since 1972 at this address.

The legacy of designs focuses mostly on the highly decorative and exquisitely finished modern known as Art Deco. But there are also tubular 1930s modern and turn-of-the-century Austrian architect's designs.

There was a high-backed squarish upholstered arm chair by Pierre Chareau covered with tapestry by Jean Lurçat for $6,000 and a stunning straw-covered table measuring 15 inches square by Jean-Michel Frank at $5,225. Jean Dunand was represented in a fireplace surround inlaid in metal in the dinanderie technique. Two chairs by Joseph M. Olbrich, the Viennese turn-of-the-century architect, in blue ash and decorated with gold are squarish precursors of Art Deco. They were $18,000 the pair.

The two chairs by Félix Aublet, a name not known outside of France, are splendid in their simplicity: black tubing bent in an exaggerated Z frames canvas seats and backs. They were $4,475 for the two.

B. FABRE & SONS

19 Rue Balzac
75008 Paris
France
Phone: (33-1) 45-61-17-52, 45-63-79-17
Hours: 9:30 A.M. to 12:30 P.M. and 2:30 to 7 P.M. Monday to Friday, by appointment Saturday

Jean-Paul Fabre, whose grandfather Basile Fabre founded the business almost a century ago, shares the management with his younger brother, Michel. They have been in charge since the death of their father, André, in 1965. Fabre's 17th- and 18th-century French chairs, tables, cabinets, desks, beds and consoles fill three floors of galleries in a 19th-century house that frames a courtyard. "We are a little bit away from most dealers, and most people come here by appointment," Jean-Paul Fabre said.

The gallery's impressive assortment of French designs range in price from $2,000 for the simpler Louis XV and Louis XVI chairs to $1 million for a Louis XIV bureau plat, a flat-topped writing table, probably by André-Charles Boulle, with curvaceous legs and drawer fronts elaborately embellished with inlay and gilded-bronze mounts.

An unusual Louis XVI guéridon, a round table with a double-decker top, has a writing surface and drawer hidden in its lower surface. A set of 12 late-18th-century Jacob side chairs include shapely, high-heeled legs and horseshoe-shaped backs.

Jacqueline Kennedy Onassis bought a set of Louis XVI chairs, painted white, during a visit to Fabre more than 20 years ago when she was decorating the White House.

"Every piece of furniture has its own story," said Jean-Paul Fabre. "Sometimes I've known a table, chair or desk for 10 to 18 years. Many return to us. It's a very small world, and we know the furniture and the people who buy it." What clients often request is total anonymity, he said. They cherish finding a piece of furniture that no one has seen for many years, a cabinet or carved table with excellent pedigree, in mint condition and a signature to add to its value. At Fabre, the brothers are often able to fulfill such requests.

Known for the best in late-18th-century furniture, the

Fabre brothers also stock examples that are more modest in quality. "Furniture must be the best—or have charm," he said.

Another specialty is period paneling, including rooms ranging in date from Louis XIV through Empire, which they restore and sometimes edit, or cut, for their clients. The J. Paul Getty Museum in Malibu, Calif., is one they have accommodated more than once. "Mr. Getty was a client of my family; this was how the museum first came to know us," the older Mr. Fabre explained. The large stock of paneling here includes Louis XIV through Empire rooms from Paris and throughout France.

JEAN GISMONDI

20 Rue Royale
75008 Paris
France
Phone: (33-1) 42-60-73-89
Hours: 3 to 7:30 P.M. Monday, 10 A.M. to 7:30 P.M. Tuesday to Saturday
Closed in August

The high-style French 17th-, 18th- and early-19th-century furniture stocked by Jean Gismondi—the inlaid cabinets, fall-front desks, gilded chairs and ormolu-embellished corner cupboards—glow with finishes as rich as when they were new.

Mr. Gismondi shares with most of his colleagues who handle the finest quality in French furniture the Gallic taste to restore everything to its original luster. Inlaid desks and cabinets in the Boulle style require the most meticulous handling to clean and polish the mother-of-pearl-inlaid surfaces so they shimmer.

Each material requires different skills, Mr. Gismondi explained, leading a visitor through his restoration workshops in Antibes in the south of France, where he has been since 1964 when he was twenty. Artisans work in a dozen rooms tending to the marble inlays of birds, fruits and flowers in an early-19th-century pietra dura tabletop; the gilded metal mounts used throughout the 18th century on a variety of pieces of furniture; the porcelain and the ivory panels on clocks, cabinets, chests and consoles, and the score of woods that veneer the surfaces of major works by French ébénistes.

Mr. Gismondi, maintains a large restoration staff to revive the 18th-century French designs (occasionally he adds an Italian marble-topped table or inlaid cabinet to his stock) that he offers at his Paris gallery. These artisans also mend tapestry coverings on 18th-century suites, like the set of six chairs and a sofa by Jean Baptiste Tilliard. Most of the period furniture stocked in Paris is shipped first to Antibes to freshen the finish or repair damage.

An Italian early-19th-century octagonal table with a pietra dura top was $24,000, and an early-19th-century ebony-inlaid marquetry-embellished Italian cabinet on a stand was $150,000.

Prices ranged from about $4,500 for a small Louis XV desk to "several million" French francs ($450,000) for a French cabinet by Charles Cressent.

KRAEMER

43 Rue de Morceau
75008 Paris
Phone: (33-1) 45-63-24-46
Hours: 11 A.M. to 7 P.M. Monday to Saturday (phone ahead in August)

Kraemer has been a name to be reckoned with in French period furniture since 1876, when Lucien Kraemer, an Alsatian born near Strasbourg, founded the family business. As a young man in the early 1870s when most of Alsace was incorporated into Germany, he went to Paris to remain a Frenchman. In Paris he worked with an uncle who was an important dealer in paintings and furniture. The small shop where he began on his own in 1876 is a far cry from the stone mansion, a hotel built in 1869, to which he moved his family and business in 1928.

Today this grand setting accommodates Kraemer's stock of lacquered, painted, gilded, marquetry-embellished and bronze-mounted French 18th-century pedigreed furniture and objects, some with royal provenance, on three floors and their private apartments on two floors.

After Lucien Kraemer's death in 1935, his son Raymond took over and headed the family business until his death in 1965. Philippe, Raymond's only son, is now in charge and shares the responsibilities of the business since the mid-1970s with his two sons, Olivier (born in 1953) and Laurent (born in 1957).

The selections on view in impressive period settings date from Louis XIV through Louis XVI. The galleries, which are embellished with 17th- and 18th-century tapestries, gilded mirrors, candelabra and porcelains, are furnished with commodes, chests, tables, desks and chairs by Boulle, Weisweiler and their contemporaries.

The Kraemers, who are extremely cordial, would not discuss prices. "We are very reasonable," Philippe Kraemer said without elaboration on what reasonable means except to say vaguely: "The price is an accident." Clients? "We never say to whom we sell and from whom we buy."

J. KUGEL

279 Rue St.-Honoré
75008 Paris
France
Phone: (33-1) 42-60-86-23, 42-60-19-45
Hours: 10 A.M. to 1 P.M. and 2:30 to 6:30 P.M. Tuesday to Saturday

Jacques Kugel preferred to be known as a general dealer, and his shop, with its 18th-century furniture, choice curios, porcelains and prized silver objects, certainly illustrated his point. The walls glittered with rococo candelabra. Tabletops groaned with Renaissance bronzes. Throughout the gallery were dozens of armillary spheres and globes, once used for studying the earth and heavens. His taste was for extraordinary objects, not the least of which were his 17th-century ivory pedestal-based cups sprouting covers with balls and spires—spires like those punctuating the skylines of his native Russia.

"I am really a collector myself and am obliged to sell to be able to buy something else," he said in an interview shortly before his death at the age of seventy-three in October 1985.

His sons, Nicolas and Alexis, both in their twenties, took over at the gallery, saying they intended to maintain it in the spirit of their father.

Jacques Kugel made it a point of telling his clients he never photographed his wares, never did research and paid only slight attention to pedigree. "For me, the art speaks for itself," he said.

His sons take a different approach. "We do a lot of research on the history of objects," Nicolas Kugel said.

He and his brother are the sixth generation of their family in the antiques business, with roots in Minsk. Their father settled in Paris in 1924 after leaving the Soviet Union with his father, who had specialized in silver and Russian objects.

The selection of antiques and art objects in the gallery, to which Jacques Kugel moved in 1971, included glittering 17th-century brass astrolabes, a pair of Chinese porcelain vases the color of lapis lazuli, tapestry-covered Louis XV armchairs and an early-18th-century Dutch cabinet with lacquered Chinese panels.

Nearby was an extraordinary pair of Louis XIV Boulle cabinets on stands. Behind the wall panels in the Kugels' office, lighted shelves display porcelain blackamoors, parrots, milk maidens and dishes. And, judging by the 18th-century ewers, trays, soup tureens, candlelabra and cups that filled a cabinet at the front of the shop, the Kugels continue to stock major works in silver.

Prices at the gallery range from about $2,000 for a French 18th-century silver beaker or wine taster's cup to "several hundred thousand dollars" for an important piece of furniture or object.

GEORGE LEFEBVRE

24 Rue du Bac
75007 Paris
France
Phone: (33-1) 42-61-19-40
Hours: 10:30 A.M. to noon and 2:30 to 6:30 P.M. Monday to Saturday
Closed in August

"My great-grandfather was an art dealer who handled everything, even jewelry," said George Lefebvre of Leon Lefebvre, adding that his grandparents founded the shop called Le Temps Jadis, 55 Rue Châteaudun, and they retired just before World War II.

Mr. Lefebvre, the fourth generation in his family to become a dealer, specializes in Chinese and European pottery, faïence and porcelain of the 16th through early 19th centuries. He said his father, Gaston, an expert with the French auction houses, bought the shop for him in 1953 when he was twenty-two, after he completed four years of studies as an art restorer at the Louvre.

The shop was chock-full of Chinese, French, German, Italian and Spanish Hispano-Moresque wares. There were Ming blue-and-white and famille verte bottles and vases, as well as China export wares, including armorial plates, bowls and cups. French Sèvres services and vases patterned with flowers were also on view. In some cases there may be as many as 50 or 60 plates of a single pattern, he said.

Some small and large Sèvres figures were on tabletops and in cabinets. The continuing revival of interest in French porcelain figures has been marked at this shop by a rapid turnover in such miniature sculptures from Vincennes and Sèvres. Now, Mr. Lefebvre said, collectors are looking more seriously at Dutch Delft and Italian majolica in response to the increased interest in bolder, more robust wares with colorful decoration. "We have one of the best stocks of Delft and majolica in Paris," he said.

The 18th-century porcelains available also include German examples—occasionally Meissen figures by Kändler, Strasbourg and Niderviller—as well as selections from French factories.

Prices range from about $350 for a French provincial faïence plate to about $55,000 for a major piece of Italian majolica.

ALAIN LESIEUTRE

55 Rue Vaneau, Second Floor
75001 Paris
France
Phone: (33-1) 42-22-79-13, 42-22-49-31
Hours: By appointment, 9 to 11 A.M.

GALERIE ALAIN LESIEUTRE

356 Rue St.-Honoré
75001 Paris
France
Phone: (33-1) 42-60-68-62, 42-97-28-63
Hours: 2 to 7 P.M.

Also at the Louvre des Antiquaires

Alain Lesieutre, an enterprising collector-turned-dealer, opened his first shop selling Art Nouveau and Art Deco in 1960. His success was swift because he had a sure eye for the most extraordinary art works and he had spent more than 30 years handling period works.

At his home, where he shows his finest pieces to collectors and museum curators by appointment only, one room was filled with works by the masters of the 20th-century decorative arts. There were silver table wares by Puiforcat, Jean Dunand's radio, Emile Gallé's glass lamps and vases. Notable too were a stunning sharkskin-covered table with ebony and palm wood by Clement Rousseau, vases in silver by Carlo Bugatti and a desk and chair by Jean-Michel Frank.

Mr. Lesieutre began collecting antiques and objects after he left the French navy in the mid-1950s when he worked for several years as a celebrated photographic model.

"I've been every day at the Drouot for 30 years," Mr. Lesieutre said. That compulsion to watch the art sales at the main auction house of Paris and buy whenever possible was awakened in 1954 when he was twenty-four and a runner for antiques dealers.

One of Mr. Lesieutre's earliest interests were the bronze and ivory figures of Demêtre Chiparus and Frederick Preiss. When he had the opportunity, he said, he bought the Chiparus atelier, which was stocked with great quantities of heads, hands, feet and busts of the figures that had been produced in unlimited editions when they were new in the 1920s. Mr. Lesieutre repaired figures that were damaged and assembled others with these parts and insisted: "Not even a professional can tell the difference."

Mr. Lesieutre is criticized for the bronzes but praised for his eye and his entrepreneurial skills. He knows where to find Paul Gauguin's ceramics, Ruhlmann's furniture, Dunand's vases, Gallé's lamps and vases, Pierre Legrain's Art Deco bookbindings and Hector Guimard's furniture.

Chiparus figures range from $4,500 to $22,200, 19th-century bronze animal figures from $2,200 to $15,000, 19th-century paintings from $7,500 to $45,000, furniture by Ruhlmann from $22,200 to $120,000 and Dunand vases from $15,000 to $45,000.

ETIENNE LÉVY

178 Rue du Faubourg St.-Honoré
75008 Paris
France
Phone: (33-1) 45-62-33-47

La Cour de Varenne
42 Rue de Varenne
75007 Paris
France
Phone: (33-1) 45-44-65-50
Hours: 10 A.M. to noon and 2 to 6:30 P.M. Monday to Saturday
Closed in August and Saturdays in January, July and September

Claude Lévy has a discriminating eye for French clocks and for virtually everything else made in France in the 18th and early 19th century: the desks, chairs, commodes, cabinets and tables made by the period's finest cabinetmakers.

"I like clocks," he said. "For me clocks are very special things, very amusing." One of the 10 timepieces he showed at the 1984 Biennale had a gilded-bronze monkey on top, another an ormolu elephant, a third was a Louis XV clock with a pendulum in a tall case that told the day as well as the minute and the hour. Clocks by such masters as Antide Janvier, Lepaute and Robin Leroy may be found here.

Mr. Lévy said his father, Etienne Lévy, founded the business in 1920 and he joined his father in 1949 at the age of nineteen. "He gave me this taste." His father retired in 1980. The gallery, in what Claude Lévy describes as a "not very old house," dating to the 19th century, is run by Claude and his wife, Anne.

After his academic studies, Mr. Lévy spent three years studying furniture-making to understand the techniques used by ébénistes (cabinetmakers), clockmakers and the bronze craftsmen who cast the metal mounts, chased the metal surfaces and gilded them.

The Lévys' taste is impressive, especially when it comes to clocks and offbeat furniture. This could be seen in a small mail table by Conrad Mauter, used for sorting mail about 1800, and an unsigned Louis XVI rolltop desk, a set of four Louis XVI chairs with lyre cutouts in their backs and an upholstered Louis XV easy chair with five legs.

Most of Mr. Lévy's stock is Louis XIV through Empire, but occasionally he shows earlier pieces. An extraordinary Italian 17th-century cabinet-on-stand has a lift-up top, inlaid lapis lazuli and agate decoration and carved faces of Roman emperors.

Prices range from $7,500 to $75,000.

GALERIE FÉLIX MARCILHAC

8 Rue Bonaparte
75006 Paris
France
Phone: (33-1) 43-26-47-36
Hours: 10 A.M. to 1 P.M. and 2:30 to 7 P.M. Monday to Saturday
Closed July 14 to Sept. 4

Félix Marcilhac was a law student in Paris in 1963 when he began buying Art Nouveau objects. In 1970 he opened a shop on Rue Bonaparte, where he holds forth today with a wide-ranging stock dating from the turn of the century to 1940. Since 1973 he has served as an expert for French auctioneers on Art Nouveau and Art Deco, areas in which he is now one of the most active dealers in the field, advising clients and museums in Europe, the United States and Japan.

Today the shop is dominated by the masters of the Art Deco movement. There were a pair of high-backed armchairs by Pierre Chareau, upholstered in plush and with seats and backs covered in pale-yellow-and-orange modern tapestry at $13,500 and two chairs by Eugène Printz at $6,750 the pair.

Nearby there were two sharkskin-covered tables by Jean-Michel Frank at $11,200, a metal floor lamp by Jean Perzel at $6,750 and a 1920s Thonet desk sheathed in shimmering nickel and glass, with three drawers on one side, a column on the other. Outstanding was a rosewood chiffonier of stunning simplicity on brass-tipped feet by Emile-Jacques Ruhlmann at $67,200. Prices here range from a low of $150 for a ceramic design by Georges

Hoentschel to $75,000 for an important work by Ruhlmann, for example.

In his role as an expert at auctions, Mr. Marcilhac authenticates works, identifies who made them and when and decides which are fakes. He sometimes is an agent for absent bidders in the sale of the most important works. At a 1985 auction of a rare lacquered furniture designed by Jean Dunand—a cube table and four chairs made in 1930 for Madeleine Vionnet, the French couturiere—Mr. Marcilhac, the expert at the sale, bid for the absent and unidentified buyer and acquired the set for $449,032, a record at auction then for 19th- and 20th-century furniture.

A year earlier in Tokyo, he rewrote the record for Art Nouveau glass at an auction of part of the collection of glass owned by the family of the manufacturer Daum, paying $290,000 for a Daum cone-shaped 1910 vase called *Nettle and the Spider—Homage to Victor Hugo.* Mr. Marcilhac made the purchase for the Kitizawa glass museum in Suwa, Nagano prefecture, a private museum established by a Japanese rubber producer that has assembled one of the finest collections of French Art Nouveau glass outside of France. Mr. Marcilhac was the adviser on that collection and wrote its catalogue.

What does Mr. Marcilhac covet for himself? The one category of works he does not offer as a dealer but collects with dedication and a connoisseur's eye is Art Deco bookbindings. He owns some extraordinary examples by Pierre Legrain, Georges Cretté, Paul Bonet, Jean Dunand and others, and, he says, he refuses to part with any of them.

NICOLIER

7 Quai Voltaire
75007 Paris
France
Phone: (33-1) 42-60-78-63
Hours: 10:30 A.M. to noon and 2:30 to 6:30 P.M. Tuesday to Saturday, appointment suggested
Closed in August

Virtually every period and style of European and Oriental ceramics made between the 9th and 19th centuries are represented at this inviting gallery. Pierre Nicolier explained that the family business was established in 1904 and has been at its Left Bank address ever since. Mr. Nicolier learned the business from his father, Jean Nicolier, and he and his brother, Philip, share the store's responsibilities.

Among the stunning assortment of ceramics lining the walls, filling the shelves and arranged on tabletops in Nicolier's warren of tiny rooms are Chinese Sung porcelain jars, European salt-glaze bowls, Italian majolica, French faïence and German 18th-century porcelains. There was a splendid pair of five-foot-tall Meissen partridges from about 1740, modeled by Kändler, the factory's sculptor.

Blue, always a favorite color for ceramics collectors in virtually every period, shows up in this shop in an assortment of extraordinary works. For example, there were a fine French 17th-century faïence sugar box from Rouen and an outsize 17th-century French faïence dish 20 inches in diameter and decorated in bold strokes of blue glaze with a memorable hunting scene from Moustiers.

French majolica, a product of Nîmes, is a rarity even at this source. Mr. Nicolier selected a 12-inch-tall 16th-century majolica vase, glazed in strong polychrome and with a head of a warrior on each side. It came from the Sigalon factory, and he called it "very important and extremely rare."

Prices start at $500 for a fine 18th-century Dutch Delft plate, a Meissen figurine or a Chinese blue-and-white dish.

PÉRINET

420 Rue St.-Honoré
75008 Paris
France
Phone: (33-1) 42-61-49-16
Hours: 11 A.M. to 7 P.M. Monday to Saturday

Michel Périnet, a jeweler since 1955 when he was fifteen years old, made new jewelry for 10 years. In 1965, people began bringing old jewelry to him so he could remove the stones, melt down the gold and create new pieces. That is how his interest in period jewelry was aroused. He began to buy period works then just as a revival of interest in jewelry of the Art Nouveau period was beginning. Over the years, Mr. Périnet became one of the most important sources in Paris for Art Nouveau, Art Deco and other period pieces.

Mr. Périnet stocks most of the major makers of the Art Nouveau period: René Lalique, Georges Fouquet and Vever. "Now they are all difficult to find," he said. The prices range accordingly from $10,000 to $100,000. During a recent visit, there was a Eugène Gaillard horn comb, ornamented with opals and a moonstone. "The artists want to see the sky, the sea and nature," Mr. Périnet said.

The dealer also handles 19th-century jewelry of the Charles X and Napoleon III periods. Later pieces include many by the major Art Deco makers—Raymond Templier, Vever, Cartier, Van Cleef and Boucheron—and works of the 1940s and 1950s as well. There were an Art Deco Cubist-style bracelet in coral and diamonds, a cameo brooch from about 1900, a bracelet that changed into a necklace, a rare Napoleon III period brooch showing African faces, an Art Nouveau horn comb with flowers; a blue aquamarine pendant by Vever from 1930 and an 1850s cross in green enamel, pink topaz and pearls.

RODOLPHE PERPITCH

52 Rue de Bac
75007 Paris
France
Phone: (33-1) 45-48-24-29
Hours: 2 to 7 P.M. Monday to Saturday

Paris decorative-arts dealers abandoned Art Nouveau by the 1980s and, by 1985, they were also looking past Art Deco to the 1950s and 1960s. The designs that Rodolphe Perpitch, a dealer since 1974, now shows in his shop at the corner of Boulevard St.-Germain are this sort of mixture, dating from 1910 through the 1960s.

There were some familiar designs: a table by Emile-Jacques Ruhlmann at $22,220, an armchair with curved arms and back by Otto Wagner at $1,480 and a straw-covered chest for a record player, 18 by 22 inches, by Jean-Michel Frank at $6,660. The designs of later periods included a 1930s hanging light fixture of glass and wood that produced ribbons of light and was designed by Minali, an Italian architect, and a 1950s pair of parchment-covered chests of drawers in treelike shapes by Biazzini Piacenza, also an Italian.

Most prices are from about $1,480 to about $45,000, Mr. Perpitch said.

JACQUES PERRIN

3 Quai Voltaire
76007 Paris
France
Phone: (33-1) 42-60-27-20
Hours: 2 to 7 P.M. Monday, 10 A.M. to 1 P.M. and 2 to 7 P.M. Tuesday to Saturday

Jacques Perrin's two-story shop overlooking the Seine is divided into small, elegantly furnished rooms. Mr. Perrin moved here in 1964, about eight years after becoming an antiques dealer, the first in his family. Now he has been joined in the business by his wife, Pierrette Nogatch, and his son, Patrick, a specialist in paintings.

The Perrin gallery offers many examples of the sort of designs that would enliven a room filled with 20th-century modern, whether it be Ludwig Mies van der Rohe's Barcelona table and chairs in gleaming steel and glass or Cini Boeri's voluptuous Italian Modern upholstery.

This is a shop for unusual furniture and paintings of the Louis XIV, XV and XVI periods. There were some wonderful offbeat tables, including a Louis XVI architect's table at about $40,000 and a Louis XVI games table fitted with many secret compartments and changeable tops for playing chess, backgammon, tric-trac and other games, at about $20,000. Even more arresting was a marble-topped, elaborately carved Louis XV console, serpentine in shape, with every leaf and shell detail painted or gilded. Mr. Perrin's price was $35,000.

Desks included a Louis XV flat-top, table-desk by Jean-François Leleu. The small desk, on cabriole legs with gilded-bronze sabots, had a sliding top that covered a leather-topped writing tablet. Another rarity was a Louis XVI fall-front cabinet-secretary embellished with a gilded-bronze frieze of rosettes, swags and foliage, its marquetry veneer depicting architectural landscapes. The interior, stamped Pierre Roussel, was special, too, decorated with trompe l'oeil trickery of still lifes and books.

Mr. Perrin, a former head of Antiquaires à Paris, the French antiques dealers' association, was among the first 14 foreign dealers to exhibit at London's Burlington House Fair, which alternates every other September with the Biennale Internationale des Antiquaires in Paris, where he also shows. At the Burlington fair in 1985, Mr. Perrin exhibited an 18th-century desk with a Versailles pedigree signed by B.V.R.B., for Bernard van Risamburgh, that carried a price tag of $750,000.

Mr. Perrin stocks period decorations, including pairs of candelabra mounted as lamps from $2,000 and as chandeliers from $10,000. The finest period furniture here may be as much as $700,000 for a superb Louis XVI ebony bureau signed by Montigny.

MAURICE SEGOURA

20 Rue du Faubourg St.-Honoré
75008 Paris
Phone: (33-1) 42-65-11-03
Hours: 9 A.M. to 7 P.M. Monday to Saturday

Like his father and grandfather before him, Maurice Segoura not only chose to become an antiques dealer but also decided to go his own way in this entrepreneurial business in which personal taste frequently spells success or failure.

The dealer's grandfather Sidi Segoura was born in Bulgaria, came to Paris in the 1880s and became a dealer in Persian art and manuscripts. His son, Vital, was an Oriental rug dealer.

In 1955, Maurice Segoura, then twenty-three and fresh from the army, decided to become a dealer in French 18th-century furniture and porcelains. "During my first 10 years I sold only to other dealers," he recalled. "I sold to the public only after I learned all the art objects of the 18th century." Mr. Segoura learned his lessons well. With this knowledge and the Segoura eye for detail, he became one of Paris's major French furniture dealers.

In 1968 Mr. Segoura opened his present gallery and has over the years handled scores of signed and unsigned pieces, many with aristocratic pedigrees. He has sold furniture to Jayne Wrightsman, widow of the oil industrialist Charles B. Wrightsman, and the J. Paul Getty Museum in Malibu, Calif.

"My specialty is Louis XVI when the legs are like the Louis XIV," he said, showing several examples during a tour of the three-story premises. "For a big connoisseur, the best of the art is Louis XIV." In the earlier Louis XIV period, he said, the basic elements of the French style are expressed most forcefully in the lacquered panels, the pietra dura surfaces and the gilded bronze mounts, details that are among the most innovative in French 18th-century furniture.

Mr. Segoura's stock included a gilded-bronze candelabra by Pierre-Philippe Thomire, a painted Louis XVI suite of six chairs and a sofa by Jean-Baptiste-Claude Sené and a Louis XIV Régence bookcase by Pierre Migeon.

The abundance of French furniture in this well-stocked gallery and in the marketplace raises the question of why there continues to be so much French 18th-century furniture available today. Mr. Segoura, drawing on his knowledge of the history of the late-18th-century French furniture trade, said: "During each year, 15,000 pieces were made; Riesener alone produced about 1,500 pieces. It was the most important industry in the second part of the 18th century."

Mr. Segoura said about 50 percent of what he sells stays in Europe, and the rest goes to the United States, "mostly to New York."

Prices range from about $2,500 for an 18th-century drawing box to about $1.2 million for a commode by B.V.R.B.—Bernard van Risamburgh.

JEAN SOUSTIEL

146 Boulevard Haussmann
75008 Paris
France
Phone: (33-1) 45-622-776
Hours: 10 A.M. to 7 P.M. (except lunchtime) Monday to Friday and by appointment
Closed in August

"We try to be 10 years ahead of the market," Jean Soustiel said, explaining that he had handled Islamic art works, turn-of-the-century Orientalist paintings of Middle Eastern subjects by Europeans, Indian miniatures and Turkish art in 1963, when these art works were out of fashion. That was the year Mr. Soustiel joined his father, Joseph Soustiel, in the family art business that his grandfather Maurice Soustiel had founded in Istanbul in 1883. The grandfather's stock included many of the same types of artworks that Jean Soustiel has handled. Joseph Soustiel retired in 1983 after 57 years in the business.

Mr. Soustiel's offbeat tastes in objects include virtually all areas of Islamic and Turkish art—manuscripts, metalwork, ceramics, calligraphy, textiles—but he does not handle rugs. The dealer prefers a modest display of what he owns in the cluttered and book-lined office that also functions as his shop. His collection of books, he says without hesitation of his library on Islamic, Persian, Middle Eastern, Indian and Turkish art, "is the greatest private library in the world of this material." The modest office offers no clue to such importance, and Mr. Soustiel says, "I am not a very famous world dealer." His clients know his eye, and he shares his knowledge freely. The prices at this gallery range from about $500 to $200,000, with most things selling for $1,000 to $3,000, he said.

BERNARD STEINITZ

4 Rue Drouot
75009 Paris
Phone: (33-1) 42-46-98-98
Hours: 9 A.M. to 5 P.M. Monday to Friday, appointment suggested
Closed in August

The palatial interiors of Bernard Steinitz's gallery, a duplex, one floor above the street in an 18th-century building, speak volumes about this dealer. The 20th-century is gently acknowledged in the lighting and telephones. Everything else echoes the 17th and 18th centuries: the elegantly formal foyer, the sweeping staircase leading to the drawing rooms above and the boiserie-lined galleries filled with pedigree furnishings in the grand style. The fittings and the furnishings are all for sale.

"It's like me—it keeps the tradition of the 18th century going," Mr. Steinitz said. He was surrounded by the proof: Louis XIV, XV and XVI commodes with lacquered fronts, lavishly carved consoles, painted chairs, imposing desks and clocks embellished with gilded-bronze mounts. Things change here frequently but the ambiance remains the same, he said.

"My father brought me to an auction when I was eight or nine years old because he liked the feeling of auctions," Mr. Steinitz said, adding that he did, too. "I said to him, 'Now I want to be an antiques dealer.'"

Mr. Steinitz was born in Dijon and his father had a textile business. Bernard Steinitz was sixteen when he went out on his own. "I started with nothing," he recalled. "I began with what I found." He married young and he and his wife, Simone, sold period silver from their home. In 1957, when he was twenty-three, he opened his first shop. Now, five children later, the Steinitzes have a business with a staff of 40 people, including two of his children, David, who is in Paris, and Mireille, who is in London.

Mr. Steinitz specializes in French furniture and decorations of the late 17th century through the early 19th century. His favorite pieces are the earliest, he said, dating from 1670 to 1720. "This is a period I like very much. It was a period of discovery," he said. "Afterward, at the end of the 18th century, the furniture becomes an obsession of production."

Mr. Steinitz learned much of what he knows about furniture during the 10 years he worked for the Paris dealer Etienne Lévy. He has counted among his clients the Metropolitan Museum of Art in New York, the J. Paul Getty Museum in Malibu, Calif., and Jayne Wrightsman. The Getty bought an ivory-veneered Louis XIV table decorated with horn.

In addition to fine French furnishings of the late 17th century and later, the gallery stocks boiserie, or period paneling, "when they are of fantastic quality." Sometimes Mr. Steinitz handles early-19th-century Empire furnishings.

Prices range from about $15,000 for a simple corner cabinet by Genty to $500,000 or more for a bureau plat that dates from about 1740, has gilding from the period and is signed by Jacques Dubois.

GALERIE VALOIS

41 Rue de Seine
75006 Paris
France
Phone: (33-1) 43-29-50-85
Hours: 2 to 7 P.M. Monday, 10 A.M. to 1 P.M. and 2 to 7 P.M. Tuesday to Saturday
Closed in August

Cheska and Bob Valois have been buying and selling Art Deco objects and furniture since 1970, first on Rue St.-Denis and since 1980 at this address. The couple handles some extraordinary examples of the style, especially the lacquered accessories and furniture by Jean Dunand, the veneered furniture and hand-woven carpets by Emile-Jacques Ruhlmann and the gilded metal chairs of Diego Giacometti.

Dunand was well represented at the shop on one visit. There was a stunning bed that was later sold to DeLorenzo in New York, where it was a major highlight in the Dunand exhibition, and a superb lemon yellow vase with a crackled glaze embellished with a pair of graceful antelopes, alert and listening, that was $30,000. Another memorable Art Deco design of the 1920s was a Cubist-inspired cigar box of lacquer inlaid with metal by Jean Goulden that cost $24,500.

The Valoises like 20th-century objects that must be touched to be fully appreciated. A case in point was a richly textured green sharkskin-wrapped Macassar box by Clement Rousseau.

Furniture here was equally inviting to collectors who enjoy the luxurious finishes that French Art Deco craftsmen excelled at. These included a table with a rectangular top covered in doelike parchment with slab legs lacquered a satin black, as well as à table-desk framed in chromed tubing by Eugène Printz that was $37,000 and a shimmering black lacquer and gilded commode with open sides by Michael Dufet that was $22,160.

Equally arresting if rougher to the touch were two of Giacometti's gilded bronze chairs, on each of which a bird perched on a lower rung. They were $30,000 each.

VANDERMEESCH

27 Quai Voltaire
75007 Paris
France
Phone: (33-1) 42-61-23-10
Hours: 10 A.M. to 12:30 P.M. and 2 to 7 P.M. Tuesday to Saturday
Closed in August

Vandermeesch has been a name to be reckoned with in period ceramics in Paris for more than a century. Three generations of this family have headed the concern that Auguste Vandermeesch founded in 1880 and that Pierre Vandermeesch headed until his death in 1983.

Now Michel Vandermeesch is in charge of this impressive shop on the main floor of the house where Voltaire lived and died, as visitors discover from the sign out front. The dealer moved here from a few doors away in 1982 and has been on the Quai Voltaire since just before World War II.

History of another sort reigns inside, where the offerings date from the 16th century to about 1830. Among the Chinese ceramics are Ming and Ch'ing wares, made for Chinese use and for export. European ceramics include hard-paste German porcelains (by Meissen and others) and the soft-paste French porcelains (by Sèvres, Strasbourg, Vincennes and others). Faïence, which is also gaining in popularity these days, is well represented here.

Although there are Meissen offerings here, including such works from the early period as tureens and figures decorated by Kändler, there is a greater demand recently for Sèvres and all soft-paste porcelains and faïence, Mr. Vandermeesch said. Until a few years ago, French dealers went to New York to buy, he noted, adding that the situation has changed dramatically. Now New Yorkers and other Americans are competing for these ceramics at auctions and in shops on both sides of the Atlantic. At this shop, he said, Americans buy about 20 percent of what is sold.

Prices ranged from about $250 for a Ch'ien Lung plate to about $60,000 for an important work of Sèvres of the 18th century, a 15th-century Italian majolica vessel or a Chinese Ming porcelain vase.

LE LOUVRE DES ANTIQUAIRES

2 Place du Royal
75001 Paris
France
Phone: (33-1) 42-97-27-00
Hours: 11 A.M. to 7 P.M. Tuesday to Sunday

Since it opened in 1978, this antiques center, where about 250 dealers exhibit, has been one of the most successful of its kind. There are specialists in periods ranging from ancient art through Art Deco and in glass, silver, ceramics, bronzes, furniture, as well as coins, African art, postcards, photography, arms and armor and marine art.

The building in which this modern showcase for antiques is housed is as historic as anything under its roof. Built in 1855 as the Grand Hôtel du Louvre, it was where Nathaniel Hawthorne and Samuel Clemens (Mark Twain) stayed when they visited Paris. Later, the shops in its arcades evolved into a department store that took over the building, and it became Les Grands Magasins du Louvre.

The British Post Office Pension Fund acquired 86 percent of the building in 1975, remodeled the interiors and opened it as an antiques center.

BIENNALE INTERNATIONALE DES ANTIQUAIRES

Grand Palais
Avenue du Général Eisenhower
75008 Paris
France
Phone: (33-1) 42-61-54-10
Hours: 11 A.M. to 11 P.M. Monday to Saturday, 10 A.M. to 8 P.M. Sunday
Admission: About $6.50

For information:
Biennale
Syndicat National des Antiquaires
11 Rue Jean Mermoz
75008 Paris
France
Phone: (33-1) 42-25-44-33

The Biennale, the fair of superlatives, is organized by the French Antiques Dealers' Association (Le Syndicat National des Antiquaires) and the French Jewelers Association (La Haute Joaillerie de France). It takes place every other year for two and a half weeks in late September and early October. Since it was started in 1962, this event has been widely regarded as Europe's most prestigious antiques bazaar. It attracts the largest attendance of all the major international antiques fairs, typically 350,000 visitors or more, and it runs the longest.

The Biennale exhibits are predominantly 18th-century French furniture, ceramics and art. But the show is also stocked with artworks from throughout Europe, the Far East and Africa, and includes Art Nouveau and Art Deco. Among the 130 exhibitors are many of the leading dealers of Paris, with scores of prominent merchants from other parts of France and from Belgium, Britain and Italy. Before the show opens to the public, the booths are reviewed by experts who order the removal of all wares that are judged not to be period or to be other than as represented.

NOUVEAU DROUOT

9 Rue Drouot
75009 Paris
France
Phone: (33-1) 42-46-17-11
Viewing hours: 11 A.M. to 6 P.M. the day before the sale, 11 A.M. to noon the day of the sale
Sales: Frequent every month except August, always at 2 P.M.
Schedules published weekly in:
Gazette Hôtel Drouot
99 Rue de Richelieu
75002 Paris
France
Phone: (33-1) 42-61-81-78

VIENNA

GALERIE BEI DER ALBERTINA

Lobkowitzplatz 1
A1010 Vienna
Austria
Phone: (43-222) 53-14-16
Hours: 9:30 A.M. to 6 P.M. Monday to Friday, 9:30 A.M. to 12:30 P.M. Saturday

Christa Zetter, a dealer since 1973, inherited her delight in period objects from her parents, who occupied this shop from 1939 until 1973, when she took over. But her interest in early-20th-century Austrian design is her own and is highly developed, as can be seen in the ceramics, toys, jewelry and furniture, including works made by the Wiener Werkstätte, the Vienna crafts workshop founded in 1903 by Josef Hoffmann and Koloman Moser with the financial backing of Fritz Wärndorfer.

The ceramics here usually include baroque figures and decorative objects by Michael Powolny, Vally Wieselthier, Eduard Klablena, Hubert Kovarik, Ena Kopriva, Gudrun Baudisch, Josef Hoffmann and Dagobert Peche. Most are unique or produced in limited editions by artists in their studios and are yet to be fully documented, Mrs. Zetter said.

These, as well as the more fully documented ceramics made by the Wiener Werkstätte in larger editions, which are also stocked here, date from about 1910 to 1930. They are priced from $700 to $5,450; Powolny's work may be as much as $10,000, and a figure by Ena Kopriva in what Mrs. Zetter calls the expressive style may be $8,200.

The carved wooden toys made by the Wiener Werkstätte are outstanding. The most memorable example seen on one visit was a 1906 Noah's Ark on a raft, its graphics anticipating Mondrian, by Mitzi von Uchatius, who studied under Carl Otto Czeschka. The bold colors and motifs of the animals and toys by Czeschka and other designers who did wonderful Nibelungen-style toy knights derive from the works of Austrian Expressionist painters and graphics designers whose postcards and Secessionist posters date to the same period. The designs are precursors of the modern wooden toys that proliferated in Europe and the United States after World War II.

Mrs. Zetter also stocks furniture and was showing a bentwood turn-of-the-century lacquered black suite designed by Gustav Siegel for the 1900 World's Fair in Paris. Josef Hoffmann's 1908 chairs designed for Purkesdorf, the Vienna sanitarium, which were cubes painted white and framed in rods, were $15,650 each. And a center table by Hoffmann was $2,725.

The prices for other objects ranged from $275 for a simple wooden toy by Ferdinand Andri to an eight-piece suite of Hoffmann furniture at about $200,000.

HERBERT ASENBAUM, KUNST UND ANTIQUITATENHANDEL

Kärntner Strasse 28
A1010 Vienna
Austria
Phone: (43-222) 512-28-47
Hours: 9 A.M. to 1 P.M. and 2 to 6 P.M. Monday to Friday, 9:30 A.M. to 1:30 P.M. Saturday

Members of the Asenbaum family have been art dealers in Vienna since 1916. In each of three generations, family members have reshaped the business to their own personalities and to the art and antiques collecting interests that developed, often with their help, in each period.

When Josef and Regina Asenbaum started in their shop in 1916, they offered all kinds of antiques, especially Baroque and Biedermeier furniture. Their son, Herbert, began in business in 1939, offering a wider range of objects, from medieval through 19th-century Biedermeier and including silver, porcelain, glass, paintings and furniture. After he retired in 1984, he became a consultant in goldwork to Vienna's Museum of Applied Art.

Stefan and Paul Asenbaum, the sons of Herbert and Inge Asenbaum, who is herself a dealer in modern and antique jewelry with a shop on the Graben called Galerie am Graben, are as independent in their thinking as their parents and grandparents were. Stefan, born in 1947, and Paul, in 1953, continue to offer the same periods as their father did and have added 20th-century furniture, art objects and decorations.

Stefan started in the business in 1963 at his father's store and in 1974, he and Paul opened the Gallery Kunstkontakte, where they stocked Thonet, Wiener Werkstätte and the early-20th-century architectural designs of Vienna. These plus Biedermeier are the Asenbaums' specialties today.

They offer 18th- and early-19th-century Meissen and Vienna porcelains as well as silver and glass from the 17th to 19th centuries. At this quietly elegant shop, the shelves, cabinets and showcases display austerely shaped porcelains awash with stripes, squares and circles; bold ruby- and cobalt-colored glass and geometric-patterned silver tableware that borrows its bold shapes from architecture. The Viennese taste for simplicity of form embellished with flashes of jewel colors and shimmering accents of gold and silver is all expressed in these objects. Prices range from about $300 for an early-19th-century Viennese small silver cup to about $10,000 for an Augsburg 17th-century tankard or a late-18th-century French gold box.

The Asenbaums handle "very select" Biedermeier, 19th- and 20th-century bentwood and architect's furniture at a gallery nearby. The spectacular examples of these classical styles, Biedermeier parlor tables, chairs and settees, as well as secretaries, chests and clothes cupboards, combine well with the furniture from almost 100 years later. Both are spare in form and have light finishes, wood in the 19th century and sometimes painted in the 20th century. From the 20th century are the more modern suites of center tables, chairs and settees, desks, nests of tables and adjustable chairs called sitting machines. The Asenbaums specialize in Otto Wagner, and Paul Asenbaum was one of four co-authors of a 1984 book on this Austrian architect's work.

Their handsomely designed, well-illustrated exhibitions and catalogues on Otto Wagner, on the Biedermeier style, on bentwood and on early-20th-century Austrian architects' designs are respected reference works.

ADIL BESIM

Dorotheergasse 5
(also at Graben 30)
A1014 Vienna
Austria
Phone: (43-222) 52-16-38
Hours: 9 A.M. to 6 P.M. Monday to Friday, 9 A.M. to noon Saturday

Oriental rugs fill three floors of the Adil Besim establishment on Dorotheergasse and four floors at its premises on the Graben, a kind of square in the middle of the downtown shopping district. "Everyone is saying we are the largest retail Oriental rug dealers in the world," Ferdi Besim said, adding that he has 25,000 clients in Europe and the United States. Besim operates its own restoration workshops and has three other stores in Austria, in Salzburg, Innsbruck and Graz, and one in Pasadena, Calif.

"We have between 7,000 and 8,000 rugs in stock," Mr. Besim said, of which 15 percent are antique, 30 percent old and the rest new. The large variety includes all standard types, Persians, Turkomans, Caucasians, Anatolians and kilims, as well as European rugs and tapestries. Most of the period weavings are 19th- and 20th-century, but Besim has some 16th-century rugs also.

The concern's origins were much more modest. Adil Besim and Friedrich Langauer, who are Austrians and cousins, were the founders in 1946 of the company that is now run by their sons. Adil Besim, born Adolf Böhm, went to Turkey in 1928, where he leased a cotton plantation and remained. He married there, became a Moslem in 1934 and changed his name. In 1943, two years after his son Ferdi was born in Istanbul, Adil Besim was called into the German army and returned to Austria. After the war, he translated the value of his prewar business in Turkey into Oriental rugs, which he brought to Vienna. He and his cousin opened a small store near the Graben. By 1949 they had moved to the Graben building. In 1968 Ferdi Besim and Fritz Langauer took over the business and continued expanding.

Prices range from about $50 for a small mat or $1,800 for a late-19th-century Afshar in blues and reds to about $60,000 for a Salor-type Turkoman rug.

GALERIE HOFSTÄTTER

Stallburggasse, at the corner of Braeunerstrasse
1010 Vienna
Austria
Phone: (43-222) 52-89-84, 52-89-85
Hours: 10 A.M. to 6 P.M. Monday to Friday, 10 A.M. to 1 P.M. Saturday

Reinhold Hofstätter, the second generation of his family in this business, became an antiques dealer in 1953. He moved in 1981 to this spacious gallery and has filled it with an impressive assortment of art and antiques, dating from antiquities through early-20th-century modern. The grand style of this establishment echoes Vienna of an earlier time.

The furniture is robust and strongly sculptural, whether it be a Henry II table on columnar legs, a Baroque library table with angled corners, an Italian 18th-century chest embellished with gilded bronzes, a Biedermeier secretary or a set of eight 1920s chairs by Otto Prutscher. He says he covers all periods and carries "from every epoch the very best."

His taste is for imposing, even regal furnishings, as could be seen in a late-17th-century Munich desk awash with inlay in the Boulle style. The dealer suggested that it "was probably made for a Bavarian king." The price was $68,120.

Mr. Hofstätter maintains a large sales staff to help shoppers (he is available by appointment), and there are 12 specialists who restore furniture, the veneered surfaces, broken hinges, gilding on bronze mounts, frames of chairs, linings of drawers and upholstery.

This is a source visited by those seeking the exotic and the extraordinary, especially outsize cabinets and armoires and banquet-size tables. The top price here is about $70,000.

GLASGALERIE MICHAEL KOVACEK

Stallburggasse 2
A1010 Vienna
Austria
Phone: (43-222) 512-99-54, 513-21-66
Hours: 10 A.M. to 6:30 P.M. Monday to Friday, 9 A.M. to 1 P.M. Saturday

Michael and Regine Kovacek, the husband-wife team who head this gallery, have become well known in recent years to collectors throughout Europe and North America for glass of the 17th century through the early 20th century. Mr. Kovacek became a dealer in 1973 and opened this shop in 1975. It offers 17th-century colorless Venetian goblets, 18th-century enameled Franconian beakers, 19th-century Bohemian ruby-red stemware and French paperweights and early-20th-century Bohemian and Austrian Art Nouveau vases.

The Kovaceks combine scholarship and an instinct for what collectors seek in glass. They have organized two major exhibitions to stimulate interest in European glass of the periods and styles they handle and have not been disappointed in the response. The exhibition in 1982 attracted more than 5,000 visitors, Mr. Kovacek reported, and in 1985 its "Glass of Four Centuries" was attended by 10,000 people. The Kovaceks' catalogue for the 1985 exhibition, published in German and English, included 260 designs, offering a comprehensive overview of the subject and of their stock.

The variety and quality of glass at this shop are impressive. Mr. Kovacek has a keen eye for the simplest utilitarian glass, as can be seen in a 17th-century greenish-yellow precursor of the thermos, a pewter-lidded cooler-flask, possibly Bohemian. Other 17th- and 18th-century bottles and flasks in brilliant red, blue, amber, clear and green colors and blown in swirled and lobed molds are arresting studies.

Highly refined crafting is seen in a wide range of works. There are stunning blown 17th-century Venetian goblets with spaghettilike handles and twisted stems. Paper-thin enameled beakers from Saxony, Franconia and Bohemia, brilliantly decorated with palettes borrowed from illuminated manuscripts and stained-glass windows, depict coats of arms, marriage scenes and allegories.

Glasses frosted with engravings included a 17th-century beaker depicting the Turkish army on the march and goblets from Silesia, Potsdam and the Black Forest that appeared to be covered with lace. Johann Mildner's 18th-century medallion glasses, black portrait silhouettes and red images framed in gold, are well represented here. And so are the delicately decorated Dresden and Vienna beakers of the early 19th century, embellished sparely with flowers or a cathedral. The weightier cut and engraved Bohemian works that followed, most of them more admirable for their craftsmanship than their art, are also found in abundance here.

Austrian and Bohemian Art Nouveau glass, far heavier than its French and American counterparts, and glass figures by or in the style of Karl Hagenauer are also available.

Prices range from about $200 for drinking glasses or Bohemian early-20th-century paperweights to about $100,000 for rare, museum-quality objects.

GALERIE METROPOL

Dorotheergasse 12
1010 Vienna
Austria
Phone: (43-222) 513-22-08
Hours: 11 A.M. to 6 P.M. Monday to Friday, 10 A.M. to noon Saturday; only by appointment in August

Georg Kargl, Christian Meyer and Wolfgang Ritschka, all Austrian art dealers, formed a partnership in 1975 to sell the works of Josef Hoffmann and Koloman Moser. In 1978 Mr. Kargl and Mr. Meyer opened the first Galerie Metropol in Vienna. The second shop followed in New York in

1981, opening on Madison Avenue under the direction of Mr. Ritschka.

In 1982, the Vienna team moved the gallery to its current address, across the street from the Dorotheum, Vienna's auction house. Mr. Kargl and Christian Meyer continue to work in association with the New York gallery but are no longer formally connected. The emphasis has been changing in recent years at the Vienna gallery, where the partners now focus more on the Austrian Secessionist and Expressionist painters Carl Moll, Egon Schiele and Gustav Klimt.

The two galleries are dramatically different in appearance. The Vienna shop looks like a jewel box with glorious early-20th-century Austrian objects arranged on softly lighted shelves. Settings elsewhere are carefully arranged with selections of Vienna's furniture. In sharp contrast, furniture is emphasized at the Madison Avenue source, and everything operates in a more casual way.

The differences reflect both the dealers' interests and shoppers' choices. "Furniture is going well in New York, but not the smaller objects," Mr. Kargl said. There are exceptions at both shops; the biggest names and the finest examples of designs might be seen in either place. He said that in Vienna there were very few people who came to buy a chair or table to fill a corner in their flat, but there were serious collectors who just acquire furniture and objects of the period and store them away.

The selection of works here might include Josef Hoffmann's cobalt-blue glass vases, Dagobert Peche's baroque silver vessels, Michael Powolny's ceramics and a variety of unsigned works in leather purses and wallets and gold jewelry inset with semiprecious stones. Accessories include pierced grillwork, such as baskets, trays, vases and such by both Hoffmann and Moser. Sterling silver flatware services by Hoffmann command increasingly higher prices, as much as $15,000 or more for a service for 12.

Prices range from about $500 for a gold-trimmed wallet by Hoffmann to between $35,000 and $50,000 for a sitting machine by Hoffmann or $60,000 for a complete room of furniture by Adolf Loos.

SEE New York: ***Galerie Metropol, page 81***

GALERIE SAILER

Dorotheergasse 7
A1010 Vienna
Austria
Phone: (43-222) 53-10-75
Hours: 9 A.M. to 6 P.M. Monday to Friday, 9 A.M. to noon Saturday

"We buy from Americans and we sell to Americans," said Roberto Barberis, director of this gallery where 16th- to early-20th-century carpets are stocked. The variety shown in this white-walled glittering modern establishment includes Turkoman, Anatolian, Caucasian and Persian carpets. The rugs are hung on walls and sliding panels on the main floor and balcony so they can be fully appreciated.

Mr. Barberis said he holds exhibitions of textiles and period rugs two or three times a year at this gallery and at his larger one in Salzburg. One catalogue included a stunning Konya, an Anatolian from about 1800, that was awash with geometric motifs. Of the several boldly patterned kilims, the most memorable was one from Tunisia that combined rows of camels, people and geometric motifs. Notable too was a bright red Yarkand weaving from East Turkestan bordered with colorfully striped triangles and patterned with bars and a medallion.

Galerie Sailer was founded by Franz Sailer in 1976 in Salzburg. Mr. Sailer, then thirty-nine years old, had been in the Oriental rug business 18 years. He opened the Vienna gallery in 1983. The Vienna Gallery was started as a gathering place for rug collectors, and it still is, Mr. Sailer said.

Although Sailer stocks antique textiles and carpets from the 16th to the early 20th centuries, most are 18th- and 19th-century.

Prices start at about $200 for saddle bags and $1,500 for kilims, although kilims can be $10,000 and even much more. Period pile rugs start at about $4,000 and go up. "There is no limit," Mr. Sailer said.

SCHULLIN

Kohlmarkt 7
1010 Vienna
Phone: (43-222) 52-62-52
Hours: 9 A.M. to 6 P.M. Monday to Friday, 9 A.M. to 12:30 P.M. Saturday

Herbert Schullin's stunning jewelry shop is a modern architectural landmark in a city more famous for its period Gothic, Baroque and turn-of-the-century masterpieces than its postwar buildings. The 1982 shop, by Hans Hollein, the Austrian architect, is a shimmering repository for modern and period jewelry with milk-white marble floors, gilded metal cylinders and lots of glass. It is one of only four architectural works by Hollein here.

Herbert Schullin is the second generation of jewelers in his family; Hans Schullin, his father, was a jeweler in Graz from 1928 until he retired in 1976, he said. The younger Mr. Schullin went on his own, moving in 1974 to Vienna, where he began showing the work of contemporary jewelers as well as period gems of the Renaissance, Art Nouveau and early-20th-century periods.

The rarities in Wiener Werkstätte jewelry that Mr. Schullin handles from time to time include silver brooches set with a variety of different-colored semiprecious stones, echoing barbarian jewelry of the 5th to 10th centuries. Examples of these designs were included in "Dream and Reality," the show held in 1985 in Vienna and Paris, and the 1986 exhibition "Vienna 1900: Art, Architecture & Design" at New York's Museum of Modern Art.

Austrian jewelry from earlier periods included several spectacular tiaras: a mid-19th-century diamond crown decorated with one gray pearl was $30,000, and another stunning early-19th-century tiara with diamond-studded flowers in silver and gold settings was $18,000. There were Austrian 17th-century enameled brooches and a necklace awash with tiny rubies as well as Hungarian and Russian gems. Notable too was a 1650s gold locket with a miniature painting inside.

Although Austrian jewelry is his specialty, Mr. Schullin also stocks French Art Nouveau and Art Deco pieces, including the work of René Lalique. Earlier pieces would be Renaissance and Baroque works made in Vienna and elsewhere in Europe.

Prices range from about $1,000 for a brooch up to $50,000 for some of the more lavish tiaras.

DOROTHEUM

17 Dorotheergasse
A1010 Vienna
Austria
Phone: (43-222) 51-56-00
Office and buying hours: 7:30 or 8 A.M. to 2 or 3 P.M. Monday to Friday
Viewing hours: 10 A.M. to 6 P.M. Monday to Friday, 8:30 A.M. to noon Saturday; some Sundays before major sales

The Dorotheum, the world's oldest auction house, combines some ancient and modern business practices these days. Founded 1n 1707 as a pawn shop to aid the poor by Joseph I, the Holy Roman Emperor, it has been at the same address for almost two centuries. It is in an eight-story palacelike Baroque building that was originally a monastery. The Government-owned auction house still operates as a pawnshop but has added retail sales and become more profitable. The number of works auctioned has declined to about half of what it was in the mid-1970s. It has about 900 auctions a year.

Specialties of interest to international buyers include Austrian Expressionist art, Wiener Werkstätte furniture, glass, ceramics, jewelry, Baroque and Biedermeier furniture, ceramics and silver.

MIDDLE EAST

JERUSALEM

RAFI BROWN

10 King David Antiquities Ltd.
10 King David Street
Jerusalem
Israel
Phone: (972-2) 234-511
Hours: 10 A.M. to 1 P.M. and 4:30 to 7:30 P.M. Sunday to Thursday, 10 A.M. to 2 P.M. Friday

Rafi Brown, one of Israel's most prestigious antiquities dealers, stocks ancient glass, jewelry, ceramics, oil lamps and archeological works. He became a private dealer in 1979.

"I was always interested in archeology and antiquities," the Israeli-born dealer said. After he served in the Israeli army, he studied archeology at Hebrew University in Jerusalem from 1962 to 1966 but did not graduate. Mr. Brown was on several excavations at Arad, between 1963 and 1966, where he studied the type of ancient works he stocks today.

In 1963 he joined the staff of the Israel Museum (Bronfman Museum of Archaeology) to work as a restorer. Two years later, he became head of restoration of antiquities at the museum. "We covered a lot: mosaics, pottery and glass," Mr. Brown recalled. "I was especially interested in research on forgeries and fakes."

"We have biblical archeology," he said. "We don't have gold. These pieces are things used in daily life in the biblical period."

People go wrong, he said, when they buy stories and not artifacts. "A good object will sell itself without any story," he commented. "Very rare items should be inspected by an expert before the purchase and not after."

At this two-story shop, where Mr. Brown has two assistants, there are works from $25 for an oil lamp to $3,000 or $4,000 for ancient glass or bronze figurines. Necklaces of glass beads, faïence, carnelians and semiprecious stones may date from 1800 B.C. to 50 or 40 B.C. They average about $500.

Glass vases and perfume bottles from the fourth century or later, the Roman or Byzantine period, are among the more sought-after types of antiquities here. There are opalescent vases and some iridescent ones, too. They run $200 to $3,000. Mr. Brown said. Pottery oil lamps with a menorah from the third or fourth century are $5,000 to $7,000. And, he warned, they are often fakes. "That's a big problem. There has to be the trust between the dealer and the client." Mr. Brown advises people at no charge, he said.

GREGORY MOMJIAN

190 Jaffa Gate
104 Muristan Road
Jerusalem
Israel
Phone: Tsolag Momjian, his son, at Jerusalem Jewelry: (972-2) 852-053, 852-054
Hours: When open, 10 A.M. to 2 P.M. ("Many days I close," the proprietor said, adding that there was no particular schedule.)

Gregory Momjian's dusty and cluttered antiquities shop in the Old City is not far from the Jaffa gate and looks like many others in this ancient city. Piled high on the floor and shelves are stacks of old pottery and shards, gleaming silver vessels, glass, brass, mosaics and jewelry.

Mr. Momjian is, however, like no other merchant in this ancient town, according to antiquities dealers, collectors and museum curators who say they have relied on his eye and knowledge to guide them for many decades.

"My shop was a school—many were learning here," Mr. Momjian said. While he sipped a cup of coffee, he spoke a bit about his past. His parents were killed in 1915 in Malatya, Turkey, and his sister, who was at least 15 years older, saved him from the massacre. Understandably, he is not quite certain about his age but thinks he was born in 1913 or 1914.

Mr. Momjian's childhood was spent in orphanages, first in Turkey. In 1921, he was transferred to the orphanage of the American Near East Relief in Nazareth. He remained there until 1927 when it closed. He was then thirteen or fourteen and moved to an Armenian convent in Jaffa, where he went to work for a Rouben Kashi, a prominent Jewish jeweler, and began to learn this business.

In 1936 when rioting broke out in the streets of Jaffa, the shop was under siege and Mr. Momjian escaped. His efforts to save the dealer and some customers who were locked in the store with him were later rewarded. Mr. Kashi gave Mr. Momjian the keys to Kashi's Jerusalem store and said that from now on it would be his shop. "I continued making jewelry until 1966-67," he said.

Antiquities had always been his private interest. "I would buy books to get more knowledge about this hobby of mine," he said. Evenually his love for ancient pottery, glass and bronzes dominated his attention, and the shop slowly changed from jewelry to antiquities about 1967. The jewelry manufacturing was transferred to another shop in the Old City under his two sons. (They have a New York outlet, Allegra Gold, on Fifth Avenue.)

"I don't know what I have," the dealer said with a wave at the bounty of archeological vessels and shiny bits of period wares that surrounded him in every direction. The statement meant only that he would not be able to recite what was on every shelf. Hand him a clay pot, a glass perfume bottle, a silver belt, however, and the vague descriptions end as he identifies, as closely as is possible, the piece in question.

Mr. Momjian's shop is a place where the knowledgeable may find works of some or great value and where the unknowledgeable may leave with a good feeling if they have been lucky enough to meet the engaging proprietor.

Prices for the least of his wares are not high. Antiques here start at $10, $20 and $30.

When Mr. Momjian finished his coffee that morning, he closed his shop. "I will play just now," he said, smiling his farewell to neighboring dealers.

SASSON ANTIQUES

King David Hotel Annex
King David Street, corner of Emile Botta Street
Jerusalem 94101
Israel
Phone: (972-2) 249 483
Hours: 10 A.M. to 1 P.M. and 4 to 7 P.M. Sunday to Thursday, 10 A.M. to 1 P.M. Friday

Gideon Sasson's shop windows are showcases filled with old coins and scarabs in modern settings and a score of ancient objects—pottery jugs and oil lamps, small sculptures, glass vessels, a gold earring or two and bronze figures. Mr. Sasson, who became an antiquities dealer in 1979 at the age of twenty-seven, is the son of an antiquities dealer, Joav Sasson, whose family was in jewelry and antiques and came to Jerusalem from Iran in 1923. Mr. Sasson studied archeology for his Master of Arts degree at the Hebrew University.

Ancient biblical objects at this shop include bronzes, pottery and glass of the fourth millennium B.C. to the end of the Persian period in Jerusalem, 400 B.C. Classical works dating from the fourth century B.C. to the seventh century include Hellenistic, Roman and Byzantine selections.

The differences between rarities and common examples of pottery and glass vessels and bronze figures can spell the difference of thousands of dollars at this shop. As knowledgeable buyers of such material know, it takes time to train the eye to choose the exceptional over the more ordinary. It is even more difficult for buyers who are not knowledgeable to separate fake contemporary works from period examples of iridescent glass vessels. Gideon Sasoon said that he certifies the authenticity of every antiquity he sells and guarantees that it is genuine. Mr. Sasson's stock of early works includes perfume and ointment vessels at $100 to $10,000 in most of the familiar and some of the less-known classical shapes.

The offerings here range from $50 for such common ancient works as Jewish and Christian pottery oil lamps, Roman glass bottles and coins to about $10,000 for a bronze statuette, Roman marble head or Roman glass vessel.

TARSHIS GALLERY

18 King David Street
Jerusalem 94101
Israel
Phone: (972-2) 228-039
Hours: 10 A.M. to 1 P.M. and 4 to 7:30 P.M. Sunday to Thursday, 10 A.M. to 1 P.M. Friday

Shaya Zadok is a dealer in antiquities and Judaica. The selection of antiques on view at this cluttered shop, where a man hummed quietly and visitors browsed undisturbed, is wide-ranging both in period and in materials. There were, for example, many animal figures, mirrors, brass jugs, silver pieces, glass vessels, ceramic oil lamps, broken bits of pottery and, in a corner, stacks of folded rugs.

Born in Sana, Yemen, Mr. Zadok said his family has been six generations in Israel and that he moved to Jerusalem in 1949 and opened the shop in 1966. He is from a family of jewelry dealers and continues as a merchant in that tradition, offering Yemeni gold and silver jewelry. He also handles Bedouin necklaces of faïence and glass beads for $20 to $100.

Coins are a specialty here and some date to the First Temple of Jerusalem, 300 B.C. to A.D. 134, and to the Byzantine period of the sixth or seventh century. One of the rarest selections was a shekel, showing the facade of the Second Temple, that was $30,000. "Good pieces you are not afraid to sell," Mr. Zadok said. Byzantine period mosaics start at about $800. The offerings start at about $100 for a kiddush cup or a candlestick. Some are period pieces while others are made today in the traditional style.

TEL AVIV

YOSSI BENYAMINOFF

Le Petit Musée
Tel Aviv Hilton
Tel Aviv
Israel
Phone: (972-3) 24-57-12
Hours: 8 A.M. to 10 P.M. Sunday to Thursday, closed at sundown Friday, 4 to 10 P.M. Saturday

Yossi Benyaminoff's shop seems more like an Oriental bazaar in miniature than a French boutique. His taste for exotic and lavishly embellished objects shows everywhere in the shop, which is abundant in different materials and period works—textiles, jewelry, decorative objects—that were produced throughout the Middle East, Africa and Europe.

Born in Jerusalem, he is the third generation of his family in Israel and in this business, which his grandfather Joseph Benyaminoff founded around 1875 and his father, Nissan, continued. His family, Kurdish Jews, were from Azerbaijan. The present shop has been in the Tel Aviv Hilton since 1979; before that he was in business in Jerusalem.

Mr. Benyaminoff set up another antiques and appraisal business in the United States in 1966, and he continues it today in New York as a private dealer.

In both places he specializes in mid-18th-century and 19th-century antiques. He stocks Judaica textiles from Persia, Turkey and Africa, many of which are fine embroideries. These range from $500 to $30,000. Islamic vessels, another interest, include brass works inlaid with gold, silver and copper from $250 to $150,000. He also handles late-19th-century American silver—Tiffany & Company and Gorham designs, including tea services from the late

Victorian Revival period and in the Art Nouveau style—at $400 to $60,000.

Jewelry selections include ethnic earrings from Iraq, filigree buttons and Yemeni rings at about $150 to jeweled offerings that may be as much as $200,000.

SCHMUEL KAUFMANN

81 Ben Juddah Street
Tel Aviv
Israel
Phone: (972-3) 234-113
Hours: 10 A.M. to 1 P.M. Sunday to Friday

Schmuel Kaufmann, a dealer in ancient glass, antique maps and Judaica, was born in Düsseldorf, Germany. He came to Israel in 1936 at the age of sixteen with the Youth Alijah group under Henrietta Szold. His parents followed in 1939. For most of the next 13 years Mr. Kaufmann was a soldier, first with the Haganah, then in the British army and finally in Israel's 1948 war.

"I used to collect stamps, coins and antiquities," Mr. Kaufmann recalled. "I couldn't afford to go to university, but I attended the open lectures there on archeology." Mr. Kaufmann worked in the government from 1950 to 1960 and gained some practical experience in archeology working on two excavations, at Hazor and Megiddo.

Mr. Kaufmann's inventory in Roman glass vessels included the typical as well as some unusual perfume bottles and vases that ranged from $100 to $1,000. Judaica, priced from $200 or $300 to $2,500, was primarily silver. On view were Hanukkah lights, silver boxes, Torah pointers and cups.

Maps have always been an absorbing interest for Mr. Kaufmann, and he stocked two kinds, European maps of the 18th and 19th centuries for $300 to $800 and maps of Old Jerusalem that date from the 16th to the 19th centuries for up to $1,500. The oldest map he ever handled, dated 1493, was a map of Jerusalem that he sold to the government of Israel.

His maps included the Holy Land by German, French and Dutch cartographers. Some were woodcuts, others copper engravings. Those from the late 19th century on are lithographs. These historical and biblical maps depict the country in the time of King Solomon, at the time of the Roman Empire and later. A 1735 hand-colored view of biblical Jerusalem was $1,500.

JOSEPH STIEGLITZ

71 Allenby Street
Tel Aviv
Israel
Phone: Office: (972-3) 29-13-89, Home: (972-3) 58-01-61
Hours: 10 A.M. to 1 P.M. and 4 to 6 P.M. Sunday to Thursday, 10 A.M. to 1 P.M. Friday

Joseph Stieglitz was born in Cracow, Poland, in 1903, two years after his father, Abraham, began the family's antiques business. The elder Mr. Stieglitz handled silver and paintings. Joseph Stieglitz and his two daughters, Eve Elovic and Miriam Marn, are carrying on the family business, specializing in antiques and paintings with Jewish themes from both Israel and elsewhere.

In 1945, Joseph Stieglitz, who said he spent World War II in jails in Poland, Germany and Hungary, went to Israel. His wife and children, who had left Siberia in 1943, joined him.

On his arrival, Mr. Stieglitz immediately began selling antiques in Tel Aviv, where he handles mostly silver Judaica, Roman glass and pottery and ethnic jewelry. His Judaica included several 18th-century works. An Augsburg cup from about 1720 was $5,000, and a Polish silver Torah crown, the ornament embellishing the top of the scroll to stress its importance as the word of God, was $4,500.

Ancient glass included some extremely fine examples, not unlike the perfume vials he sold to the Corning Museum in Corning, N.Y. Among the examples on view was a double vial in pale blue glass that was $400. Mold-blown glass vases and other vessels here range from

$50 to $2,500. A Corinthian clay vase from about the first century B.C. was $2,000. Luristan (Iran) bronzes, Persian necklaces and Islamic works range from about $100 to $500.

FAR EAST

HONG KONG

ROBERT CHANG, ANTIQUES AND JEWELRY

124 Waglan Gallery
Deck 1 Ocean Terminal
Kowloon
Hong Kong
Phone: (852-3) 672-397
Hours: 10 A.M. to 7 P.M. daily

Robert Chang, the son of a Shanghai art dealer, Chung Ying Chang, was seventeen when he went into business in China, opening a fashion boutique in a department store. In 1949 he left for Hong Kong, where he decided he preferred the antiques business and became a dealer. He shows many of the finest pieces to visiting collectors and dealers at his home.

Mr. Chang handles the finest porcelains, Sung through Ming and Ch'ing, as well as Shang bronzes, Shang jades but very little in paintings and sculpture. The dealer is one of the more active figures at auctions in Hong Kong, New York and London.

Prices range mostly from $50,000 to $1 million. Mr. Chang offers the blue-and-white Ming and later vessels, famille verte, under-glaze red and imperial yellow wares prized by all Chinese porcelain collectors, as well as much earlier works.

HANART GALLERY

40 Hollywood Road
Hong Kong
Phone: (852-5) 410-941,
Hours: 10:30 A.M. to 6:30 P.M. Monday to Saturday

Harold C. F. Wong began in art selling paintings and added antiques. Born in 1943 in Shanghai, he left the mainland with his family in 1948. The family was in shipping, but his father was an art collector, and this was the genesis of Mr. Wong's interest. In paintings, he concentrates mostly on 19th- and 20th-century artists.

Among the early pieces are works from the 15th, 16th and 17th centuries. "We always have works by various old and 20th-century calligraphers," he said. "They come in the hanging scroll, hand scroll and album format." Prices range from about $400 to $4,000.

He said he had sold to the Freer Gallery in Washington and acted as agent for the Phoenix Art Museum in making purchases at Sotheby's auctions in Hong Kong.

Most of the early scrolls and albums with calligraphy command from $15,000 to $75,000.

HONEYCHURCH ANTIQUES LTD.

29 Hollywood Road
Hong Kong
Phone: (852-5) 432-433
Hours: 10 A.M. to 6 P.M. Monday to Saturday, 2 to 5 P.M. Sunday

Close to the top of Hollywood Road, Hong Kong's antiques street, Lucille and Glenn Vessa (and their colleagues) hold forth daily in their two-story shop filled with one of the largest assortments of Oriental wares to be found hereabouts. Shelves, tabletops, cabinets and counters were chock-full of silverware, jewelry, enameled boxes, puppets and opium pots, all small enough to go into a suitcase. Even more impressive was the variety of

19th-century and later Japanese farmhouse and restaurant chests and cabinets.

Glenn Vessa likened these rural kitchen cupboards, made to store foods and necessities, to English butter safes. To Western eyes these sturdy boxes with geometric hardware, drawers and secret compartments are among the more handsomely fitted chests and cabinets anywhere. They were crafted of chestnut, pine and cypress from the 1840s to the 1920s, and Mr. Vessa has admired them since the 1950s, when he saw them on his first visit to Kyoto. The prices range, depending on age, size and fittings, from about $1,000 to about $10,000.

Both Vessas were teachers. Glenn taught at Barnard College, Columbia University, in New York, and Lucille, later in the 1950s when they lived in Japan, taught nursery and elementary schools. Their introduction to Japan came when Mr. Vessa was in the United States Navy during the Korean War. That's when, he recalled, he "got hooked" on everything about Japanese life and art and found a wonderful excuse to linger—he taught at the University of Kyoto in 1954 and 1955. While there he also became involved in publishing contemporary Japanese prints. They also went to Korea in 1960 and remained for two years and have traveled widely ever since in Vietnam, Korea, Japan and China.

The Vessas came to Hong Kong in 1969 and have had a flourishing antiques business since 1971. Among the more impressive offerings was a painted earthenware narrow-necked globular vase dating from 2200 to 1700 B.C. It was sparely painted with bold graphic designs at the neck and the waist. It was $12,000. Other items included a bowl with a rounded base, the lower half of which was glazed black, and several tall vases.

"We do have a lot of Chinese things," Mr. Vessa said, pointing out 19th-century Chinese cricket paraphernalia that included carrying gourds, porcelain watering dishes and ivory boxes.

Prices start at $20 for a Chinese silver puzzle ring from about 1820. At the high end, important examples of early Chinese ceramics may run as high as $250,000. The Vessas' son, John B. Fairman, operates a stateside outlet for their stock in a gallery at 1008 James Street, Seattle, Wash. The Vessas say he also does some esoteric and specialized exhibitions of Asian art.

CHARLOTTE HORSTMANN AND GERALD GODFREY LTD.

Ocean Ferry Terminal
Kowloon
Hong Kong
Phone: (852-3) 677-167
Hours: 9:30 A.M. to 6 P.M. Monday to Saturday

This crowded, two-level antiques establishment is the sort of treasure-filled emporium one reads about in novels but encounters rarely. At every turn there is something wonderful to touch or look at. The same is true in the separate 10,000-square-foot warehouse-gallery elsewhere in the terminal.

The shop's walls are covered with reverse glass paintings, Chinese scrolls, period embroideries, No masks and framed fragments of vintage wallpapers. Late-medieval Ming vases in dazzling colors share shelf space with 11th-century Sung jugs, awesome in their simplicity. Tabletops display curious and superbly crafted items. A gilded Japanese bronze stirrup lies next to an Anglo-Indian rosewood lap desk; a Khmer bronze stands beside a low Japanese table.

The art and antiques on view came from India, Thailand, Burma, Indonesia, China, Japan and Korea. They date from 200 B.C. to the late 20th century and represent an extraordinary mix of materials: jade, amber, porcelain, silver, glass, lacquer, bronze, wood, silk and bamboo.

Since 1955 the proprietors of this shop have built a business that is regarded internationally as singular for the broad range and rarity of its Oriental offerings. Although many objects were bought in their travels throughout the Far East, many wares are brought back from frequent visits to New York, London and Paris.

Charlotte Horstmann, who has retired, became something of a legend to the museum curators, collectors, designers, department store buyers and tourists who found many Oriental works to satisfy their taste. She was born in Berlin and taken as an infant to Beijing, where she was raised. In 1950, the antiques dealer packed up her Ming furniture and moved from Peking to Bangkok, where she remained until 1955, when she moved again, this time to Hong Kong.

Gerald Godfrey, her London-born partner, an Oxford graduate, was in business in Bangkok before going to Hong Kong in 1955 to work with Mrs. Horstmann. A short, stocky man with a sharp wit and an eye for the most refined and the most robust in art, he is now the sole owner of the business and has opened another gallery in London, Gerald Godfrey/Far Eastern Art at 104 Mount Street. There he specializes in 20th-century Chinese paintings and offers Chinese and Japanese antiques and art objects.

In Hong Kong he stocks many more objects that appeal to all types of shoppers. There are, for example, such souvenir-type objects as Japanese cherry wood boxes about the size of a pack of cigarettes, which are $5, and shards of export Ming porcelain from sunken ships found in the Gulf of Siam, which are framed in silver. They range in price from $15 to $80. There are examples of period Ming furniture and an assortment of Ming reproductions, too. Other specialties include bamboo and lacquer furniture that was made a century ago and shipped knocked down to Europe, where it was assembled. "It has become increasingly difficult to find this furniture, so we buy it abroad and ship it back here," Mr. Godfrey said.

Screens are even scarcer, so reproductions are offered along with a few old ones. Smaller exotic objects abound. A Tibetan skull cap with a silver lining was $460. A pair of gilded Japanese stirrups in bronze and iron was $3,500. A superb late-Ming silk tapestry, awash with birds and foliage, was $18,000.

TAI SING COMPANY

22 Wyndham Street
Hong Kong
Phone: (852-5) 259-365
Hours: 10 A.M. to 5:30 P.M. Monday to Saturday, by appointment on Sunday

TAI SING COMPANY

122 Hollywood Road
Hong Kong
Phone: (852-5) 491-269
Hours: 10 A.M. to 5:30 A.M. Monday to Saturday

"My father came from Canton," said Eugene Lai, speaking of C. P. Lai, who came to Hong Kong in the 1950s when Eugene Lai was five years old. One of his brothers, Andrew Lai, is a dealer in Canada who has a shop under the family name of C. C. Lai, the name C. P. Lai introduced when he began the international business at 9 Hazelton Avenue, Toronto.

In Hong Kong, Eugene Lai stocks Tang to Ch'ing ceramics, archaic jades, ancient bronzes, Ming furniture and late works: jades, decorations and furniture. The shop on Hollywood Road shows a greater variety of decorative wares, and the Wyndham Street gallery is where the finer works are shown.

"Ming furniture is not so popular in Hong Kong as in the States and Europe," Mr. Lai said, explaining that 19th-century furniture is admired here both by those who make their homes here and by tourists.

Visitors to the two Hong Kong shops of C. C. Lai will find works from $100 for a small piece of porcelain to $500,000 or more, even $1 million for a rare Ming vase or dish or a Shang or Chou wine vessel. "I don't think there is any limit," he said.

Y. F. YANG COMPANY

163-C Ocean Terminal
Kowloon
Hong Kong
Phone: (852-3) 666-921, 679-474
Hours: 10 A.M. to 6:30 P.M. Monday to Saturday, to 6 P.M. Sunday

Chinese snuff bottles became a major collectible in the 1960s and 1970s. Much of the activity that spurred the extraordinary sales and prices was caused by the British dealer Hugh Moss, who moved to Hong Kong from London and encouraged collectors to explore all possible examples of these 18th- to 20th-century wares.

The antiques business founded by Yung Fu Yang specializes in snuff bottles and supplies examples to collectors in New York, Los Angeles, Laguna Beach, Calif., Vancouver, British Columbia, and Florence.

The variety of shapes, materials and decorative devices used in these Lilliputian baubles—most are small enough to disappear in the palm of the hand—is astounding. This can best be appreciated when seeing the Yang stock. It included examples in agate, enamel on glass, porcelain, lacquer with silver inlay, yellow jade, Beijing glass and carved porcelain. To the uninitiated, the bottles with decorations painted inside seem as extraordinary and as difficult to create as ships in bottles.

Yung Fu Yang was born in 1921 in Beijing. He was seventeen when the war broke out and spent the years 1937 to 1962 in Shanghai, then moved to Hong Kong. Stanley S. K. Yang, one of his sons, moved with the rest of the family to Hong Kong in 1979 and now heads the Yang shop. His father moved to Honolulu in 1981 and now works there.

The bottles at this shop range from about $100 to $10,000, even though snuff bottles today can command prices up to about $20,000.

SOTHEBY'S

901-5 Lane Crawford House
70 Queens Road Central
Hong Kong
Phone: (853-5) 248-121
Hours: 10 A.M. to 6 P.M. Monday to Friday
Sales: May and November

Salesroom:
Furama Hotel
1 Connaught Road Central
Hong Kong
Phone: (853-5) 255-111

KYOTO

DAVID KIDD

17 Ebisudani-cho
Hi-no-oka
Yamashina-ku
Kyoto
Japan 607
Phone: (81-75) 751-8552
Hours: By appointment

"We are the back yard of New York," David Kidd said, settling down on a couch one evening after his guests had been seated in Ming chairs and were served tea in the living room of the extraordinary house he shares with Yasuyoshi Morimoto, his assistant director. The softly lighted all-wood environment, enriched by arresting examples of Ming chairs, tables and couches and by stunning rugs, wonderful porcelains, lacquers and textiles, is the most revealing showcase a dealer could create to express his taste.

Mr. Kidd has welcomed scores—hundreds, perhaps—of major American and European collectors and personalities to his home, an unofficial landmark of modern-day Kyoto. He has filled it with major examples of 17th- and 18th-century Chinese furniture and art and with examples of other works from throughout Asia, an accumulation that began in the early 1950s and became serious after he became a dealer here in early 1963.

"I was a student at the University of Michigan at nineteen and rushed off to China—I went to fabled Beijing," he recalled. Americans were not doing that in the days of Mr. Kidd's first visit in 1946. He then went to New York and got a job in 1951 teaching the history of Chinese art at the Asia Institute.

Everyone is looking for a smaller size in screens, Mr.

Kidd said. "The smaller ones were bed screens," he said, adding that he had one, an early example from the era of Tokugawa rulers (1603-1867). Japanese screens have been so much in demand there are now very few fine ones available, he said. "They are beginning to disappear." A six-panel screen, when available, can be anywhere from $15,000 to $200,000 or more, he said.

Mr. Kidd also stocks Chinese textiles—16th-, 17th- and 18th-century selections—as well as pillar carpets, which were were woven to wrap around pillars in temples and palaces. Their patterns often worked like spirals, as could be seen in one dragon example.

Although prices begin at a few thousand dollars, Mr. Kidd's art is primarily for serious collectors.

MIZUTANI—ANTIQUE ARTS AND CRAFTS

Nawate Higashi Shinmonzen
Higashiyama-ku
Kyoto
Japan
Phone: (81-75) 561-5711
Hours: 9:30 A.M. to 5:30 P.M. Wednesday to Monday
Closed Tuesday

"My father came from Shiga prefecture to Kyoto in the late 1930s," Yoko Mizutani said, recalling the history of her family. She and her brother, Shoichiro Mizutani, an art dealer, are their family's fourth generation of merchants in this field. Her great-grandfather, grandfather and father all handled antiques in the countryside of Shiga. Her father, Nisaburo Mizutani, opened a shop in Kyoto in a corner of the Takashimaya department store. During World War II, Yoko Mizutani said, many people of Kyoto moved to the countryside and sold their things. Her father, who retired at seventy-five in 1985, was very busy in those years, selling to very wealthy people and buying great works, including national treasures.

Miss Mizutani's period textiles—costumes, robes,

lengths of fabrics, embroideries—are exceptional. She also handles bamboo, wood, lacquer and dolls. She began her own business in 1977 after working with her brother for seven years. In the beginning, she said, you could still find textiles and costumes of all periods. Now it is hard to find even 18th-century Edo pieces, so most of what she sells is 19th-century late Edo and Meiji textiles.

At her shop, textiles were stacked in great piles on tables, and a bounty of costumes, old farmer's coats and vests and fireman's jackets were hung high on hooks and rods. There were many memorable selections. Farmer's coats—weighty, sturdy garments rich in texture and some decoration—were about $450, and farmer's vests were $200.

Fireman's jackets, thickly quilted short coats painted with protective images of a brave god or a fierce dragon that also show how brave a firefighter is—were $1,300 to $1,700. One fireman's coat made with the bark of an exotic tree was a deep indigo and had a large red crest. Fisherman's coats are simpler and cost about $300. Soldier's jackets are linen with metal plaque liners.

Futon covers are bought as bedspreads or wall hangings, Miss Mizutani said. They are about $570. Sashes are $20 to $30. Carpenter's sacks are about $30.

The variety of men's and women's kimonos included a woman's tie-dyed marriage robe in brown with orange-red, white and blue patterning that was $4,000. A fancier woman's robe in white, embroidered with stenciled flowers in orange and black with gold leaves and lined with orange silk, was about $6,700.

SHOICHIRO MIZUTANI

Shukodo Oriental Art
3-39 Sanjo-Sagaru
Yamtooji
Higashiyama-ku
Kyoto 605
Japan
Phone: (81-75) 531-4585
Hours: 9:30 A.M. to 6 P.M. Monday to Saturday, appointment advised

Shoichiro Mizutani began in business as an art dealer in 1970 after he graduated from Doshisha University, where he studied political science. At first he worked with his father, Nisaburo Mizutani, at his shop, selling screens, scrolls, porcelains, tea ceremony wares—everything Japanese. Yoko Mizutani, an older sister of Shoichiro Mizutani, is a dealer in antique textiles.

Mr. Mizutani stocks early Japanese ceramics, works that collectors are increasingly investigating in the West because they are more robust than the Chinese Sung porcelains of the same period. He handles scrolls and calligraphy and produced an important cultural treasure, a Momo-yama scroll, a mid-16th-century seated portrait of the founder of a temple in Kyoto. The work was purchased from a late-Meiji collector. Calligraphy here dates from the seventh century, or Nara period, and includes poetry and other calligraphy by monks and paintings.

The dealer also handles Japanese lacquer boxes and writing materials from the Kamakura period (1192-1333) through Momo-yama of the late 16th century when the craft was at its zenith in Japan, and early works of the Meiji period. Two examples that he showed were a mid-16th-century Momo-yama box, made before the Edo period, exquisitely decorated with flowers, that was $25,750 and an even rarer tiny Kamakura box of the late 12th century that was $32,195.

Mr. Mizutani said it was best to make an appointment because he goes to an auction at some point almost every day.

Prices start at about $640. "The highest price is unknown," he said.

SHOJI YAMANAKA

Yamanaka & Company
21 Sangobocho
Awataguchi
Higashiyama-ku
Kyoto
Japan
Phone: (81-75) 561-0931
Hours: 9 A.M. to 7:30 P.M. Tuesday to Sunday
Closed Jan. 1 to 3

"I think Yamanaka started about 1860," said Shoji Yamanaka on an early spring afternoon as tourists descended on the shop that is the most famous in the West for Japanese antiques.

The shop's popularity seems justified because of Yamanaka's long history in the West, even though the success of these shops ended with World War II, when they were closed, their assets confiscated and the stock sold. Mr. Yamanaka said that his great-great-grandfather sent a set of furniture to the St. Louis Exposition in 1904, a time when Japanese art was sweeping the United States and Europe. "Before the war we had three stores in the United States—in New York, Chicago and Boston." There were others elsewhere, he said, in London, Beijing and Tianjin, China.

Shoji Yamanaka, who was born in 1931, knew little of that period, but he is very much in charge of the antiquities and art works at Yamanaka's warehouses and main shop. The gallery where the tourists browse is stocked with many fine examples of Japanese, Chinese and Korean ceramics, lacquers, jades, bronzes, sculpture, screens, textiles and paintings. The range is wide in the periods covered, going from ancient Chinese works of the Shang and Chou periods through the 19th-century Chinese Ch'ing, Japanese Meiji and Korean Li works.

The price range is also broad, starting at $50 for an old ceramic dish. Mr. Yamanaka still owns great treasures for which the prices would be in six figures, including a sixth-century Chinese stone head from a cave in the Tien Shan Mountains that was $250,000.

The 19th-century founder of Yamanaka was Kichirobei Yamanaka.

SHIGEHIKO YANAGI

Shimbashi Agaru
Yamatoojidori
Higashiyama-ku
Kyoto
Phone: (81-75) 561-5676, 721-1456
Hours: 9 A.M. to 6 P.M. daily, appointment suggested

Shigehiko Yanagi or his assistants are on hand seven days a week to show the stunning screens in his inventory. Some were as early as the 15th century, but most were from the 16th to 20th centuries. Fourteenth-century screens do not come on the market, an assistant reported through an interpreter.

The gallery, where English was not spoken during that visit, offers some of the finest selections of screens available and is not a place for the casual shopper. Because screens are also fragile, Mr. Yanagi has photographed those in his stock and viewers can select from the photographs those they wish to see. Those discussed cost $8,000 to $110,000.

Mr. Yanagi will not break up important pairs of screens, which are rare in period works and therefore choice. The screens come in many sizes, two-fold, six-fold, as singles or in pairs. The variety of boldly graphic realistic images was astounding and included hunting scenes as well as nature and wildlife: monkeys, birds in flight, ocean waves, flower-filled gardens, wild beasts and quiet ponds. The depiction of skies, mountains and oceans and their bold colorings linger long in the memory.

T. YANAGI FINE ARTS AND CURIOS

Nawate Street
Shinmonzen Agaru
Higashiyama-ku,
Kyoto
Japan
Phone: (81-75) 551-1284, 561-9044
Hours: 9 A.M. to 6 P.M. every day, appointment suggested

Takashi Yanagi stocks fine examples of period Japanese wares and specializes in ceramics from the 9th to 19th centuries. There were baroque guardian figures from the 14th century, hanging scrolls, screens, lacquer wares and showcases filled with handsome examples of brown-and-white tea ceremony wares, a ninth-century Heian grayish pottery vase and many pale green stoneware vessels, greener than celadon. Adding to the variety was a porcelain bowl made for trade with the Portuguese in the 17th or 18th century that was $20,000.

A marvelous Bizen-ware teapot in reddish clay with an ash glaze showed the Japanese at their most voluptuous in the shaping of such vessels. The finer examples of these vessels are $10,000 to $20,000, Mr. Yanagi said. He also produced a box with tea-ceremony wares made in the 16th century and signed by a master from that period and by another from about 1800.

There were vaselike ceramic vessels, including one that was black inside with a checked pattern in black and gray on part of the outside. A 15th-century Negoro lacquer box, black with red on top, had marvelous strap-band hinges.

Calligraphy here includes Heian scrolls, which are from old Kyoto, some of which have drawn images. One scroll showed a Buddha surrounded by his disciples. As a foil for silver and gold, the paper was dyed indigo many times. The scroll was a sutra, or scriptural narrative, in Chinese characters executed by a Japanese.

Prices range from about $1,000 to $23,000.

TOKYO

KIRYU KITAYAMA

Kitayama Fine Arts
Kojun Building
8-7, Ginza, 6-chome
Chuo-ku
Tokyo
Japan
Phone: (81-3) 572-0701
Hours: 10 A.M. to 6:30 P.M. Monday to Saturday, appointment suggested
Closed between Christmas and New Year's

This elegant street-floor shop with mustard walls and beige carpeting stocks fine ceramics and bronzes dating from antiquity through the Ch'ing period. Kiryu Kitayama was 23 years with Mayuyama and went on his own in 1970, opening this gallery.

The stock covers the same periods and materials as Mayuyama. On view were Han mirrors and bronzes, Sung porcelains and Korean ceramics. One of the more impressive works was a late Han bronze tiger weight, small and well modeled, that was $33,000. A stunning, narrow-necked vase from the Liao period (916 to 1125) with a caramel glaze was $30,000. The prices here start at less than $3,300 for a Ch'ing plate or a Korean 18th-century brush rest.

HIRANO KOTOKEN COMPANY

3-13, Ginza, 7-chome
Chuo-ku
Tokyo 104
Japan
Phone: (81-3) 572-7371
Hours: 10 A.M. to 7 P.M. Monday to Friday, 10 A.M. to 6 P.M. Saturday
Closed the first two weeks in August and two weeks at Christmas and New Year's

HIRANO KOTOKEN COMPANY

12-21, Nishitenma, 4-chome
Kita-ku
Osaka 530
Japan
Phone: (81-6) 365-0219
Hours: 10 A.M. to 7 P.M. Monday to Friday, 10 A.M. to 6 P.M. Saturday
Closed the first two weeks in August and two weeks at Christmas and New Year's

Tatsuo Hirano heads a company stocking Japanese and Chinese stone sculpture, Chinese ceramics, ancient bronzes and scrolls. The business was founded in 1936 in Osaka by his father, Ryoji Hirano, who sold Chinese antiques. The younger Mr. Hirano became a dealer after completing his university studies in 1962, but he worked elsewhere for nine years to learn the business of handling paintings. He then joined his father in Osaka in 1971 and they opened this branch, a two-story gallery in Tokyo. He is today one of the top art dealers in Japan.

"Usually in this business we don't want to show many pieces," Mr. Hirano said. "If everyone sees it, it puts something on it, and nobody wants it." In keeping with Japanese practice, therefore, Mr. Hirano is selective in what he shows in the gallery and to clients. He suggests that people make an appointment because most of the important pieces are not on view and are brought out of storage to show.

Ancient Chinese bronzes, which have become increasingly important to collectors in the West in the last decade, are specialties here. Mr. Hirano had a number of Shang and Chou vessels, tall trumpet-shaped vases, boxlike vessels, beakers and gravy-boatlike ewers. There were Han and Tang bronzes and mirrors, 14th-century celadons and Sung through Ch'ing porcelains. Mr. Hirano said his inventory included more than 300 works.

Most of his clients, he said, are Japanese collectors and museums. He has supplied many works to the Idemitsu Museum, a private museum in Tokyo that is owned by and housed in the Tokyo headquarters of Idemitsu Kosan, a privately held petroleum company. He also does a lot of business through the dealer-controlled auctions. Foreign collectors and dealers buy about $5 million worth annually from Mr. Hirano.

Prices range from $1,000 for a Sung bowl to more than $1 million for major Ming porcelains or an ancient bronze.

GEORGE LEE

Daijindo Company
Daijindo Building, First Floor
6-12-1 Minami Aoyama
Minato-ku
Tokyo 107
Japan
Phone: (81-3) 486-5091, 486-5092
Hours: 10 A.M. to 6 P.M. Monday to Saturday
Closed the first two weeks of August and from Christmas to New Year's

George Lee, a dealer in Chinese ceramics, was born in Hong Kong and is now a Japanese citizen. He is the third generation in his family in the art business. His grandfather Sammy Y. Lee was also an author of several books on Chinese art covering ceramics, lacquer, furniture and rugs in Beijing before 1949. His father, King Tsi Lee, is a major collector of Chinese lacquer and helped form the Ataka Collection in Osaka.

When George Lee went into business on his own in 1984, he was twenty-seven and had trained as an apprentice in Japan for more than four years. Many of the Japanese buyers, including those with museums, are older men, he said. For example, one of the biggest buyers of Chinese ceramics and all art is Seijire Matsuoka, who was born in 1894. Now younger Japanese collectors are also buying these wares. About 20 to 25 percent of all his sales are to Americans, Mr. Lee reported, adding that the figure was higher when the dollar was more favorable against the yen.

Mr. Lee's offerings start at about $1,000 for Imari porcelain. Among the early ceramics on view were a big blue-and-white dish from 1403-1424, a foliated vessel embellished with chrysanthemums that was $100,000. Han dynasty tomb figures from recent excavations that have been exported from China through Macao have caused prices to fall in this market. The better pieces will be restored to their former values, he said.

Mr. Lee's main focus is Tang through Ming, with special emphasis on Sung ceramics. He did, however, have Tang pottery figures in three colors, green, caramel-brown and yellow, and also an imperial yellow bowl, a Chia-ching dish and a polychromed seven-inch Nabeshima dish awash with rhododendron in green, orange, blue and white. The Nabeshima dish was later sold to a museum.

MAYUYAMA & COMPANY

5-9, 2-chome
Kyobashi
Chuo-ku
Tokyo
Japan
Phone: (81-3) 561-5146
Hours: 10 A.M. to 6 P.M. Monday to Saturday, appointment suggested

Founded in Beijing by Matsutaro Mayuyama in 1904 when Chinese art was a new field for the Japanese to collect, this Chinese concern is now in its third generation, under the direction of Saburo Takahashi. Mr. Takahashi, born into the Mayuyama family in 1925, was adopted as a child by the Takahashi family. He has worked at Mayuyama since 1946 and has headed it since 1986.

At its founding, most Japanese collected tea-ceremony works. At that time the railroads were being built in China, and excavations unearthed great Tang works from tombs. They were not appreciated by the Chinese, so they were acquired by the famous collectors and museums in Europe and the United States and, to a lesser extent, in Japan.

Matsutaro Mayuyama concentrated his interests in ceramics, his son Junkichi Mayuyama said, adding: "My father died very young." The younger Mr. Mayuyama, who headed the business until recently and is still active as an adviser, is the older brother of Mr. Takahashi. Junkichi Mayuyama's son, Yusuhiko, was active in the business until recently.

"After the war, that moment was very important to the firm," Mr. Takahashi said. "All of the rich and important Japanese collectors came out to the market. They had to sell all the heirloom pieces." Mr. Takahashi said that Americans such as Sherman Lee, later director of the Cleveland Museum of Art, were in Japan after the war. "They had the best chance to collect many masterpieces of Chinese art in Japan. They became very good friends of ours."

The Mayuyama gallery, grayish-tan walls, caramel-colored leather armchairs, green carpeting, is the perfect backdrop for Tang ceramics as well as the earlier bronzes and later porcelains stocked here. "We don't set a minimum price," the dealer said, adding that there are offerings from about $700 up for a Sung dish.

He said the gallery stocks all periods of Chinese art, from antiquities through Ch'ing. There are ancient bronzes, ceramics of all periods, lacquer wares and jades. Japanese ceramics are also carried here, from the neolithic pots of the Jomon period to the porcelains of the Edo period. Japanese paintings and folding screens are not a specialty. "We carry them only when we find the best pieces," Mr. Takahashi said.

SETSU GATODO

3-7, 9-chome
Nihombashi
Chuo-ku
Tokyo 103
Japan
Phone: (81-3) 271-7571
Hours: 11 A.M. to 6 P.M. Monday to Friday, 11 A.M. to 6 P.M. on alternate Saturdays, appointment suggested

The entrance to this impressive four-story gallery, a soaring space with blond cypress walls and gleaming modern furniture, is dominated by an outsize 10th-century wood sculpture of a standing god.

Iwao Setso handles ceramics, sculpture, calligraphy and paintings dating from the Nara period of the seventh century through the Edo period of the 18th century.

"I built this building after I saw a fire at a lacquer store in front of our store in 1976," Mr. Setsu said. "And I felt I had to build a secure building to protect my—at the same time, our nation's—treasure from a disaster."

Mr. Setsu's father, Inosuke Setsu, established the gallery in 1931, and Mr. Setsu went to work for his father in 1960.

The sculpture and outsize ceramic vessels here are most memorable. The figures of gods, guardians and attendants of the 10th, 14th and 17th centuries in wood, bronze and stone are compelling studies. An outsize 14th-century Shigaraki stoneware vessel about 30 inches high of the Kamakura period is about $20,000.

In Japan some dealers have photographs of the art and objects they offer because they do not own the works. Mr. Setsu owns what he sells, and his clients have included several major museums in the West, including the Cleveland Museum of Art, and many of the major stateside collectors, including Mary and Jackson Burke, John Powers and John D. Rockefeller 3d. He said a major difference between Japanese dealers and those in the United States and Europe is that a Japanese dealer will always buy back anything he has sold.

Prices range from about $2,000 to to $1 million.

S. YABUMOTO COMPANY

Gallery Center Building, Seventh Floor
3-2, Ginza, 6-chome
Chuo-ku
Tokyo 104
Japan
Phone: (81-3) 572-2748
Hours: 10 A.M. to 6 P.M. Monday to Saturday
Closed the first three weeks of August, the end of December and the first week of January

Soichiro Yabumoto deals in Japanese and Chinese calligraphy, paintings, screens, sculpture, ceramics and lacquerware. Among the interesting works on view during one visit were a Zen painting from the late 16th century by the priest Fugai that was about $10,000 and a Tang figure of a woman on a horse that was about $26,000.

"Mainly we do hanging scrolls," Shunichi Yabumoto, the assistant director and the son of the president, said. "We know the client's taste." He unrolled a painting with calligraphy by Ikkyu, a 15th-century Zen monk known for his wit. And he also showed a 12th-century illustrated sutra on a dark blue ground, still bearing the seal of the temple Jingo-ji of Kyoto.

Mr. Yabumoto also handles outsize sculpture. There was a 12th-century fierce-faced, robustly carved guardian on display. Western clients are interested in paintings by artists of several schools that are highly decorative—the Bunjinga or Nanga southern school as well as the Rimpa school. Screens from the Rimpa are in the collections of the Freer Gallery of Art in Washington, Boston's Museum of Fine Arts and the Metropolitan Museum of Art in New York.

INDEX

Kunsthandel Aalderink, 139–40
Didier Aaron, 33, 183, 259–61
Aaron, Hervé, 260
Aaron, Olivier, 260
Berdj Abadjian, 34–35
Acevedo, Alexander, 37–39
Acoma kachina dolls, 17
Adam, Robert, 130
Adams, Norman, 183–5
Adler, Rose, 48
advertising signs, 40
African art, 15, 26, 123, 145, 241, 291, 292, 315
African jewelry, 16, 104, 315
Afshar rugs, 251, 299
agateware, 42
Agra rugs, 43
alabasters, 155
A la Vieille Russie, 35–36
Galerie Bei Der Albertina, 295–96
Alexander & Berendt, 186
Alexander Gallery, 37–39
Armin B. Allen, 187–88
amber, 324
America Hurrah, 39–40
American arts and crafts, 65–66, 87, 115
American folk art, 9–10, 11–12, 37, 40, 62–63, 68–69, 112–13, 116
American furniture, 12, 31, 33, 65–66, 112–13, 115, 116, 122
  country, 11–12, 62, 113
  New England, 12, 94–96, 113
  17th-century, 94–96
  18th-century, 9, 12, 94–96
  19th-century, 9, 12, 63, 94–96
American Indian art, 9, 15–17, 37–40, 74, 104–5
Albert Amor Ltd., 188–89
amulets, 235
Anatolian rugs, 248, 250, 253, 298, 303
ancient art, *see* antiquities
Andri, Ferdinand, 296
Antique Porcelain Company, 41, 189–91
antiques shows:
  Biennale Internationale des Antiquaires, 292
  Burlington House Fair, 243
  Chicago International Antiques Show, 32, 199
  Fall Antiques Show at the Pier, 114
  Grosvenor House Antiques Fair, 244–45
  International Antiques Show, 202
  Modernism: A Century of Style and Design 1860–1960, 115
  Nouveau Drouot, 293
  San Francisco Fall Antiques Show, 135
  Theta Charity Antiques Show of Houston, 16
  Tri Delta Charity Antiques Show, 10, 13
  Winter Antiques Show, 116, 188, 202
antiquities, 15, 54–55, 79–80, 110–11, 146, 148, 153, 175, 179, 227, 235–36, 241, 262, 291, 299, 309–13, 317, 337, 341
Antonacci, Giuseppe, 170–71
Fabrizio Apolloni, 167–68

architect-designed furniture, 25–27, 59, 61–62, 65–66, 77, 81–82, 115, 130, 194–95 264–65, 269, 284, 297–98
architectural drawings, 202
architectural elements, 69, 86–87, 107–8, 186, 201
Armitage, 191–92
armorial ceramics, 207–9, 275
arms and armor, 291
Aronson, David Ronny, 140
Aronson Antiquaire, 140–41
Art Deco, 20, 22, 48, 51–52, 59, 60, 84–87, 89–90, 108, 115, 143–44, 158, 159, 169, 213, 215, 219, 249, 257, 276, 279, 289, 291, 292
  furniture, 58, 59, 76–77, 89–90, 159, 166, 264–65, 268–69, 279–80, 289
  jewelry, 73, 76, 89–90, 91, 282, 304
Art Nouveau, 20, 60, 76, 84–87, 115, 143, 158, 166, 213, 249, 251–52, 257, 276, 279, 280, 292, 300–301, 316
  furniture, 76–77, 251–52, 264–65, 279–80
  jewelry, 73, 91, 252, 282, 304
arts and crafts, 115, 214
  American, 65–66, 87, 115
  Dutch, 143
  English, 87, 147, 215
Art Trading (U.S.) Ltd., 41–42
Asenbaum, Inge, 297
Herbert Asenbaum, Kunst und Antiquitatenhandel, 296–98
Asenbaum, Paul, 297
Asenbaum, Stefan, 297
Ashbee, Charles, 214
Asian art, *see* Oriental art
astrolabes, 274
Aublet, Félix, 269
Aubusson rugs, 19
auction houses:
  Butterfield & Butterfield, 135
  Christie's, 117, 245
  Christie's Amsterdam B.V., 149
  Christie's East, 117
  Christie's International, 180
  Christie's South Kensington, 245
  Dorotheum, 305
  William Doyle Galleries, 117
  Gallery Wolfgang Ketterer, 257
  Edgar Abraham Mannheimer, 176–77
  Phillips, 118, 246
  Sotheby's, 118, 246, 328
  Sotheby's Amsterdam, 149
  Sotheby's Geneva, 181
  Spink & Son Ltd., 232–33
Augsburg silver, 256
Austrian art, 22–23, 81–82, 174, 257, 295–98, 301, 302, 305
Austrian ceramics, 23, 190, 295, 297
Austrian furniture, 22–23, 27, 33, 81–82, 87, 105, 123, 158, 159, 171, 254–55, 295–98, 302
Austrian Secessionists, 158, 302
autographs, 127, 206–7
automatons, 176–77
Aveline, 261–62

Bakelite, 19–20, 67–68
Balene Inc., 15–16
Baluch rugs, 251
bamboo, 51, 141, 324–25, 331
  brush holders, 263–64
Barberis, Roberto, 303
Barker, Margery, 23
Baroque period, 54, 190, 260, 305
  furniture, 123, 170, 171, 260, 299, 305
Jacques Barrère, 262–63
Bartolozzi, Guido, 165
Bartolozzi, Massimo, 165
Guido Bartolozzi & Figlio, 165
Barye, Antoine-Louis, 179
baskets, 40, 112, 302
Bateman, Hester, 217–18
bathroom fixtures, Victorian, 108
Baudisch, Gudrun, 295
Bauhaus, 115, 158
Bayer, Herbert, 265
beadwork:
  African, 15, 104
  American Indian, 17, 38–39
Beauclaire, Isaac, 256
Beck, Martin, 191
Bedouin jewelry, 313
Behrens, Peter, 219
Beiny, Rotraut, 189–90
belle époque, 126

Galleria Luigi Bellini, 163–64
Bellini, Mario A., 163–64
Beneman, Guillaume, 230
bentwood, 22–23, 27, 81, 82, 297–98
Yossi Benyaminoff, 315–16
Berendt, Frank, 186
Bernheimer, 247–48
Bernheimer, Konrad, 247–48
Bernheimer Fine Arts Ltd., 192
Adil Besim, 298–99
Bessarabian rugs, 176, 194
Bett, Hugh, 220
Piero Betti, 168–69
Beurdeley, 263–64
Beurdeley, Jean-Michel, 263
Beurdeley, Michel, 263
Galerie Maria de Beyrie, 264–65
Bianconi, Fulvio, 90
Biedermeier, 22, 33, 87, 88, 123, 131, 165, 254–55, 296–99, 305
Biennale Internationale des Antiquaires, 292
Bijar rugs, 19, 251
Bizen-ware, 335
David Black, 193
H. Blairman, 194–95
blankets, 38–40
Doris Leslie Blau, 43–44
Vojtech Blau, 44–45
Blitz, Dries, 141–42
Blitz Antiek en Kunsthandel, 141–42
Bernard Blondeel, 151–52
Bluett, Roger B., 195–96
Bluett & Sons Ltd., 195–96
Blumka, 46–47
Blumka, Ruth, 46–47
Blumka, Victoria, 46–47
Boeri, Cini, 284
Bohemian Art Nouveau glass, 301
boiserie, 288
Bokhara rugs, 248
Bonet, Paul, 48
books, 3–4, 5–7, 23–24, 28–29, 48, 56–57, 70–71, 126–28, 206–7, 219–20, 228–29, 277
  anthropology, 229
  architecture, 229
  biographies, 206–7
  cartography, 28; *see also* maps
  economics, 126, 229
  English, 5–6, 127, 220
  European, 229
  geography, 71
  historical, 4, 28–29, 127
  Islamic, 48
  medical, 126
  medieval, 48, 128–30
  military, 220
  music, 206–7
  paleography, 128–30
  philosophy, 229
  Renaissance, 48, 128–30
  science, 71, 126, 229
  travel, 220, 229
Borms, France, 157–58
botanical drawings, 187–88
Böttger stoneware, 254
Boucheron jewelry, 76, 89, 282
Boudin, Thomas, 186
Boulle, André-Charles, 223, 270, 271, 274, 299
Boulton, Matthew, 217
Bouwnan, Wim, 139–40
Bow ceramics, 78, 189, 191
boxes, 125, 157, 175
  Art Deco, 289
  Art Nouveau, 252
  enameled, 322
  German, 256
  gold, 227, 239
  ivory, 323
  Japanese, 35, 198, 260, 332, 335
  lacquer, 141
  Russian, 237
  silver, 214, 316
boxwood figures, 151
Brandt, Edgar, 52, 77, 90, 214, 219
brass candlesticks, 131, 155
brass jugs, 313
Martin Breslauer Inc., 47–48
Breuer, Marcel, 158, 265
Bristol ceramics, 189, 205
bronzes, 71–72, 80, 85, 87, 94, 109, 141, 143, 145, 166, 167, 169, 174, 179, 186, 213, 221, 248, 249, 252, 277, 291, 310, 318, 324–25
  ancient, 311, 312, 326
  Chinese, 156, 197, 262–63, 321, 338–39, 341
  Egyptian, 80, 154
  European, 76, 230
  Greek, 55, 80

bronzes *(cont'd.)*
Oriental, 80, 233, 267, 324, 333, 337, 342
Renaissance, 148, 163, 240, 273
Roman, 55, 80
Rafi Brown, 309–10
buckles, 249
Buddhas, 123, 263
Buddhist art, medieval, 102
Bugatti, Carlo, 27, 85, 166, 266, 276
Bugatti, Ettore, 77
Bunjinga school, 343
Burlington House Fair, 243
Bustelli figures, 190
Butterfield & Butterfield, 135
butterflies, enameled, 147
B.V.R.B. (Bernhard van Risamburgh), 93, 286
Byzantine art, 79, 147, 179, 180, 310, 312, 313

Cabaret Fledermaus, 23, 82, 159
Calderoni of Rome, 215
calligraphy, 322
Chinese, 154, 343
Islamic, 203–4, 286
Japanese, 102, 332, 335, 342, 343
Turkish, 286
Cambodian art, 154, 264, 324
Camoin, 265–66
candelabra, 230, 249, 273, 274, 284, 285
candlesticks, 131, 155, 163, 171, 179, 211, 230, 313
Carlin, Martin, 262
carpenter's sacks, 331
Carrell, Russell, 116, 135
cars, 176
Carter, Anthony, 196
Cartier, 73–74, 76, 89, 147, 176, 215, 282
cash registers, 177
cassones, 164, 167
Castellanis, jewelry by, 239
Castillo, Antonio, 90
cast iron furniture, 11, 64
Caucasian rugs, 193, 194, 248, 250–51, 253, 298, 303
Celtic art, 111, 241
ceramics, 19–20, 49, 67, 91, 116, 213, 218, 240, 243, 249, 252, 277, 291, 305, 309, 313
armorial, 207–9
Austrian, 23, 295
Chinese, *see* Chinese ceramics; Chinese export
English, *see* English ceramics
European, 20, 42, 109–10, 116, 142, 148, 244, 281, 290
French, 187, 275, 292
German, 140, 187, 275
Italian, 187, 215, 275
Japanese, 102–3, 232, 332, 333, 335, 341–43
Oriental, 71–72, 93–94, 116, 132–33, 139–40, 141, 144, 232–33, 244, 281, 286, 333, 337
Spanish, 151, 275
see also porcelains; pottery
ceramic tiles, 180, 210, 249
Chait, Allan S., 49
Ralph M. Chait Galleries, 49–51
chalkware, 62
Chambers, Thomas, 62
Chambers, William, 201
Champa sculpture, 264
chandeliers, 171, 221, 224, 265, 284
Robert Chang, Antiques and Jewelry, 321
Chantilly ceramics, 190
Chareau, Pierre, 52, 77, 90, 265, 268, 269, 279
Charles X, 87, 123, 152–53, 160, 260, 282
Charnelhouse, William, 97
Chelsea ceramics, 189, 190–91
Chenevière, Antoine, 236
Cherubinus, Andrea, 165
Cheuret, Albert, 52
Chia-ching, 340
Chicago International Antiques Show, 32, 199
Ch'ien Lung dynasty, 49, 140, 232, 290
china, *see* ceramics, 218
Chinese art, 49, 53, 54, 71–73, 125, 139, 154, 160, 197–200, 202–3, 264, 266, 324–25, 329–30, 338–39, 341
bronzes, 156, 197, 262–63, 324, 338–39, 341
Ch'ing, 196, 333, 337, 341

Chou, 262, 333
Han, 198, 262, 337, 339
K'ang Hsi, 134
Ming, 73, 156, 196, 262
neolithic, 71–72, 196, 263
Shang, 197, 262, 321, 333
Sung, 139, 156, 196
Tang, 125, 132, 139–40, 156, 196–98, 262–63, 339, 343
tomb figures, 73, 161
Wei, 156, 263
Yüan, 154
Yung Lo, 146
Chinese ceramics, 9, 42, 72, 132–33, 140, 142, 148, 161, 196, 197, 208, 232–33, 248, 274, 275, 290, 323, 326, 333, 338, 339–41, 343
Ch'ien Lung, 49, 140, 232, 290
Ch'ing, 49, 140, 141, 197, 248, 290, 321, 326, 339
Chou, 326, 339
Han, 49, 132–33, 262
K'ang Hsi, 49, 248
Ming, 140–42, 148, 153–54, 196–98, 232, 262, 275, 290, 321, 324–25, 326, 339, 340
Shang, 326, 339
Sung, 49, 133, 141, 156, 196, 198, 281, 321, 324, 337, 339, 340
Tang, 49, 132, 156, 161, 196, 232, 263, 326, 340, 341
Chinese export:
ceramics, 9, 208, 233, 275, 290
furniture, 156
porcelains, 50–51, 233
silver, 50
tableware, 91
Chinese furniture, 54, 125–26, 161, 262, 267, 326, 329–30
Chinese rugs, 35, 250
Ch'ing dynasty, 49, 140, 141, 196, 197, 248, 262, 290, 321, 326, 333, 337, 339, 341
chinoiserie, 223, 233
Chiparus, Demêtre, 213, 277
Chippendale, 12, 96, 99, 106, 154, 184, 201, 221–22, 225
Chou dynasty, 262, 326, 333, 339
Christie's, 117, 245
Christie's Amsterdam B.V., 149
Christie's East, 117
Christie's International, 180
Christie's South Kensington, 245
cigarette cases, 159, 249, 256
Gallery Bob Claes, 152–53
Clichy ceramics, 190
Cliff, Clarice, 90, 218–19
clocks, 146, 148, 170, 171, 176–77, 226, 237, 266, 272, 278
cloisonné, 141, 262
Cnudde, André, 161
Coard furniture, 27, 268–69
coats of arms, 174, 208, 257
coffeepots, 256–57
Coger, Henry, 9–10
coins, 232–33, 291, 312, 313
Colinet, C. R., 166
Colnaghi (U.S.A.) Ltd., 203
Colnaghi Oriental, 202–3
columns, 89, 108
marble, 107, 172
stone, 172
commedia dell'arte figures, 190, 254
Copier, Andries D., 144
coral, 17, 198
cornhusk bags, 40
coromandel, 267–68
screens, 131, 226, 262
costumes, Oriental, 330
country furnishings, 11–12, 30, 40, 62, 113, 114
see also folk art
Coustou, Nicolas, 186
creamware, 205, 210
Cressent, Charles, 178, 272
Gisèle Croës, 155–56
Crow Indians, 38
Martha Lanman Cusick, 17–18
Czechoslovak glass, 241
Czeschka, Carl Otto, 23, 296

Dali, Salvador, 169
Ariane Dandois, 267–68
Danish furniture, 134
Danish silver, 249
Dante folding chairs, 164
Daum glass, 52, 90, 166, 214, 215, 219, 249
Christian de Bruyn, 157
de Bruyn, Germaine, 157
decoys, 9, 40
de Feure, Georges, 77
Degas, Edgar, 179

de Lamerie, Paul, 97, 217, 227
Delft, 148, 154
  Dutch, 140, 144, 275, 281
  English, 41, 78, 209, 210, 231
Della Robbia, 163
DeLorenzo, 51
DeLorenzo, Anthony, 51–53
DeLorenzo 1950, 51–53
Demachy, Alain, 265
Derby ceramics, 78, 189, 191
Deruta vessels, 163
Desforges furniture, 260
de Stijl furniture, 143–44
Galerie DeWindt, 157–58
DeWindt, Jacques, 157–58
di Castro, Alberto, 170
di Castro, Franco, 170
Alberto di Castro & Figlio, 169–70
Dillingham, Gaylord, 119–20
Dillingham & Company, 119–20
Directoire, 88, 123, 237
dolls, 37, 331
  kachina, 15, 17
Domergue, Robert, 121–22
Robert Domergue & Company, 121–22
Dominique furniture, 27
Dorotheum, 305
William Doyle Galleries, 117
drawings, 23, 93, 146, 187–88
  architectural, 25, 202
  Art Nouveau, 143
  botanical, 187–88
Dresden beakers, 301
Drum, John, Jr., 122
Drum & Company, 122–23
Dubois, Jacques, 169, 288
Dufet, Michael, 289
Dunand, Jean, 51–52, 90, 158, 166, 268, 269, 276, 277, 280, 289
durries, 194
Dutch art, 142–44, 174
Dutch arts and crafts, 143
Dutch Delft, 140, 144, 275, 281
Dutch furniture, 59, 120, 140–41, 143–45, 148
Galerie Jean-Jacques Dutko, 268–69
Anne-Sophie Duval, 269

Eames, Charles, 259
Easter eggs, 35–37, 176, 238–39
Edo period, 331, 341, 342
Antonacci Efrati, 170–71
Egyptian art, 80, 111–12, 145, 154, 168, 172, 179, 236
Egyptian Revival, 85, 87
Elizabethan Revival, 91, 98, 108
Elizabethan tableware, 91, 98
Elliott, Scott, 25–26
Ellis, Harvey, 65–66
Robert H. Ellsworth Ltd., 53–54
embroideries, 141, 194, 315, 324, 331
André Emmerich, 54–55
Empire, 147, 152–53, 261, 279
  furniture, 62, 87, 88, 121, 152–53, 173, 178, 212, 230, 237, 271, 288
enamels, enameled, 35–37, 151, 174, 227
  boxes, 32
  candleholders, 179
  glass, 174–75
  jewelry, 147
  medieval, 93
English art, 99, 221, 223, 232
English arts and crafts, 87, 147, 215
English ceramics, 41–42, 65, 77–79, 99, 109, 189–91, 209–10, 221, 223, 230–31, 244
  Bow, 78, 189, 191
  Bristol, 78, 189, 205
  Chelsea, 78
  Delft, 41, 78, 209, 210, 231
  Derby, 78, 189, 191
  Longton Hall, 78
  medieval, 209–10
  17th-century, 209
  18th-century, 31, 78, 205, 209
  19th-century, 31, 78, 205, 209
  Spode, 78
  Worcester, 31, 78
English furniture, 21–22, 31, 33, 98–101, 105–6, 119–20, 130–31, 154, 175, 183–85, 201, 212, 221–25, 240, 243, 244, 266
  17th-century, 21–22, 99, 151, 215–16, 226, 231
  18th-century, 9, 58, 99, 120, 123, 130–31, 183, 215–16, 221, 223, 226, 231
  19th-century, 9, 21–22, 99, 120, 183, 215–16, 223, 226
English silver, *see* silver
engravings, 99, 208

Eskenazi, 197–99
Eskenazi, Giuseppe, 197–98
Eskimo art, 146
Esthetic Movement, 194–95
Esthetic Realism, 63
Etruscan art, 80, 179
European art, 60, 115, 142, 157, 158, 178, 223, 292, 315
European ceramics, 20, 109–10, 116, 142, 148, 244, 281, 290
  porcelains, 91–92, 133–34, 144, 186, 189–91, 223, 230
European furniture, 59, 109–10, 115, 116, 119–20, 122, 125–26, 130–31, 133–34, 140–41, 144, 148, 157, 158, 169, 186, 222–23, 229–30, 243, 244, 266, 267
  17th-century, 121, 226
  18th-century, 30, 121, 178, 226, 248
  19th-century, 30, 88, 121, 178, 226
  20th-century, 26–27, 283
European porcelains, *see* European ceramics
European rugs, 19, 35, 298
European silver, *see* silver
European tapestries, 250, 298
export wares, 207–8; *see also* Chinese export

Fabergé, Peter Carl, 35–37, 238–39
Fabergé eggs, 176, 238–39
Fabre, Jean-Paul, 270
Fabre, Michel, 270
B. Fabre & Sons, 270–71
Faenza vessels, 163
Fahrenson, Monika, 249
faïence, 41, 148, 187, 198, 276, 281, 290, 310, 313
Fallani, Paola, 166
Fallani, Roberto, 166
Fallani Best, 166
Fall Antiques Show at the Pier, 114
farmer's coats, 331
Federal furniture, 63
Feld, Stuart P., 61–63
Joseph W. Fell, 18
Louis D. Fenton, 123–24
Ferahan rugs, 35, 43
Field, Erastus Salisbury, 62, 69
fireman's jackets, 331
fireplaces, 108
fisherman's coats, 331
flatware, 98, 215, 217, 302; *see also* tableware
John F. Fleming Inc., 56–57
Flemish furniture, 154, 260
Flüli glasses, 174
Fly By Nite, 19–20
folk art, 37, 67, 114
  American, 9–10, 11–12, 37, 40, 62–63, 68–69, 112–13, 116
  French, 9–10
  Japanese, 102–3
Folter, Roland, 70
Fong, Charles Luke, 132–33
Fouquet, Georges, 73, 76, 90, 213, 215, 282
Frank, Jean-Michel, 27, 52, 77, 90, 265, 269, 276, 279, 283
Frankenthal porcelains, 190
Franklin, Paul, 21–22
Malcolm Franklin Inc., 20
Michael Franses, 199–200
Freeman, Arthur, 228
French & Company, 57–59
French art, 151, 157, 158, 170, 174, 223, 278, 284, 292
French ceramics, 113, 187, 241, 275, 292
  porcelains, 93–94, 148, 153, 223, 273, 290
French folk art, 9–10
French furniture, 33, 59, 101, 105–6, 109–10, 120, 123, 125, 155, 170, 171, 223–25, 240, 248, 259, 266, 272–73, 278–79, 284, 285–86
  Baroque, 123, 170–71, 299, 305
  Charles X, 87, 123, 152–53, 160, 260, 262
  Empire, 87, 88, 121, 152–53, 173, 178, 212, 230, 271, 288
  Louis XIII, 155
  Louis XIV, 123, 160, 186, 230, 270, 273, 274, 284, 285, 287
  Louis XV, 129, 169, 173, 186, 230, 248, 259–60, 266, 270, 272, 274, 279, 284, 287
  Louis XVI, 88, 101, 173, 175, 186, 225, 230, 248, 261, 270, 273, 278, 284, 285, 287
  Napoleon III, 88, 160, 176
  17th-century, 121, 148, 270,

French furniture *(cont'd.)*
271–72, 288
18th-century, 30, 33, 36, 58, 93, 120, 121, 148, 160, 186, 212, 223, 253, 259–61, 266, 270, 271–72, 288, 292
19th-century, 27, 30, 87, 120, 121, 160, 175–76, 212, 223, 259–61, 271–72, 288
20th-century, 27, 283
French ivory, 47, 157
French porcelains, *see* French ceramics
French silver, *see* silver
Friedman, Audrey, 89–90
Friedman, Barry, 89
Barry Friedman Ltd., 59–61
Frishmuth, Harriet W., 85
Fulper pottery, 65
Funk, Mathäus, 178
furniture, 52, 59, 67, 75, 76, 101, 146, 148, 152, 165–67, 169, 170, 172, 173, 175, 176, 194–95, 201, 214, 261–62, 269, 273–74, 277, 291, 296–98, 299–300, 305
see also specific countries and types of furniture
futon covers, 331

Gaillard, Eugène, 282
Gallé, Emile, 59–60, 77, 85, 166, 214, 249, 276, 277
Gallery Vienna, 22–23
Galuchat, 159–60
Gamboni, Guido, 215
Garcia, Robert R., 133
gargoyles, 108
Garthorne, George, 233
Gauguin, Paul, 277
Genty furniture, 288
George, Anne Margaret, 188
Georgian styles, 21, 91, 97, 98
furniture, 21, 120, 123, 126, 212, 222
Germain, Thomas, 227
German art, 142, 145, 174, 249, 252, 257, 260
German ceramics, 140, 187, 275
porcelains, 148, 253–54, 281, 290
German furniture, 123, 131, 155, 171, 211, 248
Biedermeier, 22, 33, 87, 88, 123, 131, 165, 254–55, 296–99, 305
18th-century, 9, 253
19th-century, 9, 87
German porcelains, *see* German ceramics
Giacometti, Diego, 27, 52, 289
Giambologna, 179
Christopher Gibbs Ltd., 201–2
Jean Gismondi, 271–72
Giuliano, Carlo, 147
Giulianos, jewelry by, 239
glass, 62, 67, 85, 91, 99, 145, 159, 166, 174–75, 180, 198, 213–14, 218–19, 276, 291, 296, 300–301, 304, 305, 310, 313, 324
ancient, 111, 309, 311, 312, 316, 317–18
Austrian, 23, 301
European, 68, 142, 174, 223
French, 122, 142, 300
German, 142, 145
Italian, 68, 142, 175, 241
medieval, 145, 241
Roman, 142, 316, 317
Scandinavian, 241
Venetian, 38, 47, 104, 300–301
glass paintings, reverse, 324
Gleicher, Michael, 22
Gleicher, Norbert, 22
Gerald Godfrey/Far Eastern Art, 204, 325
Godwin, Edward William, 195
Michael Goedhuis Ltd., 202–4
gold, 256, 313
ancient, 312
boxes, 227, 239
jewelry, 180, 302
Oriental, 71
Gorham silver, 315
Gothic, *see* medieval period
Goulden, Jean, 289
Galerie am Graben, 297
Graham, Michael, 205
Graham & Oxley, 205
Galerie Grandes Epoques, 173
Gray, Eileen, 52, 90, 158, 268
Greek art, 112–12, 179–80, 236
bronzes, 55, 80
sculpture, 80, 112, 201

Greek Codices, 129
Greene, Charles Sumner, 62
Greene, Henry Mather, 62
Greenstein, Blanche, 112–13
Grendey, Giles, 216
Griffith, Patsy Lace, 9
William Griffith Antiques, 9–10
Grosvenor House Antiques Fair, 244–45
Groult, André, 268
Grueby pottery, 65
Gubbio vessels, 163
Guimard, Hector, 59, 264–65, 277

Otto Haas, 206
Haas-Stoclet, Nele, 159
Hagenauer, Franz, 67
Hagenauer, Karl, 301
Hakuin, 264
Hamill, Frances, 23
Hamill & Barker, 23–24
Hanart Gallery, 322
Han dynasty, 49, 132-33, 198, 262, 337, 339
Hanukkah lights, 316
Harcourt, Paul, 219–20
Harding, Robert, 220
Hardy, Ed, 124–26
Ed Hardy/San Francisco, 124–26
Hathaway, Rufus, 62
hat pins, 249
Heian period, 335
Heirloom & Howard, 207–9
Hellenistic art, 55, 312
Henry II, 155, 299
Henry VIII, 97
Hepplewhite furniture, 184
heraldry, 207–9
Herbaut, Christian, 88–89
Herbst, René, 158, 265
Heriz rugs, 18–19, 35, 248
Herner, Richard, 203
Eberhart, Herrmann, 250–51
Herter Brothers, 63–64
Hill, Geoffrey, 211
Hill, John, 211
Hill, Michael, 211–12
Hindu Javanese sculpture, 145
Hirano, Tatsuo, 338
Hirano Kotoken Company, 338–39
Hirschl & Adler Folk Inc., 61–63
Hirschl & Adler Galleries Inc., 61
Hirschl & Modern Inc., 61
Hispano-Moresque ceramics, 151, 275
Hittite scupltures, 80
Höchst porcelains, 190
Hoentschel, Georges, 279–80
Hoffmann, Josef, 23, 27, 59, 77, 81–82, 85, 90, 159–60, 214, 218, 249, 295, 296, 301–2
Galerie Hofstätter, 299–300
Hofstätter, Reinhold, 299
Hohokam Indians, 15–16
Holbein, Hans, 202
B.C. Holland Inc., 26–27
Honeychurch Antiques Ltd., 322–23
hooked rugs, 40, 112
Hopi Indians, 17
Jonathan Horne, 209–10
Horner, R.J., 63
Horstmann, Charlotte, 324–25
Charlotte Horstmann and Gerald Godfrey Ltd., 324–25
Horta, Victor, 77
Howard, David Sanctuary, 207–9
Howe, Marion C., 49
Huari people, 80
Hudson River School, 37
Hunter-Stiebel, Penelope, 93
Hunzinger, George, 63
Huseby, James G., 133

icons, 35–37, 163
Ikkyu, 343
illuminated manuscripts, 4, 48, 71, 220
Imari period, 169, 205, 340
incunabula, 71
Indian art, 54, 104, 146, 202–3, 267, 286, 324
  Mogul, 105, 146, 156, 200
  Naga, 104
  Pahari, 146
Indian furniture, 105
Indonesian art, 139, 264, 324
Indonesian textiles, 139
Brand Inglis Ltd., 210-11
intaglios, 235
intarsia, 164
International Antiques Show, 202
Iribe, Paul, 265
Irish furniture, 101, 105
iron:
  furniture, 11, 64, 90

iron *(cont'd.)*
grillwork, 107
hardware, 47
ironstone, 9, 205
Iroquois beadwork, 38
Islamic art, 26, 48, 202–4, 232, 286, 315, 318
Italian art, 168, 170, 171, 174
Renaissance, 148, 163, 167, 260
Italian ceramics, 187, 215, 275
Italian furniture, 47, 90, 101, 121, 170, 171, 267, 272
18th-century, 299
19th-century, 27, 125
20th-century, 27, 283
Modern, 59–60, 284
Renaissance, 155, 163–64
ivory, 51, 141, 146, 151, 196, 198, 213, 215, 277, 323
French, 47, 157

Jacob, Georges, 133, 173, 178, 180, 270, 321, 324
jade, 154, 156, 196, 197, 204, 326, 333, 341
Janvier, Antide, 278
Japanese art, 54, 102–3, 139, 198, 202–3, 262, 264, 324, 325, 331, 332, 338–39, 341, 343
Edo, 331, 342
Kamakura, 332
Meiji, 233, 331, 333
Nara, 332, 342
Japanese ceramics, 102–3, 232, 332, 333, 335, 341–43
Edo, 341
Heian, 335
Imari, 169, 205, 340
Jomon, 341
Kakiemon, 262
Kamakura, 342
porcelains, 141–42, 262–63, 332, 335
Shigaraki, 103
Tokoname, 103
Japanese furniture, 102–3, 105–6, 156, 267
Japanese porcelains, *see* Japanese ceramics
Japanese pottery, 335
Japanese screens, 154, 161, 169, 198, 267–68, 330, 332, 343
Japanese scrolls, 161
Japanese tea ceremony wares, 139, 332, 335
jaspé, 113
Javanese sculpture, 264
Jellinek, Tobias, 231
Jenkins, John Holmes, 3–4
The Jenkins Company, 3–4
Jensen, Georg, 90, 158, 214–15, 249
Jeremy Ltd., 211–12
Jesse, John, 213
John Jesse and Irina Laski Ltd., 213–14
jewelry, 15–16, 19–20, 52, 67, 73–74, 76–77, 90, 146–147, 158, 166, 176, 179, 213–14, 227, 232, 239, 241–42, 249, 302, 305, 313, 315, 317, 322
African, 16, 104–5, 315
American Indian, 15–17, 38, 74, 104–5
ancient, 146–47, 236, 309–10
Art Deco, *see* Art Deco
Art Nouveau, *see* Art Nouveau
Australian, 104
Austrian, 295, 304
Baroque, 305
Egyptian, 80
European, 158, 315
Hungarian, 304
Indian, 105
Mexican, 68, 90
Oriental, 104, 139, 315, 322
Persian, 318
pre-Columbian, 79
Renaissance, 227, 305
Russian, 36, 238–39, 304
South American, 104
tribal, 104–5
Yemeni, 313, 316
Margot Johnson Inc., 63–64
Jomon period, 341
Jordan, Vance, 65
Jordan Volpe Gallery, 65-66
Judaica, 313, 315–17
Jugendstil, 20, 249

kachina dolls, 15, 17
Kakiemon period, 262
Kamakura period, 332, 342
Kammerer, Marcel, 82
Kändler, 190, 275, 281, 290

K'ang Hsi dynasty, 49, 134, 248
Lewis M. Kaplan Associates, 214–15
Muriel Karasik, 67–68
Kargl, Georg, 81, 301–2
Kashan rugs, 35
Schmuel Kaufmann, 316–17
Kazak rugs, 248
John Keil Ltd., 215–16
Kelmscott Gallery, 25–26
Kelsterbach, 190
Kemp furniture, 230
Kent, William, 201
Gallery Wolfgang Ketterer, 257
Keverne, Roger, 232
Khecheong, 50
Khmer art, 154, 264, 324
David Kidd, 329–30
kilims, 19, 83–84, 176, 193, 194, 199, 248, 251, 298, 303
kimonos, 331
Kiryu Kitayama, 337
Kjaerholm, Poul, 158
Klablena, Eduard, 295
Klimt, Gustav, 302
Max Knöll Antiquités, 174
Knox, Archibald, 214
Kohn furniture, 23
Konya rugs, 43, 303
Koopman, Jacques, 216–18
E. & C. T. Koopman & Son Ltd., 216–18
Kopp, Joel, 39–40
Kopp, Kate, 39–40
Köpping, Karl, 219
Kopriva, Ena, 295
Korean art, 324, 333, 337
Gerald Kornblau, 68–69
Glasgalerie Michael Kovacek, 300–301
Kovacek, Regine, 300
Kovarik, Hubert, 295
Kraemer, 272–73
Kraemer, Philippe, 273
Kramer, Sam, 90
H.P. Kraus, 70–71
Kraus, Hans P., 70
J. Kugel, 273–74
Kugel, Alexis, 274
Kugel, Nicolas, 274
Kurdish rugs, 19, 251

lacquer wares, 51–52, 71–72, 102, 139, 142, 158, 166, 196, 262–63, 267, 272, 289, 324–25, 331, 333, 335, 341, 343
  boxes, 141, 198, 260, 332
  furniture, 101, 120, 125, 131, 134, 146, 223–25, 230, 232, 260, 261, 267, 272, 280, 287
  mirrors, 108, 179
  panels, 169, 274
Lacroix (Roger Vandercruse), 93
Lai, Eugene, 326
Lalique, René, 73–74, 76, 85, 90, 147, 214, 219, 282, 304
Lally, James J., 71–73
J. J. Lally & Company Oriental Art, 71–73
Frides Laméris, 142
lamps, 176, 195, 276, 277,
  oil, 309–10, 312, 313
  Tiffany, 59–60, 76–77, 85
  see also lighting fixtures
Lane, Raymond E., 41–42
Langlois, Pierre, 212
Lannuier, Paul, 211
Lanvin perfume bottles, 215
lapis lazuli, 133, 237
Larch, Raoul, 249
Laski, Irina, 213
Latin Codices, 129
Latz, Jean-Pierre, 93
leather, 302
Lebeau, Chris, 144
George Lee, 339–40
Leerdam glass, 143, 144
George Lefebvre, 275–76
Lefebvre, Leon, 275
Legrain, Pierre, 48, 265, 277
Frans Leidelmeijer, 143–44
Fred Leighton, 73–74
Leleu, Jean-François, 284
Leleu, Jules, 77
Lencker, Christoph, 178
Lepaute clocks, 278
Lepinne clocks, 171
Leroy, Robin, 278
Alain Lesieutre, 276
Galerie Alain Lesieutre, 276–77
Etienne Lévy, 278–79
Lévy, Claude, 278
Levy, George, 194
Bernard & S. Dean Levy Inc., 74–76
Li period, 333

Liao period, 337
lighting fixtures, 25, 52, 59, 62, 66, 67, 81, 86, 158, 170, 249, 251–52, 269; *see also* lamps
Limoges enamels, 151
literature, *see* books
L'Odéon, 218–19
Loetz glass, 214, 219
Loloma, Charles, 17
London Silver Vaults, 241–42
Longton Hall ceramics, 189, 191
Loos, Adolf, 23, 27, 82, 265, 302
Lorenz, Anton, 265
Louis XIII furniture, 155
Louis XIV, 262, 273, 284, 287
  furniture, 123, 160, 186, 230, 270, 273, 274, 284, 285, 287
Louis XV, 176, 230, 278–79, 284, 287
  furniture, 125, 169, 173, 186, 230, 248, 259–60, 266, 270, 272, 274, 279, 284, 287
Louis XVI, 88, 273, 284, 287
  furniture, 88, 101, 173, 175, 186, 225, 230, 237, 248, 261, 270, 273, 278, 284, 285, 287
Le Louvre des Antiquaires, 291
Luce, Jean, 90
Ludwigsburg, 190
Lurçat, Jean, 269
Luri rugs, 251
Gianfranco Luzzetti, 167

McCormick, Balene, 15
Milly McGhee, 11–12
Mackintosh, Charles Rennie, 59, 195, 236
Macklowe, Barbara, 76
Macklowe, Lloyd, 76
Macklowe Gallery, 76
Macret, Pierre, 173
Madonnas, 163
Maggs, Bryan, 219
Maggs, John, 219
Maggs Bros. Ltd., 219–20
Maitland, Peter, 221
majolica, 47, 148, 163, 164, 167, 187, 241, 248, 275–76, 281, 290
Majorelle, Louis, 59, 77, 85, 249, 264
malachite, 169, 237, 266
Mallet-Stevens, Robert, 77, 158, 265, 268
Mallett & Son Antiques Ltd., 221
Mallett at Bourbon House Ltd., 221–23
Mamluk rugs, 253
Manheim, Millie, 77–79
D. M. & P. Manheim Antiques Corporation, 77–79
Manishevitz, Haim, 89–90
Edgar Abraham Mannheimer, 176–77
manuscripts, 5–6, 24, 28, 126
  illuminated, 4, 48, 71, 220
  Islamic, 286
  medieval, 71, 128–30
  music, 206–7
  Renaissance, 128–30
  Turkish, 286
maps, 4, 28–29, 316–17
marble, 108, 167, 171, 312
  columns, 107, 172
  fountains, 169
  Hellenistic, 55
  Roman, 55, 170
  sculpture, 163, 171, 180, 224, 236
  vases, 168, 169, 186
Galerie Félix Marcilhac, 279–80
Marcotte, Leon, 63
marine art, 291
Marinot, Maurice, 90
Martin Brothers, 65–66
Martinez, Maria, 17
masks, 15, 324
Matégot, Mathieu, 52
Mauter, Conrad, 278
Mayer, George, 25
Mayuyama & Company, 340–41
medieval period:
  art, 46–47, 80, 92–94, 110–11, 145–46, 154, 179, 231, 235–36, 241, 296, 324
  books, 48, 128–30
  Buddhist art, 102
  illuminated manuscripts, 4, 48, 71, 220
  text manuscripts, 71, 128–30
  sculpture, 201, 248
  tapestries, 45, 46, 80, 151–52
meditation stones, 51
Meiji period, 233, 331, 333
Meisel, Louis, 90
Meisel, Susan, 90

Meisel-Primavera, 89
Meissen porcelains, 93, 148, 190, 254, 275, 281, 290, 297
Mellotti ceramics, 215
Edward H. Merrin, 79–80
metal wares, 218–19, 223, 244, 252, 286
Galerie Metropol, 301–2
Galerie Metropol Inc., 81–82
H. V. Metz & Company, 265
Mexican wedding dresses, 74
Meyer, Christian, 81, 301–2
Mickey Mouse figures, 37
Mies van der Rohe, Ludwig, 284
Migeon, Pierre, 285
Miklos, Gustave, 169
Mildner, Johann, 301
Marian Miller, 83–84
Minali designs, 283
Ming dynasty, 54, 73, 125–26, 140–42, 148, 153–54, 156, 196–98, 232, 262, 267, 275, 290, 321, 324–25, 326, 339, 340
mirrors, 108, 143, 170, 171, 180, 201, 224, 230, 260, 273, 313, 337, 339
  Venetian, 105–6
mission-style furniture, 65
Shoichiro Mizutani, 332
Mizutani, Yoko, 330
Mizutani—Antique Arts and Crafts, 330–31
Modernism: A Century of Style and Design 1860–1960, 115
Mogul art, 105, 146, 156, 200
Molino, Carl, 90, 241
Moll, Carl, 302
Gregory Momjian, 310–11
Mondschein, Murray, 73
Montigny furniture, 284
Morgan, Brian, 196
Morpurgo, Joseph M., 144–45
Morpurgo, Rebecca, 144–45
mortars, Japanese, 103
mosaics, Byzantine, 313
Moser, Koloman, 23, 59–60, 81–82, 90, 159, 218, 295, 301–2
Mouille, Serge, 52
Mucha, Alfonso, 214
Munn, Geoffrey, 239
Munves, Edward, Jr., 91
Murano goblets, 142
Murdock, David H., 99
musical instruments, 177, 226
musical manuscripts, 206–7

Naga jewelry, 104
Nanga school, 343
Napoleon III, 88, 160, 176, 282
Nara period, 332, 342
Lillian Nassau, 84–86
Nassau, Paul, 85
Nathan, Jeremiah, 256
Navajo Indians, 15, 17
Nazca people, 80
Ndebele jewelry, 104
Kenneth Nebenzahl Inc., 28–29
Ferdinand Neess, 251–52
neo-classical style, 89, 122, 171, 217
  furniture, 122, 130–31, 170, 171, 201, 254, 259
Neo-Gothic furniture, 240
netsukes, 139, 198–99
Newbon, David B., 41
Newel Art Galleries, Inc., 86–87
Newman, Bruce M., 86–87
Nickerson, David G. F., 222–23
Nicolier, 281
Nicolier, Philip, 281
Nicolier, Pierre, 281
Niderviller porcelains, 275
Nieuwe Kunst, 143
Nogaret furniture, 122
Nogatch, Pierrette, 284
No masks, 324
Jeremy Norman & Company, 126–28
Richard Norton, 29–30
Norton, Martin, 227
Nottingham pottery, 210
Nouveau Drouot, 293
Nymphenburg porcelains, 190

Oberson, Bernard, 173
Oerley, Robert, 23, 160
Ohr, George, 65
oil lamps, 309–10, 312, 313
Olbrich, Joseph M., 77, 269
Old Master paintings, 33, 58, 152, 164, 167, 168, 203, 243, 260–61
Olmec sculpture, 79
onyx, Egyptian, 168

opium pots, 322
Oriental art, 15, 26, 49, 53, 71–73, 134, 139–40, 141, 145, 146, 161, 195–98, 203, 232–33, 236, 243, 262–64, 292, 315, 322–25, 333; *see also specific countries*
Oriental ceramics, 71–72, 93–94, 116, 132–33, 139–40, 141, 144, 232–33, 244, 281, 286, 333, 337; *see also specific countries*
Oriental furniture, 116, 139, 169, 244, 267, 322–23, 325; *see also specific countries*
Oriental rugs, 18–19, 26, 34–35, 43–45, 145, 193–94, 248, 250–53, 298–99
  Afshar, 251, 299
  Anatolian, 248, 250, 253, 298, 303
  Baluch, 251
  Bessarabian, 176, 194
  Bijar, 19, 251
  Bokhara, 248
  Caucasian, 193, 194, 248, 250–51, 253, 298, 303
  Chinese, 35, 250
  Ferahan, 35, 43
  Heriz, 18–19, 35, 248
  Kashan, 35
  Kazak, 248
  kilims, 19, 83–84, 176, 193, 194, 199, 248, 251, 298, 303
  Konya, 43, 303
  Kurdish, 19, 251
  Luri, 251
  Mamluk, 253
  Persian, 18–19, 35, 194, 298, 303
  Qashqai, 194, 251
  Senneh, 251
  Shirvan, 253
  Sultanabad, 35, 42, 43, 45
  Tabriz, 18, 35, 43, 248
  Tibetan, 251
  Turkestan, 303
  Turkish, 35, 251, 315
  Turkoman, 19, 194, 248, 250–51, 253, 298–99, 303
  Usak, 19, 43
  Uzbekistan, 251
ormolu, 212, 261, 271
Ostler, Herbert, 252
Galerie Ostler G.M.B.H. "Alte Und Neue Kunst," 252–53
Oxley, Joseph, 205

Pahari school, 146
paintings, 33, 60, 62, 66, 93, 163, 170, 221, 232, 260, 266, 296, 322
  American, 37, 62, 69, 116
  Chinese, 266, 325, 343
  French, 284
  Japanese, 102, 332, 342, 343
  miniature, 146, 203, 227
  modern, 26–27
  Old Masters, 164, 167, 168, 203, 243, 260–61
  Oriental, 139, 145, 146, 203, 264, 333
  reverse glass, 324
Palissy pottery, 241
pamphlets, 29
Pannini, 165
paper goods, 20
Partridge, John, 223–25
Partridge (Fine Arts) Ltd., 223–25
pastille burners, 42
patina, importance of, 184, 216
Fritz Payer, 177–78
Peche, Dagobert, 160, 295, 302
pedestal sinks, 108
Pelham Galleries, 225–26
perfume bottles, 68, 214, 215, 310–12, 316
Périnet, Michel, 282
Rodolphe Perpitch, 283
Perriand, Charlotte, 268
Jacques Perrin, 283–84
Perrin, Patrick, 284
Persian art, 179–80
  miniature paintings, 203
Persian rugs, *see* Oriental rugs
Perzel, Jean, 269, 279
pewter, 214
pharmacy jars, 148
Phillips, 118, 246
Phillips, Ammi, 62
S. J. Phillips Ltd., 226–27
photography, 291
Piacenza, Biazzini, 283
Piñeda, Antonio, 90
Plains Indians, 17, 38
plastic, 67, 147, 158, 213

Kunsthandel J. Polak, 145–46
Polak, Jaap, 145–46
Poli, Flavio, 90
Pomodoro, Arnaldo, 166
Ponti, Gio, 27, 90
porcelains, 36, 41–42, 62, 143, 146, 148, 176, 187, 188, 212, 252, 273, 296, 324
  Chinese, 49–51, 140, 156, 161, 198, 248, 274, 281, 321, 323, 326, 337, 340, 341
  English, 31, 77–79, 91–92, 99, 189–91, 205, 223
  European, 91–92, 133–34, 144, 186, 189–91, 223, 230
  French, 92–94, 148, 153, 223, 273, 290
  German, 148, 253–54, 281, 290
  Japanese, 141–42, 262–63, 332, 335
  Oriental, 93–94, 144
  see also ceramics; pottery
Juan Portela Antiques, 88–89
Portuguese furniture, 120
postcards, 291
posters, 25, 60, 67, 143
poster stamps, 20
pottery, 15, 65–66, 151–52, 187, 310
  American, 17–18, 40, 113
  ancient, 311, 312, 317
  English, 41–42, 209–10, 221, 230–31
  French, 113, 241
  Hispano-Moresque, 151–52
  medieval, 231
  Oriental, 262, 335, 340
  stoneware, 210, 254, 335, 342
  see also ceramics; porcelains
Pottier & Stymus, 63
Powolny, Michael, 23, 32, 249, 295
pre-Columbian art, 15, 54–55, 79, 180, 199–200, 257
Preiss, Frederick, 213, 219, 277
Pre-Raphaelite paintings, 60
Primavera, 89
prints, 28–29, 99, 249
Printz, Eugène, 90, 268, 279, 289
Prouvé, Jean, 52
Prutscher, Otto, 23, 299
Puiforcat silver, 214–15, 276
puppets, 122, 322
purses, 302

Qashqai rugs, 194, 251
Bernard Quaritch Ltd., 228–29
Queen Anne, 21–22, 97, 99, 183, 184, 218, 221, 233
quillwork, American Indian, 38
quilts, 39–40, 62, 112–13

Ramsden, Omar, 233
Rappaport, Julius, 176
William Redford, 229–30
redware, 42
Regency style, 62, 88, 99, 101, 106, 109, 126, 175, 183, 184, 194–95, 201, 212, 226
reliquaries, 47
Renaissance art, 46–47, 86, 92–94, 111, 122, 146, 157, 163, 177–78
  books, 48, 128–30
  bronzes, 240, 273
  furniture, 155, 167, 248
  Italian, 148, 260
  jewelry, 227, 305
  manuscripts, 128–30
  sculpture, 248
  tapestries, 46
reproductions, 109
Restoration furniture, 153
Révillon wallpapers, 131
Revival, 88, 114, 115, 122, 194–95
  Egyptian, 85, 87
  Elizabethan, 91, 98, 108
  Renaissance, 122
Riesener, Jean-Henri, 160, 186, 266
Rietveld, Gerrit, 60–61, 143–44, 265
Rimpa school, 343
Ritschka, Wolfgang, 81, 301
Robb, Robyn, 189
robes, Oriental, 102, 330
James Robinson Inc., 91–92
rococo, 122, 169–71, 179, 190, 201, 217, 224, 259, 273
Rodin, Auguste, 179
Gerhard Roebbig, 253–54
Roentgen, David, 261
Rohlfs, Charles, 65
Roman art, 111–12, 165, 168, 170, 179–80, 236, 310, 312
  bronzes, 55, 80
  glass, 316, 317
  pottery, 317
  sculpture, 55, 80, 112, 154, 201

Galerie Römer, 178–79
Römer, Roland, 178
Römer-du Carrois, Heidi, 178
Römer glass, 174
Rookwood pottery, 65
Rörstrand vases, 19–20
Rosenberg & Stiebel, 92–94
Bernard M. Rosenthal, 128–30
Rosenthal, Albi, 206–7
A. Rosenthal Ltd., 206–7
Rossi, Jean-Marie, 261
Rothschild, Jacob, 203
Rouen ceramics, 187, 281
Rousseau, Clement, 276, 289
Roussel, Pierre, 284
Roux, Alexandre, 63
Royère, Jean, 52
Rozenburg porcelains, 143
Rubin, Alan, 225–26
Rubin, Davida, 126
Rudinoff, Willibald, 23
rugs, 42–43, 52, 224, 313
  European, 19, 35, 45, 298,
  hooked, 40, 112
  Oriental, *see* Oriental rugs
Ruhlmann, Emile-Jacques, 27, 52, 77, 166, 215, 265, 268, 277, 279–80, 283, 289
Russian art, 35–37, 153, 238–39, 304
Russian furniture, 36, 89, 101, 105–6, 121, 134, 153, 176, 212, 236–37, 267

Saadat, Rahim, 191–92
Sabino furniture, 268
Sack, Israel, 12
Israel Sack Inc., 94–96
saddle bags, 303
Galerie Sailer, 303
St. Cloud porcelains, 190
salt cellars, 192
salt glaze, 41, 42, 281
Alastair Sampson Antiques, 230–31
San Francisco Fall Antiques Show, 135
Sarraute-Mourchette, Gilbert, 160
sashes, 331
Sassanian art, 80
Sasson, Gideon, 312
Sasson Antiques, 312
Saunier, Claude Charles, 261
Savonarola folding chairs, 164
Savonnerie rugs, 19
scarabs, 145, 312
Schaffer, Paul, 35–36
Schaffer, Peter, 35–36
Schaffer, Ray, 35–36
Schechter, Leonard, 107
Scheers, Alfons, 153
Schellink, Sam, 143
Schiele, Egon, 23, 302
Schlapka, Axel, 254–55
Schlapka Kg, 254–55
Schneider, Andreas, 166
Schullin, 304–5
Schullin, Herbert, 304
sconces, 230, 266
screens, 333–35, 341
  Chinese, 343
  Japanese, 154, 161, 169, 198, 267–68, 330, 332, 343
scrolls, 322, 324, 332, 335, 338, 343
sculpture, 52, 54, 62, 67, 86, 94, 105, 116, 125–26, 143, 163, 165, 171, 172, 178–80, 186, 201, 213, 236, 249, 259, 266
  African, 241
  ancient, 51, 112, 312
  Chinese, 54, 264, 338, 343
  Egyptian, 80, 112
  Greek, 80, 112, 201
  Indian, 54, 267
  Japanese, 54, 102, 198, 338, 342, 343
  medieval, 201, 248
  Oriental, 54, 80, 139, 145, 263–64, 333
  pre-Columbian, 79
  Renaissance, 86, 248
  Roman, 80, 112, 154, 168, 201
Maurice Segoura, 285–86
Kunsthandlung H. W. Seling, 256–57
Seling, Helmut, 256
Sené, Jean-Baptiste-Claude, 285
Senneh rugs, 251
Setsu, Iwao, 342
Setsu Gatodo, 342
Sèvres, 93, 187, 190–91, 275, 290
Shaker wares, 15, 112–13
Shang dynasty, 197, 262, 321, 326, 333, 339
Shapiro, Gil, 107
Sheffield, 227, 242

Norman Shepherd, 130–31
Shigaraki period, 103
Shinto painting, 264
Shirvan rugs, 253
S. J. Shrubsole, 96–98
Shrubsole, Eric Norman, 96–97
Siamese pottery, 263–64
Siegel, Gustav, 296
signs, advertising, 40
silver, 63, 91, 146, 148, 154, 159, 174–76, 214, 215, 239–43, 273, 274, 276, 291, 296, 302, 305, 313, 316, 322, 324
  American, 97–98, 116, 315-16
  ancient, 311
  Chinese export, 50
  Dutch, 144
  English, 97-98, 191-92, 211, 217–18, 221, 223–25, 227, 232–33, 244, 256
  European, 116, 133, 140, 148, 155, 159–60, 177–78, 191–92, 227, 244, 256
  French, 217–18, 223–25
  German, 211
  Irish, 97–98
  Judaica, 317
  Mexican, 68
  Oriental, 71, 80, 116, 244, 322
  Renaissance, 146, 177–78
  Russian, 35–36
  Victorian, 62, 242
  see also jewelry
sitting machines, 23, 82, 159, 302
slipware, 41, 42, 210, 231
Snowman, A. Kenneth, 238
snuff bottles, snuff boxes, 120, 227, 327
soapstone, 141, 198
Socorro pots, 15–16, 18
soldier's jackets, 331
Sotheby's, 118, 246, 328
Sotheby's Amsterdam, 149
Sotheby's Geneva, 181
Jean Soustiel, 286–87
Spanish ceramics, 151, 275
Spink & Son Ltd., 232-33
spongeware, 40, 113
Spratling, William, 68
Spriet, Winston, 158
Staffordshire, 210, 231
stained glass, 46, 62, 108, 174
  lamps, 59–60, 65, 76–77, 85
  windows, 25–26, 107
Stair & Company, 98–100, 234
Stam, Mart, 143, 144
statuary, 154, 172; *see also* sculpture
Bernard Steinitz, 287–88
Steinitz, David, 288
Steinitz, Mireille, 288
Garrick C. Stephenson, 100–101
Steuben glass, 85
Stickley, Gustav, 65–66
Stiebel, Eric, 93
Stiebel, Gerald, 93
Stiegl glass, 174
Joseph Stieglitz, 317–18
Jacob Stodel, 234
Kunsthandel Inez Stodel, 146–47
Stodel, Inez, 146–47
Salomon Stodel Antiquités, 148
stoneware, *see* pottery
stonework, 51, 108, 172, 180; *see also* sculpture
Storr, Paul, 211, 217
Strasbourg, 275, 290
Sue et Mare, 77, 90
Sugimoto, 102–3
Sugimoto, Hiroshi, 102
Sullivan, Louis, 65
Sullivan, Mary Ann, 22
Sultanabad rugs, 35, 42, 43, 45
House of Sung, 132–33
Sung dynasty, 49, 133, 139, 141, 156, 196, 198, 281, 321, 324, 337, 339, 340
Susi Singer figurines, 19
Swedish furniture, 36, 101, 121, 123, 125, 131, 134
Swedish glass, 68
Symbolism, 60
Robin Symes, 235–36
Le Syndicat National des Antiquaires, 292

tableware, 91–92, 159, 189, 249, 252, 276; *see also* glass; porcelains; silver
Tabriz rugs, 18, 35, 43, 248
Tai Sing Company, 326
Takahashi, Saburo, 341
Tambaran, 103–5
Tang dynasty, 49, 125, 132, 133, 139–41, 156, 161, 196–98, 232, 262–63, 263, 326, 339,

Tang dynasty *(cont'd)*
340, 341, 343
Tanner, Terence, 23–24
tapestries, 45, 146, 155, 157, 163, 171, 180, 240, 248
Coptic, 200
English, 223
European, 250, 298
Flemish, 151–52
French, 178, 223, 273
German, 200
medieval, 45, 46, 80, 151–52
Ming, 325
Renaissance, 46
Tournai, 151
Tarshis Gallery, 313
Taylor, Walter Thomas, 5–7
W. Thomas Taylor Bookseller, 5–7
tazzas, 146, 177–78
tea ceremony wares, 139, 332, 335
teapots, 42, 256–57, 335
Templier, Raymond, 282
terra cottas, 166, 179, 180, 236
textiles, 15, 179, 248, 315
African, 123, 315
Chinese, 199–200, 330
Coptic, 80, 179, 180, 199–200
European, 315
French Gothic, 199–200
Indian, 200
Islamic, 203, 286
Japanese, 331, 332
Judaica, 315
Oriental, 139, 200, 250, 315, 330–31, 333
Persian, 199–200, 315
Peruvian, 79, 80
pre-Columbian, 79, 199–200
Scandinavian, 199–200
Turkish, 286, 315
Thai art, 264, 324
Therien & Company, 133–34
Theta Charity Antiques Show of Houston, 16
Thomire, Pierre-Phillippe, 261, 285
Thonet furniture, 23, 160, 279, 297
tiaras, 304
Tibetan art, 123–24, 325
Tibetan rugs, 251
Tiffany, Louis Comfort, 59–60, 64, 76–77
Tiffany & Company, 73, 76, 85, 89, 176, 214, 315
tiger's lapis lazuli, 133
tiles, 180, 210, 249
Tilliard, Jean Baptiste, 272
Toby jugs, 42
Tokoname ceramics, 103
tomb figures, Chinese, 161, 197, 340
Tomc, Thomas Martin, 19–20
Toorup, Jan, 143
Topino furniture, 146
Torah items, 316, 317
Tournai tapestries, 151
Tovey, Noël, 218
toys, 37–38, 108
dolls, Oriental, 331
puppets, 122, 322
trains, 37–38
Wiener Werkstätte, 295–96
wooden, 11
Tremayne, Bruce G., 133
tribal art, 15, 104–5, 145, 257
Tri Delta Charity Antiques Show, 10, 13
trompe l'oeil decoration, 89
Galleria Antiquaria "F. Tuena," 172
Tuena, Massimo, 172
Turkestan rugs, 303
Turkish art, 204, 286
Turkish furniture, 88, 105–6
Turkish rugs, 35, 251, 315
Turkoman rugs, 19, 194, 248, 250–51, 253, 298–99, 303
twig furniture, 11, 87
Tyson, Gene, 105–6
Gene Tyson Antiques Inc., 105–6
Tzigany Fine Arts, 236–37

Urban Archaeology, 107–8
Urbino majolica, 148, 163
Usak rugs, 19, 43
Uzbekistan rugs, 251

Galerie Valois, 289
Valois, Bob, 289
Valois, Cheska, 289
Van Cleef & Arpels, 73–74, 76, 89, 215, 282
van der Cingel, Daan, 143
Vandercruse, Roger (Lacroix), 93
Vandermeesch, 290
Vandermeesch, Michel, 290
Van Mulders, Luc, 161

van Risamburgh, Bernard, (B.V.R.B.), 93, 286
Venetian art, 168
Venetian furniture, 87, 131, 176, 266
Venetian glass, 38, 47, 104, 300–301
Venetian mirrors, 105–6
Venini glass, 90, 219
Veracruz sculpture, 79
Veraguas (Panama) gold, 79
Vermoutier, Antoine de, 231
Axel Vervoordt, 153–54
Vessa, Glenn, 322
Vessa, Lucille, 322
Vever, Henri, 73
Vever, Paul, 73
Vever jewelry, 282
Victoria, Anthony G., 109–10
Frederick P. Victoria & Son Inc., 109–10
Victorian wares, 192, 316
  bathroom fixtures, 108
  furniture, 62–64
  glass, 62
  jewelry, 74, 91
  porcelain, 62
  silver, 62, 242
Viennese art, 22–23, 297
Viennese furniture, 27, 159, 297
Viennese porcelains, 190, 297
Viking art, 241
Villars, 160–61
Vincennes porcelains, 187, 190, 290
Heidi Vollmoeller, 179–80
Volpe, Todd, 65
Vos, Theo, 143

Wagner, Otto, 27, 59, 77, 283, 297
Wagner, Richard, 48
wallets, 302
wallpapers, 131, 324
Walton, John, 42
Michael Ward, 110–12
Wartski, 238–39
watches, 158, 176
watercolors, 23, 69; *see also* paintings
weathervanes, 9, 11, 40, 62
Wei dynasty, 156, 263
Weiner, Ed, 90
Whieldonware, 42, 210, 231
Whittington, Stewart, 183–85
wicker furniture, 64
Wiener Werkstätte, 20, 22–23, 77, 81–82, 115, 218, 249, 295, 297, 304, 305
Wieselthier, Vally, 23, 295
Willaume, David, 154
William and Mary, 21, 98, 222
William IV, 226
Taylor B. Williams, 30–32
Williams, Robert, 187
Wilson, John D., 32
windup toys, 37
Winter Antiques Show, 116, 188, 202
Wong, Harold C. F., 322
Wood, Ralph, 42
Woodard, Thomas K., 112–13
Thos. K. Woodard Antiques Corporation, 112–13
wood carvings, 15, 17, 148, 157
Worcester, 31, 189, 191, 205
Wouda, Hendrik, 144
Wright, Frank Lloyd, 25–26, 59, 62, 65–66
Würzburg furniture, 171

Yabumoto, Soichiro, 343
S. Yabumoto Company, 343
Shoji Yamanaka, 333
Shigehiko Yanagi, 334
Yanagi, Takashi, 335
T. Yanagi Fine Arts and Curios, 335
Yang, Yung Fu, 327
Y.F. Yang Company, 327
yellowware, 40
Yemeni jewelry, 313, 316
Yüan dynasty, 154
Yung Lo dynasty, 146

Zadok, Shaya, 313
Zarember, Maureen, 103–4
J. Zeberg N.V., 155
Zen Gallery, 161
Peter Zervudachi, 175–76
Zetter, Christa, 295
Rainer Zietz, 240–41
Zigzag chairs, 61, 144
Zimet, Martin J., 58–59
Zuñi jewelry, 15